THE MASONIC BOOK CLUB

VOL. 7

The Signers of the Constitution of the United States

David C. Whitney

Westphalia Press
An Imprint of the Policy Studies Organization
Washington, DC

The Signers of the Constitution of the United States

Westphalia Press
An imprint of Policy Studies Organization
1367 Connecticut Avenue NW
Washington, D.C. 20036
info@ipsonet.org

ISBN: 978-1-63723-559-1

Daniel Gutierrez-Sandoval, Executive Director
PSO and Westphalia Press

Updated material and comments on this edition
can be found at the Westphalia Press website:
www.westphaliapress.org

The Masonic Book Club

The *Masonic Book Club* (MBC) was formed in 1970 by two Illinois Masons, Alphonse Cerza, 33°, and Louis L. Williams, 33°. The MBC primarily reprinted out-of-print Masonic books with scholarly introductions; occasionally they would print additional texts as "bonuses" (though none were marked specifically as such on the title pages); sometimes a reprint would be marked "Masonic Book Club Edition"; often an unnumbered bonus was published jointly with the Illinois Lodge of Research or the Supreme Council, 33°, NMJ, USA.

Most of the MBC volumes indicated on the title page, "Volume [*Number*] of the Publications of the Masonic Book Club," some were misnumbered, and some were unnumbered. Indeed, the numbering of the early volumes was inconsistent. For example, *A Serious and Impartial Enquiry* is "Volume Five" (1974) but *Masonic Membership of the Founding Fathers* is "The Masonic Book Club Edition" (1974). Then, *Masonry Dissected* is "Volume Eight" (1977), *The Trestleboard* is "Volume 8A" (1978), and *Anderson's Constitutions of 1738* is "Volume Nine" (1978). If nothing else, MBC books keep bibliophiles on their toes.

The first volumes had deckle-edged paper and pages of slightly different sizes, though eventually the MBC settled into a 6″×9″ trimmed-page format for their books. The books were bound in a dark blue fabric with gold lettering. Listed below are the fifty-nine MBC volumes published 1970–2010 with bonuses. N.B.: A number and letter, e.g. "Volume 8A," is a numbering for this reprint series.

The club originally was limited to 333 members, but the number grew to nearly 2,000, with 1,083 members when it dissolved in 2010. In 2017 MW Barry Weer, 33°, the last president of the MBC, transferred the MBC name and assets to the Supreme Council, 33°, SJ, USA. Under the editorship of Arturo de Hoyos, 33°, G∴C∴, and S. Brent Morris, 33°, G∴C∴, the revived Masonic Book Club has the goal of publishing classic Masonic books while supporting Scottish Rite, SJ, USA philanthropies.

Publications of the Masonic Book Club, 1970–2010

1	1970	*The Regius Poem*	Masonic Book Club
2	1971	*The Constitutions of the Free-Masons*	Benjamin Franklin
3	1972	*Ahiman Rezon*	Laurence Dermott
4	1973	*Illustrations of Masonry*	William Preston
5	1974	*A Serious and Impartial Enquiry into the Cause of the Present Decay of Free-Masonry in the Kingdom of Ireland*	Fifield D'Assigny
5A	1974*	*Masonic Membership of the Founding Fathers*	Ronald E. Heaton

6	1975	*The Signers of the Declaration of Independence*	David C. Whitney
7	1976	*The Signers of the Constitution of the United States*	David C. Whitney
7A	1976*	*Masonic Symbols in American Decorative Art*	Louis L. Williams & Alphonse Cerza
8	1977	*Samuel Prichard's Masonry Dissected, 1730*	Harry Carr
8A	1978*	*Trestle-Board (A facsimile of the original Trestle Board by the Baltimore Masonic Convention of 1843)*	Dwight L. Smith
9	1978	*Anderson's Constitutions of 1738*	Lewis Edward & W. J. Hughan
10	1979	*Sufferings of John Coustos*	Wallace McLeod
11	1980	*The Revelations of a Square*	George Oliver
11A	1980	*Biblical Characters in Freemasonry*	John H. Van Gorden
11B	1980*	*A Masonic Reader's Guide*	*Guide* Alphonse Cerza & Thomas Warden
12	1981	*Three Distinct Knocks and Jachin and Boaz*	Harry Carr
13	1982	*Masonic Almanacs and Anti-Masonic Almanacs*	Plez A. Transou
13A	1982*	*Stephen A. Douglas: Freemason*	Wayne C. Temple
14	1983	*The Beginnings of Freemasonry in America*	Melvin M. Johnson
14A	1983*	*Bespangled, Painted & Embroidered: Decorated Masonic Aprons in America, 1790–1850*	Scottish Rite Masonic Museum & Library
14B	1983*	*Making a Mason at Sight*	Louis L. Williams
15	1984	*Masonic Concordance of the Holy Bible*	Charles Clyde Hunt
15A	1984*	*By Square and Compasses: The Building of Lincoln's Home and Its Saga*	Wayne C. Temple

16	1985	*The Old Gothic Constitutions*	Wallace McLeod
16A	1985*	*Modern Historical Characters in Freemasonry*	John H. Van Gorden
17	1986	*The Rise and Development of Organised Freemasonry*	Roy A. Wells
17A	1986*	*Ancient and Early Medieval Historical Characters in Freemasonry*	John H. Van Gorden
18	1987	*The Lodge in Friendship Village and Other Stories*	P. W. George
18A	1987*	*Masonic Charities*	John H. Van Gorden & Stewart M. L. Pollard
18B	1987*	*Medieval Historical Characters in Freemasonry*	John H. Van Gorden
18C	1987*	*George Washington in New York*	Allan Boudreau & Alexander Bleimann
19	1988	*Records of the Hole Crafte and Fellowship of Masons*	Edward Conder, Jr.
20	1989	*A Candid Disquisition of the Principles and Practices of the Most Ancient and Honourable Society of Free and Accepted Masons*	Wellins Calcott
20A	1989*	*Freemasonry and Nauvoo, 1839–1846*	Robin L. Carr
21	1990	*Masonic Odes and Poems*	Rob Morris
22	1991	*Lessing's Masonic Dialogues*	Gotthold Lessing
22A	1991*	*ABC of Freemasonry: A Book for Beginners*	Delmar D. Darrah
23	1992	*The Folger Manuscript*	S. Brent Morris
24	1993	*Freemasonry and Christianity: Lectures from Two Ages*	T. De Witt Peake & John J. Murchison
25	1994	*The Constitutions of St. John's Lodge*	Robin L. Carr
25A	1994*	*The Mystic Tie and Men of Letters*	Robin L. Carr
26	1995	*Recollections of a Masonic Veteran*	S. Brent Morris

27	1996	*The Freemason's Monitor or Illustrations of Masonry in Two Parts*	Thomas Smith Webb
28	1997	*The Masonic Ladder or the Nine Steps to Ancient Freemasonry*	John Sherer
28A	1997*	*Freemasonry and Democracy: Its Evolution in North America*	Allen E. Roberts & Wallace McLeod
29	1998	*The Masonic Harp: Collection of Masonic Odes, Hymns, Songs*	George Wingate Chase
30	1999	*Symbolic Teachings of Masonry and Its Message*	Thomas Milton Stewart
31	2000	*Freemasonry Its Meaning and Significance, An Exposition of its Ethics, Religion and Philosophy*	Otto Caspari
32	2001	*K. R. Cama Masonic Jubilee Volume*	Jivanji Jamshedji Modi
33	2002	*Caementaria Hibernica*	W. J. Chetwode Crawley
34	2003	*A Daily Advancement in Masonic Knowledge*	Wallace McLeod & S. Brent Morris
35	2004	*The Craftsman, and Templar's Textbook and, also, Melodies for the Craft*	Cornelius Moore
36	2005	*The Text Book of Freemasonry*	Retired Member of the Craft
37	2006	*Orations of the Illustrious Brother Frederick Dalcho Esq., M.D.*	Frederick Dalcho
38	2007	*Antiquities of Freemasonry Comprising Illustrations of the Five Grand Periods of Masonry from the Creation of the World to the Dedication of King Solomon's Temple*	George Oliver
39	2008	*Diogenes' Lamp or an Examination of our Present-Day Morality and Enlightenment*	Adam Weishaupt
40	2009	*Proofs of Conspiracy Against All the Governments of Europe*	John Robison
41	2010	*The Evolution of Freemasonry*	Delmar Darrah

** indicates a bonus book*

The Signers of the Constitution of the United States

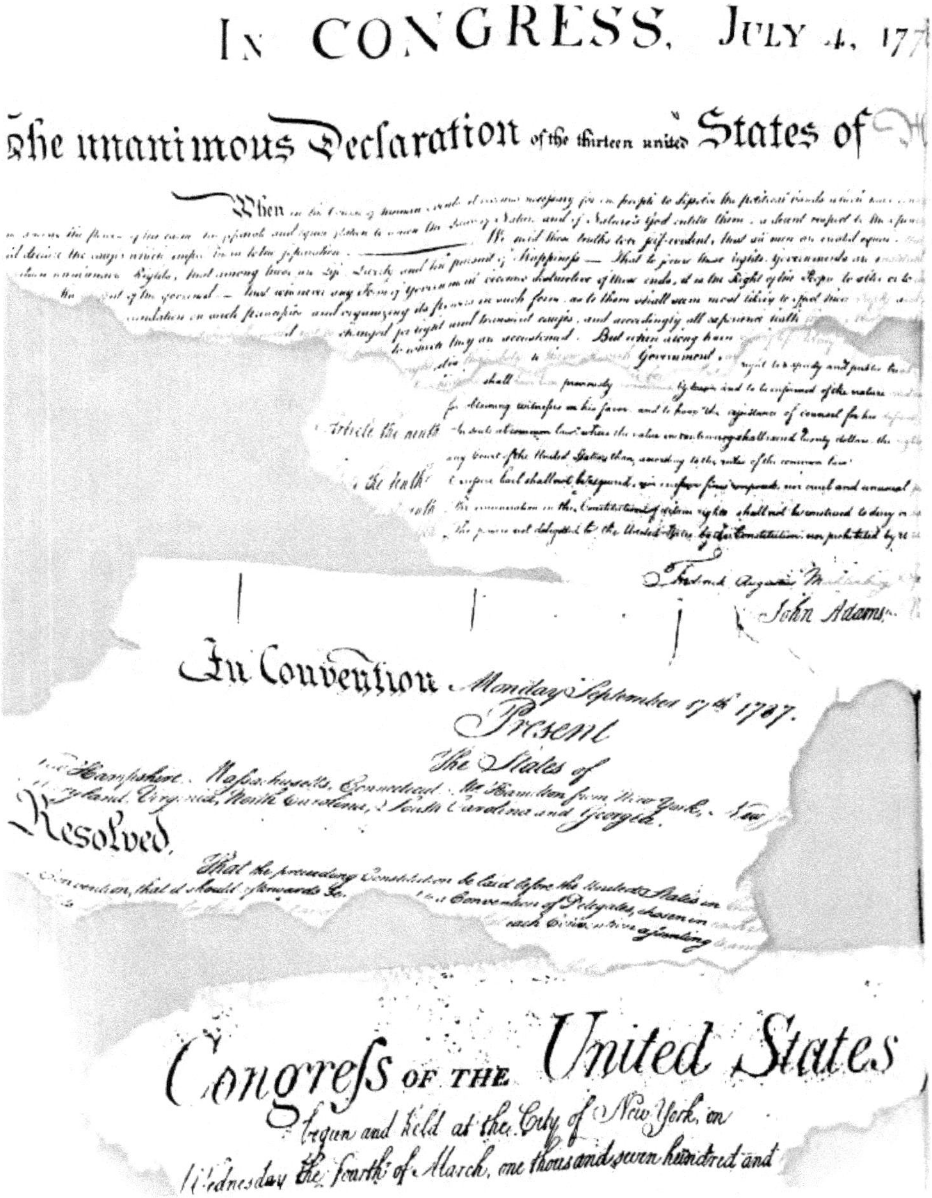
IN CONGRESS, JULY 4, 177
The unanimous Declaration of the thirteen united States of
John Adams
In Convention Monday September 17th 1787.
Present
The States of

Virginia, North Carolina, South Carolina and Georgia.

Resolved,

That the preceding Constitution be laid before the United States in Congress assembled, and that it should afterwards be submitted to a Convention of Delegates, chosen in each State...

Congress OF THE United States
begun and held at the City of New-York, on
Wednesday the fourth of March, one thousand seven hundred and

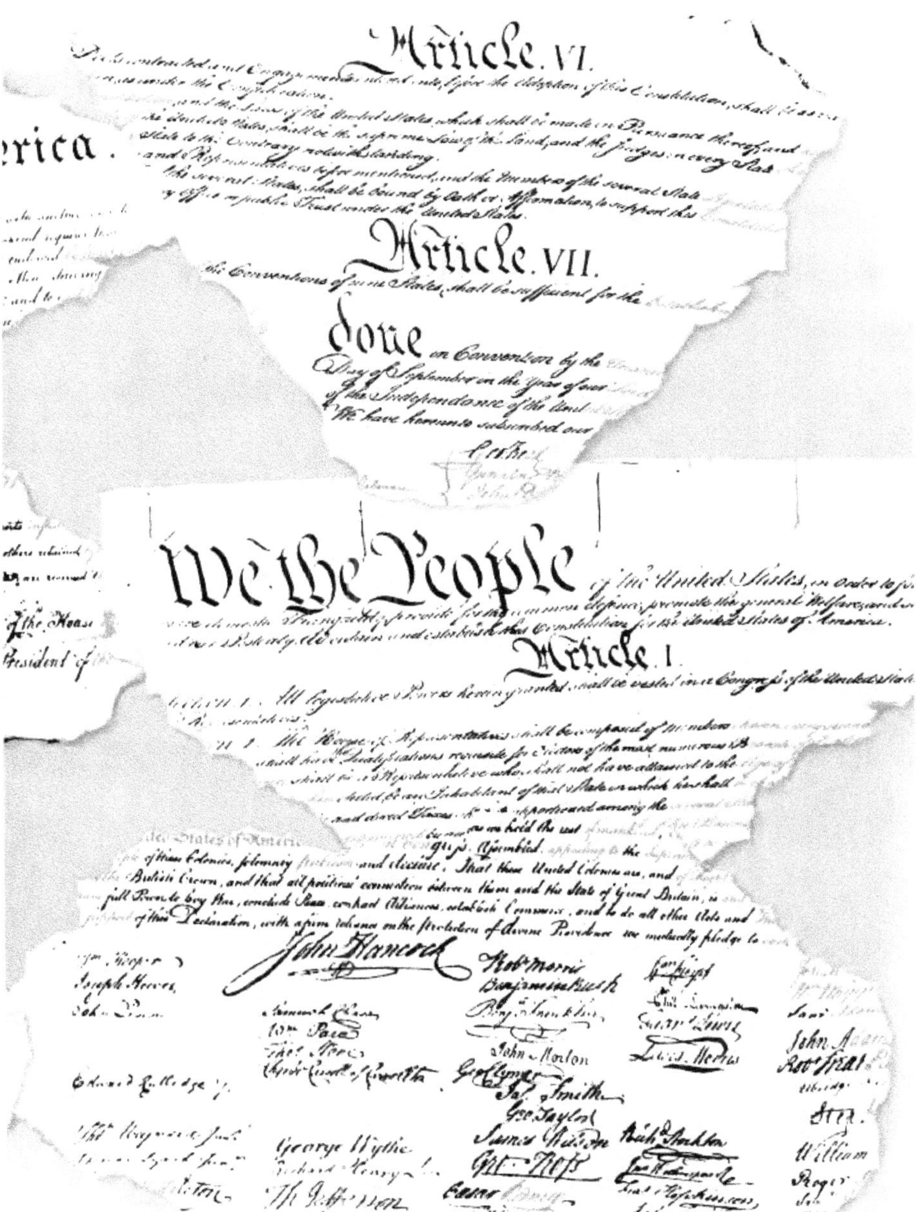
Article. VI.
Article. VII.
done
We the People
Article. I
John Hancock

THE MASONIC BOOK CLUB EDITION

of

The Signers of the Constitution of the United States

VOLUME SEVEN

of the Publications of

THE MASONIC BOOK CLUB

Distributed by

THE MASONIC BOOK CLUB

A Not-for-Profit Corporation of Illinois

Bloomington, Illinois

1976

This Edition has been
bound and distributed solely
for the Members of
The Masonic Book Club
and is limited to
999 copies
of which this is

No. 810

[This text appeared in the original publication.]

PREFACE

Many years ago William E. Gladstone, eminent British statesman, described the Constitution of the United States as "the most wonderful work ever struck off at a given time by the brain and purpose of man." The men who created the document have been described by enthusiastic speakers as "divinely inspired" and also as being "demi-gods." But an examination of their lives will disclose that although they had different backgrounds, each was familiar with the lessons of history and the functioning of government. And they each possessed an important characteristic that is essential for success in any human activity; the spirit of compromise. A consideration of the proceedings of the Constitutional Convention discloses that the members were prompted by high ideals, but that they were also practical minded men who recognized the need of a charter that would work.

Montesquieu, a Mason, in his book "The Spirit of the Law", had described three basic functions of government: the Executive, the Legislative, and the Judicial. This idea was incorporated into the Constitution of the United States with its familiar checks and balances. Being a child of revolution, and reflecting the recognition that with the passage of time there would be need for change, the document provides for making changes as needed. The periodic election of the executive and the members of the legislative branch affords constant renewal of the exercise of the will of the people. This opportunity for change by the majority makes it unnecessary to engage in violent revolution whenever those who govern are no longer responsive to the will of the people.

Recognizing that the will of the majority can be tyrannical, certain basic rights are protected in the Bill of Rights. Freemasonry has as its foundation stone the worth of the individual. Since the Constitution of the United States also recognizes the worth of the individual person it can be described as a Masonic document. Under our system every person is free to make choices and act as he pleases, being restricted only from acting in a manner that will interfere with the similar rights of others.

At the time of the Constitutional Convention, George Washington was fifty-five years old, and as the presiding officer, was the great pacifier when the debates became heated. Benjamin Franklin at the time was eighty-one years old, and his wise counsel entitles him to the description of the elder statesman. Without the presence of these two Masons it is doubtful if the convention would have succeeded.

The Foreword has been written by Brother Wendell K. Walker, 33°, a professional librarian and a graduate of Columbia University. He joined the New York Masonic Library in 1931, and interrupted his work during World War II to serve in the armed forces in France rising to the rank of Captain. After the war he resumed his duties as Librarian and later was elected Grand Secretary of the Grand Lodge of New York. He has written extensively for the *New York Masonic Outlook*, the *Empire State Mason* and other Masonic periodicals. He has been active in the American Lodge of Research, serving as Worshipful Master in 1951, 1954, and 1955. He is also a Fellow of the Philalethes Society and a Blue Friar.

Since this book was originally prepared for general circulation, it has no direct Masonic references. And, since persons make an organization, Brother Walker describes the Masons who were members of the Constitutional Convention. This book will prove valuable during this Bicentennial period and for many years to come, as it contains in words and pictures all that is of primary importance relating to the fundamental charter of our beloved United States.

Alphonse Cerza
Louis L. Williams

FOREWORD

The Signers of the Declaration of Independence, some of whom were Masons, gave the world and our country a challenging statement of political freedom. The Signers of the Constitution, some of the same men and Masons, and some others, met the challenge with a necessary outline of political organization. The document they produced has been rated "above every other written constitution" and its acceptance identified as the event which "made the American people a nation".

The Signers of the Constitution, with George Washington at their head, as well as the Signers of the Declaration led by John Hancock, are remembered for their public rather than their private virtues. Masonic membership, then as now, was private rather than public, and the lives of the signers, as presented in this book and in historical publications generally, do not mention Masonic activity even when known; hence this Foreword.

The Masons who were signers, like the signers who were not Masons, deserve to be remembered with public admiration and gratitude. In addition, the signers who were Masons deserve to have the public sentiment with which they are remembered augmented by fraternal pride and affection. The historical bases for sorting the Masons from the others have been best presented in a Masonic Service Association publication by Ronald E. Heaton, *Masonic Membership of the Founding Fathers.*

The greatest of all the Signers of the Constitution, and perhaps of all Americans, George Washington, was not only first in war and peace and in his countrymen's hearts but also in fraternal esteem, which he appreciated. He wrote to two Masons in 1782: "For your affectionate vows, permit me to be grateful; and offer mine for true Brothers in all parts of the world."

We do not have so much direct evidence from most of the other Masonic signers; from some not even enough to identify them certainly as Masons; but from several we have very impressive Masonic records, and from the others quite respectable indications of good standing in the Fraternity.

We have most from Benjamin Franklin, who was the oldest Mason at the Constitutional Convention and probably the oldest signer. He had entered the Craft in 1731, at the age of 25, in St. John's Lodge at the Tun Tavern, Water Street, Philadelphia. The following year he was elected Junior Grand Warden, and in 1734 Grand Master. In that year he published the first Masonic book in America, a reprint of the first London edition of Anderson's Constitutions of the Free-Masons. In 1749 he accepted an appointment as Provincial Grand Master of Pennsylvania, and the following year as Deputy Grand Master. In 1754 he attended a Grand Lodge communication in Boston, and in 1760 another in London. He was still an active Mason during his ambassadorial service in Paris, and there in 1778 assisted in initiating Voltaire into the famous Lodge of the Nine Muses. His later years in Philadelphia do not appear to have been active Masonically, but it was he who proposed opening each session of the Constitutional Convention with prayer.

Roger Sherman of Connecticut, who was associated with Franklin in the proposal for prayer at the Constitutional Convention, was one of the signers for whom we have no Masonic information, although it has been long sought. Two of his sons were Masons in Connecticut, and "his" apron at Yale University may have belonged to one of them.

Robert Morris of Pennsylvania is another very distinguished signer to whom has been attributed the ownership of a Masonic apron, this one the gift of no less a personage than George Washington, but without any surviving record to confirm either ownership or membership.

One more doubtful case is that of John Langdon, whose brother Woodbury was a member of St. John's Lodge No. 1 in Portsmouth, New Hampshire, but whose own connection with the Fraternity has not been established.

Lack of surviving record does not always mean doubtful membership, even when the doubt is compounded by that so often fanciful attribution of having been made "in a military Lodge during the Revolutionary War". Lodge No. 19 of Pennsylvania is supposed to have been the scene in the case of David Brearley of New Jersey, but without confirmation this would have left his membership as much in doubt as that of many others whom we cannot claim as brothers. In his case subsequent confirmation is abundant; David Brearley was most emphatically one of us. His original Lodge may or may not have been Pennsylvania's No. 19, but in 1786 he was not only recognized as a Mason but was elected first Grand Master of the Grand Lodge of New Jersey, and he served in that exalted office until his death in 1790.

Another New Jersey Masonic signer with an unknown record of initiation was Jonathan Dayton. He was a much younger man, but old enough to have been a member before the signing. He attended the Grand Lodge of New Jersey in December 1788 from "No. 1 Lodge", probably the one in his native Elizabethtown.

A third New Jersey signer, William Paterson, did not become a Mason until several years after the Constitutional Convention, receiving his three degrees in Trenton Lodge No. 5 in 1791.

One from Maryland, James McHenry, waited still longer. His initiation in Spiritual Lodge No. 23 was not until 1806 and lasted only to 1809.

Most of the Masonic signers had been members of the Fraternity for several years before they attended the Constitutional Convention. In fact, a majority received their degrees while the war was in progress, although not usually in military Lodges. Only three were pre-war members: George Washington, Benjamin Franklin, and John Blair of Virginia.

Nicholas Gilman, on or before March 20, 1777, became a member of St. John's Lodge No. 1, Portsmouth, New Hampshire.

John Dickinson, of Pennsylvania and Delaware, became a member of Lodge No. 18 (Pennsylvania) located in Dover, Delaware, in 1780.

Jacob Broom, also of Delaware, has been identified as a member and officer of Lodge No. 14 (Pennsylvania) at Christiana Ferry (Wilmington), elected Secretary and Treasurer June 24, 1780, Junior Warden June 25, 1781, and again Treasurer December 18, 1783.

Daniel Carroll of Maryland, one of the few Catholic delegates at the Constitutional Convention, was also a Mason. He received the first two degrees in 1780, and the third the following year, in Lodge No. 16, Baltimore. As one of three Commissioners of the new capital district, and as a Freemason, he participated in two famous cornerstone ceremonies, one for the Capital on April 14, 1791 and the other for the Capitol on September 18, 1793, President Washington presiding at the latter.

Gunning Bedford, Jr. was another member of Lodge No. 14, Christiana Ferry (Wilmington), Delaware, having received the degrees in 1782. Years later, when the Delaware Lodges formed their own Grand Lodge, 1806, Gunning Bedford was elected the first Grand Master, and was re-elected in 1807 and again in 1808.

One Masonic signer, long on the doubtful list because of records unknown, was Rufus King of Massachusetts, later New York. His initiation date is still not known, but he was in attendance as a member in St. John's Lodge, Newburyport, Massachusetts, in 1781 and 1782; as Treasurer in 1782; and as Junior Warden in 1783 and 1784. He was fined three shillings for unexcused absence December 27, 1783. His later years in New York appear to have been without Masonic activity.

After Washington and Franklin, the senior Mason in the Constitutional Convention, and one of the most distinguished, was John Blair of Virginia. He was already a Past Grand Master, having been elected at the organization of the Grand Lodge of Virginia, October 13, 1778, and served until 1784. He had been initiated in 1762 in a Lodge at the Crown Tavern in Williamsburg, and was a charter member of the new Williamsburg Lodge No. 6 in 1773. He succeeded Peyton Randolph as Master of this Lodge four years before becoming Grand Master.

Not much need be said in this Foreword of the greatest man and Mason of them all, George Washington, about whom we know most and admire most. He was a member all his adult life, first in the Lodge at Fredericksburg (now No. 4, Virginia) and then nearer Mount Vernon at Alexandria (No. 39, Pennsylvania; No. 22, Virginia; now Alexandria-Washington Lodge 22) where he was the first Master under the Virginia charter. He was nominated for General Grand Master of the United States, and if a national Grand Lodge had ever been organized he would undoubtedly have been elected. He visited American Union Lodge, in the army, and Solomon's Lodge No. 1, Poughkeepsie, and was an honorary member of the Holland Lodge (now No. 8) New York. As already mentioned, he presided at the most prestigious public Masonic ceremony in American history, the laying of the cornerstone of the national Capitol, September 18, 1793, and was the central figure in an even more prestigious ceremony, not Masonic but with important Masonic participants, the first presidential inauguration, April 30, 1789.

The Signers of the Constitution completed their work in the fall of 1787 and saw it ratified by a requisite number of states in 1788, but it was not until the spring of 1789 that their accomplishment was finally and formally immortalized as the fundamental law of the land, with the former president of their convention duly installed as the first President of the United States under the Constitution. There have been many presidential inaugurations since that first one, and Masons as citizens have participated to some degree in all, but never so extensively or so intimately as on that 30th day of April 1789, a day which ranks with July 4th, 1776, in American historical significance. The two parade marshals, Majors (afterward Major Generals) Jacob Morton and Morgan Lewis, were Masons, one the Master of his Lodge at the time and each to be elected later as Grand Master. The official who administered the presidential oath, Chancellor Robert R. Livingston, was then and had been and would be for years the Grand Master of Masons in the State of New York. Finally, the Bible on which the oath was taken was the altar Bible of St. John's Lodge No. 1, borrowed for the occasion by its Master, Worshipful Jacob Morton, from the Lodge room then located near Federal Hall, Broad and Wall Streets, New York City.

How many of the signers, Masons and others, may have been attending President Washington that fateful April 30th, either officially in Federal Hall or with the thousands of fellow citizens who lined the roofs and filled the streets as far as the eye could see, we do not know, but they must have been proud. All the signers must have been proud, even those few with lingering misgivings about the future adequacy of the Constitution, and we are proud of them, and grateful. We who are Masons are perhaps warmest in our proud memories of our brothers, but we salute all the signers, every one.

WENDELL K. WALKER
New York, 1976

[This text appeared in the original publication.]

COLOPHON

Nine hundred and ninety-nine copies of this special Masonic limited edition were manufactured by the Pantagraph Press of Bloomington, Illinois, which gathered, sewed, and bound the printed sheets furnished by J. G. Ferguson Publishing Company of Chicago, Illinois.

The typeface chosen for the special Preface and Foreword for this edition was Linotype Caledonia. The book covers are made of Columbia Mills' Riverside vellum over boards and stamped in gold.

All volumes of The Masonic Book Club series are designed and prepared by Louis L. Williams, Alphonse Cerza, and Fred A. Dolan.

Courtesy of the Boston Athenaeum. Currently on loan to Museum of Fine Arts, Boston.

Pat Lyon at the Forge
By John Neagle

The Capitol, Washington, D.C. Photograph by Davis Studio.

The Scene at the Signing of the Constitution
By Howard Chandler Christy
(This mural appears in the South Wing of the Capitol, Washington, D.C.)

FOUNDERS OF FREEDOM

IN AMERICA

Courtesy: New York Public Library.

James Madison

FOUNDERS OF FREEDOM
IN
AMERICA

Lives of The Men Who Signed

The Constitution of The United States

And So Helped To Establish

The

UNITED STATES OF AMERICA

By

DAVID C. WHITNEY

Encyclopedia Editor and Historian

Coordinating Editor

THOMAS C. JONES

Editor of Prints and Photographs

KATHRINE B. SANBORN

Published By

J. G. FERGUSON PUBLISHING COMPANY

Chicago, Illinois

1974

ISBN: 0-385-06355-5
LIBRARY OF CONGRESS CATALOG CARD NUMBER 65-13057

LITHOGRAPHED IN THE UNITED STATES OF AMERICA
by
PHOTOPRESS, INC. · BROADVIEW, ILLINOIS

COMMENTS and ACKNOWLEDGMENTS . . .

There were fifty-six signers of the Declaration of Independence, and thirty-nine signers of the Constitution, six signers of both. Without any doubt, these eighty-nine signers qualify as "founding fathers." There were many others, to be sure, whose leadership, daring, and energy contributed to the establishment of the republic we know today as the United States of America, but the signers were the ones directly responsible for converting a dream into a reality.

Surmising the intentions of the "founding fathers" in writing the Constitution has been a prominent part of the national, political, and judicial scene since 1787. The Madison papers throw light upon many of the varying viewpoints that led to disagreements and ultimate compromises. It was generally agreed that the loosely knit Articles of Confederation served only to increase confusion and decrease the chance to consolidate the great opportunities made possible by the hard-won military victory and the resulting freedom. There were widely divergent views as to how to achieve the desired result, namely: a federal government that preserved the essential features of republics for the colonies, yet strong enough to function as a nation in terms of treaties, fiscal matters, defense, international trade, communications, and many other rapidly expanding spheres of development.

Sixty delegates were appointed to the Constitutional Convention; fifty-five attended at least some of the sessions. The average age of the members was about forty-two. A large majority were lawyers with private practice. Only a few had seen military service in the Revolution. As a group, they were able, practical men who were keenly aware of the defects of the existing system.

The great political cleavage at that time was between the large and small states rather than between sections of the country. It was agreed that each state would have one vote on all issues. Seven states constituted a quorum. Nothing spoken in the convention was to be published or communicated without consent. It was hoped that this secrecy would eliminate later arguments when the Constitution would be submitted for ratification.

The Virginia delegation met in caucus frequently and, on May 29, 1787, submitted the Virginia Plan for the consideration of all the delegates. It provided for three departments of government—legislative, executive, and judicial. A legislature of two houses in which the representation of states should be proportional, either to quotas of taxes or to free population, the members of the lower house to be elected by the people and those of the upper house by the lower house from persons nominated by the state legislatures; an executive to be chosen by the legislature and to be ineligible for a second term; and a judicial department to consist of a supreme court and inferior courts. The federal legislature was to have power to pass on the constitutionality of state laws. The laws of the federal legislature were to be subject to review by the excutive and part of the judiciary. The final draft of the Constitution was essentially evolved from this plan.

The so-called Pinckney Plan was probably referred to by the delegates, but was never taken very seriously. No actual copy of this plan has ever been found. That which appears on pages 247 and 248 cannot be regarded as anything but a probable approximation of this Plan.

On June 15, 1787, the New Jersey delegation submitted a Plan designed to be more favorable to the small states. The legislature was to be unicameral with each state having one vote. Congress would have added powers in taxation and commerce. The executive would be chosen by Congress and there would be a supreme court. Acts of Congress and treaties were to be the supreme law of the states. The judiciary of the states would be bound by the laws and decisions of the Congress. The federal executive was authorized to use force if necessary to execute federal acts or treaties.

The delegates carefully considered the various viewpoints and evolved a basis of government that has endured for one hundred, seventy-five years. To be sure, the amendments and interpretations have resulted in broadened applications, but the essential features remain in force as the basis of the republic.

James Madison said in *The Federalist:*

"The truth is that the principles of the Constitution proposed by the Convention may be considered less as absolutely new than as the expansion of principles which are found in the Articles of Confederation . . . If the new Constitution be examined with accuracy and candor, it will be found that the change which it proposes consists much less in the addition of NEW POWERS to the Union, than in the invigoration of its ORIGINAL POWERS."

On the subject of representation, Madison reports James Wilson as saying:

"It was necessary to observe the twofold relation in which the people would stand. 1. as Citizens of the Genl. Govt. 2. as Citizens of their particular State. The Genl. Govt. was meant for them in the first capacity; the State in the second. Both Govts. were derived from the people—both meant for the people—both therefore ought to be regulated on the same principles. The same train of ideas which belonged to the relation of the Citizens to their State Govts. were applicable to their relation to the Genl. Govt. and in forming the latter, we ought to proceed by abstracting as much as possible from the idea of State Govts. with respect to the province and objects of the Genl. Govt., they should be considered as having no existence . . . The Genl. Govt. is not an assembly of States but of individuals for certain political purposes—it is not meant for the States, but for the individuals composing them; the individuals therefore not the States, ought to be represented in it."

In these biographies, Mr. Whitney tells the story of each signer in an appealing direct, style making generous use of quotations from contemporaries of the subjects. He brings together much basic information that has not previously been included in a single source. It is perhaps no coincidence that in most of the biographies there is a natural emergence of values of citizenship that should be emulated. Indeed for the most part these patriots were men of substance whose lives should serve as examples of conduct for the citizen and leader of today.

These articles have particular value to the junior high and high school junior citizens. Above all, the general nature of the material has a close affinity and application to this time in the history of the republic.

In the preparation of this work, there have been many organizations and individuals who graciously cooperated with us. With grateful pleasure, we list below those to whom we are indebted. David Whitney, Kathrine B. Sanborn, Herbert J. Sanborn, Norma Rehder, Jean Eisinger, Walter Luchman, Elizabeth Roth, Grace Jameson, Suzanne T. Cooper, Francis G. Mayer, Dale Jansen, Mrs. Samuel Edelson, Arthur K. Scott, Don Swann, Mrs. H. K. D. Peachy, Mr. and Mrs. Nigel Brunt, Mrs. Overton W Price, Eric Muller, Edward R. Pool, John H. Mitchell, Constance Stuart Larrabee, George H. Van Anda, The Library of Congress, The New York Public Library, Colonial Williamsburg, The Davis Studio, National Archives, The Detroit Public Library, The Historical Society of Delaware, Bowdoin College Museum of Art, Eastern National Park and Monument Association, Mount Vernon Ladies Association, Independence National Historical Park Collection, Historical Society of Pennsylvania, Cooper Dawson, The Baltimore Museum of Art, The Old Print Shop, N. Y., Sanborn Studios, Princeton University Library, William Blount Mansion Association, Grand Lodge F&AM, Trenton, N. J., Frick Art Reference Library, The Pennsylvania Museum of Fine Arts, Peale Museum, Phillips Studios, Rutgers University, The Metropolitan Museum of Art, N. Y., The Corcoran Gallery of Art, Washington, D.C., Phillips Exeter Academy, Museum of Fine Arts, Boston, National Gallery of Art, Washington, D.C., Museum of the City of New York, The Boston Atheneum, Society for the Preservation of New England Antiquities, Boston, Columbia University, N. Y., Yale University Art Gallery, The Long Island Historical Society, Essex Institute, The Pennsylvania Academy of Fine Arts, Thomas Gilcrease Institute of American History and Arts, Tulsa, Oklahoma, American Scenic and Historic Preservation Society Collection, Carolina Art Association, Charleston, S. C., Worcester Art Museum, Massachusetts, Marler Potos, Alexandria, Va., Louisiana State Museum; George Lohr Studios, Washington, D.C., National Collection of Fine Arts, Smithsonian Institution, Maryland Historical Society, The Beck Engraving Company, Inc., G. R. Grubb & Company, A-1 Composition Company, Photopress, Inc., and A. C. Engdahl & Company.

It is possible that we have inadvertently omitted the names of some people and organizations who have helped us in the preparation of this work. We shall be glad to add any omissions to future printings upon notification.

THOMAS C. JONES, *for the publisher*

TABLE OF CONTENTS

A LISTING OF BLACK-AND-WHITE ILLUSTRATIONS

A LISTING OF COLORED ILLUSTRATIONS

The I. N. Phelps Stokes Collection of American Historical Prints, New York Public Library.

Baltimore, Maryland, 1752

STEPS LEADING TO THE CONSTITUTIONAL CONVENTION

By JAMES MADISON, *Fourth President of the United States*

The following article, written by James Madison, the "Father of the Constitution," was found among his papers after his death in 1836. It sets forth the developments that led to the Constitutional Convention of 1787.

There are many examples of associations of men under common authority.

As the weakness and wants of man naturally lead to an association of individuals under a common authority, whereby each may have the protection of the whole against danger from without, and enjoy in safety within the advantages of social intercourse, and an exchange of the necessaries and comforts of life; in like manner feeble communities, independent of each other, have resorted to a union, less intimate, but with common councils, for the common safety against powerful neighbours, and for the preservation of justice and peace among themselves. Ancient history furnishes examples of these confederate associations, though with a very imperfect account of their structure, and of the attributes and functions of the presiding authority. There are examples of modern date also, some of them still existing, the modifications and transactions of which are sufficiently known.

It remained for the British Colonies, now United States of North America, to add to those examples, one of a more interesting character than any of them; which led to a system without an example ancient or modern. A system founded on popular rights, and so combining a federal form with the forms of individual republics, as may enable each to supply the defects of the other and obtain that advantage of both.

Growth of the colonies tempted the British.

Whilst the Colonies enjoyed the protection of the parent country, as it was called, against foreign danger, and were secured by its superintending control against conflicts among themselves, they continued independent of each other, under a common, though limited, dependence on the parental authority. When, however, the growth of the offspring in strength and in wealth awakened the jealousy, and tempted the avidity of the parent, into schemes of usurpation and exaction, the obligation was felt by the former of uniting their counsels and efforts, to avert the impending calamity.

As early as the year 1754, indications having been given of a design in the British government to levy contributions on the Colonies without their consent, a meeting of Colonial deputies took place at Albany, which attempted to introduce a compromising substitute, that might at once satisfy the British requisitions, and save their own rights from violation. The attempt had no other effect, than, by bringing these rights into a more conspicuous view, to invigorate the attachment to them, on the one side; and to nourish the haughty and encroaching spirit on the other.

In 1774, the progress made by Great Britain in the open assertion of her pretensions, and the apprehended purpose of otherwise maintaining them by legislative enactments and declarations, had been such that the Colonies did not hesitate to assemble, by their deputies, in a formal Congress, authorized to oppose to the British innovations whatever measures might be found best adapted to the occasion; without, however, losing sight of an eventual reconciliation.

The dissuasive measures of that Congress being without effect, another Congress was held in 1775, whose pacific efforts to bring about a change in the views of the other party being equally unavailing, and the commencement of actual hostilities having at length put an end to all hope of reconciliation, the Congress finding, moreover, that the popular voice began to call for an entire and perpetual dissolution of the political ties which had connected them with Great Britain, proceeded on the memorable Fourth of July, 1776, to declare the thirteen Colonies *Independent States*.

During the discussions of this solemn act, a Committee, consisting of a member from each Colony, had been appointed, to prepare and digest a form of Confederation for the future management of the common interests, which had hitherto been left to the discretion of Congress, guided by the exigencies of the contest, and by the known intentions or occasional instructions of the Colonial Legislatures.

Origin of the Articles of Confederation.

It appears that as early as the twenty-first of July, 1775, a plan, entitled "Articles of Confederation and *perpetual* union of the Colonies," had been sketched by Doctor Franklin, the plan being on that day submitted by him to Congress; and though not copied into their Journals, remaining on their files in his handwriting. But notwithstanding the term "perpetual" observed in the title, the Articles provided expressly for the event of a return of the Colonies to a connection with Great Britain.

This sketch became a basis for the plan reported by the Committee on the twelfth of July, now also remaining on the files of Congress in the hand-

The Repeal of the Stamp Act
One of the many cartoons depicting the funeral of this hated legislation.

Library of Congress.

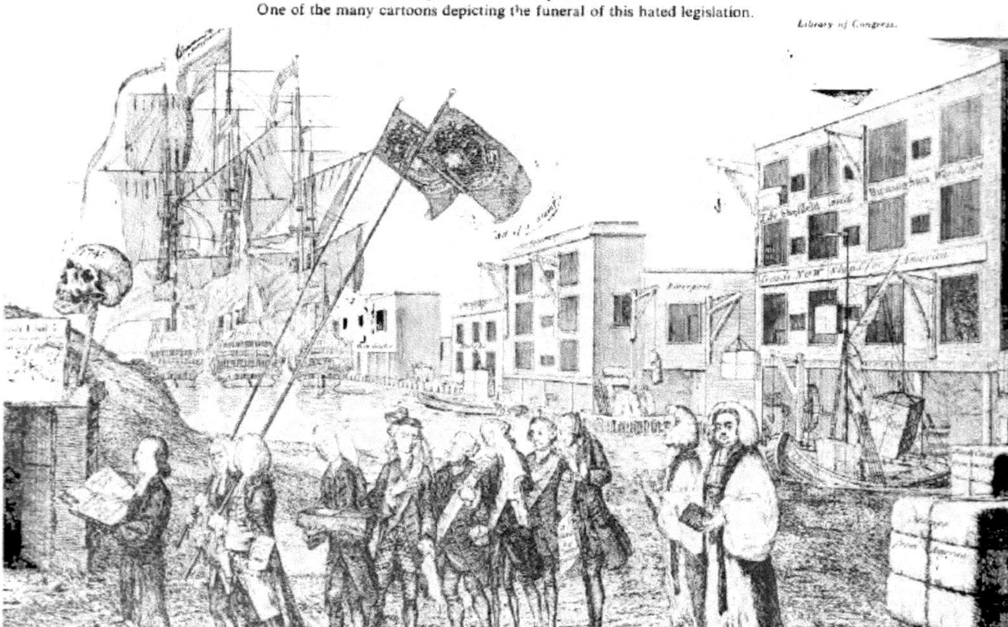

writing of Mr. Dickinson. The plan, though dated after the Declaration of Independence, was probably drawn up before that event; since the name of Colonies, not States, is used throughout the draught. The plan reported was debated and amended from time to time, till the seventeenth of November, 1777, when it was agreed to by Congress, and proposed to the Legislatures of the States, with an explanatory and recommendatory letter. The ratifications of these, by their delegates in Congress, duly authorized, took place at successive dates; but were not completed till the first of March, 1781, when Maryland, who had made a prerequisite that the vacant lands acquired from the British Crown should be a common fund, yielded to the persuasion that a final and formal establishment of the Federal Union and Government would make a favorable impression, not only on other foreign nations, but on Great Britain herself.

Ratification of the Articles of Confederation.

The great difficulty experienced in so framing the Federal system, as to obtain the unanimity required for its due sanction, may be inferred from the long interval, and recurring discussions, between the commencement and completion of the work; from the changes made during its progress; from the language of Congress when proposing it to the States, which dwelt on the impracticability of devising a system acceptable to all of them; from the reluctant assent given by some; and the various alterations proposed by others; and by a tardiness in others again, which produced a special address to them from Congress, enforcing the duty of sacrificing local considerations and favorite opinions to the public safety, and the necessary harmony; nor was the assent of some of the States finally yielded without strong protests against particular Articles, and a reliance on future amendments removing their objections. It is to be recollected, no doubt, that these delays might be occasioned in some degree by an occupation of the public councils, both general and local, with the deliberations and measures essential to a voluntary struggle; but there must have been a balance for these causes in the obvious motives to hasten the establishment of a regular and efficient government; and in the tendency of the crisis to repress opinions and pretensions which might be inflexible in another state of things.

Necessity forced an acceptance.

The principal difficulties which embarrassed the progress, and retarded the completion, of the plan of Confederation, may be traced to—first, the natural repugnance of the parties to a relinquishment of power; secondly, a natural jealousy of its abuse in other hands than their own; thirdly, the rule of suffrage among parties whose inequality in size did not correspond with that of their wealth, or of their military or free population; fourthly, the selection and definition of the powers, at once necessary to the federal head, and safe to the several members.

To these sources of difficulty, incident to the formation of all such confederacies, were added two others, one of a temporary, the other of a permanent nature. The first was the case of the Crown lands, so called because they had been held by the British Crown, and being ungranted to individuals when its authority ceased, were considered by the States within whose charters or asserted limits they lay, as devolving on them; whilst it was contended by the others, that being wrested from the dethroned authority by the equal exertions of all, they resulted of right and in equity to the benefit of all. The lands being of vast extent, and of growing value, were the occasion of much discussion and heart-burning; and proved the most obstinate of the impediments to an earlier consummation of the plan of federal government. The State of Maryland, the last that acceded to it, held out as already noticed, till the first of March, 1781; and then yielded only to the hope that, by giving a stable and authoritative character to the Confederation, a successful termination of the contest might be accelerated. The dispute was happily compromised by successive surrenders of portions of the territory by the States having exclusive claims to it, and acceptances of them by Congress.

Articles of Confederation proved unsatisfactory.

The other source of dissatisfaction was the peculiar situation of some of the States, which, having no convenient ports for foreign commerce, were subject to be taxed by their neighbours, through whose ports their commerce was carried on. New Jersey, placed between Philadelphia and New York, was likened to a cask tapped at both ends; and North Carolina, between Virginia and South Carolina, to a patient bleeding at both arms. The Articles of Confederation provided no remedy for the complaint; which produced a strong protest on the part of New Jersey, and never ceased to be a source of dissatisfaction and discord, until the new Constitution superseded the old.

But the radical infirmity of the "Articles of Confederation" was the dependence of Congress on the voluntary and simultaneous compliance with its requisitions by so many independent communities, each consulting more or less its particular interests and convenience, and distrusting the compliance of the others. Whilst the paper emissions of Congress continued to circulate, they were employed as a sinew of war, like gold and silver. When that ceased to be the case, and the fatal defect of the political system was felt in its alarming force, the war was merely kept alive, and brought to a successful conclusion, by such foreign aids and temporary expedients as could be applied; a hope prevailing with many, and a wish with all, that a state of peace, and the sources of prosperity opened by it, would give to the Confederacy, in practice, the efficiency which had been inferred from its theory.

The close of the war, however, brought no cure for the public embarrassments. The States, relieved from the pressure of foreign danger, and flushed with the enjoyment of independent and sovereign power, instead of a diminished disposition to part with it, persevered in omissions and in measures incompatible with their relations to the Federal Government, and with those among themselves.

An obligation to avert a calamity.

Having served as a member of Congress through the period between March, 1780, and the arrival of peace, in 1783, I had become intimately acquainted with the public distresses and the causes of them. I had observed the successful opposition to every attempt to procure a remedy by new grants of power to Congress. I had found, moreover, that despair of success hung over the compromising principle of April, 1783, for the public necessities, which had been so elaborately planned and so impressively recommended to the States. Sympathizing, under this aspect of affairs, in the alarm of the friends of free government at the threatened danger of an abortive result to the great, and perhaps last, experiment in its favor, I could not be insensible to the obligation to aid as far as I could in averting the calamity. With this view I acceded to the desire of my fellow citizens of the County, that I should be one of its representatives in the Legislature, hoping that I might there best contribute to inculcate the critical posture to which the Revolutionary cause was reduced, and the merit of a leading agency of the State in bringing about a rescue of the Union, and the blessings of liberty staked on it, from an impending catastrophe.

It required but little time after taking my seat in the House of Delegates in May, 1784, to discover, that, however favorable the general disposition of the State might be towards the Confederacy, the Legislature retained the aversion of its predecessors to transfers of power from the State to the Government of the Union; notwithstanding the urgent demands of the Federal Treasury, the glaring inadequacy of the authorized mode of supplying it, the rapid growth of anarchy in the Federal system, and the animosity kindled among the States by their conflicting regulations.

The temper of the Legislature, and the wayward course of its proceedings, may be gathered from the Journals of its sessions in the years 1784 and 1785.

Repeated disagreements forced a meeting to work out a more effective system.

The failure, however, of the varied propositions in the Legislature, for enlarging the powers of Congress; the continued failure of the efforts of Congress to obtain from them the means of providing for the debts of the Revolution, and of countervailing the commercial laws of Great Britain, a source of much irritation, and against which the separate efforts of the States were found worse than abortive; these considerations, with the lights thrown on the whole subject by the free and full discussion it had undergone, led to a general acquiescence in the Resolution passed on the twenty-first of January, 1786, which proposed and invited a meeting of Deputies from all the States, as follows:

"*Resolved*, that Edmund Randolph, James Madison, Jr., Walter Jones, St. George Tucker, and Meriwether Smith, Esquires, be appointed Commissioners, who, or any three of whom, shall meet such Commissioners as may be appointed in the other States of the Union, at a time and place to be agreed on, to take into consideration the trade of the United States; to examine the relative situations and trade of said States; to consider how far a uniform system in their commercial regulations may be necessary to their common interest and their permanent harmony; and to report to the several States such an act, relative to this great object, as when unanimously ratified by them, will enable the United States in Congress, effectually to provide for the same."

Travels in the United States and Canada, by De Roos.

A stop on the stagecoach between Baltimore and Washington

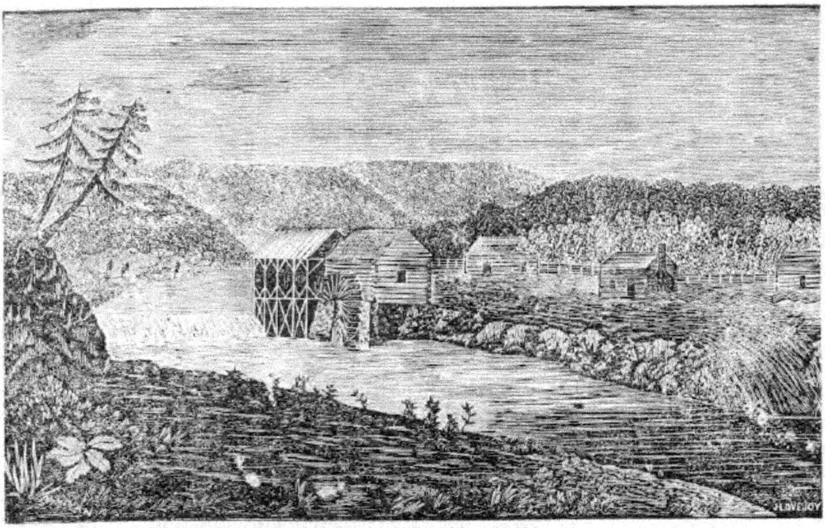

An Early Settlement in Ohio (1789)
This is a print of the Wolf Creek Mills at the time George Washington became President.

The Resolution had been brought forward some weeks before, on a failure of a proposed grant of power to Congress to collect a revenue from commerce, which had been abandoned by its friends in consequence of material alterations made in the grant by a Committee of the Whole. The Resolution, though introduced by Mr. Tyler, an influential member,—who, having never served in Congress, had more the ear of the House than those whose services there exposed them to an imputable bias,—was so little acceptable, that it was not then persisted in. Being now revived by him, on the last day of the session, and being the alternative of adjourning without any effort for the crisis in the affairs of the Union, it obtained a general vote; less, however, with some of its friends, from a confidence in the success of the experiment, than from a hope that it might prove a step to a more comprehensive and adequate provision for the wants of the Confederacy.

Acknowledged need of uniformity in several matters

It happened also, that Commissioners, appointed by Virginia and Maryland to settle the jurisdiction on waters dividing the two States, had, apart from their official reports, recommended a uniformity in the regulations of the two States on several subjects, and particularly on those having relation to foreign trade. It appeared at the same time, that Maryland had deemed a concurrence of her neighbours, Delaware and Pennsylvania, indispensable in such a case; who, for like reasons, would require that all of their neighbours. So apt and forcible an illustration of the necessity of an uniformity throughout all the States could not but favor the passage of a resolution which proposed a Convention having that for its object.

Norfolk, Virginia
By Benjamin Henry Latrobe

New York Public Library. Photo by Francis G. Mayer.

U. S. Frigate, *The President*, off the Port of Marseilles, France, 1806

The Commissioners appointed by the Legislature, and who attended the Convention, were Edmund Randolph, the Attorney of the State, St. George Tucker and James Madison. The designation of the time and place to be proposed for its meeting, and communicated to the States, having been left to the Commissioners, they named, for the time the first Monday in September, and for the place the city of Annapolis, avoiding the residence of Congress, and large commercial cities, as liable to suspicions of an extraneous influence.

Representatives of only five states attended the meeting.

Although the invited meeting appeared to be generally favored, five States only assembled; some failing to make appointments, and some of the individuals appointed not hastening their attendance; the result in both cases being ascribed mainly to a belief that the time had not arrived for such a political reform as might be expected from a further experience of its necessity.

But in the interval between the proposal of the Convention and the time of its meeting, such had been the advance of public opinion in the desired direction, stimulated as it had been by the effect of the contemplated object of the meeting, in turning the general attention to the critical state of things, and in calling forth the sentiments and exertions of the most enlightened and influential patriots, that the Convention, thin as it was, did not scruple to decline the limited task assigned to it, and to recommend to the States a Convention with powers adequate to the occasion. Nor had it been unnoticed that the commission of the New Jersey deputation had extended its object to a general provision for the exigencies of the Union. A recommendation for this enlarged purpose was accordingly reported by a committee to whom the subject had been referred. It was drafted by Col. Hamilton, and finally agreed to in the following form:

A resolution to meet as states empowered to act in developing a uniform system of government.

"To the Honorable, the Legislatures of Virginia, Delaware, Pennsylvania, New Jersey, and New York, the Commissioners from the said States, respectively, assembled at Annapolis, humbly beg leave to report:

"That, pursuant to their several appointments, they met at Annapolis, in the State of Maryland, on the eleventh day of September instant; and having proceeded to a communication of their powers, they found that the States of New York, Pennsylvania and Virginia, had, in substance, and nearly in the same terms, authorized their respective Commissioners 'to meet such commissioners as were, or might be, appointed by the other States of the Union, at such time and place as should be agreed upon by the said Commissioners, to take into consideration the trade and commerce of the United States; to consider how far an uniform system in their commercial intercourse and regulations might be necessary to their common interest and permanent harmony; and to report to the several States such an act, relative to this great object, as, when unanimously ratified by them, would enable the United States in Congress assembled effectually to provide for the same.'

"That the State of Delaware had given similar powers to their Commissioners, with this difference only, that the act to be framed in virtue of these powers is required to be reported 'to the United States in Congress assembled, to be agreed to by them, and confirmed by the Legislature of every State.'

"That the State of New Jersey had enlarged the object of their appointment, empowering their commissioners, 'to consider how far an uniform system in their commercial regulations, and *other important matters,* might be necessary to the common interest and permanent harmony of the several States;' and to report such an act on the subject, as, when ratified by them, 'would enable the United States in Congress assembled effectually to provide for the exigencies of the Union.'

Bowdoin College Museum of Art. Bequest of James Bowdoin III.

President James Madison
(1805)
By GILBERT STUART

"That appointments of Commissioners have also been made by the States of New Hampshire, Massachusetts, Rhode Island, and North Carolina, none of whom, however, have attended; but that no information has been received by your Commissioners of any appointment having been made by the States of Maryland, Connecticut, South Carolina or Georgia.

"That the express terms of the powers to your Commissioners supposing a deputation from all the States, and having for object the trade and commerce of the United States, your Commissioners did not conceive it advisable to proceed on the business of their mission under the circumstances of so partial and defective a representation.

"Deeply impressed, however, with the magnitude and importance of the object confided to them on this occasion, your Commissioners cannot forbear to indulge an expression of their earnest and unanimous wish, that speedy measures may be taken to effect a general meeting of the States in a future Convention, for the same and such other purposes, as the situation of public affairs may be found to require.

"If, in expressing this wish, or in intimating any other sentiment, your Commissioners should seem to exceed the strict bounds of their appointment, they entertain a full confidence, that a conduct dictated by an anxiety for the welfare of the United States will not fail to receive an indulgent construction.

"In this persuasion, your Commissioners submit an opinion, that the idea of extending the powers of their Deputies to other objects than those of commerce, which has been adopted by the State of New Jersey, was an improvement on the original plan, and will deserve to be incorporated into that of a future Convention. They are the more naturally led to this conclusion, as, in the course of their reflections on the subject, they have been induced to think that the power of regulating trade is of such comprehensive extent, and will enter so far into the general system of the Federal Government, that to give it efficacy, and to obviate questions and doubts concerning its precise nature and limits, may require a correspondent adjustment of other parts of the Federal system.

Acknowledging defects in the system.

"That there are important defects in the system of the Federal Government, is acknowledged by the acts of all those States which have concurred in the present meeting. That the defects, upon a closer examination, may be found greater and more numerous than even these acts imply, is at least so far probable, from the embarrassments which characterize the present state of our national affairs, foreign and domestic, as may reasonably be supposed to merit a deliberate and candid discussion, in some mode which will unite the sentiments and councils of all the States. In the choice of the mode, your Commissioners are of opinion, that a Convention of deputies from the different States, for the special and sole purpose of entering into this investigation, and digesting a plan for supplying such defects as may be discovered to exist, will be entitled to a preference, from considerations which will occur without being particularized.

"Your Commissioners decline an enumeration of those national circumstances on which their opinion, respecting the propriety of a future Convention with more enlarged powers, is founded; as it would be an useless intrusion of facts and observations, most of which have been frequently the subject of public discussion, and none of which can have escaped the penetration of those to whom they would in this instance be addressed. They are, however, of a nature so serious, as, in the view of your Commissioners, to render the situa-

To provide a federal government adequate to the exigencies.

tion of the United States delicate and critical, calling for an exertion of the united virtue and wisdom of all the members of the Confederacy.

"Under this impression, your Commissioners, with the most respectful deference, beg leave to suggest their unanimous conviction, that it may essentially tend to advance the interests of the Union, if the States by whom they have been respectively delegated would themselves concur, and use their endeavours to procure the concurrence of the other States, in the appointment of Commissioners, to meet at Philadelphia on the second Monday in May next, to take into consideration the situation of the United States; to devise such further provisions as shall appear to them necessary to render the constitution of the Federal Government adequate to the exigencies of the Union; and to report such an act for that purpose, to the United States in Congress assembled, as, when agreed to by them, and afterwards confirmed by the Legislatures of every State, will effectually provide for the same.

"Though your Commissioners could not with propriety address these observations and sentiments to any but the States they have the honor to represent, they have nevertheless concluded, from motives of respect, to transmit copies of this Report to the United States in Congress assembled, and to the Executives of the other States."

The recommendation was well received by the Legislature of Virginia, which happened to be the *first* that *acted on* it; and the example of her compliance was made as conciliatory and impressive as possible. The Legislature were unanimous, or very nearly so, on the occasion. As a proof of the magnitude and solemnity attached to it, they placed General Washington at the head of the deputation from the State; and as a proof of the deep interest he felt in the case, he overstepped the obstacles to his acceptance of the appointment.

Tarrytown, New York (c. 1780)
This is the site where Major Andre was captured.

Library of Congress. Itineraire Pittoresque, J. Milbert.

The Detroit Public Library, Burton Historical Collection.

A View of Detroit
(July 25, 1794)

The law complying with the recommendation from Annapolis was in the terms following:

"Whereas, the Commissioners who assembled at Annapolis, on the fourteenth day of September last, for the purpose of devising and reporting the means of enabling Congress to provide effectually for the commercial interests of the United States, have represented the necessity of extending the revision of the Federal system to all its defects; and have recommended that deputies for that purpose be appointed by the several Legislatures, to meet in Convention in the City of Philadelphia, on the second Monday of May next,—a provision which seems preferable to a discussion of the subject in Congress, where it might be too much interrupted by the ordinary business before them, and where it would, besides, be deprived of the valuable counsels of sundry individuals who are disqualified by the constitution or laws of particular States, or restrained by peculiar circumstances, from a seat in that Assembly:

Setting the date of the Convention.

"And whereas, the General Assembly of this Commonwealth, taking into view the actual situation of the Confederacy, as well as reflecting on the alarming representations made from time to time, by the United States in Congress, particularly in their act of the fifteenth day of February last, can no longer doubt that the crisis is arrived at which the good people of America are to decide the solemn question, whether they will, by wise and magnanimous efforts, reap the just fruits of that independence which they have so gloriously acquired, and of that union which they have cemented with so much of their common blood; or whether, by giving way to unmanly jealousies and prejudices, or to partial and transitory interests, they will renounce the auspicious blessings prepared for them by the Revolution, and furnish to its enemies an eventual triumph over those, by whose virtue and valour, it has been accomplished:

"And whereas, the same noble and extended policy, and the same fraternal and affectionate sentiments, which originally determined the citizens of this Commonwealth to unite with their brethren of the other States, in establishing a federal government, cannot but be felt with equal force now, as motives to lay aside every inferior consideration, and to concur in such farther concessions and provisions, as may be necessary to secure the great objects for which that government was instituted, and to render the United States as happy in peace, as they have been glorious in war.

"Be it, therefore, enacted, by the General Assembly of the Commonwealth of Virginia, That seven Commissioners be appointed by joint ballot of both Houses of Assembly, who, or any three of them, are hereby authorized as Deputies from this Commonwealth, to meet such Deputies as may be appointed and authorized by other States, to assemble in Convention at Philadelphia, as above recommended, and to join with them in devising and discussing all such alterations and farther provisions, as may be necessary to render the Federal Constitution adequate to the exigencies of the Union; and in reporting such an act for that purpose, to the United States in Congress, as when agreed to by them, and duly confirmed by the several States, will effectually provide for the same.

"And be it further enacted, That in case of the death of any of the said deputies, or of their declining their appointments, the Executive are hereby authorized to supply such vacancies; and the Governor is requested to transmit forthwith a copy of this act to the United States in Congress, and to the Executives of each of the States in the Union."*

A general constitutional convention was not a new idea.

A resort to a General Convention, to re-model the Confederacy, was not a new idea. It had entered at an early date into the conversations and speculations of the most reflecting and foreseeing observers of the inadequacy of the powers allowed to Congress. In a pamphlet published in May, 1781, at the seat of Congress, Pelatiah Webster, an able though not conspicuous citizen, after discussing the fiscal system of the United States, and suggesting, among other remedial provisions, one including a national bank, remarks, that "the authority of Congress at present is very inadequate to the performance of their duties; and this indicates the necessity of their calling a *Continental Convention* for the express purpose of ascertaining, defining, enlarging and limiting, the duties and powers of their Constitution."

On the first day of April, 1783, Colonel Hamilton, in a debate in Congress, observed, that "he wished, instead of them (partial Conventions), to see a general Convention take place; and that he should soon, in pursuance of instructions from his constituents, propose to Congress a plan for that purpose, the object of which would be to strengthen the Federal Constitution." He alluded probably, to the resolutions introduced by General Schuyler in the Senate, and passed unanimously by the Legislature of New York in the summer of 1782, declaring, that the Confederation was defective, in not giving Congress power to provide a revenue for itself, or in not investing them with funds from established and productive sources; and that it would be advisable for Congress to recommend to the States to call a general Conven-

*Drawn by J. Madison, passed the House of Delegates November 9th, the Senate November 23d— and Deputies appointed December 4th, 1786.

tion to revise and amend the Confederation." It does not appear, however, that his expectation had been fulfilled.

A union of states is essential.

In a letter to James Madison from R. H. Lee, then President of Congress, dated the twenty-sixth of November, 1784, he says: "It is by many here suggested as a very necessary step for Congress to take, the calling on the States to form a Convention for the sole purpose of revising the Confederation, so far as to enable Congress to execute with more energy, effect and vigor the powers assigned to it, than it appears by experience that they can do under the present state of things." The answer of Mr. Madison remarks: "I hold it for a maxim, that the union of the States is essential to their safety against foreign danger and internal contention; and that the perpetuity and efficacy of the present system cannot be confided in. The question, therefore, is, in what mode, and at what moment, the experiment for supplying the defects ought to be made."

Richard Henry Lee
From an early engraving

In the winter of 1784-5, Noah Webster, whose political and other valuable writings had made him known to the public, proposed, in one of his publications, "a new system of government which should act, not on the States, but directly on individuals, and vest in Congress full power to carry its laws into effect."

Courtesy: Eastern National Park & Monument Association
William Jackson Secretary of Congress
By Charles Willson Peale

The proposed and expected Convention at Annapolis, the first of a general character that appears to have been realized, and the state of the public mind awakened by it, had attracted the particular attention of Congress, and favored the idea there of a Convention with fuller power for amending the Confederacy.

It does not appear that in any of these cases the reformed system was to be otherwise sanctioned than by the Legislative authority of the

States; nor whether, nor how far, a change was to be made in the structure of the depository of Federal powers.

The act of Virginia providing for the Convention at Philadelphia was succeeded by appointments from the other States as their Legislatures were assembled, the appointments being selections from the most experienced and highest standing citizens. Rhode Island was the only exception to a compliance with the recommendation from Annapolis, well known to have been swayed by an obdurate adherence to an advantage which her position gave her, of taxing her neighbours through their consumption of imported supplies, an advantage which it was foreseen would be taken from her by a revisal of the Articles of Confederation.

As the public mind had been ripened for a salutary reform of the political system, in the interval between the proposal and the meeting of the Commissioners at Annapolis, the interval between the last event and the meeting of deputies at Philadelphia had continued to develop more and more the necessity and the extent of a systematic provision for the preservation and government of the Union. Among the ripening incidents was the insurrection of Shays, in Massachusetts, against her government; which was with difficulty suppressed, notwithstanding the influence on the insurgents of an apprehended interposition of the Federal troops.

Shays' Rebellion highlighted the need for union.

At the date of the Convention, the aspect and retrospect of the political condition of the United States could not but fill the public mind with a gloom which was relieved only by a hope that so select a body would devise an adequate remedy for the existing and prospective evils so impressively demanding it.

It was seen that the public debt, rendered so sacred by the cause in which it had been incurred, remained without any provision for its payment. The reiterated and elaborate efforts of Congress to procure from the States a more adequate power to raise the means of payment, had failed. The effect of the ordinary requisitions of Congress had only displayed the inefficiency of the authority making them, none of the States having duly complied with them, some having failed altogether, or nearly so; while in one instance, that of New Jersey, a compliance was *expressly* refused; nor was more yielded to the expostulations of members of Congress depused to her Legislature, than a mere repeal of the law, without a compliance. The want of authority in Congress to regulate commerce had produced in foreign nations, particularly Great Britain, a monopolizing policy, injurious to the trade of the United States, and destructive to their navigation; the imbecility, and anticipated dissolution, of the Confederacy extinguishing all apprehensions of a countervailing policy on the part of the United States. The same want of a general power over commerce led to an exercise of the power, separately, by the States, which not only proved abortive, but engendered rival, conflicting and angry regulations. Besides the vain attempts to supply their respective treasuries by imposts, which turned their commerce into the neighbouring ports, and to coerce a relaxation of the British monopoly of the West India navigation, which was attempted by Virginia, the States having ports for foreign commerce, taxed and irritated the adjoining States, trading through them, as New York, Pennsylvania, Virginia, and South Carolina. Some of the States, as Connecticut, taxed imports from others, as from Massachusetts, which complained in a letter to the Executive of Virginia, and doubtless to those of other States. In sundry instances, as of New York, New Jersey, Pennsylvania and Maryland, the navigation laws treated the citizens of other States as aliens. In certain cases the authority of

Federal finances required authority to tax.

The I. N. Phelps Stokes Collection of American Historical Prints, New York Public Library.

An east view of the city of Philadelphia, taken by George Heap, from the Jersey Shore, under the direction of Nicholas Skull, Surveyor General of the Province of Pennsylvania. (c. 1754)

the Confederacy was disregarded, as in violation, not only of the Treaty of Peace, but of treaties with France and Holland; which were complained of to Congress. In other cases the Federal authority was violated by treaties and war with Indians as by Georgia; by troops raised and kept up without the consent of Congress, as by Massachusetts; by compacts without the consent of Congress, as between Pennsylvania and New Jersey, and between Virginia and Maryland. From the Legislative Journals of Virginia it appears, that a vote refusing to apply for a sanction of Congress was followed by a vote against the communication of the compact to Congress. In the internal administration of the States, a violation of contracts had become familiar, in the form of depreciated paper made a legal tender, of property substituted for money, of instalment laws, and of the occlusions of the courts of justice, although evident that all such interferences affected the rights of other States, relatively creditors, as well as citizens creditors within the State. Among the defects which had been severely felt was want of an uniformity in cases requiring it, as laws of naturalization and bankruptcy, a coercive authority operating on individuals, and a guarantee of the internal tranquility of the States.

A general decay of confidence.

As a natural consequence of this distracted and disheartening condition of the Union, the Federal authority had ceased to be respected abroad, and dispositions were shown there, particularly in Great Britain, to take advantage of its imbecility, and to speculate on its approaching downfall. At home it had lost all confidence and credit; the unstable and unjust career of the States had also forfeited the respect and confidence essential to order and good government, involving a general decay of confidence and credit between man and man. It was found, moreover, that those least partial to popular government, or most distrustful of its efficacy, were yielding to anticipations, that from an increase of the confusion a government might result more congenial with their taste or their opinions; whilst those most devoted to the principles and forms of Republics were alarmed for the cause of liberty itself, at stake in the American experiment, and anxious for a system that would avoid the inefficacy of a mere confederacy, without passing into the opposite extreme of a consolidated government. It was known that there were individuals who had betrayed a bias towards monarchy, and there had always been some not unfavorable to a partition of the Union into several confederacies; either from a better chance of figuring on a sectional theatre, or that the sections would require stronger governments, or by their hostile conflicts lead to a monarchial consolidation. The idea of dismemberment had recently made its appearance in the newspapers.

A constitutional government sanctioned by the people.

Such were the defects, the deformities, the diseases and the ominous prospects, for which the Convention were to provide a remedy, and which ought never to be overlooked in expounding and appreciating the constitutional charter, the remedy that was provided.

As a sketch on paper, the earliest, perhaps, of a Constitutional Government for the Union (organized into the regular departments, with physical means operating on individuals) to be sanctioned by *the people of the States*, acting in their original and sovereign character, was contained in the letters of James Madison to Thomas Jefferson of the nineteenth of March; to Governor Randolph of the eighth of April; and to General Washington of the sixteenth of April, 1787, for which see their respective dates.

The feature, in these letters which vested in the general authority a negative on the laws of the States, was suggested by the negative in the head of the British Empire, which prevented collisions between the parts and the whole, and between the parts themselves. It was supposed that the substitution of an elective and responsible authority, for an hereditary and irresponsible one, would avoid the appearance even of a departure from Republicanism. But although the subject was so viewed in the Convention, and the votes on it were more than once equally divided, it was finally and justly abandoned, as, apart from other objections, it was not practicable among so many States, increasing in number, and enacting, each of them, so many laws. Instead of the proposed negative, the objects of it were left as finally provided for in the Constitution.

On the arrival of the Virginia Deputies at Philadelphia, it occurred to them, that, from the early and prominent part taken by that State in bringing about the Convention, some initiative step might be expected from them. The Resolutions introduced by Governor Randolph were the result of consultation on the subject, with an understanding that they left all the Deputies entirely open to the lights of discussion, and free to concur in any alterations or modifications which their reflections and judgments might approve. The Resolutions, as the Journals show, became the basis on which the proceedings of the Convention commenced, and to the developements, variations and modifications of which the plan of government proposed by the Convention may be traced.

Serving the cause of liberty throughout the world.

The curiosity I had felt during my researches into the history of the most distinguished confederacies, particularly those of antiquity, and the deficiency I found in the means of satisfying it, more especially in what related to the process, the principles, the reasons, and the anticipations, which prevailed in the formation of them, determined me to preserve, as far I could, an exact account of what might pass in the Convention while executing its trust; with the magnitude of which I was duly impressed, as I was by the gratification promised to future curiosity by an authentic exhibition of the objects, the opinions, and the reasonings, from which the system of government was to receive its peculiar structure and organization. Nor was I unaware of the value of such a contribution to the fund of materials for the history of a Constitution on which would be staked the happiness of a people great even in its infancy, and possibly the cause of liberty throughout the world.

In pursuance of the task I had assumed, I chose a seat in front of the presiding member, with the other members on my right and left hands. In this favorable position for all that passed, I noted, in terms legible and in abbreviations and marks intelligible to myself, what was read from the Chair or spoken by the members; and losing not a moment unnecessarily between the adjournment and reassembling of the Convention, I was enabled to write out my daily notes during the session, or within a few finishing days after its close, in the extent and form preserved in my own hand on my files.

In the labor and correctness of this I was not a little aided by practice, and by a familiarity with the style and the train of observation and reasoning which characterized the principal speakers. It happened, also, that I was not absent a single day, nor more than a casual fraction of an hour in any day, so that I could not have lost a single speech, unless a very short one.

It may be proper to remark, that, with a very few exceptions, the speeches were neither furnished, nor revised, nor sanctioned, by the speakers, but written out from my notes, aided by the freshness of my recollections. A further remark may be proper, that views of the subject might occasionally be presented, in the speeches and proceedings, with a latent reference to a compromise on some middle ground, by mutual concessions. The exceptions alluded to were,—first, the sketch furnished by Mr. Randolph of his speech on the introduction of his propositions on the 29th day of May; secondly, the speech of Mr. Hamilton, who happened to call on me when putting the last hand to it, and who acknowledged its fidelity, without suggesting more than a very few verbal alterations which were made; thirdly, the speech of Gouverneur Morris on the second day of May,* which was communicated to him on a like occasion, and who acquiesced in it without even a verbal change. The correctness of his language and the distinctness of his enunciation were particularly favorable to a reporter. The speeches of Doctor Franklin, excepting a few brief ones, were copied from the written ones read to the Convention by his colleague, Mr. Wilson, it being inconvenient to the Doctor to remain long on his feet.

There never was an assembly of men of purer motives.

Of the ability and intelligence of those who composed the Convention the debates and proceedings may be a test; as the character of the work which was the offspring of their deliberations must be tested by the experience of the future, added to that of nearly half a century which has passed.

But whatever may be the judgment pronounced on the competency of the architects of the Constitution, or whatever may be the destiny of the edifice prepared by them, I feel it a duty to express my profound and solemn conviction, derived from my intimate opportunity of observing and appreciating the views of the Convention, collectively and individually, that there never was an assembly of men, charged with a great and arduous trust, who were more pure in their motives, or more exclusively or anxiously devoted to the object committed to them, than were the members of the Federal Convention of 1787, to the object of devising and proposing a constitutional system which should best supply the defects of that which it was to replace, and best secure the permanent liberty and happiness of their country.

*Probably refers to July 2nd.

WRITING THE CONSTITUTION

More than a dozen hard and bitter years elapsed from 1776 to 1789, between the adoption of the Declaration of Independence and the establishment of the federal government of the United States of America under the Constitution. During this period, the Founding Fathers learned on the battlefield and in their legislative halls the necessity of working together as a single nation instead of as thirteen sovereign states. Yet they also learned how necessary it was to preserve the rights of the states and of individual citizens from a too powerful national government. The lessons of the times resulted in the writing of the United States Constitution with its concept of a set of checks and balances among the executive, legislative, and judicial branches of the government.

The theory of checks and balances resulted from the lessons of the times.

During most of the Revolutionary War, the Congress had no established authority and operated largely by making specific requests to the separate states. It had great difficulty raising enough men or enough money to fight the war. The leaders of the Revolutionary War recognized that a national government was needed, but the states were loath to give up their sovereign powers to Congress.

Only eight days after the adoption of the Declaration of Independence, on July 12, 1776, John Dickinson presented Congress with the first draft of the Articles of Confederation. The delegates to Congress argued over the Articles for more than a year, until November 15, 1777, when the Articles were approved and sent to the states for ratification. Twelve of the states soon approved the Articles, but unanimous ratification was required, and Maryland held off final approval for more than three years in a disagreement with other states about claims to western lands. Thus, the Articles of Confederation did not become effective until Maryland's ratification on March 1, 1781.

The single house system of the Confederation lacked power of enforcement.

The Articles of Confederation centered all the powers of the national government—executive, legislative, and judicial—in the single-house Congress of the Confederation. Congress was given the powers to declare war, to establish armed forces, to direct foreign relations, to issue money, to borrow money, to sell public land, and to administer Indian affairs. However, the national government under the Articles of Confederation was very weak. It did not have the power to enforce its decisions, nor did it have the powers to levy taxes or to regulate trade. An even more fatal weakness of the Articles of Confederation lay in the provision that no amendment to the Articles could become effective without the unanimous consent of all the states; thus, a single state could prevent any change in the Articles.

After the peace treaty ending the Revolutionary War had been signed with Great Britain in 1783, it rapidly became apparent that the Congress of the Confederation was ill-equipped to cope with national problems in peacetime. Business conditions grew more and more chaotic as each state set tariffs against the import of products from neighboring states. Congress could issue money, but it lacked the reserves to make the money worth its face value. The United States had assumed heavy war debts to France and the Netherlands, but Congress could not levy taxes to pay the debts. Farmers rebelled at the high taxes imposed by the states and demanded that all debts be abolished.

Early in 1786 the Virginia legislature issued an invitation to the other states to join in a conference at Annapolis, Md., in September, 1786, to discuss what might be done to straighten out the worsening trade relations between

Mount Vernon Ladies' Association, Mount Vernon, Virginia.

A print showing Mount Vernon as it was during the lifetime of George Washington.

the states. George Washington, then in retirement at Mount Vernon, lent his support to such a convention, but felt that conditions in the country were likely going to have to get worse before the states would take positive action to improve the structure of government. In a letter to John Jay in May, 1786, Washington wrote: "That it is necessary to revise and amend the Articles of Confederation, I entertain no doubt; but what may be the consequences of such an attempt is doubtful. Yet something must be done, or the fabric must fall, for it certainly is tottering."

"Something must be done, or the fabric must fall."

Only five states sent delegates to the Annapolis Convention, thus preventing any far-reaching agreement on amending the Articles of Confederation. The delegates who did attend, including James Madison of Virginia and Alexander Hamilton of New York, were in agreement that concerted action must be taken to overhaul the national government. The Convention adjourned after approving a report written by Hamilton calling on all the states to send representatives to a convention in Philadelphia in May, 1787. The report stated that the purpose of this convention would be "to take into consideration the situation of the United States, to devise such further provisions as shall appear to them necessary to render the constitution of the federal government adequate to the exigencies of the Union; and to report such an act for that purpose to the United States in Congress assembled, as, when agreed to by them, and afterwards confirmed by the legislatures of every State will effectually provide for the same."

The call for a Constitutional Convention was approved by Congress, but, meanwhile, the situation in the country grew worse, particularly in New England where mobs and riots were the order of the day. Reading with alarm of Shays' Rebellion in Massachusetts and of other disorders, George Washington wrote to James Madison in November, 1786: "Without some alteration in our political creed, the superstructure we have been seven years raising at the expense of so much blood and treasure, must fall. We are fast verging to anarchy and confusion."

Washington led the Virginia delegation.

The state of Virginia chose Washington to lead its delegation to the Constitutional Convention. Washington was worshipped throughout the country for his leadership in the Revolutionary War, and his acceptance of the appointment brought great pressure on the other states to send delegates to the Convention. When Washington arrived in Philadelphia on May 13, the day before the convention was to open, he was greeted by admiring crowds and the ringing of the city's bells. But other delegates were slower in arriving, so it was not until May 25, 1787, that the Constitutional Convention opened in Independence Hall with representatives present from seven states, a majority of the thirteen. On the opening day, the delegates unanimously elected Washington to preside over the Convention. Washington's strength and his determination that the Convention would succeed in its purpose was one of the most important factors, if not the most important factor, in the ultimate construction of the Constitution. A contemporary view of his role appeared in an article in the newspaper *Pennsylvania Packet*: "We behold him at the head of a chosen band of patriots and heroes, arresting the progress of American anarchy, and taking the lead in laying a deep foundation for preserving that liberty by a good government, which he had acquired for his country by his sword."

Library of Congress.

Fort Harmar, 1790

Fifty-five representatives from twelve states.

Once the convention got underway, more delegates kept arriving, until finally there were fifty-five representatives from twelve states. Only Rhode Island refused to attend. The delegates included many of the distinguished men of the time, including Benjamin Franklin and six other signers of the Declaration of Independence. Some notable names were missing, however, from the roll of delegates, including John Adams, Thomas Jefferson, Patrick Henry, and John Jay. Although not famous nationally, James Madison, a 36-year-old delegate from Virginia, played the leading role in drafting the Constitution – so much so that he has generally become known as the "Father of the Constitution."

At the outset of the Convention, the delegates began studying a plan for the Constitution that had been drafted by Madison. This "Virginia Plan," as it was called, incorporated many constitutional features that had previously been adopted in various state constitutions, notably the Massachusetts constitution written by John Adams and the New York constitution that had been written in large part by John Jay. Madison's plan provided for a balance of power between the legislative, executive, and judicial branches of the federal government. The larger states favored the "Virginia Plan" because it embodied the principle that representation in the national legislature should be based on the size of the population in each state, thus giving the larger states a bigger voice in Congress. The smaller states, fearing they would have little say in such a national government, favored instead the New Jersey Plan that would give each state an equal representation in the national legislature.

The Convention came close to breaking down over this argument between the large states and the small states. "The greatest difficulty lies in the affair of representation," Madison wrote. "And if this could be adjusted, all others

The American Pioneer.

Courthouse and Jail, Marietta, Ohio (c. 1798)

would be surmountable." The solution was provided by Roger Sherman, a delegate from Connecticut who had been a signer of the Declaration of Independence. Sherman's "Connecticut Compromise" called for a Congress of two houses—with each state having equal representation in one house and representation based on population in the other house.

Thirty-nine signers plus the secretary.

Finally, on September 17, 1787, the delegates reached agreement on the Constitution and signed it. Only forty-one delegates remained, fourteen having gone home during the summer. Thirty-eight delegates signed the document, and the name of a thirty-ninth who was absent, John Dickinson, was signed by proxy. William Jackson, the secretary of the Convention, signed the Constitution to attest the signatures of the delegates, but he generally is not counted among the signers of the Constitution because he was not an official delegate from any state. Three delegates—George Mason, Elbridge Gerry, and Edmund Randolph—refused to sign the Constitution.

National Archives. Copy by O. W. Boudet after Hesselius. Courtesy: Cooper Dawson

George Mason

Maryland Historical Society.

Richmond, Virginia
By B. H. Latrobe
(May, 1796)

New York Public Library. Photo by Francis G. Mayer.

The Presidio, San Francisco, 1816

Washington's letter of transmittal of the Constitution to Congress ably summarized the problems and conflicts that the new plan of government hoped to solve:

"Sir,

"We have now the honor to submit to the consideration of the United States in Congress assembled, that Constitution which has appeared to us most advisable.

"The friends of our country have long seen and desired, that the power of making war, peace and treaties, of levying money and regulating commerce, and the correspondent executive and judicial authorities should be fully and effectually vested in the general government of the Union: but the impropriety of delegating such extensive trust to one body of men is evident–Hence results the necessity of a different organization.

Washington's letter of transmittal.

"It is obviously impracticable in the federal government of these States, to secure all rights of independent sovereignty to each, and yet provide for the interest and safety of all–Individuals entering into society, must give up a share of liberty to preserve the rest. The magnitude of the sacrifice must depend as well on situation and circumstances as on the object to be obtained. It is at all times difficult to draw with precision the line between those rights which must be surrendered, and those which may be reserved; and on the present occasion this difficulty was increased by a difference among the several States as to their situation, extent, habits, and particular interests.

"In all our deliberations on this subject we kept steadily in our view, that which appears to us the greatest interest of every true American, the consolidation of our Union, in which is involved our prosperity, felicity, safety, perhaps our national existence. This important consideration, seriously and deeply impressed on our minds, led each State in the Convention to be less rigid on points of inferior magnitude, than might have been otherwise expected; and thus the Constitution, which we now present, is the result of a spirit of amity, and of that mutual deference and concession which the peculiarity of our political situation rendered indispensable.

"That it will meet the full and entire approbation of every State is not perhaps to be expected; but each will doubtless consider, that had her interest alone been consulted, the consequences might have been particularly disagreeable or injurious to others; that it is liable to as few exceptions as could reasonably have been expected, we hope and believe; that it may promote the lasting welfare of that country so dear to us all, and secure her freedom and happiness, is our most ardent wish."

The Constitutional Convention had met in secrecy throughout the summer of 1787, allowing no word of its deliberations to be released to the public; and now, with the draft of the Constitution made public for the first time, a great controversy began to rage as each state began to deliberate on whether to ratify the Constitution. Richard Henry Lee of Virginia, who had presented the resolution calling for independence from Great Britain on June 7, 1776, became one of the leading opponents of the Constitution. He feared that the Constitution did not adequately protect the rights of the states and that it was planned to make the states into "one consolidated government." He was supported by Patrick Henry, who had refused to attend the Constitutional Convention, and by George Mason, one of the delegates who had refused to sign the Constitution. In a famous series of articles first published in New York newspapers from October, 1787, to May, 1788, James Madison, Alexander Hamilton, and John Jay defended the merits of the Constitution. These articles, later published in book form under the title of *The Federalist*, continue to provide lawyers and political scientists the most thorough analysis of the meaning of the Constitution available.

Because the concept of federalism is perhaps the most important contribution to government made by the Constitution—the concept of sovereign states giving up part of their powers to a national government. It is particularly interesting to read Madison's reply to Lee's arguments in paper No. 39 of *The Federalist* in which he concludes:

Delaware was the first state to ratify the Constitution.

"The proposed Constitution, therefore, is, in strictness, neither a national nor a federal Constitution, but a composition of both. In its foundation it is federal, not national; in the sources from which the ordinary powers of the government are drawn, it is partly federal and partly national; in the operation of these powers, it is national, not federal; in the extent of them, again, it is federal, not national; and, finally, in the authoritative mode of introducing amendments, it is neither wholly federal nor wholly national."

On December 7, 1787, less than three months after the Constitutional Convention adjourned, Delaware became the first state to ratify the Constitution. A little more than six months later, on June 21, 1788, New Hampshire became the ninth state to approve ratification, assuring that the new government would go into operation. Shortly after, Virginia and New York became the tenth and eleventh states to ratify, but North Carolina and Rhode Island refused approval, largely because the Constitution did not include a Bill of Rights.

The first Congress under the new Constitution met in 1789, in New York City. On April 30, George Washington was inaugurated as the first President of the United States. The Supreme Court of the United States was first organized on February 2, 1790, with John Jay as Chief Justice.

James Madison led in obtaining approval for the Bill of Rights.

James Madison, who had been elected as a Representative from Virginia to the new Congress, took leadership in obtaining approval for the first ten amendments to the Constitution containing a Bill of Rights. Assured of protection of their rights and fearful that the new United States government would begin treating them as foreign powers, North Carolina joined the Union on November 21, 1789, and Rhode Island became the thirteenth state on May 29, 1790. The Bill of Rights amendments were ratified by the states and became effective on December 15, 1791.

The United States Constitution has stood the test of time as one of the greatest documents ever written by men. The remarkable achievement of the writers of the Constitution was deservedly praised by historian Charles Beard who said:

"It is not merely patriotic pride that compels one to assert that never in the history of assemblies has there been a convention of men richer in political experience and in practical knowledge, or endowed with a profounder insight into the springs of human action and the intimate essence of government. It is indeed an astounding fact that at one time so many men skilled in statecraft could be found on the very frontiers of civilization among a population numbering about four million whites. It is no less a cause for admiration that their instrument of government should have survived the trials and crises of a century that saw the wreck of more than a score of paper constitutions."

SOME POLITICAL VIEWS on the CONSTITUTION By The Signers

ABRAHAM BALDWIN believed in a strict interpretation of the Constitution within the terms of the words written in it. He discouraged attempts to enlarge or narrow its provisions by any theory not specifically stated in the Constitution. He refused to support any measures that intruded on the reserved powers and rights of the states or of the people.

DAVID BREARLEY was so alarmed at the disproportionate representation by the populous states and the sparsely populated states that he favored erasing all boundaries and making a new partition of the whole into thirteen equal parts.

JACOB BROOM joined his colleague from Delaware in advocating a nine-year term for Senators. He favored apportioning membership in the House of Representatives according to population, provided only that he expected the delegates from the larger states to give an equal voice to the smaller states in the Senate.

PIERCE BUTLER objected to having representatives to the Congress elected directly by the people. He was a strong advocate of states rights. He supported the idea of a single person rather than a council as chief executive. He opposed giving the chief executive the power of veto. He urged that the number of representatives a state had in Congress should be based upon its wealth. He stated his theory succinctly as "money is power." He opposed plans for a Congress to appoint federal judges, believing state courts should handle all judicial matters. He believed in the right of all to vote, stating, "There is no right of which the people are more jealous than that of suffrage." He took a cynical view of the Bill of Rights sponsored by James Madison, stating, "If you wait for substantial amendments, you will wait longer than I wish you to do speaking *interestedly*. A few *milk-and-water* amendments have been proposed by Mr. M., such as liberty of conscience, a free press, and one or two general things already well secured. I suppose it was done to keep his promise with his constituents, to move for alterations; but, if I am not greatly mistaken, he is not hearty in the cause of amendments."

DANIEL CARROLL advocated a strong national government and he believed as much democracy as possible should be granted by the Constitution. He believed the President should be elected directly by the people. He called the Constitution "the best form of government which has ever been offered to the world." He played an important role in getting Congress to adopt the First Amendment to the Constitution providing for religious freedom.

GEORGE CLYMER felt that the Constitution was making the Senate too powerful a body.

JONATHAN DAYTON was the youngest man to sign the Constitution (27). He feared the overwhelming power of the large state vs. the small state.

JOHN DICKINSON strongly supported the provision in the Constitution that the members of the House of Representatives should be elected by the people and that the Senate should be elected by the State Legislatures. He believed that Congress should be the strongest branch of the Federal Government and tried to give Congress the power to remove the President or Federal Judges at will.

WILLIAM FEW was enough of a realist to say that the Constitution would not altogether please everybody, but it was agreed to be the most expedient that could be devised and approved.

THOMAS FITZSIMONS was apparently the first Roman Catholic ever elected to public office in the Colony of Pennsylvania. Until his time, a "test oath" had been required of all public officials, an oath that all Roman Catholics refused to swear to. He represented Philadelphia's bankers and merchants at the Constitutional Convention and in so doing seconded a motion by Gouverneur Morris to insure that the ownership of property would be a requirement for voting in congressional elections.

BENJAMIN FRANKLIN was the oldest signer of the Constitution (81). He favored a unicameral legislature and an executive power residing in the hands of several men rather than in a single president. Concerning the Constitution itself, he said, "We must not expect, that a new government may be formed, as a game of chess may be played, by a skilful hand, without a fault. The players of our game are so many, their ideas so different, their prejudices so strong and so various, and their particular interests, independent of the general, seeming so opposite, that not a move can be made that is not contested; the numerous objections confound the understanding; the wisest must agree to some unreasonable things that reasonable ones of more consequence may be obtained; and thus chance has its share in many of the determinations, so that the play is more like . . . with a box of dice."

At the beginning of the Constitutional Convention, he said, "I therefore beg leave to move —that henceforth prayers imploring the assistance of Heaven, and its blessings on our deliberations, be held in this Assembly every morning before we proceed to business, and that one or more of the clergy of this city be requested to officiate in that service."

Franklin's motion was seconded by Roger Sherman of Connecticut; but, in the discussion that followed, Alexander Hamilton pointed out that the public would suspect that the disagreements in the Convention were greater than they actually were, and Hugh Williamson remarked that there were no funds available to pay the clergymen. Therefore, the matter of prayer was dropped without a vote.

NATHANIEL GORHAM was elected chairman of the committee of the whole, the next most important office to that of George Washington, who was president of the convention. He felt that the thirteen states should be divided equally to prevent unequal distribution of power. He opposed Gouverneur Morris' attempt to limit voting rights to property owners. He said, "The people have been long accustomed to this right in various parts of America, and will never allow it to be abridged. We must consult their rooted prejudices if we expect their concurrence in our propositions."

On the last day of the Convention, he introduced the proposal to increase the number of representatives in Congress to one in every thirty thousand people rather than one in every forty thousand people. George Washington, for the first time during the four months of deliberations, rose and spoke in favor of Gorham's motion, which was then adopted unanimously, the last change in the Constitution before it was signed by the delegates.

DANIEL OF ST. THOMAS JENIFER proposed that members of the House of Representatives be elected every three years instead of every two years because too great frequency of elections rendered the people indifferent to them and made the best men unwilling to serve in so precarious a service.

WILLIAM SAMUEL JOHNSON speaking in behalf of the Constitution said, "Our commerce is annihilated; our national honour, once in so high esteem is no more. We have got to the very brink of ruin; we must turn back and adopt a new system. . . . As to the old system, we can go no further with it; experience has shown it to be utterly inefficient."

RUFUS KING favored a strong central government. "He conceived that the import of the term 'States,' 'sovereignty,' 'national,' and 'federal,' had been often used and implied in the discussions inaccurately and delusively. The States were not 'sovereigns' in the sense contended for by some. They did not possess the peculiar features of sovereignty,— they could not make war, nor peace, nor alliances, nor treaties. Considering them as political beings, they were dumb, for they could not speak to any foreign sovereign whatever."

JOHN LANGDON said, "The General and State Governments are not enemies to each other, but different institutions for the good of the people of America. As one of the people, I can say, the National Government is mine, the State Government is mine. In transferring power from one to the other, I only take out of my left hand what it cannot so well use, and put it into my right hand where it can be better used."

JAMES MADISON favored a two-house legislature with a separate executive to execute the laws and a separate judiciary. Most of these ideas came from what was known as the Virginia Plan, with many added details.

JAMES MCHENRY wrote in his diary: "Being opposed to many parts of the system I make a remark why I signed it and mean to support it. 1stly. I distrust my own judgment, especially as it is opposite to the opinion of a majority of gentlemen whose abilities and patriotism are of the first cast; and as I have already frequent occasions to be convinced that I have not always judged right. 2dly. Alterations may be obtained, it being provided that the concurrence of ⅔ of the Congress may at any time introduce them. 3dly. Comparing the inconveniences and the evils which we labor under and may experience from the present confederation, and the little good we can expect from it, with the possible evils and probable benefits and advantages promised us by the new system, I am clear that I ought to give it all the support in my power . . ."

GOUVERNEUR MORRIS believed thoroughly in the system of checks and balances. "One interest must be opposed to another interest. Vices, as they exist, must be turned against each other. In the second place, it must have great personal property; it must have the aristocratic spirit; it must love to lord it through pride. Pride is, indeed, the great principle that actuates both the poor and the rich. It is this principle which in the former resists, in the latter abuses, authority. In the third place it should be independent. In religion the creature is apt to forget its Creator."

CHARLES PINCKNEY was the originator of the so-called Pinckney Plan for a Constitution. After signing the Constitution, he stated the following: "The advantages of a republic are, liberty—exemption from needless restrictions—equal laws—public spirit—averseness to war—frugality—above all, the opportunities afforded to men of every description, of producing their abilities and counsels to public observation.

"The citizens of the United States would reprobate, with indignation, the idea of a monarchy. But the essential qualities of a monarchy—unity of council—vigor—secrecy—and despatch, are qualities essential in every government."

CHARLES COTESWORTH PINCKNEY. According to the Madison papers, his thoughts concerning the Constitution were as follows: "General Pinckney wished to have a good National Government, and at the same time to leave a considerable share of power in the States. An election of either branch by the people, scattered as they are in many States, particularly in South Carolina, was impracticable."

GEORGE READ favored a strong central government. He said, "Too much attachment is betrayed to the State Governments. We must look beyond their continuance. A National Government must soon of necessity swallow them all up."

JOHN RUTLEDGE spoke out strongly for the interests of the slave states, stating, "If the Convention thinks that North Carolina, South Carolina, and Georgia, will ever agree to the plan, unless their right to import slaves be untouched, the expectation is vain. The people of those States will never be such fools, as to give up so important an interest."

ROGER SHERMAN firmly opposed a popular election, insisting that public officers should be elected by the State Legislatures. The objects of the Union, he thought were few: first, defence against foreign danger; secondly, against internal disputes, and a resort to force; thirdly, treaties with foreign nations; fourthly, regulating foreign commerce, and drawing revenue from it.

GEORGE WASHINGTON—"It is obviously impracticable in the federal government of these States, to secure all rights of independent sovereignty to each, and yet provide for the interest and safety of all—Individuals entering into society, must give up a share of liberty to preserve the rest. The magnitude of the sacrifice must depend as well on situation and circumstances as on the object to be obtained. It is at all times difficult to draw with precision the line between those rights which must be surrendered, and those which may be reserved; and on the present occasion this difficulty was increased by a difference among the several States as to their situation, extent, habits, and particular interests.

"In all our deliberations on this subject we kept steadily in our view, that which appears to us the greatest interest of every true American, the consolidation of our Union, in which is involved our prosperity, felicity, safety, perhaps our national existence. This important consideration, seriously and deeply impressed on our minds, led each State in the Convention to be less rigid on points of inferior magnitude, than might have been otherwise expected; and thus the Constitution, which we now present, is the result of a spirit of amity, and of that mutual deference and concession which the peculiarity of our political situation rendered indispensable."

JAMES WILSON favored direct election of both houses of Congress, saying, "No government can long subsist without the confidence of the people."

He moved that the executive power of the government be vested in a single person. He said, "One fact has great weight with me. All the thirteen States, though agreeing in scarce any other instance, agree in placing a single magistrate at the head of the government. The idea of three heads had taken place in none."

He was a strong advocate of proportional representation in Congress based on population. He said, "Can we forget for whom we are forming a Government? Is it for *men*, or for the imaginary beings called *States?*"

The Signers of the

Name	Born	Died	Birthplace	Age at Signing of Constitution
Abraham Baldwin	November 22, 1754	March 4, 1807	North Guilford, Conn.	32
Richard Bassett	April 2, 1745	September 15, 1815	Cecil County, Md.	42
Gunning Bedford, Jr.	1747	March 30, 1812	Philadelphia	40
John Blair	1732	August 31, 1800	Williamsburg, Va.	55
William Blount	March 26, 1749	March 21, 1800	Bertie County, N.C.	38
David Brearley	June 11, 1745	August 16, 1790	Spring Grove, N.J.	42
Jacob Broom	1752	April 25, 1810	Wilmington, Del.	35
Pierce Butler	July 11, 1744	February 15, 1822	County Carlow, Ireland	42
Daniel Carroll	July 22, 1730	May 7, 1796	Upper Marlboro, Md.	56
George Clymer	March 16, 1739	January 23, 1813	Philadelphia	48
Jonathan Dayton	October 16, 1760	October 9, 1824	Elizabethtown, N.J.	26
John Dickinson	November 8, 1732	February 14, 1808	Talbot County, Md.	54
William Few	June 8, 1748	July 16, 1828	Baltimore County, Md.	39
Thomas FitzSimons	1741	August 26, 1811	Ireland	46
Benjamin Franklin	January 17, 1706	April 17, 1790	Boston, Mass.	81
Nicholas Gilman	August 3, 1755	May 2, 1814	Exeter, N.H.	32
Nathaniel Gorham	May, 27, 1738	June 11, 1796	Charlestown, Mass.	49
Alexander Hamilton	January 11, 1755/1757	July 12, 1804	Charlestown, West Indies	30/32
Jared Ingersoll	October 27, 1749	October 31, 1822	New Haven, Conn.	38
Daniel of St. Thomas Jenifer	1723	Nov. 16, 1790	Charles County, Md.	64

United States Constitution

Colony Represented	University or College	Profession	Later Achievements	Age at Death
Georgia	Yale	Lawyer	U. S. Senator from Georgia 1799-1807	52
Delaware		Lawyer	Governor of Delaware 1799-1800	70
Delaware	Col. of New Jersey (Princeton)	Lawyer	U. S. District judge 1789-1812	64
Virginia	William and Mary	Lawyer	Associate justice, Supreme Court of U. S. 1789-1796	68
North Carolina		Politician	President, Tennessee state constitutional convention 1796	50
New Jersey		Lawyer	U. S. District judge 1789-1790	45
Delaware		Businessman	Built first cotton mill in Wilmington, Del.	58
South Carolina		Soldier-Planter	U. S. Senator from South Carolina 1789-1796, 1802-1806	77
Maryland	Educated in France	Landowner	U. S. Representative from Maryland 1789-1791	65
Pennsylvania	Col. of Philadelphia (U. of Pennsylvania)	Banker	U. S. Representative from Pennsylvania 1789-1791	73
New Jersey	Col. of New Jersey (Princeton)	Lawyer	U. S. Representative from New Jersey 1791-1799; U. S. Senator 1799-1805	63
Delaware	Studied law in England	Lawyer	President of Delaware 1781-1782; President of Pennsylvania 1782-1785	75
Georgia		Politician	U. S. Senator from Georgia 1789-1795	80
Pennsylvania		Businessman	U. S. Representative from Pennsylvania 1789-1795	64
Pennsylvania		Publisher	Retired	84
New Hampshire		Politician	U. S. Representative 1789-1797; U. S. Senator 1805-1814	58
Massachusetts		Businessman	Became a land speculator	58
New York	King's Col. (Columbia U.)	Lawyer	Secretary of the Treasury 1789-1795	47 or 49
Pennsylvania	Yale	Lawyer	Federalist candidate for Vice-President of U. S. in 1812	73
Maryland		Landowner	Retired	67

The Signers of the

(CONTINUED)

Name	Born	Died	Birthplace	Age at Signing of Constitution
William Samuel Johnson	October 7, 1727	November 14, 1819	Stratford, Conn.	59
Rufus King	March 24, 1755	April 29, 1827	Scarboro, Mass. (later Maine)	32
John Langdon	June 25, 1741	September 18, 1819	Portsmouth, N.H.	46
William Livingston	November 30, 1723	July 25, 1790	Albany, N.Y.	63
James Madison, Jr.	March 16, 1751	June 28, 1836	Port Conway, Va.	36
James McHenry	November 16, 1753	May 3, 1816	Balymena, Ireland	33
Thomas Mifflin	January 10, 1744	January 20, 1800	Philadelphia	43
Gouverneur Morris	January 31, 1752	November 16, 1816	Morrisania, N.Y. (now part of Bronx)	35
Robert Morris	January 31, 1734	May 8, 1806	Liverpool, England	53
William Paterson	December 24, 1745	September 9, 1806	County Antrim, Ireland	42
Charles Pinckney	October 26, 1757	October 29, 1824	Charleston, S.C.	29
Charles Cotesworth Pinckney	February 25, 1746	August 16, 1825	Charleston, S.C.	41
George Read	September 18, 1733	September 21, 1798	North East, Md.	53
John Rutledge	1739	July 18, 1800	Charleston, S.C.	48
Roger Sherman	April 19, 1721	July 23, 1793	Newton, Mass.	66
Richard Dobbs Spaight	March 25, 1758	September 6, 1802	New Bern, N.C.	29
George Washington	February 22, 1732	December 14, 1799	Westmoreland County, Va.	55
Hugh Williamson	December 5, 1735	May 22, 1819	West Nottingham, Pa.	51
James Wilson	September 14, 1742	August 21, 1798	St. Andrews, Scotland	44

United States Constitution

(CONTINUED)

Colony Represented	University or College	Profession	Later Achievements	Age at Death
Connecticut	Yale	Lawyer-Educator	President of Columbia College 1787-1800	92
Massachusetts	Harvard	Lawyer	U. S. Senator from New York 1789-1796, 1813-1825	72
New Hampshire		Shipowner	Governor of New Hampshire 1805-1809, 1810-1812	78
New Jersey	Yale	Lawyer	Governor of New Jersey 1776-1790	66
Virginia	Col. of New Jersey (Princeton)	Politician	President of U. S. 1809-1817	85
Maryland		Physician	Secretary of War 1796-1800	62
Pennsylvania	Col. of Philadelphia (U. of Pennsylvania)	Politician	Governor of Pennsylvania 1790-1799	56
Pennsylvania	King's Col. (Columbia U.)	Lawyer	U. S. Senator from Pennsylvania 1800-1803	64
Pennsylvania		Financier	U. S. Senator from Pennsylvania 1789-1795	72
New Jersey	Col. of New Jersey (Princeton)	Lawyer	Associate justice of Supreme Court of U. S. 1793-1806	61
South Carolina	Educated in England	Lawyer	Governor of South Carolina 1789-1792; 1796-1798; 1806-1808	67
South Carolina	Educated in England	Lawyer	Federalist candidate for President of U. S. 1804 and 1808	79
Delaware		Lawyer	Chief justice of Delaware 1793-1798	65
South Carolina	Educated in England	Lawyer	Chief justice of the United States 1795	61
Connecticut		Merchant-lawyer	U. S. Senator from Connecticut 1791-1793	72
North Carolina	U. of Glasgow	Politician	Governor of North Carolina 1792-1795	44
Virginia		Soldier-planter	President of U. S. 1789-1797	67
North Carolina	Col. of Philadelphia (U. of Pennsylvania)	Physician	U. S. Representative from North Carolina 1790-1793	73
Pennsylvania	U. of Edinburgh	Lawyer	Associate justice of Supreme Court of U. S. 1789-1798	55

Thomas Jefferson
By Charles Willson Peale

ABRAHAM BALDWIN of GEORGIA

Abraham Baldwin, signer of the United States Constitution and founder of the University of Georgia, devoted his life to public service. On his deathbed, at the age of fifty-two, he boasted to friends that the few days of his last illness accounted for his first absence from official duties in his twenty-two years of membership in Congress.

The outstanding nature of Baldwin's character was well-described by his brother-in-law Joel Barlow, the poet and diplomat, who said of him:

"The annals of our country have rarely been adorned with a character more venerable, or a life more useful than that of Abraham Baldwin. War brings its animation, and creates its own heroes; it often rears them up to fame with as little assistance from native genius as from study, or from moral and political virtue. It is in times of peace that an illustrious name is hardest earned, and most difficult to be secured, especially among enlightened republicans, where an equality of right and rank leaves nothing to the caprice of chance; where every action is weighed in its proper balance, and every man compared not only with his neighbor, but with himself; his motives being tested by the uniform tendency of his measures."

Entered Yale at thirteen

Baldwin was born in North Guilford, Conn., on November 22, 1754. An exceptionally bright boy, he entered Yale College in New Haven at the age of thirteen. He was a good student, particularly in the classics and in mathematics. Graduating in 1772 at the age of seventeen, he decided to remain on at Yale, studying law and acting as a tutor for other students.

ABRAHAM BALDWIN

- **1754 (Nov. 22) Born in North Guilford, Conn.**
- **1772 Graduated from Yale.**
- **1775-1779 Taught at Yale.**
- **1784 Admitted to bar at Savannah, Ga.**
- **1784-1785 Member of Georgia state legislature; drew up charter for and became founder of the University of Georgia.**
- **1786-1789 Member of the Congress of the Confederation.**
- **1786 Delegate to the Annapolis Convention.**
- **1787 Member of the Constitutional Convention and signer of the United States Constitution.**
- **1789-1799 U.S. Congressman from Georgia.**
- **1799-1807 U.S. Senator from Georgia.**
- **1807 (March 4) Died in Washington, D.C.**

Late in the Revolutionary War, he and Joel Barlow, a college chum, became chaplains for Connecticut troops. In 1781, Barlow married Baldwin's sister Ruth. Baldwin himself never married, but he liked young people and helped finance the education of his own sisters and half-brothers.

When independence had been won, Baldwin decided to go to Georgia to seek his fortune. He arrived in Savannah, Ga., in 1784, and shortly afterward he was admitted to the bar. He charmed new acquaintances, winning so many friends that he was elected to the state legislature only three months after his arrival.

Started the University of Georgia

During the year he spent as a state legislator, Baldwin performed a lasting service for his adopted state by originating the plan for a University of Georgia and drawing up its charter. The legislature approved the charter on January 27, 1785, making the University of Georgia the first such institution of higher education chartered by a state. Baldwin's charter endowed the university with 40,000 acres of land, the rents from which paid for buildings and salaries for the faculty.

Abraham Baldwin

National Archives. Courtesy: Historical Society of Pennsylvania.

The I. N. Phelps Stokes Collection, New York Public Library.

A View of Annapolis, Maryland

(Original watercolor drawing by an unknown artist, c. 1800.)

From left to right: 1. A corner of Reynold's Tavern. 2. The Maynadier House, site of the present U. S. Post Office. 3. The Cupola of McDowell Hall, now the main building of St. John's College. 4. St. Anne's Church. 5. Maryland's famous State House. 6. "The Green House" Mansion.

His success as a state legislator won Baldwin increased popularity, and, in his second year in residence in Georgia, he was elected to represent the state in the Congress of the Confederation. Henceforward, for the rest of his life, Baldwin represented Georgia in Congress.

In 1786, Baldwin was appointed as a delegate from Georgia to the Annapolis Convention—the preliminary meeting of a few states to decide what might be done to strengthen the national government under the Articles of the Confederation. Baldwin joined James Madison and Alexander Hamilton in supporting the need for a national constitutional convention.

Tolerant of the opinions of others

At the Constitutional Convention in Philadelphia in 1787, Baldwin was one of the representatives from Georgia. He distinguished himself with his simple, forcible oratory, and his tolerant examination of even the wildest opinions of some of the other delegates. To the end of his life, he regarded his services at this convention and his signing of the United States Constitution as the crowning achievements of his career.

In the national elections of 1788, he was elected to the House of Representatives, an office he held through 1799, serving throughout the critical period that the new United States government was being formed under President George Washington. With James Madison, he was a member of the congressional committee that drew up the Bill of Rights amendments, guaranteeing the rights of the states and individuals under the Constitution. He served on many other important committees, including that which prepared legislation establishing the executive departments of Foreign Affairs, War, and Treasury.

Baldwin believed in a strict interpretation of the Constitution within the terms of the words written in it. He discounted attempts to enlarge or narrow its provisions by any theory not specifically stated in the Constitution. He refused to support any measures that intruded on the reserved powers and rights of the states or of the people. Pointing out that "every particle of law-making power in the Constitution granted, was vested in Congress," he was particularly watchful to prevent the executive branch of the government from taking on legislative powers.

In 1798, Baldwin was elected as a United States Senator from Georgia, taking his seat in the upper house in 1799. He was re-elected as a senator in 1804, but did not live to complete his second term. After an illness of only eight days, Baldwin died on March 4, 1807.

RICHARD BASSETT of DELAWARE

Richard Bassett, a lawyer and statesman, was one of the signers of the United States Constitution for the state of Delaware. A friendly, wise, and conservative man, Bassett was one of Delaware's first two United States senators. He started a unique dynasty in which he, his son-in-law, two grandsons, his great-grandson, and his great-great-grandson all became U. S. senators from Delaware. Bassett was active in the establishment of the Methodist church in the United States, and was a close friend of Francis Asbury, the first Methodist bishop.

Inherited an estate of six thousand acres

Bassett was born in Cecil County, Maryland, on April 2, 1745. He was the son of a tavern-keeper, but at an early age he was adopted by a wealthy lawyer by the name of Lawson. His adopted father educated him and trained him to be a lawyer. Upon Lawson's death, his adopted son inherited a six-thousand-acre estate known as Bohemia Manor on the Elk River near the Delaware-Maryland boundary line.

Bassett married twice. His first wife was Ann Ennals, a member of a prominent Maryland family. When his first wife died, he married again; this time, the attractive daughter of the Bruff family of Talbot County, Maryland. Bassett had only one child, a daughter.

Although Bassett maintained his estate of Bohemia Manor in Maryland as his chief residence, his law practice largely was in Delaware where he had houses at both Dover and Wilmington.

During the Revolutionary War, Bassett was captain of a Dover troop of light-horse militia.

The Baltimore Museum of Art, Bequest of Ellen H. Bayard.
Richard Bassett
By CHARLES B. J. FEVRET DE SAINT-MEMIN

He was not particularly active in the fighting, however, because he was elected to the state legislature in 1776. He served in the legislature for the next ten years and also was a delegate to the state constitutional convention.

A distinguished record of government service

Bassett took as his protege a young law student by the name of James Bayard who married Bassett's only daughter. Bassett and his son-in-law, who was more than twenty years his junior, developed a close family, professional, and political friendship that lasted until their deaths in the same year. They are reported to have carried on many friendly arguments with Bassett's saying, "All you know I taught you;" and Bayard replying, "You taught me all you knew, and, all I know besides, I taught myself." Bayard became Delaware's first member of the U. S. House of Representatives in 1789 while Bassett served in the U. S. Senate; and Bayard provided the decisive Federalist vote that gave the presidency to Thomas Jefferson in his contest with Aaron Burr in 1801. Bayard later served as U. S. senator from Delaware from 1805 to 1813. Bassett's grandsons Richard Bay-

RICHARD BASSETT

1745 (April 2) Born in Cecil County, Maryland.
1776-1786 Member of Delaware legislature.
1786 Delegate to Annapolis Convention.
1787 Represented Delaware at United States Constitutional Convention and signed the United States Constitution.
1789-1793 U. S. Senator from Delaware.
1793-1799 Chief justice of the court of common pleas of Delaware.
1797 Presidential elector; voted for John Adams.
1799-1801 Governor of Delaware.
1801 Appointed a federal circuit court judge by President Adams.
1815 (Sept. 15) Died at Bohemia Manor, Md.

Travels in the United States and Canada, by De Roos.

Bristol on the Delaware
(c. 1800)

ard and James Bayard II both represented Delaware as U. S. senators. His great-grandson Thomas Bayard served in the U. S. Senate from 1869 to 1885, then became Secretary of State under President Grover Cleveland. His great-great-grandson Thomas Bayard II served in the U. S. Senate from 1922 to 1929.

In 1778, Bassett first met Francis Asbury at the home of Judge Thomas White in Maryland. At that time, Methodists were generally regarded as Tories, and Bassett was alarmed that White would invite a Methodist to be a guest in his house. However, after conversing with Asbury, Bassett became impressed with the wisdom of the English missionary and was convinced that the principles of Methodism had no bearing on the political struggle with Great Britain.

Repulsed mob violence

The story is told that in 1779 White came to visit Bassett at his home in Dover; a crowd gathered in front of the house demanding that White be turned over to them for punishment because he was a known Methodist and consequently that made him a Tory. Bassett put on his uniform as a captain in the militia and went to the door carrying his sword and pistols. He told the mob that White was not a Tory and that they would have to kill him first if they wanted to take White. Upon hearing this, the mob dispersed.

Asbury wrote of a visit he made to Bassett's home in February, 1780: "Went home with Lawyer Bassett, a very conversant and affectionate man, who from his own acknowledgment appears to be sick of sin."

Bassett financed the construction of a Methodist church in Dover in 1784, and himself became a Methodist lay preacher. In his sermons he vigorously attacked skeptics who refused to have faith in anything they could not see or touch. He said he could not understand "how a man could believe by this rule that he had a back, as he could not see it unless he had a neck like a crane or a goose."

By Alexander Lawson after Lewis Krimmel.
Courtesy: The Old Print Shop, N. Y.

Election Day At The State House

Favored a stronger national government

After the Revolutionary War, Bassett became a leader of those in his state who believed it was necessary to revise the Articles of Confederation in order to strengthen the national government. In 1786, he attended the Annapolis Convention as a delegate from Delaware, and the next year he was elected as a representative to the Constitutional Convention in Philadelphia. After helping write and signing the United States Constitution, Bassett took an important role in the Delaware state convention that ratified the Constitution in December, 1787, the first state to do so.

On October 24, 1788, Bassett and George Read, another signer of the Constitution, were chosen as the state's first two U. S. senators. The new senate was supposed to convene on March 4, 1789, but many of the senators, including Bassett, were late in arriving. It was not until April 6, 1789, that enough senators were present to make a quorum.

Cast the first vote in favor of Washington as capital

Bassett took part in many important committees in the Senate as laws were established under which the new government of the United States would operate. He was one of eight members appointed to a committee to draw up a bill "organizing the Judiciary of the United States." The committee made the important decision to establish federal lower courts instead of relying on state courts as lower courts. Bassett also was active in the consideration of whether the President should be given the power to remove from office persons that he had appointed. Bassett favored the addition of a clause granting the President this right in bills establishing the executive departments. Opponents of the measure felt that the President inherently had the power through his right of appointment, and that the addition of the clause would indicate that the Senate could withdraw the power of Presidential removal if they desired to do so. In a close vote, Bassett's viewpoint won out. Bassett also was an advocate of moving the capital from New York City, and, when the measure to establish the District of Columbia on the Potomac River was voted upon in the Senate, Bassett had the privilege of being the first senator to cast his vote in favor of the bill.

Served as governor of Delaware

Retiring from the U. S. Senate in 1793, Bassett devoted the rest of his life to affairs within the state of Delaware. In 1793, he was appointed chief justice of the court of common pleas of Delaware, a position that he held for six years. During this period, he served as a presidential elector in 1797, casting his vote for John Adams for President. At the age of 53, Bassett received the highest honor the state of Delaware could confer, being elected governor for the term of 1799 to 1801.

Bassett played a minor role in the famous case of *Marbury vs. Madison* that established the power of the Supreme Court to rule on the constitutionality of congressional legislation. President John Adams, in one of his last acts before turning the presidency over to Thomas Jefferson in 1801, appointed Bassett and a number of other Federalists as circuit court judges. These appointees became known as "midnight judges" because of their last-minute appointments, and Jefferson refused to recognize their rights to the offices. In the case of Marbury vs. Madison, the Supreme Court upheld Jefferson's right to refuse to recognize the appointments, and, more importantly, it ruled that the Judiciary Act of 1789 was unconstitutional.

In the last years of his life, Bassett spent most of his time at his Bohemia Manor estate. In 1808 and 1809 he held two large Methodist camp-meetings on his estate. He particularly enjoyed listening to Negro spirituals at the camp meetings. Bassett had become partially paralyzed and found it difficult to travel. Methodist Bishop Asbury, who visited him in 1815, wrote: "My long-loved friend Judge Bassett, some time past a paralytic, is lately stricken on the other side and suffers much in his helpless state." Shortly after, on September 15, 1815, Bassett died at the age of 70.

Courtesy: Colonial Williamsburg.

Bruton Parish Church and William & Mary College, Williamsburg, Virginia

Courtesy: Wilmington Historical Society.

Gunning Bedford, Jr.

Courtesy: Wilmington Historical Society.

Mrs. Gunning Bedford, Jr.

Courtesy: The Frederick S. Hicks Collection. Photo by George Lohr Studios, Washington, D.C.

The First Steamboat, *The Fulton*

GUNNING BEDFORD, JR. of DELAWARE

Gunning Bedford, Jr., a lawyer and judge, was one of the signers of the United States Constitution for the state of Delaware. After the government of the United States was organized in 1789, Bedford was appointed by President George Washington as the first United States district judge for Delaware.

This distinguished patriot was born in Philadelphia in 1747. His father, Gunning Bedford, Sr., was a Philadelphia architect who served as a captain in the French and Indian War, and also was an alderman in the city of Philadelphia. His mother's maiden name was Susannah Jacquett. He was the fifth of eleven children.

A Princeton classmate of James Madison

When he was twenty years old, Gunning Bedford, Jr., entered the College of New Jersey, now Princeton University. One of his classmates was James Madison, who later became the "Father of the Constitution" and the fourth President of the United States. Perhaps because he was older than his other classmates, Bedford made an excellent scholastic record, graduating at the head of his class and giving the valedictory address.

Bedford also was different from the other members of his class in that he already was married, and at the graduation ceremony his wife was present with their first baby. His wife was Jane Ballaroux Parker, daughter of the editor of the New York *Post Boy*. Her father, James Parker, had been an apprentice printer with Benjamin Franklin in Boston, and he and Franklin had exchanged the first silver dollars they ever earned. Franklin's first dollar was preserved by Parker and made into a punch strainer that later was given to the Historical Society of Delaware by Bedford's daughter.

GUNNING BEDFORD, JR.

1747 Born in Philadelphia.

1771 Graduated from College of New Jersey (now Princeton University).

1783-1786 Represented Delaware in the Continental Congress.

1784-1789 Attorney General of the state of Delaware.

1786 Delegate to the Annapolis Convention.

1787 Member of the United States Constitutional Convention and signer of the Constitution.

1789-1812 United States district court judge for Delaware.

1812 (March 30) Died in Wilmington, Delaware.

After his graduation in 1771, Bedford returned to Philadelphia where he studied law with a prominent attorney, Joseph Reed. About eight years later he moved to Dover, Del. On August 4, 1779, he was admitted to the bar and began practicing law in Dover.

An Aide-de-Camp of George Washington

No authentic record has been found of Bedford's activities during the Revolutionary War. However, in the will of his daughter, Henrietta Jane Bedford, filed in 1871, he was described as an "Aide-de-Camp to General Washington in the Revolutionary War." The will left a pair of pocket pistols to the Smithsonian Institution and gave their history as follows: "During the Revolutionary War, General Washington, desiring my father to go from Trenton to New York on some important secret embassy at night, and fearing that he was not sufficiently armed with the pistols in his holsters, presented him with a pair of pocket-pistols with a view to his protection and greater security."

Bedford has sometimes been confused with a cousin five years older than himself who had the same name. This other Gunning Bedford was born in New Castle, Del., in 1742. He had served in

Gunning Bedford, Jr.
From Orville Peets
The Historical Society of Delaware, Wilmington. Photo by Sanborn Studio.

The Historical Society of Delaware, Wilmington.
Photo by Sanborn Studio.

"Lombardy," The Country Residence of Gunning Bedford, Jr.

the French and Indian War, and had held the rank of major at the beginning of the Revolutionary War. He rose to the rank of lieutenant colonel with a Delaware regiment and was wounded in the battle of White Plains. In 1795, he was elected governor of Delaware and served in that office until his death in 1797.

By the time the peace treaty had been signed with Great Britain in 1783, Gunning Bedford, Jr., was living in Wilmington, Del. That year he was elected as a member of the Continental Congress where he served until 1785. It is not difficult to imagine that considerable confusion arose over the fact that his cousin of the same name also represented Delaware in the Continental Congress during the same period.

On April 26, 1784, Gunning Bedford, Jr., was appointed as attorney general for the state of Delaware. He held this office until 1789, and is said to have served with distinction.

A delegate from Delaware at the Annapolis Convention

Bedford recognized that the country was in serious difficulty because of the inadequacy of the powers delegated to the national government by the Articles of Confederation, so he was a logical choice as one of Delaware's five delegates to the Annapolis Convention in 1786. That meeting had been called to discuss ways in which trade relationships between the states might be improved, and it ended by calling for a Constitutional Convention to revise the Articles of Confederation.

In 1787, Bedford was appointed, with the same delegates who had attended the Annapolis Convention, as a representative of Delaware to the Constitutional Convention in Philadelphia. He became one of the most vocal spokesmen for the interests of the small states against the large states. The forcefulness of his arguments and his eloquence have been credited with being important factors in the decision to give each state two senators in the upper house of the national Congress. When he returned home after signing the United States Constitution, Bedford worked diligently and successfully to have Delaware become the first state to ratify the Constitution.

First U. S. district judge for Delaware

Bedford devoted the rest of his life to public service. On October 24, 1788, his name was placed in nomination before the legislature to be one of the state's first U. S. senators, but Richard Bassett and George Read, two other signers of the Constitution, were selected instead. The next year, President George Washington, recognizing Bedford's outstanding legal talents, named him as the first United States district judge for the state of Delaware, a position he held until his death. Newspaper accounts of the times show that Bedford handled one of the earliest cases ever to be tried in a United States federal court—the conviction of a smuggler in May, 1790.

In 1793, Bedford purchased a 250-acre estate near Wilmington which he named Lombardy. There he and his family lived in a large two-story mansion. Bedford died at the age of sixty-four on March 30, 1812. His wife and two children survived him. Buried in the graveyard of the First Presbyterian Church of Wilmington, Del., Bedford's body lies beneath a marble monument whose inscription says in part:

"His form was goodly, his temper amiable,
his manners winning, and his discharge
of private duties exemplary.
Reader, may his example stimulate you
to improve the talents—be they five or two,
or one—with which God has entrusted you."

As a footnote to Bedford's death, it is interesting to read a letter that was sent four days later to Henry M. Ridgely, one of the U. S. senators from Delaware:

"Dear Sir,

"The Wilmington papers which arrived the evening before last, announced the death of Judge Bedford; —this unfortunate event, unfortunate for his family, happened on Monday last. Several of my friends have urged me to an application for the vacancy occasioned by his demise. I have always thought that a personal application for a judgeship, was a matter of indelicacy and inconsistent with the modesty, which such a candidate ought to profess. I have, however, thought on reflecting how the loaves and fishes are now distributed, that there can be but one rival, and but one man, on the same political side, whose pretensions are in any way superior to mine; but in nothing else can I yield to him . . ."

This eagerness for appointment was exhibited by John Fisher, Secretary of State of Delaware, who shortly afterward received Bedford's judgeship by appointment of President James Madison.

Nassau Hall and President's House, Home of John Witherspoon
Engraved by Dawkins after drawing by Tennant (1763)

Princeton University Library. Life in America, by Davidson.

JOHN BLAIR of VIRGINIA

A distinguished Virginia lawyer and jurist and long-time friend of George Washington, John Blair signed and supported the United States Constitution. He was appointed by Washington as one of the first associate justices of the Supreme Court of the United States. Blair was a strong faced, blue-eyed patriot whose hair had been red until he became bald. His portraits made him appear stern, as though he never smiled. A fellow-delegate to the Constitutional Convention described him as "one of the most respectable Men in Virginia, both on account of his Family as well as fortune . . . his good sense, and most excellent principles, compensate for other deficiencies."

John Blair was born in Williamsburg, Va., in 1732, the same year that Washington was born. His father, whose name also was John Blair, was an important merchant and political leader of the colony. He served as president of the Virginia governor's council and became acting governor of the state in 1758. The elder Blair also was the owner of the Raleigh Tavern that became famous as a meeting place for patriotic legislators.

Attended William and Mary College

Young John grew up in Williamsburg, and naturally learned to take an active interest in colonial politics through his father's associations with the government. As soon as he was old enough, he attended William and Mary College, which had been founded by his grand-uncle, James Blair.

After his graduation from college, John Blair was sent to England, where he studied law at the Middle Temple in London. Upon his return to Williamsburg in the late 1750's, he became a member of the bar and won a good reputation as a lawyer. He was aided in obtaining a large practice through the political influence of his father. He married Jean Balfour, and they had two daughters.

Originally opposed Patrick Henry's resolutions

Elected to the House of Burgesses, Blair at first took a stand against the American patriots. In 1765 he voted against Patrick Henry's resolutions that denounced the British Stamp Act. But four years later, in 1769, he joined with Henry, Washington, and other patriotic Virginia legislators in signing a non-importation agreement in protest against British taxes. He also signed a new non-importation agreement drafted in 1770. Blair's important standing at this time is evidenced by his appointment as one of the executors of the estate of Lord Botetourt, the British governor of Virginia, who died in 1770.

The Revolution was swiftly approaching. Blair represented William and Mary College in the final

JOHN BLAIR

1732 Born in Williamsburg, Va.
c.1752 Graduated from William and Mary College.
c.1753-1757 Studied law at the Middle Temple in London.
1765-1775 Member of the Virginia House of Burgesses.
1776 Member of Virginia state constitutional convention.
1776-1777 Member of Virginia's governor's council.
1778 Elected grand master of Virginia's Masons.
1778 Elected judge of the general court of Virginia, and later became its chief justice.
1780 Became judge of Virginia's high court of chancery and justice of the high court of appeals.
1787 Member of Virginia's delegation to the Constitutional Convention; signed the United States Constitution.
1788 Member of Virginia's constitutional ratification convention.
1789-1796 Associate justice of the United States Supreme Court.
1800 (Aug. 31) Died in Williamsburg, Va.

John Blair
National Archives. Courtesy: Mrs. H. K. D. Peachy.

Courtesy: Colonial Williamsburg.

Archibald Blair House

session of the Virginia House of Burgesses; and in the Virginia patriotic convention of 1776, he was a member of the committee that drew up Virginia's Declaration of Rights and state constitution. He took no part in the Continental Congress, but was related by marriage to Carter Braxton, one of the signers of the Declaration of Independence. Carter's brother George Braxton Jr., was the first of three husbands of John Blair's sister Mary. In the early years of the Revolution, Blair was a member of the executive council that advised Virginia's first state governor, Patrick Henry.

John Blair began his judicial career in 1778 at the age of forty-six, when he was appointed to the newly-formed general court of Virginia. Shortly afterward he became its chief justice. Two years later, in 1780, he was elected a judge of Virginia's high court of chancery and as a member of the state's first court of appeals.

One of three Virginia signers of the Constitution

His reputation as a wise and honorable judge and statesman won him election in 1787 as a member of Virginia's delegation to the Constitutional Convention in Philadelphia. His participation in the convention was overshadowed by that of other Virginia delegates, so much so that James Madison's journal of the debates in the convention hardly makes mention of him. He occasionally opposed Washington and Madison, and voted against the establishment of a president as a single executive to administer the laws of the United States. But at the close of the convention, Blair, Washington, and Madison were the only members of the Virginia delegation to sign the United States Constitution.

Blair rode home to Virginia from the convention with George Washington. On the way, they had a narrow escape from accident, when one of the carriage horses fell through the flooring of an old bridge while crossing a flooded river. But Blair and Washington had crossed the bridge on foot and were not injured in the accident.

In 1788, Blair was elected from York County as a delegate to Virginia's constitutional ratification convention. There he spoke warmly in favor of the Constitution, despite the opposition of his old friend Patrick Henry.

Mrs. John Blair
(Jean Balfour)
National Archives. Courtesy: Mrs. H. K. D. Peachy.

An Associate Justice of the first Supreme Court

Because of Blair's judicial ability, and as a reward for his support of the Constitution, President Washington appointed him an associate justice of the first Supreme Court of the United States, signing Blair's commission on September 30, 1789. After serving more than five years, Blair resigned from the Supreme Court on January 27, 1796, because of illness.

Blair's last years were spent in pain and sickness, which he vividly described in a letter to his sister shortly before his death: "I was . . . struck with a strange disorder to which I know not how to give a name, since the Doctor does not allow it to be paralytic, the effects of which are to me most melancholy depriving me of nearly all the powers of mind. The effect was very sudden and instantaneous. I happened to be employed in some algebraical exercises (of which kind of amusement I was very fond) when all at once a torpid numbness seized my whole face and I found my intellectual powers much weakened and all was confusion. My tongue partook of the distress and some words I was not able to articulate distinctly and a general difficulty of remembering words at all. There are intervals when all these distresses abate considerably; but there are times when I am unable to read and am obliged to lay aside a newspaper or whatever else I may happen to be engaged in. I am very awkward in writing, which, of course, is an unpleasant employment. . . ." Blair died on August 31, 1800 at the age of sixty-eight, and his body was interred at Bruton Parish Churchyard in Williamsburg.

WILLIAM BLOUNT of NORTH CAROLINA

Unlike most of the Founding Fathers, William Blount was more interested in what his country could do for him than in what he could do for his country. Although he was born to a wealthy family of landowners, he had an insatiable desire to own more and more land and to become more and more powerful. His determination helped him acquire millions of acres of land and to become U. S. Senator from Tennessee, a state that he helped found. But his greed led to his exposure as an unscrupulous conspirator and his downfall as the first man ever impeached by the U. S. House of Representatives and expelled from the U. S. Senate.

A handsome, dark-haired man who enjoyed high living, Blount had no ethics that he let interfere with serving his personal interests. He freely used bribery, fraud, or any other underhanded method to attain his ends. Yet his appearance and manners were those of a southern gentleman, and this led one of his fellow delegates to the Constitutional Convention of 1787 to describe him as "plain, honest, and sincere."

Born to the wealth of an aristocratic family

William Blount was born on Easter Sunday, March 26, 1749, at his grandfather's estate of Rosefield in Bertie County in northeast North Carolina. His father was Jacob Blount, a well-to-do landowner, and his mother was Barbara Gray Blount, the daughter of an aristocratic southern

---

WILLIAM BLOUNT

1749 (March 26) Born in Bertie County, N. C.

1781, 1783-1784 Member of North Carolina house of representatives.

1782-1787 Delegate to the Continental Congress.

1787 Member of the Constitutional Convention; signed the United States Constitution.

1788-1789 Member of North Carolina state senate.

1789 Member of North Carolina convention that ratified the United States Constitution.

1790-1796 Governor and superintendent of Indian affairs for the U.S. territory south of the Ohio River.

1796 President of the Tennessee state constitutional convention.

1796-1797 U.S. Senator from Tennessee; impeached by U.S. House of Representatives and expelled by the U.S. Senate.

1798-1799 Served as speaker of the Tennessee state senate.

1800 (March 21) Died in Knoxville, Tenn.

National Archives. Attributed to Charles Willson Peale.

William Blount

family. When William was four years old, Jacob Blount moved his family to Craven County, just south of Pamlico Sound. There Jacob Blount built a large home called Blount Hall that was surrounded by a cotton and tobacco plantation worked by many slaves. Jacob Blount also became an important merchant and politician in nearby New Bern, the colonial capital of North Carolina.

William Blount and his brothers and sisters grew up without benefit of much formal education because there was no school at New Bern. He and his brothers, John Gray, Thomas, and Reading, learned a great deal more about how to choose a good race horse, how to buy or sell a piece of land, or how to keep accurate business records, than they did about fine arts or literature. When William was fourteen, his mother died. Two years later in 1765, his father married a young widow,

Hannah Salter Baker, who brought her son Ned Baker to live at Blount Hall. She and Jacob had two more sons, Willie Blount and Jacob Blount Jr.

Served as paymaster for the Continental Army

As the eldest son, William Blount worked closely with his father in the sale and purchase of land throughout North Carolina. He also was a frequent observer at the colonial legislature where his father was a member. With the coming of the Revolutionary War, his father arranged an appointment for him in 1776 as paymaster for the Third North Carolina battalion of the Continental Army. Thus, Blount drew the pay of an officer; but, since he did not have to take part in the fighting, he was free to continue to make money as a land speculator, as a merchant, and as an investor in shipping.

In 1778, he married Mary "Molsey" Grainger, a well-to-do heiress, who added considerably to the fortune that he was accumulating. They had a family of seven children.

When General Horatio Gates became commander of the southern armies in 1780, Blount won the post of chief commissary agent, managing all the purchases of supplies for the army. As was the custom, he made a substantial profit on the food and clothing that he bought for the army.

Entered politics in 1781

Blount began his career as a politician in 1781. He resigned as an army paymaster to accept election to the North Carolina state legislature. He served for one session in the North Carolina house of representatives. Then in 1782 he won appointment as a member of the state's delegation to the Continental Congress. He attended the sessions of Congress in Philadelphia fairly regularly, but was more impressed with the social and business opportunities in the national capital than he was with the work of running the government. He returned to North Carolina in March, 1783, resigned his seat in Congress, and again won election to the state legislature.

Blount and his brother, John Gray Blount, who also was a member of the legislature, set about to make themselves immensely wealthy by dealing in the millions of acres of land that were claimed by North Carolina west of the Appalachian Mountains. They succeeded in having the legislature open up the western lands for sale at about 5 cents an acre. They organized the Muscle Shoals Company to settle lands owned by the Cherokee Indians at the great bend of the Tennessee River, and they sent men to establish trading posts in the pathway for westward expansion. Blount traveled to Georgia in 1784 and convinced the legislature of that state that they should give him and his associates title to about 300,000 acres of land in the Muscle Shoals area. Then, believing that if the national government controlled the western lands they would rise in value, Blount returned to the North Carolina legislature, resumed his seat, and obtained passage of legislation ceding western North Carolina to the national government.

Personally popular despite land deals

When the North Carolina legislature met in the fall of 1784, Blount was elected speaker of the house. However, opposition to his wide-scale dealing in land had built up to the point that his opponents succeeded in repealing the legislation that had ceded the western lands to Congress. Although Blount was unable to control the state representatives on the land measure, his personal popularity was undimmed and he was re-elected as a delegate to Congress by the largest vote of any candidate. However, Blount regarded the election to Congress strictly as an honor—his business interests occupying him too much to allow him time to travel north for attendance at Congress.

The Blount brothers suffered several blows to their western land ambitions in 1785. John Sevier and other residents of western North Carolina organized the area as a separate state that they called Franklin, renouncing North Carolina's control. Congress also was taking an interest in the area, and sent a group of commissioners to Georgia to make treaties with the Indian tribes on the frontier. In an effort to make sure that the Indian treaties would be favorable to his interests, Blount obtained an appointment as an Indian agent for North Carolina and received an appropriation to buy goods to influence the Indians. Blount went to Georgia to sit in on the discussions with the Indians and the congressional commission. The commissioners were unsympathetic to Blount's pleas to make the Indians give up more of their land for the use of land speculators and western settlers, and the Indians were not influenced by the goods he offered them.

Having been re-elected to Congress, Blount traveled to New York City in 1786, where Congress then was meeting, in an effort to block the ratification of the Indian treaties. However, by the time he arrived, the treaties had been approved. Since there were no other measures before Congress that interested him, he conducted some business in the sale of tobacco and returned home in June.

Had ambitions to be president of the Congress

Learning that Congress might elect a southerner as its next president, and desiring the office for himself, Blount returned to New York in November, 1786. He found that Congress was unable to meet because a quorum of delegates was not present. He waited until January when enough Congressmen finally showed up to permit balloting to begin. The election dragged on for two weeks and in the end Blount was defeated, and Arthur St. Clair of Pennsylvania became president. The disappointed Blount blamed his defeat on the delegates from New York whom he called "antifederal peasants." Blount found it advantageous to continue to attend this session of Congress because the legislature of North Carolina had embarked on an extensive investigation of land speculation. Many speculators, including Blount's brother Reading, were arrested for fraud.

Blount's influence in North Carolina remained high, and he was elected a delegate to attend the Constitutional Convention meeting in Philadelphia. He took his seat at the Convention on June 20, 1787, about a month after it had convened. Blount was not particularly impressed by the Convention, and he broke its rule of secrecy by sending copies of the constitutional plans home to his friends in North Carolina. He wrote in July that in his opinion "we shall ultimately and not many years hence be separated and distinct governments perfectly independent of each other." After staying in Philadelphia only two weeks, he returned to New York and resumed his seat in Congress on July 4, 1787.

Hoped to stimulate western settlement

In New York, Blount worked diligently to increase the interest in migration to the western frontier in order to raise the value of the lands he owned. He inserted letters in New York and London newspapers urging settlers to go west. During

Courtesy: William Blount Mansion Association.

William Blount Mansion

Library of Congress.

Main Street, Charleston, West Virginia
(Early Nineteenth Century)

this time he carried on extensive correspondence with his brothers advising them on various land deals.

Blount returned to the Philadelphia Convention in August and remained until the United States Constitution had finally been drafted and approved by the Convention. He signed it with the other delegates on September 17, 1787, explaining that his signature did not mean that he approved of the Constitution, but merely showed that he had been present.

Becoming convinced that a strong federal government would provide better opportunities for the development of the West, Blount returned to North Carolina and campaigned for ratification of the Constitution. However, Anti-Federalist sentiments were strong in North Carolina, and Blount was defeated in the election for delegates to the state ratification convention in 1788. The convention was controlled by Anti-Federalists, and it rejected ratification of the Constitution.

When the United States government organized under the Constitution in 1789 without the participation of North Carolina or Rhode Island, the people of North Carolina began to have second thoughts about trying to remain outside the Union. Blount and other Federalists won control of a new state ratification convention called in mid-November, 1789, and this time the United States Constitution was approved.

Defeated for the U. S. Senate

Blount had been elected to the state senate in 1788 and 1789, and he used his power here to have many bills passed designed to aid his business associates and increase the value of his western lands. He was defeated on only one important issue—his campaign to become one of the U. S. Senators elected by the legislature. The state of Franklin had been dissolved, and Blount's friend and secret business associate John Sevier, the former governor of Franklin, had taken a seat in the North Carolina senate. Blount and his friends saw to it that the legislature ceded the western lands to the United States government.

Throughout the spring of 1790, Blount traveled from county to county throughout North Carolina buying and selling land and securities. His powerful influence in the state government and his contacts with members of Congress gave him an important inside edge on other businessmen. His friends in the state capital helped him evade paying taxes on the land which he bought and his friends in Congress informed him that certain money certificates issued during the Revolutionary War that had become worthless were likely to be redeemed. Blount bought up thousands of dollars of these securities from people who thought they were worthless.

Appointed governor of Tennessee territory

Political pressure by his friends in Congress won Blount the appointment in June, 1790, as governor of the newly formed Territory of the United States South of the Ohio River—a territory that included the western part of North Carolina in which Blount had so much of his money invested. Blount wrote to say that his appointment by President Washington gave him more pleasure "than any other in the Gift of the President could have been."

After settling various pressing business matters and having new clothes made for himself, Blount set out for his new post in September, 1790. He went somewhat out of his way in order to stop at Mount Vernon and personally thank President Washington for his appointment. He arrived in the territory in October, and established his temporary capital in a log cabin in the place that is now Knoxville, Tenn. Blount traveled west to Nashville in December where he swore in various territorial officials, including 23-year-old Andrew Jackson as attorney general for the western part of the territory. Jackson, who later became President of the United States, was one of Blount's vigorous supporters in the years that followed.

As governor of the territory, Blount had unlimited opportunities to expand his interests in land speculation. He and his brothers dealt in millions of acres of land that they bought for little money and sold at a profit. Throughout his administration, he constantly endeavored to have the Indians who held much of the land sign new treaties giving up their hunting grounds for land development. He pressured President Washington to launch an all-out war on the Indians, and when the federal government refused to act he turned against the administration and became an Anti-Federalist. Blount built the most lavish mansion in the territory, a two-story house with hand-carved woodwork and a large ballroom.

Elected to the U. S. Senate from Tennessee

Blount became convinced that his lands would become even more valuable if he could win statehood for the territory. His land development policies had been so successful that the population of the territory had more than doubled in the five years from 1790 to 1795, increasing from about 35,000 to more than 77,000 residents. Blount called a state constitutional convention in Knoxville in January, 1796, and he was elected president of the convention. The convention quickly drew up a constitution, and Blount was elected as one of the new state's first U. S. Senators. On June 1, 1796, Congress admitted Tennessee as a state.

Wars in Europe between England and France and between England and Spain cut off the flow of immigrants to the United States in 1796. Land speculators such as Blount were hard hit because all of their dealings were contingent upon steadily increasing land values caused by the western flow of settlers. Only his immunity from arrest as a Senator saved Blount from being thrown into jail for debt.

In a desperate attempt to find a new way of increasing western land values, Blount entered into a conspiracy with John Chisholm, a soldier of fortune, and Dr. Nicholas Romayne, a land speculator. The plan called for stirring up an Indian war against the Spanish territories that lay south of Tennessee and include present-day Mississippi, Alabama, Louisiana, and Florida. The war against the Spaniards was to be aided by their enemies the British. One of the main objects was to prevent the Louisiana territory from falling into the hands of the French.

Threatened with impeachment for conspiracy

On July 3, 1797, the conspiracy was exposed in the United States Senate. Blount had written an indiscreet letter to a fellow-conspirator that outlined the plan and said in part that Blount would probably be "at the head of the business on the part of the British." A copy of the letter had come into the possession of President John Adams who forwarded it to the Senate with an opinion that it offered grounds for impeachment against Blount. The Senator from Tennessee was pale and shaken as he heard the letter he had written read aloud before the entire Senate. It said in part:

"I have advised you, in whatever you do, to take care of yourself. I have now to tell you to take care of me too, for a discovery of the plan would prevent the success, and much injure all parties concerned . . . To such complaints against me, if such there are, it may be said by my friends, at proper times and places . . . that I was by the President instructed to purchase much more land than the Indians would agree to sell. This sort of talk will be throwing all the blame off me upon the late President, and as he is now out of office, it will be of no consequence how much the Indians blame him . . . When you have read this letter over three times, then burn it."

Impeached by the House of Representatives

The panic-stricken Blount attempted to escape from Philadelphia by ship, but the Senate ordered the ship and all Blount's personal belongings and papers seized. Feeling against him ran so strong in the capital city that even Abigail Adams, the wife of the President, complained that it was too bad that Pennsylvania "keeps no Gallows." On July 7, 1797, the House of Representatives impeached Blount by a vote of 41 to 30, and the next day the Senate expelled him by a vote of 25 to 1. After posting a bond of $500 guaranteeing to appear for his trial before the U. S. Senate on the impeachment charges, Blount fled by backroads to North Carolina to avoid his creditors.

In Tennessee, Blount's friends began an active campaign for his support, pointing out that the entire conspiracy had been for the benefit of Tennessee, and that the action of the U. S. Senate had been a political move directed by the Federalists. This campaign appealed to the Anti-Federalist people of Tennessee, who felt that Federalist President Adams was following a weak policy in refusing to use federal troops in an all out war against the Indians in the state.

Regarded as a hero in Tennessee

When Blount returned to Knoxville, Tenn., in September, 1797, he was escorted into the city as a hero by Knoxville's founder, General James White and by the speaker of the state house of representatives James Stuart. Blount was urged to run for re-election to his seat in the U. S. Senate; but he declined, and his friend Andrew Jackson was elected to fill the office. The following year, Blount was elected to the state senate and was further honored by being made speaker of the senate.

The first impeachment trial in the history of the United States got underway in Philadelphia on December 17, 1798. However, Blount, the subject of the trial, was not present. The Senate had sent its sergeant at arms to Knoxville to arrest him, but the suave Blount had entertained this gentleman in his lavish home and politely refused to accompany him back to Philadelphia. Blount employed attorneys to represent him at the trial. Finally, on January 11, 1799, the U. S. Senate voted 14 to 11 to dismiss the impeachment on the basis that Senators are not impeachable civil officers.

In March, 1800, Blount's wife, three of his children, and his mother-in-law were stricken with malaria. Blount overworked himself caring for his sick family. He caught a severe cold that developed into a serious illness, and on the evening of March 21, just five days before he would have reached the age of 51, Blount died in his Knoxville mansion. His death may have saved him from further disgrace, because his brother John Gray Blount was brought to trial for fraud in their land speculations. Or it may have prevented a political comeback that might have carried him to greater power, for in the next year the Anti-Federalists under Thomas Jefferson won control of the national government.

DAVID BREARLEY of NEW JERSEY

An officer of the Continental Army during the Revolutionary War and then Chief Justice of New Jersey, David Brearley claimed the distinction of being the first delegate elected by any state to the Constitutional Convention. He signed the United States Constitution, and presided over the constitutional ratification convention that made New Jersey the third state to approve the new form of government.

David Brearley was born in Spring Grove, New Jersey, on June 11, 1745. His grandfather, John Brearley, had emigrated from England to New Jersey in 1680. Young David was one of five children of David and Mary Clark Brearley.

After studying law, Brearley was admitted to the bar at the age of twenty-one, and began practicing law in Allentown, N.J. That same year, 1767, he married Elizabeth Mullen, by whom he had four children. She died in 1777.

With the approach of the Revolution, Brearley became an outspoken patriot; so much so that he was arrested for treason. His friends rescued him from the arresting officers. After the outbreak of fighting with the British, he was appointed a captain in the New Jersey militia. In 1776, he was promoted to lieutenant colonel in the 4th New Jersey regiment. The next year, he was transferred at the same rank to the 1st New Jersey regiment.

Helped establish the principle of unconstitutionality

Brearley was enroute to put down an Indian uprising in the Wyoming Valley of Pennsylvania in 1779, when he was elected by the state legislature as Chief Justice of New Jersey. He resigned his army commission and, at the age of thirty-four, took office as the state's highest justice. His most famous ruling as chief justice helped establish the power of a supreme court to decide whether a law is constitutional. The decision, handed down in the case of Holmes vs. Walton on September 7, 1780, became known as "the New Jersey Precedent," establishing the principle of "the judicial guardianship of the organic law against attempted or inadvertent encroachment by the ordinary law."

Brearley won popularity as chief justice, and three times he was presented as a candidate for governor. But each time he was defeated by William Livingston, who had guided New Jersey's fortunes throughout the Revolutionary War. Brearley married for a second time in 1783. This wife was Elizabeth Higbee, by whom he had three more children. An ardent Episcopalian, Brearley was a delegate to the national convention of the Episcopal Church in Philadelphia in 1786, and

DAVID BREARLEY

1745 (June 11) Born in Spring Grove, N.J.
1767 Admitted to the bar.
1776-1779 Served as a lieutenant colonel in the Continental Army.
1779-1789 Chief Justice of the Supreme Court of New Jersey.
1786 Delegate to the national convention of the Episcopal Church in Philadelphia; helped compile the Episcopal Book of Common Prayer.
1787 Delegate from New Jersey to the Constitutional Convention in Philadelphia; signed the Constitution of the United States.
1787 President of the New Jersey constitutional ratification convention.
1789 Presidential elector for New Jersey; voted for George Washington.
1789-1790 U.S. District Court Judge for New Jersey.
1790 (Aug. 16) Died at Trenton, N.J.

David Brearley
Courtesy: Grand Lodge F & AM, Trenton, New Jersey

he helped compile the Episcopal *Book of Common Prayer*. He also was elected grand master of the New Jersey Masons for the years 1788 to 1790.

A passionate plea for equality between states

New Jersey was the first state to elect delegates to a national convention to revise the Articles of Confederation, and Brearley was the first man elected to the state's delegation. At the Philadelphia convention in 1787, Brearley's most dramatic speech came in June when he denounced efforts by Virginia and the large states to control Congress under the new government. His speech was reported by James Madison as follows:

"He was sorry, he said, that any question on this point was brought into view. It had been much agitated in Congress at the time of forming the Confederation, and was then rightly settled by allowing to each sovereign State an equal vote. Otherwise, the smaller States must have been destroyed instead of being saved. The substitution of a ratio, he admitted, carried fairness on the face of it; but on a deeper examination was unfair and unjust. Judging of the disparity of the States by the quota of Congress, Virginia would have sixteen votes, and Georgia but one. A like proportion to the others will make the whole number ninety. There will be three large States, and ten small ones. The large States, by which he meant Massachusetts, Pennsylvania and Virginia, will carry everything before them. It had been admitted, and was known to him from facts within New Jersey that where large and small counties were united into a district for electing representatives for the district, the large counties always carried their point, and consequently the States would do so. Virginia with her sixteen votes will be a solid column indeed, a formidable phalanx. While Georgia with her solitary vote, and the other little States, will be obliged to throw themselves constantly into the scale of some large one, in order to have any weight at all. He had come to the Convention with a view of being as useful as he could, in giving energy and stability to the Federal Government. When the proposition for destroying the equality of votes came forward, he was astonished, he was alarmed. Is it fair, then, it will be asked, that Georgia should have an equal vote with Virginia? He would not say it was. What remedy, then? One only, that a map of the United States be spread out, that all the existing boundaries be erased, and that a new partition of the whole be made into thirteen equal parts."

Approved the Constitution as written

Brearley's proposal of establishing new boundaries for the thirteen states was never seriously discussed by the Constitutional Convention. However, Brearley was satisfied with the compromise of the two houses of Congress that was worked out to safeguard the rights of both large and small states, and he signed the Constitution with other members of the New Jersey delegation. He strongly supported the new Constitution in New Jersey and was elected president of the state ratification convention that approved the document on December 18, 1787.

As a presidential elector for New Jersey, Brearley cast his vote for George Washington for President in 1789. In November of that year, Brearley was appointed by Washington the U.S. District Judge for New Jersey, and he resigned as Chief Justice of New Jersey. He served less than a year as a federal judge, dying at the age of forty-five at Trenton, N.J., on August 16, 1790. His body was buried in St. Michael's Episcopal Church graveyard in Trenton.

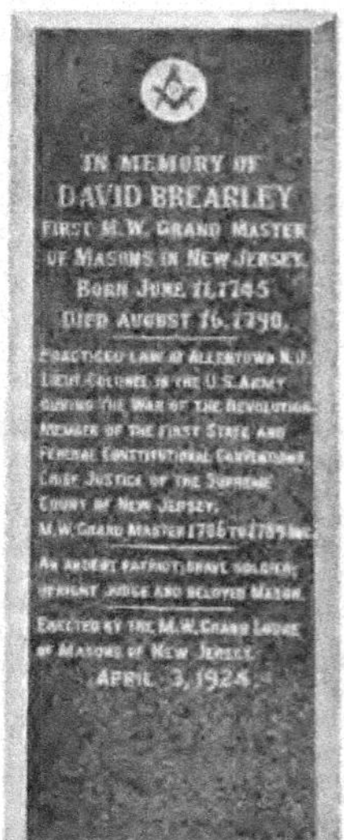

Grand Lodge of Masons, Trenton, New Jersey.

Memorial to David Brearley

JACOB BROOM of DELAWARE

A civic leader and successful businessman, Jacob Broom made his greatest contribution to the Constitutional Convention of 1787 with a strong appeal that the delegates must agree on some new plan of government, even if only by a bare majority. His appeal came at a time when the Convention seemed at the point of breaking up and a motion was before it to adjourn *sine die*, with no date set for taking further action. The only Delaware-born delegate to sign the United States Constitution, Broom was described as a quiet, serious man who enjoyed reading history.

Jacob Broom was born in Wilmington, Delaware, in 1752. His father had started his career as a blacksmith, but had acquired large land holdings and had become one of the most important men of the community. His mother was a devout member of the Society of Friends. Broom was said to be a direct descendant of the royal Plantagenet family, who lost the throne of England with Richard II in 1399. The Broom family adopted the Plantagenet axiom, "Illiterate, base nobles are the clowns of heraldry."

Young Jacob was educated at the old Wilmington Academy, where he took a particular interest in mathematics. Like young George Washington, the fondness for mathematics led Broom to learn surveying. He became surveyor for New Castle County, Delaware, and later, during the Revolutionary War, one of the maps he drew was used by George Washington during the Battle of Brandywine Creek.

In 1773, when he was twenty-one years old, Broom married Rachel Pierce. They had a family of eight children – three sons and five daughters. Two of his sons later became Congressmen, and one of them was named as a candidate for President by the Know-Nothing party.

JACOB BROOM

1752 Born in Wilmington, Del.

1776-1785 Burgess of Wilmington, or member of town council.

1784-1786 Member of Delaware state legislature.

1785-1802 Member of board of trustees of Wilmington Academy.

1787 A founder and treasurer of Wilmington library.

1787 Delaware delegate to the Constitutional Convention; signed the United States Constitution.

1790-1792 First postmaster of Wilmington.

1795 Built first cotton spinning mill in Wilmington.

1806-1810 Director of the Bank of Delaware.

1810 (April 25) Died in Philadelphia.

Wrote the address welcoming Washington after the war

When Broom was twenty-four years old, he was elected as assistant burgess of the borough of Wilmington, corresponding to a member of the town council. He was annually elected as a burgess from 1776 to 1785, serving for the last four years as chief burgess. In this last capacity, Broom composed an accomplished address to General George Washington on the occasion of his passing through Wilmington on his way to resign his commission to Congress at the end of the Revolutionary War. On December 15, 1783, Washington arrived at the city at nightfall and was welcomed with a 13-gun salute, bonfires, and an "elegant supper." Brown's address, delivered the next day, was as follows:

"MAY IT PLEASE YOUR EXCELLENCY– The Burgesses and Common Council of the Borough of Wilmington, in behalf of themselves and the inhabitants thereof–

"Being penetrated with sentiments of the most perfect respect, beg leave to approach and to be permitted to congratulate your Excellency, that your glorious endeavors to rescue our country from a determined plan of oppression have been not only attended with the most brilliant success, but crowned with the noble rewards of liberty, independence, and the final accomplishment of an honorable peace.

"When we reflect on the magnitude of the object for which we contended, and the greatness of the power we had to oppose, the boldest among us have sometimes shuddered at the prospect, while your magnanimity was our invincible shield on the most gloomy occasions.

"Convinced that our humble talents cannot express in language suitable to the subject, either the grateful sensations we feel in the contemplation of your great and eminent services, or the love and admiration of your many amiable virtues which fill the bosom of the friends of freedom in America and in distant nations, yet, rather than wound that delicacy which would receive with reluctance even less than our duty and inclination prompt us to mention, we will conclude with em-

Historical Society of Delaware. Photo by Sanborn Studio.

"Hagley," Residence of Jacob Broom, built in Christiana Hundred, Delaware, in 1795.

bracing this opportunity of joining the general voice of America, which hails you as 'the deliverer of our country'; and we flatter ourselves you will believe that our most fervent wishes will accompany your illustrious and long meditated retirement, with the enjoyment of health, tranquility, and every other felicity.

"And permit us to indulge the pleasing hope, that even in the serene enjoyment of that retirement which will astonish mankind little less than the splendor and greatness of your services; that with a parental consideration, your excellency will occasionally contribute your advice and influence to promote that harmony and union of our infant governments which are so essential to the permanent establishment of our freedom, happiness, and prosperity."

In 1784, Broom was elected to the lower house of the Delaware legislature. He continued to serve in that body for the next five years.

Favored apportionment in the House

At the age of thirty-five, Broom was elected as one of Delaware's five delegates to the Constitutional Convention in Philadelphia. He was present at the opening of the meeting on May 25, 1787, and cast his vote along with all the other delegates in electing Washington as President of the Convention. Broom apparently took his first part in the debates on June 26 when he seconded a motion by George Read, a fellow-delegate from Delaware, that called for a nine-year term for Senators. He is not mentioned again in James Madison's records of the debates in the Convention until July 10, when Broom made a brief speech explaining that he had voted in favor of apportioning membership in the House of Representatives among the states according to population only with the reservation that he expected the delegates from the larger states to give an equal voice to all states in the Senate.

Helped break the Convention deadlock

The Convention reached a crisis on July 16, and Broom helped prevent its dissolution by a timely appeal. The day began with the states voting 5 to 4 to accept a two-house Congress with representation based on population in one house, and equal representation for all states in the other house. This was a victory for the small states, causing Edmund Randolph of the large state of Virginia to ask for an immediate adjournment "in the present solemn crisis." William Paterson of New Jersey jumped up to say that there was no

Courtesy: The Brooklyn Museum.

Baltimore in 1802
By Francis Guy

The Peale Museum, Baltimore. Gift of Mrs. Harry White.

Exhuming the first American Mastadon
By Charles Willson Peale

possibility of the small states' accepting any other compromise, and, that so far as he was concerned, if Randolph wished to move for a *sine die* adjournment and remove the rule of secrecy on the delegates he would second it—in effect, end the Convention. An attempt was then made to adjourn the convention temporarily to the next day, and this failed by a 5 to 5 vote—indicating *sine die* adjournment would be the next step. At this point, Jacob Broom rose, representing the smallest state present. He declared that he believed *sine die* adjournment "would be fatal" and that "something must be done by the Convention, though it should be by a bare majority." This plea seems to have been very effective, for shortly afterward, the Convention agreed to adjourn to the next day and continue hammering out a Constitution.

For the remainder of the Convention, Broom made no important speeches, although he seconded various measures proposed by other delegates. He supported proposals that the President be chosen by Electors appointed by the state legislatures and that he should serve for life "during good behavior." He also seconded a motion by Charles Pinckney that Congress should have the power to veto any legislation passed by a state legislature. Finally, on September 17, 1787, Broom signed the United States Constitution, and then returned home to Delaware.

Interested in civic affairs

Broom took no further part in state or national affairs for the rest of his life, devoting his attention to his business and to civic duties in Wilmington. He helped found Wilmington's first library in 1787, and was treasurer of the library company with a beginning capital of fifty dollars. He became Wilmington's first postmaster from 1790 to 1792, and he also headed up the city's water, sewer, and street departments. He also served for seventeen years as trustee of the city's leading school, the Wilmington Academy.

In 1795, Broom opened the first cotton mill in Wilmington, utilizing the old Wilmington Academy building where he had once gone to school. A visitor to this mill in the year it opened described it as follows :

"This is an improvement that exceeds anything I have yet seen. It is without doubt very compleat, all the carding, woofing and spinning is done by machines, which are excellent in their performance. A very few such excellent cotton stuffs are imported as those made here."

National Archives.

Ann Broom
(Oldest daughter of Jacob Broom)
By JAMES PEALE

In 1797, Broom built a larger cotton mill north of Brandywine Creek, but this mill burned and he did not rebuild it. In 1802, Broom sold the site to Eleuthere I. du Pont, who constructed a new cotton mill in 1814. This site is now the location of the Hagley Museum, which has exhibits of American industrial history.

Broom also took part in many other important enterprises. In 1801, he was chairman of a town hall meeting that initiated petitions for the establishment of the Chesapeake & Delaware Canal, a project that was not completed until 1829. In 1806, he became a director of the Wilmington Bridge Company that constructed a toll bridge across Christina Creek, and that same year he became a director of the Bank of Delaware.

At the age of fifty-eight Broom died in Philadelphia, and was buried in the graveyard of Christ Church in that city. His sense of civic responsibility was exhibited in his will, in which he left money to the Female Benevolent Society, an organization to help needy women, and to "The Wilmington Association for Promoting the Education of People of Color," an association that maintained a school for the teaching of Negro children.

American Stage Wagon

Library of Congress. Travels Through North America, 1795-97, by Isaac Weld.

PIERCE BUTLER of SOUTH CAROLINA

The son of an Irish nobleman, Pierce Butler came to America shortly before the Revolutionary War, married a wealthy plantation owner's daughter, sold his commission as a British army major, and became a South Carolina political leader. As a delegate to the Constitutional Convention of 1787, Butler was an ardent spokesman for the Southern slave-holders, believing that the number of representatives from each state in Congress should be based on the wealth of the state rather than on its population. He also proposed the wording in the Constitution that insured that runaway slaves escaping to another state would be returned to their owners. Butler went on to serve his state in the United States Senate where he expressed the philosophy that "a member of the Senate should not only have a handsome income, but should spend it all."

Pierce Butler was born on July 11, 1744, in County Carlow, Ireland. He was the son of Sir Richard Butler, an Irish baron who was descended from the Dukes of Ormonde. Young Butler received a good education. Then, because he was one of the younger sons and not likely to inherit the title, his family purchased a commission for him in the British army.

A dashing figure in uniform

Sent to America in his twenties, Butler cut a swath in South Carolina society, where his noble lineage and well-tailored uniform made him a much sought-after guest by mothers with eligible daughters. In 1771, he succumbed to the charms of one of the daughters of Thomas Middleton, a wealthy plantation owner of Prince William's Parish. Two years later he sold his commission in the British army, and settled down to plantation life with his wife.

With the coming of the Revolutionary War, Butler supported the patriotic cause, and in 1778 was elected as a representative in the state legislature. He continued to serve in that body almost continuously for the next ten years. In 1779, he was appointed adjutant general of the state. In state politics, he opposed the interests of the wealthy coastal families who had generally controlled the South Carolina government before the war, and was instrumental in having the state capital moved from Charleston to Columbia in 1790.

In 1787, Pierce was elected by the legislature as a member of its delegation to the Congress of the Confederation in New York, and also as one of its delegates to the Constitutional Convention in Philadelphia. He traveled by boat to Philadelphia with Charles Cotesworth Pinckney, arriving there on May 24, the day before the Convention began its sessions.

Pierce Butler

Courtesy: Mr. and Mrs. Nigel Brant.
Photographer: Kinocrat House, London.

PIERCE BUTLER

1744 (July 11) Born in County Carlow, Ireland.

1773 Resigned commission as major in the British army.

1778-1782, 1784-1789 Representative in the South Carolina legislature.

1779 Appointed adjutant general of South Carolina.

1787 Delegate from South Carolina to the Constitutional Convention; signed the United States Constitution.

1789-1796, 1802-1804 United States Senator from South Carolina.

1822 (Feb. 15) Died in Philadelphia.

A Charleston Sketchbook, by Charles Fraser.

St. Andrew's Church in St. Andrew's Parish,
near Charleston, South Carolina.
(c. 1800)

Believed in wealth as criterion for representation

At the Convention, Butler was quite vocal on any point in which he thought the representatives of the Northern States were trying to get the best of their Southern colleagues. In the first month of the Convention, he objected to having representatives to Congress elected directly by the people; spoke out against taking away the states' rights by the stronger national government; supported the idea of a single person, rather than a council, as chief executive; opposed giving the chief executive veto power on legislation; and urged that the number of representatives a state had in Congress should be based on its wealth, pointing out that "money is power."

In July, when Hugh Williamson of North Carolina proposed a compromise in determining representation in Congress based on a census that would count each slave as three-fifths of a person, Butler angrily denounced the measure. He declared "that the labor of a slave in South Carolina was as productive and valuable, as that of a freeman in Massachusetts; that as wealth was the great means of defence and utility to the nation, they were equally valuable to it with freemen; and that consequently an equal representation ought to be allowed for them in a government which was instituted principally for the protection of property, and was itself to be supported by property." Later that same month, he opposed plans for the Congress to appoint federal judges, believing state courts should handle all judicial matters.

Despite his strong beliefs in property rights, Butler opposed a proposal by Gouverneur Morris that the Constitution should include a clause restricting voting rights to property owners. "There is no right of which the people are more jealous than that of suffrage," Butler said. "Abridgments of it tend to the same revolution as in Holland, where they have at length thrown all power into the hands of the Senates, who fill up vacancies themselves, and form a rank aristocracy."

Favored restrictions on immigrant political participation

Although Butler himself had lived in America less than twenty years, he denounced plans for removing any restrictions on immigrants being allowed to sit in Congress. He said that foreigners "bring with them, not only attachments to other countries, but ideas of government so distinct from ours, that in every point of view they are dangerous." He said that if he himself had been allowed to sit in Congress shortly after arriving in America that his own "foreign habits, opinions, and attachments, would have rendered him an improper agent in public affairs."

In the closing weeks of the Convention, Butler made strenuous efforts to prevent Congress from having the power to tax exports. On August 22, he said he "would never agree to the power of taxing exports." He also objected to a clause in the Constitution obligating the Congress to "discharge the debts of the United States." He pointed out that speculators had bought up much of the war debt obligations, and he did not feel that Congress should be forced to pay "the blood-suckers who had speculated on the distresses of others."

Responsible for the slavery clause in the Constitution

On August 29, Butler moved and the Convention accepted the insertion in the Constitution of the following sentence: "If any person bound to service or labor in any of the United States, shall escape into another State, he or she shall not be discharged from such service or labor, in consequence of any regulations subsisting in the State to which they escape, but shall be delivered up to the person justly claiming their service or labor."

The acceptance of this provision by the northern states seems to have removed Butler's objections to other provisions of the Constitution, for he signed it with the other delegates on September 17. Then, he went to New York City with the other members of Congress who had been attending the Convention, and proceeded to insure that the Constitution was approved by Congress and forwarded to the states for ratification.

In 1788, Butler attended a session of the South Carolina legislature where considerable controversy raged as to whether or not a convention should be called to ratify the Constitution. Butler and other delegates to the Constitutional Convention spoke warmly in favor of their accomplishment, and the legislature finally voted 76 to 75 to call the ratification convention.

One of South Carolina's first U. S. Senators

Butler was elected by the South Carolina legislature as one of the state's first two United States senators, and although he was elected as a Federalist he soon became a member of the Democratic-Republican party. Butler was disturbed by the petty politics that he found in the Senate, and wrote to a friend: "I am materially disappointed. I find locality and partiality reign as much in our Supreme Legislature as they could in a county court or State legislature. . . . I find men scrambling for partial advantages, State interests, and in short, a train of those narrow, impolitic measures that must, after a while, shake the Union to its very foundation . . ." However, a fellow-Senator from Pennsylvania described Butler himself as "ever and anon crying out against local views and partial proceedings; and that the most local and partial creature I ever heard open his mouth."

When the Constitutional Convention had been considering the pay for members of Congress in 1787, Butler had proposed that Senators should be paid no salary. But when the same matter was taken up in the Senate in 1789, he supported a motion that Senators should be paid eight dollars a day, although the bill presented by the House of Representatives called for only six dollars a day. In urging this increase, Butler said that "a member of the Senate should not only have a handsome income, but should spend it all." After much discussion, the pay for Senators was set at seven dollars a day and that for Representatives at six dollars a day.

Took a dim view of the Bill of Rights

Butler took a cynical view of the efforts by James Madison to draw up the Bill of Rights amendments to the Constitution. He wrote to a friend in 1789:

"If you wait for substantial amendments, you will wait longer than I wish you to do, speaking *interestedly*. A few *milk-and-water* amendments have been proposed by Mr. M., such as liberty of conscience, a free press, and one or two general things already well secured. I suppose it was done to keep his promise with his constituents, to move for alterations; but, if I am not greatly mistaken, he is not hearty in the cause of amendments."

Butler continued to serve in the Senate until 1796, when he resigned to attend to his personal affairs in South Carolina. He was returned to the Senate in 1802, but resigned again after serving only two years.

In his old age, Butler lived in Philadelphia, and died there at the age of seventy-seven on February 15, 1822. Disappointed because his wife had borne no sons, Butler had persuaded a young Philadelphian who married one of his daughters to name his oldest son Pierce Butler on condition that he would inherit the family estate. This grandson married the English actress Fanny Kemble in 1834 and took her to live on his South Carolina plantation. But she was so shocked by the conditions of slavery that she divorced him, and wrote her experiences in "Journal of a Residence in America."

190 Journals *of the* Aſſembly. *A.* 1778.

Articles of Confederation *and* Perpetual Union,

between the States of New-Hampſhire, Maſſachuſetts-Bay, Rhode-Iſland *and* Providence Plantations, Connecticut, New-York, New-Jerſey, Pennſylvania, Delaware, Maryland, Virginia, North-Carolina, South-Carolina, *and* Georgia.

ARTICLE I. THE ſtile of this confederacy ſhall be "The UNITED STATES of *AMERICA*."

ART. II. Each ſtate retains its ſovereignty, freedom and independence, and every power, juriſdiction and right, which is not by this confederation expreſſly delegated to the united ſtates in congreſs aſſembled.

ART. III. The ſaid ſtates hereby ſeverally enter into a firm league of friendſhip with each other, for their common defence, the ſecurity of their liberties, and their mutual and general welfare, binding themſelves to aſſiſt each other againſt all force offered to, or attacks made upon them, or any of them, on account of religion, ſovereignty, trade, or any other pretence whatever.

ART. IV. The better to ſecure and perpetuate mutual friendſhip and intercourſe among the people of the different ſtates in this union, the free inhabitants of each of theſe ſtates, paupers, vagabonds, and fugitives from juſtice excepted, ſhall be entitled to all privileges and immunities of free citizens in the ſeveral ſtates; and the people of each ſtate ſhall have free ingreſs and regreſs to and from any other ſtate, and ſhall enjoy therein all the privileges of trade and commerce, ſubject to the ſame duties, impoſitions and reſtrictions, as the inhabitants thereof reſpectively, provided that ſuch reſtriction ſhall not extend ſo far as to prevent the removal of property imported into any ſtate, to any other ſtate of which the owner is an inhabitant; provided alſo, that no impoſition, duties or reſtriction, ſhall be laid by any ſtate, on the property of the united ſtates, or either of them.

If any perſon guilty of, or charged with treaſon, felony, or other high miſdemeanor in any ſtate, ſhall flee from juſtice, and be found in any of the united ſtates, he ſhall, upon demand of the governor or executive power of the ſtate from which he fled, be delivered up and removed to the ſtate having juriſdiction of his offence.

Full faith and credit ſhall be given in each of theſe ſtates to the records, acts and judicial proceedings of the courts and magiſtrates of every other ſtate.

ART. V. For the more convenient management of the general intereſts of the united ſtates, delegates ſhall be annually appointed in ſuch manner as the legiſlature of each ſtate ſhall direct, to meet in congreſs on the firſt *Monday* in *November*, in every year, with a power reſerved to each ſtate, to recall its delegates, or any of them, at any time within the year, and to ſend others in their ſtead, for the remainder of the year.

No ſtate ſhall be repreſented in congreſs by leſs than two, nor by more than ſeven members; and no perſon ſhall be capable of being a delegate for more than three years, in any term of ſix years; nor ſhall any perſon, being a delegate, be capable of holding any office under the united ſtates, for which he, or another for his benefit receives any ſalary, fees or emolument of any kind.

Each ſtate ſhall maintain its own delegates in a meeting of the ſtates, and while they act as members of the committee of the ſtates.

In determining queſtions in the united ſtates in congreſs aſſembled, each ſtate ſhall have one vote.

Freedom of ſpeech and debate in congreſs ſhall not be impeached or queſtioned in any court, or place out of congreſs, and the members of congreſs ſhall be protected in their perſons from arreſts and impriſonments during the time of their going to and from, and attendance on congreſs, except for treaſon, felony, or breach of the peace.

ART. VI. No ſtate without the conſent of the united ſtates in congreſs aſſembled, ſhall ſend any embaſſy to, or receive any embaſſy from, or enter into any conference, agreement, alliance or treaty, with any king, prince or ſtate; nor ſhall any perſon holding any office of profit or truſt under the united ſtates, or any of them, accept of any preſent, emolument, office or title of any kind whatever, from any king, prince or foreign ſtate; nor ſhall the united ſtates in congreſs aſſembled, or any of them, grant any title of nobility.

The Articles of Confederation as printed by John Dunlap, Philadelphia, 1782

DANIEL CARROLL of MARYLAND

A wealthy landowner and merchant, Daniel Carroll of Maryland signed two important documents of American history—the Articles of Confederation and the United States Constitution. Although the dignified, dark-haired Carroll represented the aristocracy of his state, he believed strongly in democracy. He endeavored unsuccessfully to have the Constitution provide that the President of the United States should be directly elected by the people. After the adoption of the Constitution, Carroll served as a U. S. Representative in the first United States Congress and then was appointed by President Washington as one of the three commissioners responsible for supervising the surveying and construction of the capital city at Washington, D.C.

A Roman Catholic whose brother was the first Bishop

Daniel Carroll was born in Upper Marlboro, Md., on July 22, 1730. His father, also named Daniel, was a rich merchant and planter who owned thousands of acres of land and many slaves. His mother, Eleanor Darnall Carroll, was the daughter of a wealthy landowner. Young Daniel was one of seven children. His younger brother, John Carroll, later became the first Roman Catholic bishop in the United States, and then became the first archbishop.

The boy received his early education at home, because the laws of Maryland at that time forbade Catholics from educating their children in parochial schools. At the age of twelve, he was sent to France, where he went to school at St. Omer, an English Jesuit college. He returned to America in 1748, when he was eighteen.

DANIEL CARROLL

1730 (July 22) Born in Upper Marlboro, Md.
1742-1748 Attended school in France.
1777-1781 Member of Maryland Council of State.
1781-1783 Delegate to Continental Congress; signed the Articles of Confederation.
1782-1791 Member of Maryland state senate, serving in 1787 and 1788 as president of the senate.
1787 Delegate to the Constitutional Convention; signed the United States Constitution.
1789-1791 Member of U.S. House of Representatives from Maryland.
1791-1795 Commissioner of the federal district supervising the laying out of the new capital city.
1796 (May 7) Died at Rock Creek, Md.

Served as an interpreter with the Indians

In 1751, his father died, leaving the twenty-one-year-old Daniel the management of the family's business and land holdings. In the next year, he married a distant relative, Eleanor Carroll. By this marriage, he received a dowry of about three thousand pounds and became a cousin of Charles Carroll of Carrollton, one of the richest men in the American colonies. He and his wife had two children, Daniel II, and Mary. Mrs. Carroll died in 1763.

In the fifteen years prior to the Revolutionary War, Daniel Carroll increased his fortune by buying and selling land and slaves. He also operated a successful mercantile business, importing manufactured goods and exporting tobacco. He speculated in land purchases on the western frontier and promoted the settlement of the area west of the Appalachian Mountains. When he was twenty-six, he was appointed as an interpreter to aid in the negotiation of a treaty with the Cherokee and Catawba Indians. He had learned their languages from tribes living near his land.

Mrs. Daniel Carroll (Eleanor) of Upper Marlboro, and her son, Daniel Carroll, Jr.
Frick Art Reference Library. Artist: John Wollaston the younger.

Frick Art Reference Library. Artist: John Wollaston the younger.
Daniel Carroll of Upper Marlboro

During the Revolutionary War, Carroll continued to build his wealth by purchasing the condemned property of Loyalists who supported the British cause, and by speculating in the various securities and monetary certificates issued by the states. As a merchant, he helped supply the army with clothing, food, and equipment.

At the age of forty-seven, Daniel Carroll was elected by the state legislature to his first public office, as a member of the Maryland Council of State, a five-man advisory board to the state governor. He served in this office from 1777 to 1781, making particular use of his knowledge as a merchant in obtaining supplies for the militia during this critical phase of the war.

Signed the Articles of Confederation

In 1781, the state legislature elected Carroll as a delegate to the Continental Congress, and he had the pleasure of taking to Congress his state's final ratification of the Articles of Confederation. Maryland had withheld approval of the articles until other states gave assurances that they would give up their claims to western lands and allow the national government to administer them for the benefit of all the states. On March 1, 1781, Carroll signed the Articles of Confederation, providing the approval of the thirteenth state that was needed to place the Articles in effect as the national law.

For the next ten years Carroll was quite active in governmental affairs, serving most of the time in a dual role in both the state and national government. He continued to serve as a delegate to Congress until 1783; but in 1781 he was elected by the legislature as a member of the state senate, an office that he held from 1782 to 1791. At various times in 1787 and 1788 Carroll was elected as president of the state senate, at that time a fifteen-man body.

After the Revolutionary War, Carroll was associated with George Washington in the Potomac Company that was organized in 1784 to develop a canal to improve the navigation of the Potomac River. Carroll was particularly interested in this project because of his large landholdings near the proposed site of the canal.

Maryland did not send any delegates to the Annapolis Convention of 1786 that was called to consider what might be done to change the Articles of Confederation to improve the trade relations between the states. Carroll wrote a letter to James Madison of Virginia explaining why Maryland would not take part: "The proposition from yr Assembly, for a meeting of Commissioners from all the States, to adjust a general commercial system, reach'd us not long before the conclusion of the Session—Our House of Delegates propos'd Commissioners for that purpose; the measure appear'd to the Senate tho' undoubtedly adopted . . . to have a tendency to weaken the authority of Congress, on which the *Union*, & consequently the Liberty, & Safety of all the states depend."

Appointed as a delegate to the Constitutional Convention

In 1787, Daniel Carroll was appointed as one of the delegates to the Constitutional Convention, replacing his cousin Charles Carroll, the signer of the Declaration of Independence, who had declined the office. Because of his ill health, Daniel Carroll did not relish the thought of travelling to Philadelphia to attend the meeting, and he wrote to a friend:

"As this appointment was neither wish'd for, or

expected by me, & I have been detained from home all last winter, & 6 weeks this Spring, it will be some time before I can enter on the execution of this Trust. I dare not think of residing in Phila. during the Summer months. My health, thank God, is much better than it has been for several years past. Moderate (but constant dayly) exercise, temperance and attention, have in a great measure conquer'd my nervous complaints, without the aid of Medicine."

Advocated a strong national government

Carroll finally took his seat in the Constitutional Convention on July 9, 1787, nearly two months after the meeting had begun. James Madison's *Journal of the Constitutional Convention* shows that Carroll advocated a strong national government, and that he believed as much democracy as possible should be granted by the Constitution. He objected to a proposal that the Congress elect the President; and, when he was unsuccessful in convincing the Convention that the President should be elected directly by the people, he supported a system of presidential selectors to be elected by the people. Carroll believed strongly that all thirteen states should be required to ratify the Constitution, but the other delegates felt this would jeopardize the possibility of ever getting the Constitution into effect. He signed the United States Constitution with other delegates on September 17, 1787.

Carroll helped convince the people of Maryland that they should ratify the Constitution, which he called "the best form of government which has ever been offered to the world"; then he successfully ran for election on the Federalist ticket, winning one of Maryland's six seats in the first United States House of Representatives. Carroll played an important role in getting Congress to adopt the First Amendment to the Constitution providing for religious freedom; he declared that "many sects have concurred in opinion that they are not well secured under the present Constitution." He served only one term in Congress, from 1789 to 1791.

Appointed to help design Washington, D. C.

At the conclusion of his term of office as Congressman, on March 4, 1791, Carroll accepted an appointment by President Washington as one of three commissioners to oversee the surveying, design, and construction of the new federal district and national capital on the Potomac River. Carroll was quite active in his work as a federal district commissioner, attending meetings several days a week. His detractors claimed that his zeal was merely a result of the fact that several of his relatives owned large amounts of land in the area designated as the new federal district, and that his own estate was nearby.

Carroll's ill health forced him to resign as a federal district commissioner on May 21, 1795; and less than a year later, on May 7, 1796, he died at the age of sixty-five at Rock Creek, Md. Confusion exists as to Carroll's burial place because of the number of men called Daniel Carroll who lived at the time.

The State House at Annapolis

Library of Congress. Owner: Count Paul de Leusse.

View of the Bridge and of the Town of York, Pa.

GEORGE CLYMER of PENNSYLVANIA

EDITOR'S NOTE: *Because George Clymer was one of the six men who signed both the Declaration of Independence and the United States Constitution, a biography of his life is included in Volume I of* FOUNDERS OF FREEDOM, *and the following article is concerned only with his role in the writing of the United States Constitution.*

A successful merchant and former member of the Continental Congress, 48-year-old George Clymer was serving in the Pennsylvania legislature as a representative at the same time he was a member of his state's delegation to the Constitutional Convention of 1787. Because he was busy in the legislature, he took little part in the writing of the Constitution during the first three months of the Convention. But after he was appointed on August 18 to the Grand Committee of Eleven that was formed to decide whether the new national government should assume the war debts of the states, he began to take a more active role in the debates.

On August 21, in a debate on whether the national government or the state governments should have the power to tax exports, Clymer moved that this power be left to the states, with the provision that such taxes on exports might be only for the purpose of raising revenue. James Madison's journal says: "Mr. Clymer remarked, that every State might reason with regard to its particular productions in the same manner as the Southern States. The Middle States may apprehend an oppression of their wheat, flour, provisions, &c.; and with more reason, as these articles were exposed to a competition in foreign markets not incident to tobacco, rice, &c. They may apprehend also combinations against them, between the Eastern and Southern States, as much as the latter can apprehend them between the Eastern and middle. He moved, as a qualification of the power of taxing exports, that it should be restrained to regulations of trade, by inserting, after the word "duty," Article 7, Section 4, the words, "for the purpose of revenue." However, Clymer's motion was defeated, being supported only by the votes of New Jersey, Pennsylvania, and Delaware; and, when agreement could not be reached,

GEORGE CLYMER

1739 (March 16) Born in Philadelphia.

1775-1776 Served as one of first Continental treasurers for the United Colonies.

1776-1777 Delegate to the Continental Congress from Pennsylvania; signed the Declaration of Independence.

1777-1778 Served as special commissioner of Congress to investigate Indian massacres on Pennsylvania's western frontier.

1780-1782 Member of Congress of Confederation from Pennsylvania.

1784-1788 Representative in Pennsylvania state legislature.

1787 Delegate to Constitutional Convention; signed United States Constitution.

1789-1791 U.S. Representative from Pennsylvania in first United States Congress.

1791-1794 Chief U.S. collector in Pennsylvania for excise tax on alcoholic beverages during period of the Whiskey Rebellion.

1795-1796 Member of commission appointed by President Washington that negotiated a peace treaty with Creek Indians in Georgia.

1813 (Jan. 23) Died in Morrisville, Pa.

George Clymer
By CHARLES WILLSON PEALE
The Pennsylvania Museum of the Fine Arts. Photograph by Phillips Studio.

Book of the Signers, by William Brotherhead.

Residence of George Clymer
Located on Chestnut Street near Seventh Avenue, Philadelphia

it was decided to have the Grand Committee of Eleven study the matter and come back with further recommendations.

Protested use of the word "slaves" in the Constitution

On August 25, Clymer agreed with Roger Sherman of Connecticut in protesting the use of the word "slaves" in the Constitution, and as a result Gouverneur Morris withdrew his proposal that the word be included.

On August 28, after the convention by a 6 to 5 vote had agreed to prohibit the states from taxing either imports or exports, Gouverneur Morris pointed out that it was possible that unless some further restrictions were written into the Constitution, the Atlantic States might use the power of taxation to prevent Western States from making free use of the Mississippi River. At this point, Madison reported: "Mr. Clymer thought the encouragement of the Western country was suicide on the part of the old States. If the States have such different interests that they cannot be left to regulate their own manufactures, without encountering the interests of other States, it is a proof that they are not fit to compose one nation."

Favored power in government to regulate navigation

The next day, August 29, Clymer spoke in defense of the recommendation of the Committee of Eleven that no restrictions should be placed on the powers of the new government to regulate shipping. "The diversity of commercial interests," he said, "of necessity, creates difficulties which ought not to be increased by unnecessary restrictions. The Northern and Middle States will be ruined, if not enabled to defend themselves against foreign regulations." Despite the vigorous opposition of the Southern States, who wanted a restriction written ino the Constitution to prevent Congress from passing any navigation act without a two-thirds majority, the committee's recommendation was accepted.

Clymer felt that the Constitution was making the Senate too powerful a body; and on September 6, he declared that he could never agree to "the aristocratic part" that gave the Senate the power of appointment to federal offices.

In the final days of the convention, Clymer successfully opposed a plan submitted by Alexander Hamilton that the Congress of the Confederation should approve of the new Constitution before submitting it to individual states for ratification. Clymer, and a majority of the delegates, felt that it was a maneuver to defeat the adoption of the Constitution.

After signing the Constitution, Clymer returned to his work in the Pennsylvania state legislature. He next served as a U.S. Representative from Pennsylvania in the first Congress of the United States under the Constitution from 1789 to 1791. President Washington, in 1791, appointed him collector of federal excise taxes for Pennsylvania. In this position Clymer received much abuse during the Whisky Rebellion of 1794.

JONATHAN DAYTON of NEW JERSEY

The youngest man to sign the United States Constitution, Jonathan Dayton was graduated from college at the age of fifteen, then served for seven years as an officer in the Continental Army during the Revolutionary War. After attending the Constitutional Convention at the age of twenty-six, Dayton held public office as a legislator for twenty years in the New Jersey legislature, in the U. S. House of Representatives, and in the U. S. Senate. Dayton's public career was largely ruined by his association with Aaron Burr in a scheme to take Mexico and combine it with the western territories into an independent empire. Dayton was charged with treason, and, although he was never brought to trial, he never again held high office. In his old age, Dayton continued to wear the three-cornered hats of Revolutionary War days and became known as "the last of the cocked hats."

Library of Congress. Artist: Charles B. J. Fevret de Saint Memin.

Jonathan Dayton

Jonathan Dayton was born on October 16, 1760, at Elizabethtown, New Jersey. He was the son of Elias Dayton, who distinguished himself as a colonel of New Jersey troops in the Continental Army during the Revolutionary War. A bright boy, young Jonathan received his bachelor's degree from the College of New Jersey (now Princeton University) in 1776, when he was only fifteen.

Fought at Yorktown under Lafayette

Immediately after his graduation, Dayton joined the Continental Army as a paymaster for the third battalion of New Jersey troops that his father commanded. He soon was assigned to the staff of Brigadier General William Maxwell, commander of the New Jersey brigade, and in this capacity he took part in the many actions of Washington's troops in New Jersey and Pennsylvania. In 1779, while he was still only eighteen, Dayton was assigned as aide-de-camp to Major General John Sullivan and was given the temporary commission of major. He accompanied Sullivan and his army on the expedition against the Indian tribes of the Six Nations in northern Pennsylvania. The next year he rejoined the New Jersey brigade with the rank of captain, but shortly after was captured by the British at Elizabethtown, New Jersey. After a short imprisonment, Dayton was released and rejoined the New Jersey troops. As did Alexander Hamilton, he served under the Marquis de Lafayette at the siege of Yorktown in 1781, and distinguished himself by leading his troops in storming a British redoubt. Three days after his twenty-first birthday, Dayton was present at the surrender of Lord Cornwallis.

JONATHAN DAYTON

1760 (Oct. 16) Born at Elizabethtown, N. J.
1776 Graduated from the College of New Jersey (now Princeton University).
1776-1783 Fought in the Revolutionary War.
1787-1790 Member of the New Jersey state legislature.
1787 Delegate from New Jersey to the Constitutional Convention; signed the United States Constitution.
1790 Speaker of the New Jersey house of representatives.
1791-1799 U. S. Representative from New Jersey.
1795-1799 Speaker of the U. S. House of Representatives.
1797 Dayton, Ohio, named for him.
1798 Appointed brigadier general in the United States Army.
1799-1805 U. S. Senator from New Jersey.
1807 Indicted for treason with Aaron Burr, but never brought to trial.
1814-1815 Member of the New Jersey legislature.
1824 (Oct. 9) Died at Elizabethtown, N. J.

Was a late arrival at Constitutional Convention

After the war was over, Dayton began studying law, was admitted to the bar, and at the age of twenty-six won election to the New Jersey state

Miami University

From the Magazine of History, Rutgers University.

Home of Jonathan Dayton

legislature in 1787. When delegates for the Constitutional Convention were chosen by the legislature, Colonel Elias Dayton declined his nomination in favor of his son. There was some delay in confirming the younger Dayton's election, and he did not take his seat at the Philadelphia meeting until June 21, 1787, nearly a month after the Convention had begun.

Dayton took an active part in the Constitutional Convention during its remaining three months, where he was described by a fellow-delegate as having "an impetuosity in his temper that is injurious to him." This comment may have been based on a speech Dayton made only a little over a week after taking his seat in the Convention when he attacked proposals by the large states that were trying to prevent an equal voice for each state in the new Senate. James Madison reported Dayton's speech as follows:

"When assertion is given for proof, and terror substituted for argument, he presumed they would have no effect, however eloquently spoken. It should have been shown that the evils we have experienced have proceeded from the equality now objected to; and that the seeds of dissolution for the State Governments are not sown in the General Government. He considered the system on the table as a novelty, an amphibious monster; and was persuaded that it never would be received by the people."

After signing the Constitution, Dayton returned to New Jersey where he resumed his seat in the legislature and urged ratification of the Constitution. He continued to be re-elected to the legislature for the next three years, and in 1790 he was chosen as speaker of the state house of representatives.

Supported Hamilton against Madison and Jefferson

In 1791, Dayton was elected as a U. S. Representative to the Second Congress, and remained a member of the House of Representatives until 1799. There he supported the financial policies of Alexander Hamilton, becoming a leader of the Congressional forces that opposed Thomas Jefferson and James Madison. At the age of thirty-four, Dayton was elected speaker of the house of representatives, an office that he held for four years.

When an undeclared war with France began in 1798, President John Adams rushed plans for national defense. A new United States Army was born with George Washington named as commander in chief, and Alexander Hamilton as second in command. Because of his outstanding Revolutionary War record, Dayton received a commission as a brigadier general. But the war scare soon passed without the necessity of Dayton's serving on active duty.

Dayton now began a friendship with Aaron Burr that led to his fall from political power. The legislature of New Jersey elected Dayton to a six-year term in the United States Senate from 1799 to 1805, and during the last four years of this term Burr presided over the Senate as Vice-President of the United States. Burr undoubtedly called upon Dayton's parliamentary experience as speaker of the house of representatives to aid him in his office, and he also asked the well-to-do Dayton for loans to aid him in his personal financial difficulties. The friendship was so close that when De Witt Clinton, the mayor of New York City, cast some aspersions at Burr, Dayton challenged Clinton to a duel, but friends intervened to prevent bloodshed.

Indicted for treason along with Aaron Burr

After retiring from the Senate in 1805, Dayton became even more closely involved in Burr's schemes. Dayton had speculated heavily in western land and owned some quarter of a million acres in and around Dayton township in Ohio, which had been named in his honor. He was intrigued with Burr's plans for creating an empire that would consolidate Mexico and the western territories of the United States. Dayton was indicted for treason along with Burr in 1807, but while Burr was tried and found not guilty, Dayton was never brought to trial.

Although Dayton was elected to the New Jersey legislature in 1814 to 1815, his public career was destroyed by his association with Burr. He remained an active member of the Society of Cincinnati, the organization of veterans of the Continental Army. When the Marquis de Lafayette visited America in 1824, Dayton entertained his old commander. Later that year, on October 9, 1824, just a week short of his sixty-fourth birthday, Dayton died at his home in Elizabethtown.

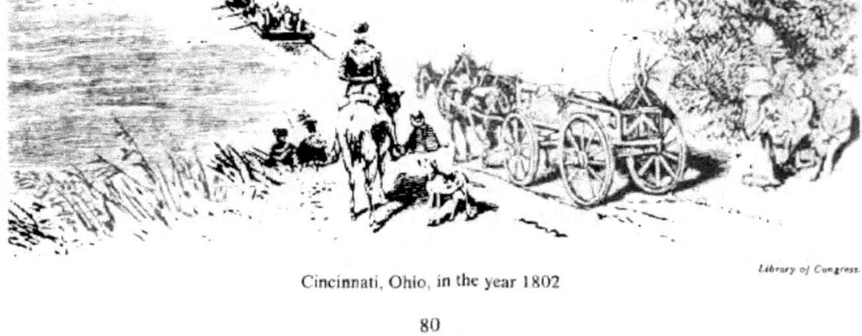

Library of Congress

Cincinnati, Ohio, in the year 1802

View by Moonlight, near Fayetteville
By J. Shaw

Courtesy: The Historical Society of Pennsylvania, Philadelphia.

Market Street Ferry
By D. J. Kennedy *(after Birch)*

JOHN DICKINSON of DELAWARE and PENNSYLVANIA

Known as the "Penman of the Revolution," John Dickinson was a distinguished lawyer who wrote one historic document after another for more than thirty years during the Revolutionary period of American history. Because he maintained homes in both Delaware and Pennsylvania, he also had the unusual distinction of serving both these states alternately as a legislator, as a Congressional representative, and as chief executive officer.

Before the Revolutionary War, Dickinson's "Declaration of Rights" adopted by the Stamp Act Congress of 1765 helped stir patriots to anger over unfair British taxation. Two years later his "Letters from a Farmer in Pennsylvania to the Inhabitants of the British Colonies" made it clear to British leaders that the colonists were not ignorant farmers who could be fooled by parliamentary maneuvers, but that they were represented by legal minds as capable as any practicing in England. Dickinson's "Petition to the King" adopted by the first Continental Congress in 1774 clearly stated the oppressive measures that were pushing the colonies toward rebellion and pleaded with the British king to reverse the course of events while there was still time. Finally, his "Declaration on the Causes and Necessity of Taking Up Arms" that was adopted by the Continental Congress in 1775, presented the steps that had led to actual fighting in Massachusetts and the continued willingness of the colonists to lay down their arms and accept a reasonable solution to the difficulties.

JOHN DICKINSON

1732 (Nov. 8) Born in Talbot County, Maryland.

1760-1762 Member of the Delaware colonial assembly.

1762-1765 Member of the Pennsylvania colonial assembly.

1765 Delegate from Pennsylvania to the Stamp Act Congress: wrote the "Declaration of Rights" of the Congress.

1767-1768 Wrote "Letters from a Farmer in Pennsylvania to the Inhabitants of the British Colonies" opposing the Townshend Acts.

1770-1776 Member of the Pennsylvania assembly.

1774 Delegate to the Continental Congress; wrote the "Petition to the King" and the "Address to the Inhabitants of Quebec."

1775 Delegate to the Continental Congress; wrote the "Declaration on the Causes and Necessity of Taking Up Arms."

1776 Delegate to the Continental Congress; wrote the draft of the Articles of Confederation; refused to sign the Declaration of Independence.

1776-1778 Served in the militia, first as a private, then as a brigadier general.

1779-1780 Delegate from Delaware to Congress; signed the Articles of Confederation.

1781-1782 President of Delaware.

1782-1785 President of Pennsylvania.

1783 Donated land for the establishment of Dickinson College at Carlisle, Pa.

1786 Chairman of the Annapolis Convention.

1787 Member of the Constitutional Convention; signed the United States Constitution by proxy.

1808 (Feb. 14) Died in Wilmington, Del.

Refused to sign the Declaration of Independence

Having received his law education in England, Dickinson had a deep understanding and belief in the British system of parliamentary government. He was sure that the British people would ultimately recognize the folly of the parliament's policies toward the colonies, and that the colonists would be granted self-government within the British empire. Therefore, he opposed the adoption of the Declaration of Independence in 1776 and refused to sign it. When accused of timidity, he replied, "If the present day is too warm for me to be calmly judged, I can credit my country for justice some years hence."

When Independence had been declared, Dickinson devoted all his energies to helping win the war and set up a workable government. He drafted the Articles of Confederation that provided the early government of the United States. He joined the militia and fought the British on the battlefield. Then he helped write the Constitution of the United States, which resulted in the most stable republic in the history of the world.

A member of the Society of Friends

John Dickinson was born in Talbot County, Maryland, on November 8, 1732. His father was Samuel Dickinson, a wealthy landowner and lawyer, and his mother was Mary Cadwalader Dickinson, daughter of a prominent Pennsylvania family. His parents both were Quakers and they brought their son up with a strong belief in the faith of the Society of Friends.

When John was about eight years old, his father was appointed judge of the court of common

The Historical Society of Pennsylvania. Artist: Charles Willson Peale.
John Dickinson

pleas in Kent County, Delaware. The boy grew up on his father's estate, Kingston-upon-Hull, near Dover, Delaware. He was educated by private tutors, and by reading in his father's library.

John Dickinson began the study of law in Philadelphia under attorney John Moland. When he was twenty, he was sent to London where he continued the study of law in the Middle Temple. Upon his return from England in 1757, Dickinson began practicing law in Philadelphia.

Served in legislatures of both Delaware and Pennsylvania

In 1760, Dickinson began his long career of public service as a legislator and representative of Delaware and Pennsylvania. At that time the two colonies had separate legislatures, but shared the same governor. Dickinson first served in the Delaware assembly from 1760 to 1762, and then he served three years in the Pennsylvania assembly.

Dickinson first rose to prominence among colonial patriots when he attended the Stamp Act Congress in New York City in 1765 as a delegate from Pennsylvania. He wrote the famed "Declaration of Rights and Grievances of the Colonists of America" adopted by the Stamp Act Congress. This declaration stated in part: "That it is inseparably essential to the freedom of a people, and the undoubted rights of Englishmen, that no taxes be imposed on them but with their own consent, given personally, or by their representatives." Because of the united stand taken by the colonists, the British parliament withdrew the Stamp Tax.

A moderate in his views

After the British government imposed new taxes on the colonies in the Townshend Acts, Dickinson rose to even greater fame in the colonies and in Europe for his series of essays called "Letters from a Farmer in Pennsylvania to the Inhabitants of the British Colonies." In these articles published in 1767 and 1768, Dickinson freely acknowledged that Great Britain had the right to regulate the trade of the colonies, but disputed its right to tax the colonies merely to raise money. These essays cautioned the colonists to be wary of agitators who might try to split them away from Britain, saying:

"I hope, my dear countrymen, that you will, in every colony, be on your guard against those, who may at any time endeavour to stir you up, under pretense of patriotism, to any measures disrespectful to our Sovereign and our mother country. Hot, rash, disorderly proceedings, injure the reputation of a people, as to wisdom, valour, and virtue, without procuring them the least benefit."

In the five years before the Revolutionary War, Dickinson served as a representative in the Pennsylvania assembly, and won increasing prominence as a lawyer representing many of the wealthiest merchants of Philadelphia. Among his friends and clients were Robert Morris and George Clymer, who were to become prominent as financiers of the Revolution.

Dickinson added to his fortune in 1770 by marrying thirty-year-old Mary Norris, the only child of Isaac Norris, who was one of Philadelphia's wealthiest men and the speaker of the Pennsylvania general assembly. Through his wife, Dickinson inherited Fairhill, a huge country estate with an elaborate mansion and formal gardens. Dickinson and his wife had two daughters.

'The minds of the people are exasperated'

With the passage by the British parliament of the Tea Act in 1773, Dickinson hotly wrote "Two Letters on the Tea Tax" that said in part: "Five Ships, loaded with Tea, on their Way to America, and this with a View not only to enforce the Revenue Act, but to establish a Monopoly for the East India Company, who . . . hope to repair their broken fortunes by the Ruin of American freedom and Liberty! No Wonder the Minds of the People are exasperated . . . hackneyed as they are in Murders, Rapine, and Cruelty, [they] would sacrifice the Lives of Thousands to preserve their Trash, and enforce their measures."

Dickinson became a leading member of the first Continental Congress, which met in the fall of 1774 to determine a course of action to aid the people of Boston. His election as a delegate from Pennsylvania was delayed, and he did not take a seat in the Congress until October 17, almost six weeks after the meeting had begun. Patrick Henry of Virginia had written a petition to the king stating the grievances of the colonies, but many delegates felt that it was too belligerent. Therefore, Dickinson, whose conservative views were well known, was asked to rewrite the document.

After Dickinson presented his version of the "Petition to the King," considerable debate ensued. John Adams in his later writings reported that at one point in the debate Dickinson followed him out of the meeting hall and said angrily, "What is the reason, Mr. Adams, that you New England men oppose our measures of reconciliation? There now is Sullivan, in a long harangue, following you in a determined opposition to our petition to the king. Look ye! If you don't concur with us in our pacific system, I and a number of us will break off from you in New England, and we will carry on the opposition by ourselves in our own way." Adams said that he was "in a very happy temper," and therefore was able to reply calmly, "Mr. Dickinson, there are many things which I can very cheerfully sacrifice to harmony, and even to unanimity; but I am not to be threatened into an express adoption or approbation of measures which my judgment reprobates. Congress must judge, and if they pronounce against me, I must submit, as, if they determine against you, you ought to acquiesce."

"We ask but for peace, liberty and safety."

The Continental Congress accepted and adopted Dickinson's petition, which said in part: "We ask but for peace, liberty, and safety. We wish not a diminution of the prerogative, nor do we solicit the grant of any new right in our favor. Your royal authority over us, and our connection with Great Britain, we shall always carefully and zealously endeavor to support and maintain."

The Historical Society of Pennsylvania. Artist: Charles Willson Peale.

Mrs. John Dickinson and daughter

John Adams had the last word when he wrote later about these debates:

"There is no greater mortification than to sit with half a dozen wits, deliberating upon a petition, address, or memorial. These great wits, these subtle critics, these refined geniuses, these learned lawyers, these wise statesmen, are so fond of showing their parts and powers as to make their consultations very tedious."

When Congress adjourned on October 26, 1774, after also adopting Dickinson's "Address to the Inhabitants of Quebec" that called upon Canadians to support the patriotic cause of the rest of the colonies, Dickinson wrote to a friend expressing his satisfaction with the results:

"The first act of violence on the part of administration in America, or the attempt to reinforce General Gage this winter or next year will put the whole continent in arms, from Nova Scotia to Georgia . . . A determined and unanimous resolution animates this continent firmly and faithfully to support the common cause to the utmost extremity in this great struggle for the blessing of liberty—a blessing that can alone render life worth holding . . ."

By the time the Continental Congress met again in May, 1775, the fighting had begun at Lexington and Concord; and now Dickinson was called upon to write the "Declaration on the Causes and Necessity of Taking Up Arms" which was adopted by Congress on July 6, 1775. This document, which was read to the troops of the Continental Army, set forth in detail the steps that had led to the outbreak of fighting. It went on to say in part:

"Our cause is just. Our union is perfect."

"Our cause is just. Our union is perfect. Our internal resources are great, and, if necessary, foreign assistance is undoubtedly attainable . . . the arms we have been compelled by our enemies to assume, we will, in defiance of every hazard, with unabating firmness and perseverance, employ for the preservation of our liberties; being, with one mind, resolved to die freemen rather than like slaves.

"Lest this Declaration should disquiet the minds of our friends and fellow-subjects in any part of the Empire, we assure them that we mean not to dissolve that union which has so long and so happily subsisted between us, and which we sincerely wish to see restored . . . We have not raised armies with ambitious designs of separating from Great Britain, and establishing independent states. We fight not for glory or for conquest. We exhibit to mankind the remarkable spectacle of a people attacked by unprovoked enemies, without any imputation or even suspicion of offence. They boast of their privileges and civilization, and yet proffer no milder conditions than servitude or death.

"In our own native land, in defence of the freedom that is our birthright, and which we ever enjoyed till the late violation of it; for the protection of our property, acquired solely by the honest industry of our forefathers and ourselves, against violence actually offered, we have taken up arms. We shall lay them down when hostilities shall cease on the part of the aggressors, and all danger of their being renewed shall be removed, and not before . . ."

Historical Society of Delaware. Photo by Sanborn Studio.

Wilmington Home of John Dickinson
Corner of Market and Kent (Eighth) Streets

The views of John Adams prevailed

When Richard Henry Lee's resolutions calling for independence were called up for debate by the Congress on July 1, 1776, Dickinson led the opposition to their adoption. He said he believed the time was not right to declare the colonies free from British rule. He pointed out that the previous documents he had written, which had been adopted by Congress, had given assurance that complete independence from Great Britain was not one of the goals of the struggle. He felt that a declaration of independence at this time would weaken the cause of the colonies in the eyes of the rest of the world. John Adams, "the Atlas of American independence," debated Dickinson and won the argument.

When the resolutions for independence came up for a vote the next day, Dickinson and Robert Morris, his fellow-delegate from Pennsylvania, stayed away from the meeting. Dickinson could not bring himself to vote *for* independence at this time, but neither could he bring himself to vote *against* it. The purposeful absence of Dickinson and Morris enabled Pennsylvania to cast its vote for the independence resolutions. As a matter

Library of Congress.

"Lancastre"
An early view of Lancaster, Pennsylvania

of principle, Dickinson also refused to sign the Declaration of Independence.

In the spring of 1776, while Thomas Jefferson was busy writing the Declaration of Independence, Dickinson was at work writing the Articles of Confederation—the document that was to provide the first formal federation of the colonies. On July 12, 1776, Dickinson presented his draft of the Articles of Confederation to Congress. A few days later, Dickinson left Congress, having failed to be re-elected as a delegate by the Pennsylvania assembly.

Joined the Delaware militia

Dickinson soon gave proof to anyone who might doubt his patriotism by joining the Delaware militia as a private. His company helped capture Elizabethtown, N.J., from the British in January, 1777, and fought in defense of Philadelphia later that year. In October, 1777, he accepted an appointment by the president of Pennsylvania as a brigadier general in the militia.

Dickinson returned to service as a legislator in 1779, accepting election by the Delaware legislature as a delegate to Congress. There, he had the pleasure of signing the Articles of Confederation, which had finally been adopted by Congress after considerable debate and some modifications.

In the next several years, Dickinson had the unusual experience of serving consecutively as the chief executive officer of the two states of Delaware and Pennsylvania. In 1780, Dickinson was elected to the Delaware assembly, and the next year he was elected president of Delaware by the state legislature. After he served as president of Delaware from 1781 to 1782, the legislature of Pennsylvania elected him as president of that state's executive council, an office that he held until October, 1785.

Helped found Dickinson College

While president of Pennsylvania, Dickinson helped found Dickinson College at Carlisle, Pa., in 1783. The college was named in his honor, and he served as the first president of its board of trustees. Dickinson contributed 700 acres of land, $500, and a collection of books to the college.

Recognizing the inadequacies of the Articles of Confederation as the basis of a strong central government, Dickinson became a leading figure in the movement to strengthen or revise the Articles. He represented Delaware and was chairman of the Annapolis Convention of 1786 that initiated the calling of a Constitutional Convention. The Delaware legislature elected him in 1787 as one of their delegates to the Constitutional Convention.

Supported popular election of House of Representatives

Dickinson became an important spokesman for the rights of the smaller states in the Constitutional Convention. Believing that it would help preserve state rights, he strongly supported the provision in the Constitution that the members of the House of Representatives should be elected by the people and that the Senate should be elected by the state legislatures—a provision that remained in the Constitution until 1913. He believed that Congress should be the strongest branch of the federal government, and he endeavored to give Congress the power to remove the President or federal judges at will. Dickinson also believed that the Constitution should forbid the importation of slaves, not leaving this question to the decision of individual legislatures. Dickinson was unable to attend the ceremony at the signing of the United States Constitution on September 17, 1787, but he authorized his fellow-delegate from Delaware George Read to sign his name by proxy.

As arguments swirled through the states in succeeding months, Dickinson lent his support to the Constitution by publishing nine letters signed by the name "Fabius." These letters were influential in obtaining early ratification of the Constitution by Delaware and Pennsylvania.

Dickinson accepted his last election to public office at the age of sixty when he became a delegate to the Delaware state constitutional convention of 1792. There, Dickinson took leadership in drawing up a new state constitution that provided a governor as the chief executive officer, abolishing the office of president which he had held.

During his last years, Dickinson retired to private life in Wilmington, Del., but he continued to take an active interest in national affairs. In 1797, he published another series of letters over the signature "Fabius" that expressed his views on current problems of President John Adams's administration. These letters were not as well written as some of his earlier works, and Dickinson apologized for this fact, saying, "neither my time, nor my infirmities, will permit me to be attentive to style, arrangement, or the labors of consulting former publications." In 1804, he sharply criticized Chief Justice John Marshall for crediting Richard Henry Lee with writing the "Petition to the King" of the first Continental Congress. "The Chief Justice has cast a reflection upon my character, and a very serious one it is," Dickinson wrote. Marshall apologized for his mistake.

'An estimable man and a true patriot'

On February 14, 1808, Dickinson died at the age of seventy-five in Wilmington, Del. Upon his death, Thomas Jefferson wrote this of Dickinson:

"A more estimable man or truer patriot could not have left us. Among the first of the advocates for the rights of his country when assailed by Great Britain, he continued to the last the orthodox advocate of the true principles of our new government, and his name will be consecrated in history as one of the great worthies of the Revolution. We ought to be grateful for having been permitted to retain the benefit of his counsel to so good an old age; still the moment of losing it, whenever it arrives, must be a moment of deep-felt regret. For himself, perhaps, a longer period of life was less important, allowed as the feeble enjoyments of that age are with so much pain. But to his country, every addition to his moments was interesting. A junior companion of his labors in the early part of our Revolution, it has been a great comfort to me to have retained his friendship to the last moment of his life."

WILLIAM FEW of GEORGIA

A farmboy who educated himself by taking his books into the field while plowing, William Few served as a lieutenant colonel in the Revolutionary War and was admitted to the bar to practice law "although I had never spent one hour in the office of an attorney to prepare for the business, nor did I know anything of the practice." Few signed the United States Constitution, served as one of Georgia's first United States Senators, and became a judge. In his fifties he moved to New York City where he began a new career as a state legislator, political appointee, and banker.

"Felt the spirit of an American"

In his old age, Few wrote a short autobiography which includes most of the facts that are known about him. In telling why he threw himself into the revolutionary cause, he explains what must have been the attitude of many of the lesser known heroes who took up their muskets: ". . . during that period the American Revolutionary War commenced, and with it commenced my political life. Although at that time I knew but little of politics, nor had I much studied the principles of free governments, I felt the spirit of an American, and without much investigation of the justice of her cause, I resolved to defend it."

William Few was born on a farm in Baltimore County, Maryland, on June 8, 1748. His father was a Quaker farmer, his mother was a Roman Catholic, and he later became a Methodist. Few described his earliest education: "When about six or seven years of age, I was sent to a country school of the lowest grade. The teacher was an ill-natured, arbitrary man, who punished with rigor, and enforced his precepts by terror. This man was to me the most dreadful of all mankind. I detested the man, the school and the books, and spent six or eight months at that school in terror and anxiety, with very little benefit."

Moved south to a warmer climate

When Few was about ten years old, his father became disgusted with living in the climate of Maryland, "having lost the greatest part of two or three crops by frost." So the Few family loaded all their possessions "in a wagon drawn by four horses and in a cart drawn by two horses" and moved to new land in North Carolina where "not a tree had been cut" and where "there were no schools, no churches or parsons, or doctors, or lawyers; no stores, groceries or taverns." Few de-

WILLIAM FEW

1748 (June 8) Born near Baltimore, Md.
1758 Went with family to North Carolina.
1776 Moved to Georgia.
1777 Member of Georgia state constitutional convention.
1777-1780 Member of Georgia legislature.
1778-1779 Served in Georgia militia, rising to rank of lieutenant colonel.
1780-1783 Delegate to Congress from Georgia.
1784-1786 Member of Georgia legislature.
1784 Admitted to bar to practice law in Georgia.
1786-1789 Delegate to Congress from Georgia.
1787 Member of Georgia delegation to Constitutional Convention; signed the United States Constitution.
1789-1793 United States Senator from Georgia.
1795 Member of Georgia legislature.
1796-1799 State district court judge in Georgia.
1799 Moved to New York.
1801-1804 Member of New York legislature.
1802-1812 Inspector of state prison in New York.
1804-1816 Commissioner of loans in New York.
1804-1814 Director of Manhattan Bank in New York City.
1813-1814 Alderman in New York City.
1814-1816 President of the City Bank of New York City.
1828 (July 16) Died at Fishkill-on-Hudson, N. Y.

William Few
Eastern National Park and Monument Association.

scribed his beginnings as a frontier farmer: "An axe was put into my hands, and I was introduced to a hickory tree about twelve or fifteen inches diameter, and was ordered to cut it down and cut off all the branches. . . . My hands blistered, and the business progressed very slowly. . . . I dared not to resist the order I had received . . . and found that practice every day made the labor more agreeable . . ."

Formal education cost five dollars

Few received his second and final year of schooling when he was twelve years old. He later recalled this as "one of the most happy years of my life," saying: "In the year 1760 a schoolmaster appeared and offered his services to teach the children of the neighborhood for twenty shillings each per year. He was employed, and about thirty scholars were collected and placed under his tuition.... This schoolmaster was a man of a mild and amiable disposition. He governed his little school with judgment and propriety, wisely distinguishing the obedient, timid child from the obstinate and contumacious; judiciously applying the rod when necessary. He possessed the art of making his pupils fear, love and esteem him. At this school I spent one of the most happy years of my life. I had the highest respect for my preceptor, and delighted in his society and instruction, and learned with facility. With him I finished my education, the whole expense of which did not exceed five dollars."

When Few was sixteen, his family moved to Hillsboro, N. C., the county seat of Orange County, which was then a small village of about thirty to forty people. There was no school, and Few said he "had no other way or means of learning but by attending the courts and hearing the principles of law discussed and settled." After reading his father's small collection of books, which included a Bible, a dictionary, and a bound set of Joseph Addison's *Spectator* magazine, Few borrowed books from the lawyers he met at the county court.

Self educated through reading

At the age of nineteen, Few was given a piece of farm land by his father. "It became my duty every Monday morning to go to the farm and remain until Saturday, and I was employed at the

The Metropolitan Museum of Art, New York, Rogers Fund, 1942.

Merrymaking at a Wayside Inn
By PAVEL (PAUL) PETROVICH SVININ

plow. It was my practice every Monday to take with me a book which I read at leisure hours, and took it with me to the fields, and when fatigued I retired to a shade and read. By those means labor became pleasant and agreeable, while the mind was amused and the understanding improved."

In about 1761 Few's father "had now unfortunately got entangled in the law" and was unable to meet the demands of his creditors; so while his father took the rest of the family to Georgia, the twenty-year-old Few was left to straighten out his father's affairs which "introduced me to a more intimate acquaintance with courts, sheriffs, clerks and lawyers."

At the outbreak of the Revolutionary War, Few was "among the first" to help form a volunteer infantry company in Hillsboro. The next year, in 1776, a patriotic convention was called at the county seat, and Few reported that "there I first learned the principles of our controversy with Great Britain, and began to think on politics." He was offered a commission as a captain in the North Carolina militia, but declined because he had wound up his father's business and had decided to rejoin his family at their new farm in Richmond County, Georgia.

A representative at the Georgia Constitutional Convention

At the age of twenty-nine, in 1777, Few "although but little acquainted with the people" was elected to the convention in Savannah that drew up the state's first constitution. He then was elected as a member of the state's first legislature, and apparently must have impressed his colleagues with the learning he had dug out of books for he was chosen by his fellow-legislators as a member of the governor's sixteen-man advisory council.

During 1778, Few went with the militia on a military expedition to attack British forces in Florida, but the mission failed because so many of the troops fell ill with fever in the hot, mosquito-infested swamps. Then Few successively held the offices of surveyor general of the state, commissioner of confiscated estates, and senior justice for Richmond County, offices he described as "appointments of more honor than profit."

The British captured the Georgia state capital of Savannah on December 28, 1778; and during the next year Few served with the militia as a lieutenant colonel, helping carry out guerilla warfare against the British, as well as fighting off Indian attacks in the western part of the state.

Frick Art Reference Library.

Mrs. William Few
By John Ramage

"I was struck with veneration and respect"

When the state legislature met in Augusta, Ga., in January, 1780, Few was elected as a delegate to the Continental Congress, an office he held for the next three years. Few was awed by the highly educated men of the other colonies that he met in Philadelphia. As he described it: "There I was introduced to the President and members of the most dignified and respectable assembly of Statesmen and Patriots that perhaps ever adorned a nation, and directed its operations in the most perilous times. When I looked round on the ancient sages—the selected wisdom of the States—sitting in council and deliberating on the most important national concerns, I was struck with veneration and respect."

After completing his service in Congress, Few resumed his seat in the Georgia legislature in 1784; but, because he "possessed not much property," he "found it necessary to commence some kind of business for support." And so: "I therefore determined to commence the practice of the law, although I had never spent one hour in the office of an attorney to prepare for the business, nor did I know anything of the practice, but I well understood the general principles of law, and I had acquired a tolerable proficiency in public speaking. I had no difficulty in getting admittance to the Bar, and at the same time commenced the study and practice of the law." He quickly prospered at his new profession; as he said, "my pecuniary prospects were very flattering."

In 1786, Few was again elected by the Georgia legislature as a delegate to Congress; and at the same time he was appointed to represent Georgia before Congress in a dispute with South Carolina over claims to western lands. In May, Few took his seat in Congress, then meeting in New York City. He soon recognized that under the Articles of Confederation "the dignity and consequence of that assembly had greatly diminished." He joined with James Madison and others who were agitating for a revision of the Articles and a strengthening of the national government.

Elected as a member of Georgia's delegation to the Constitutional Convention of 1787, Few took little active part in the Philadelphia meeting. He attended for about the first month, but left to New York to attend the Congress then in session, returning only to sign his name to the United States Constitution, which, as he said, "did not altogether please anybody, but it was agreed to be the most expedient that could be devised and agreed to."

According to Bible records on microfilm in the Georgia Department of Archives, William Few was married July 8, 1788, in New York, to Catherine Nicholson, daughter of Commodore James Nicholson, known as the first commander of the American navy. They had three daughters.

Supported the policies of Thomas Jefferson

At the age of forty, Few was elected by the state legislature as one of Georgia's first two United States senators. He apparently spent the winter in New York City, and was among the first of the members of Congress to take their seats in the spring of 1789. He witnessed the swearing in of President George Washington, joining in the "universal acclamations" which, he said, "with the roaring of cannon and martial music, inspired the most pleasing sensations." In the Senate, Few joined with the southern senators who supported Thomas Jefferson's policies against those of Alexander Hamilton.

After completing his term in the Senate in 1793, Few returned to Georgia where he settled on a plantation in Columbia County, hoping "to find that tranquility and happiness which could not be found in public life." But when a corrupt Georgia legislature sold thousands of acres of state-owned land on the Yazoo River to speculators, Few was "again drawn into the political vortex." His neighbors elected him to the next session of the legislature, which voted to rescind the Yazoo Act; but the speculators refused to give up their claims to the land.

Few attempted to win re-election as a U. S. Senator in 1796, but was defeated in "one of the greatest mortifications I had ever experienced." But on later consideration Few decided that this was "one of the most fortunate events" of his life, because "if I had obtained that appointment I should have most probably spent the remainder of my days in the scorching climate of Georgia, under all the accumulating evils of fevers and Negro slavery, those enemies to humane felicity."

Moved to New York and elected to the legislature

After serving three years as a district court judge in Georgia from 1796 to 1799, Few moved to New York City where he and a friend purchased a five-acre farm on Greenwich lane for $15,000. By 1801, he had won enough friends in New York politics that he won election to the New York legislature. He was re-elected each year for the next three years. In 1802, he was appointed inspector of the state prison, an office he described as "arduous and troublesome" and without "pay or emolument," but which he held for ten years as he "labored to correct and improve the system." In 1804, he was appointed as the state's commissioner of loans, a position that paid $2,000 a year, and which he held for twelve years. Few served as a director of the Manhattan Bank from 1804 to 1814, and then was appointed president of the City Bank from 1814 to 1816. Also during this period he won election as an alderman for New York City from 1813 to 1814.

When Few retired at the age of sixty-eight, he estimated that his personal fortune amounted to "upwards of one hundred thousand dollars" and the annual income from his investments at about six thousand dollars. In the remaining years of his life, he said he conceived "it a duty incumbent on me to duly economize in my expenses and endeavor to increase the sum that must be applied to charitable purposes." He died at the age of eighty, on July 16, 1828, at the home of his son-in-law at Fishkill-on-Hudson, N. Y.

THOMAS FITZSIMONS of PENNSYLVANIA

The first Roman Catholic to be elected to public office in Pennsylvania, Thomas FitzSimons (sometimes spelled Fitzsimmons or Fitzsimins) was an Irish immigrant who became a Revolutionary War statesman and soldier, a leading merchant and banker, and a signer of the United States Constitution. He served as a Pennsylvania representative in the first United States Congress under the Constitution; then in the last years of his life he went bankrupt because of the credit he had extended to his fellow-signer of the Constitution Robert Morris, and because of his own land speculations. Upon his death, the following comments were included in his obituary in the Philadelphia *Gazette:*

"He was justly considered one of the most enlightened and intelligent merchants in the United States and his opinions upon all questions connected with commerce were always regarded with respect and even homage, by the mercantile part of the community. He filled many important stations, both in the General and State Governments with great reputation during the Revolutionary War. In private life he was eminently useful. Hundreds in various occupations owe their establishment in business to his advice and good offices. His friendships were steady, ardent and disinterested. He possessed an uncommon firmness of mind upon all occasions except one and that was when his friends solicited favors from him. From his inability to resist the importunities of distress he suffered a reversal of fortune in the evening of his life. Even in this situation his mind retained its native goodness and hence it may be truly said, after many and great losses he died in the esteem, affection and gratitude of all classes of his fellow citizens."

THOMAS FITZSIMONS

1741 Born in Ireland.

1774 Elected to Pennsylvania's provincial congress and member of Philadelphia's committee of correspondence.

1775-1777 Captain of a company of militia in the Revolutionary War.

1781-1803 Director of the Bank of North America.

1782-1783 Delegate from Pennsylvania to the Congress of the Confederation.

1783-1784 Member of Pennsylvania's council of censors.

1785-1789 Member of the Pennsylvania state legislature.

1786 Delegate from Pennsylvania to the Annapolis Convention.

1787 Member of Pennsylvania's delegation to the Constitutional Convention: signed the United States Constitution.

1789-1795 Representative of Pennsylvania in the first United States Congress under the Constitution.

1811 (Aug. 26) Died in Philadelphia.

Born in Ireland

Thomas FitzSimons was born in 1741 in Ireland, perhaps in the city of Limerick. While still a boy, he immigrated to America with his parents, three brothers, and a twin sister. His father, who had established a store in Philadelphia, died when Thomas was sixteen, leaving the boy a third of his estate. Presumably FitzSimons completed his education by serving an apprenticeship as a clerk in one of Philadelphia's mercantile houses.

When FitzSimons was twenty, he married Catharine Meade, the daughter of a well-to-do merchant. He then became a partner of his brother-in-law in the firm George Meade and Company.

Thomas FitzSimons
Attributed to GILBERT STUART
Courtesy, Mrs. Samuel Edelson. Photo by Phillips Studio.

The business prospered, and within a few years FitzSimons became one of Philadelphia's most respected merchants and traders.

First Roman Catholic elected to public office

As difficulties mounted between the colonies and Great Britain, FitzSimons became active in the patriotic movement. In May, 1774, he was appointed a member of Philadelphia's committee of correspondence; and in July he was elected as a delegate to Pennsylvania's first provincial congress that was called to elect a delegation to the first Continental Congress. He was apparently the first Roman Catholic ever elected to public office in the colony. Until this time a "test oath" had been required of all public officials—an oath that Roman Catholics refused to swear.

When word reached Philadelphia of the fighting that had begun at Lexington and Concord in 1775, FitzSimons formed a company of militia for the defense of Philadelphia. As a captain of this company, he marched to New Jersey to aid George Washington's forces in the summer of 1776, and again in the winter of 1776-1777. FitzSimons was appointed a member of Pennsylvania's eleven-man navy board, to advise on the equipping and manning of warships for the state.

Helped Robert Morris organize the Bank of North America

During the war years, FitzSimons' business obtained supplies for the American forces and their allies, and FitzSimons' advice on financial and business affairs was sought by the leaders of the government. In 1781 he helped Robert Morris organize the Bank of North America, and was one of its directors for the next twenty-two years.

FitzSimons was elected by the Pennsylvania legislature as a delegate to the Congress of the Confederation in 1782-1783. A year later, he served for a year as member of the Pennsylvania council of censors, whose duty it was to observe the functioning of the state government and report any violations of the state constitution. From 1785 to 1789 he was a member of the Pennsylvania state legislature.

Because of his experience as a businessman and legislator, FitzSimons was chosen as one of Pennsylvania's delegation to the Annapolis Convention in 1786, where the stage was set for the calling of a convention to revise the Articles of Confederation. Then, in 1787, the Pennsylvania legislature elected FitzSimons as a delegate to the Constitutional Convention.

Favored requirement of property ownership for voting

At the Constitutional Convention, FitzSimons represented the financial interests of the Philadelphia bankers and merchants. He seconded a motion by Gouverneur Morris in an effort to insure that the ownership of property would be a requirement for voting in congressional elections. He also seconded the motion of James Wilson in an effort to require that the House of Representatives as well as the Senate should approve foreign treaties. However, FitzSimons apparently took relatively little part in the debates. On September 17, 1787, he signed the United States Constitution with the other seven delegates from Pennsylvania.

Running on the Federalist ticket, FitzSimons was elected as one of Pennsylvania's U.S. representatives in the first Congress under the Constitution in 1789. He also was re-elected twice, serving until 1795. During his terms in Congress, FitzSimons became chairman of many important committees, particularly those dealing with matters of finance, on which he represented the views of Secretary of the Treasury Alexander Hamilton. When he was defeated for re-election in November, 1794, James Madison wrote to Thomas Jefferson that it was a "stinging change for the aristocracy."

Lost his fortune through loans and speculation

FitzSimons took part in many civic activities, as well as continuing to increase the size and importance of his business. He was a trustee of the College of Philadelphia (now the University of Pennsylvania) from 1789 to 1791, and he was president of the Philadelphia chamber of commerce for a number of years. When George Washington retired as President of the United States, FitzSimons was co-chairman of a large farewell dinner.

In his later years as a merchant and banker, FitzSimons made hundreds of thousands of dollars of loans to friends, among them Robert Morris. He also plunged heavily in speculation on western lands. As Morris and others of his debtors lost their fortunes, FitzSimons, too, was finally forced to declare himself bankrupt at the age of sixty-four in 1805. He made efforts to recoup his losses, but died in relative obscurity on August 26, 1811.

BENJAMIN FRANKLIN of PENNSYLVANIA

EDITOR'S NOTE: *Because Benjamin Franklin was one of the six men who signed both the Declaration of Independence and the United States Constitution, a biography of his life is included in Volume I of* FOUNDERS OF FREEDOM. *The following article is concerned only with his role in the writing of the United States Constitution.*

At the age of eighty-one, Benjamin Franklin was the oldest man to attend the Constitutional Convention of 1787, and the oldest to sign the United States Constitution. Because of the respect in which he was held, his name on the Constitution was a major factor in winning its ratification by the states. Franklin was also serving as President of the state of Pennsylvania at the time of the Convention.

Because it was raining heavily on May 25, the first day on which a quorum of the delegates was present, Franklin remained at home to protect his health. As he was the only man other than George Washington who might logically have been chosen to preside over the Convention, Franklin arranged that Robert Morris nominate Washington for President of the Convention. Franklin took his seat when the meeting got down to business on Monday, May 28, and he remained active in the debates throughout the summer, although he had his longer speeches read for him by other members of the Pennsylvania delegation. Franklin's sedan chair, carried by trusted convicts, was a familiar sight on the streets of Philadelphia as he was borne back and forth from his home to the State House, now Independence Hall. William Pierce, a delegate to the Convention from Georgia, described Franklin as follows:

"He does not shine much in public Council,—he is no Speaker, nor does he seem to let politics engage his attention. He is, however, a most extraordinary Man, and tells a story in a style more engaging than anything I ever heard."

Excited great curiosity

Manasseh Cutler, a clergyman from Massachusetts who visited Franklin during the course of the Convention, provided a fuller description of Franklin at this time:

"We found him in his Garden, sitting upon a grass plat under a very large Mulberry, with several other gentlemen and two or three ladies. There was no curiosity in Philadelphia which I felt so anxious to see as this great man, who has been the wonder of Europe as well as the glory of America. . . . In short, when I entered his house, I felt as if I was going to be introduced to the presence of an European Monarch. But how were my ideas changed, when I saw a short, fat, trunched old man, in a plain Quaker dress, bald pate, and short white locks, sitting without his hat under the tree. . . . His voice was low, but his countenance open, frank, and pleasing. . . . I was highly delighted with the extensive knowledge he seemed to have of every subjct, the brightness of his memory, and clearness and vivacity of all his mental faculties. . . . He has an incessant vein of humor, accompanied with an uncommon vivacity, which seems as natural and involuntary as his breathing."

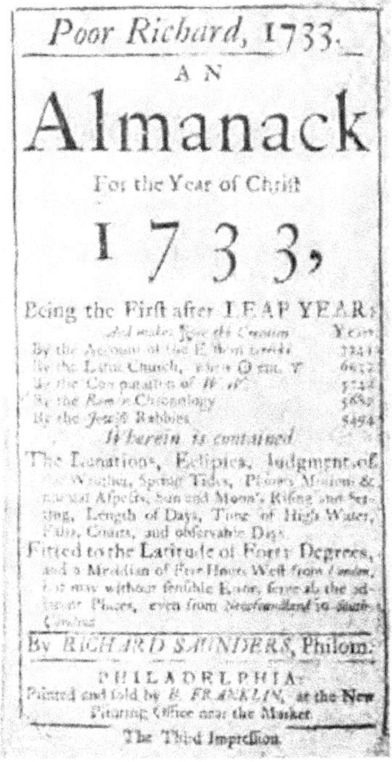

Poor Richard, 1733.

AN

Almanack

For the Year of Christ

1733,

Being the First after LEAP YEAR:

Wherein is contained

The Lunations, Eclipses, Judgment of the Weather, Spring Tides, Planets Motions & mutual Aspects, Sun and Moon's Rising and Setting, Length of Days, Time of High Water, Fairs, Courts, and observable Days.

Fitted to the Latitude of Forty Degrees, and a Meridian of Five Hours West from *London*, but may without sensible Error, serve all the adjacent Places, even from *Newfoundland* to *South-Carolina*.

By *RICHARD SAUNDERS*, Philom.

PHILADELPHIA:
Printed and sold by *B. FRANKLIN*, at the New Printing-Office near the Market.

The Third Impression.

The Corcoran Gallery of Art, Washington, D. C.

Benjamin Franklin
By JOSEPH WRIGHT

Favored a unicameral legislature

If Franklin alone had been responsible for writing the United States Constitution, the federal form of government might have been vastly different. He would have set up or established a unicameral legislature, and he would have placed the executive power of the government in the hands of a council of several men, rather than in a single president. However, he was more concerned that a new stronger central government be formed than with the details of the organization of the government. He expressed his opinion on the necessity of compromise several months after the Constitution had been signed:

"We must not expect, that a new government may be formed, as a game of chess may be played, by a skilful hand, without a fault. The players of our game are so many, their ideas so different, their prejudices so strong and so various, and their particular interests, independent of the general, seeming so opposite, that not a move can be made that is not contested; the numerous objections confound the understanding; the wisest must agree to some unreasonable things, that reasonable ones of more consequence may be obtained; and thus chance has its share in many of the determinations, so that the play is more like . . . with a box of dice."

BENJAMIN FRANKLIN

1706 (Jan. 17) Born in Boston.
1716-1718 Helped father make candles and soap.
1718-1723 Apprentice printer working for his brother James Franklin.
1723 Ran away to Philadelphia at the age of 17.
1724-1726 Worked as a printer in London, England.
1726 Returned to Philadelphia.
1729 Began publishing the newspaper the Pennsylvania Gazette.
1731 Founded the first subscription library, the Library Company of Philadelphia.
1733-1758 Published Poor Richard's Almanac.
1736-1751 Clerk of the Pennsylvania colonial legislature.
1737-1753 Deputy postmaster of Philadelphia.
1740 Invented the Franklin stove.
1744-1754 Representative in the Pennsylvania colonial legislature.
1747 Discovered positive and negative electricity.
1749 Invented the lightning rod.
1749 Helped found the Academy of Philadelphia that later became the University of Pennsylvania.
1752 Used a kite to prove that lightning is electricity.
1753-1774 Deputy postmaster general of the American colonies.
1753 Received honorary masters degrees from Harvard and Yale.
1754 Represented Pennsylvania in the Albany Congress; wrote the Albany Plan of Union for the colonies.
1757-1762 Represented the Pennsylvania colonial legislature in London.
1762 Awarded honorary degree of doctor of civil law by Oxford University.
1763 Made a 1,600-mile tour of the American colonies inspecting post offices.
1764-1775 Represented Pennsylvania, Georgia, New Jersey, and Massachusetts in London.
1775 Appointed postmaster general by the Continental Congress.
1775-1776 Member of the Pennsylvania Committee of Safety; delegate from Pennsylvania to the Continental Congress; signed the Declaration of Independence.
1776 President of the Pennsylvania state constitutional convention.
1776-1785 Represented the Continental Congress in Paris; negotiated and signed the treaty of alliance with France in 1778; negotiated and signed the treaty of peace with Great Britain in 1783.
1785-1788 President of the state of Pennsylvania.
1787 Delegate from Pennsylvania to the Constitutional Convention; signed the United States Constitution.
1788 Elected president of the first anti-slavery society in the United States.
1790 (April 17) Died in Philadelphia.

Opposed payment of salaries to government executives

On June 2, 1787, while the delegates were still discussing the Virginia Plan that had been presented by Edmund Randolph, Franklin made a speech opposing the payment of salaries to executives of the new government:

"Sir, it is with reluctance that I rise to express a disapprobation of any one article of the plan for which we are so much obliged to the honorable gentleman who laid it before us. From its first reading I have borne a good will to it, and in general wished it success. In this particular of salaries to the Executive branch, I happen to differ: and as my opinion may appear new and chimerical, it is only from a persuasion that it is right, and from a sense of duty, that I hazard it. The Committee will judge of my reasons when they have heard them, and their judgment may possibly change mine. I think I see inconveniences in the appointment of salaries; I see none in refusing them, but, on the contrary, great advantages.

"Sir, there are two passions which have a powerful influence on the affairs of men. These are ambition and avarice; the love of power, and the love of money. Separately, each of these has great force in prompting men to action; but when united in view of the same object, they have in many minds the most violent effects. Place before the

Library of Congress. From Klinckowstrom's Atlas, 1809.

Bridge over the Schuylkill River near Philadelphia

eyes of such men a post of *honor*, that shall be at the same time a place of *profit*, and they will move heaven and earth to obtain it. The vast number of such places it is that renders the British government so tempestuous. The struggles for them are the true sources of all those factions, which are perpetually dividing the nation, distracting its councils, hurrying sometimes into fruitless and mischievous wars, and often compelling a submission to dishonorable terms of peace.

Men of strong passions and selfish pursuits

"And of what kind are the men that will strive for this profitable pre-eminence, through all the bustle of cabal, the heat of contention, the infinite mutual abuse of parties, tearing to pieces the best of characters? It will not be the wise and moderate, the lovers of peace and good order, the men fittest for the trust. It will be the bold and the violent, the men of strong passions and indefatigable activity in their selfish pursuits. These will thrust themselves into your government, and be your rulers. And these, too, will be mistaken in the expected happiness of their situation: for their vanquished competitors, of the same spirit, and from the same motives, will perpetually be endeavouring to distress their administration, thwart their measures, and render them odious to the people.

The more taxes, the greater the need

"Besides these evils, Sir, though we may set out in the beginning with moderate salaries, we shall find that such will not be of long continuance. Reasons will never be wanting for proposed augmentations. And there will always be a party for giving more to the rulers, that the rulers may be able in return to give more to them. Hence, as all history informs us, there has been in every state and kingdom a constant kind of warfare between the governing and governed, the one striving to obtain more for its support, and the other to pay less. And this has alone occasioned great convulsions, actual civil wars, ending either in dethroning of the princes, or enslaving of the people. Generally, indeed, the ruling power carries its point, the revenues of princes constantly increasing; and we see that they are never satisfied, but always in want of more. The more the people are discontented with the oppression of taxes, the greater need the prince has of money

Courtesy: Wilmington Historical Society.
Benjamin Franklin

Courtesy: Wilmington Historical Society.
Marquis de Lafayette

Photo by Morler.

Stabler Leadbeater's Apothecary Shop Alexandria, Virginia (Established in 1792)

Courtesy: The Historical Society of Pennsylvania, Philadelphia.

Fourth of July Celebration in Center Square, Philadelphia, 1819
By John Lewis Krimmel

to distribute among his partizans, and pay the troops that are to suppress all resistance, and enable him to plunder at pleasure. There is scarce a king in an hundred, who would not, if he could, follow the example of Pharaoh, get first all the people's money, then all their lands, and then make them and their children servants for ever. It will be said, that we don't propose to establish kings. I know it; but there is a natural inclination in mankind to kingly government. It sometimes relieves them from aristocratic domination They had rather have one tyrant than five hundred. It gives more of the appearance of equality among citizens, and that they like. I am apprehensive, therefore, perhaps too apprehensive, that the government of these States may in future times end in a monarchy. But this catastrophe I think may be delayed, if in our proposed system we do not sow the seeds of contention, faction, and tumult, by making our posts of honor, places of profit. If we do, I fear that, though we do employ at first a number, and not a single person, the number will in time be set aside; it will only nourish the foetus of a king, as the honorable gentleman from Virginia very aptly expressed it, and a king will the sooner be set over us.

Proof of service without pay

"It may be imagined by some that this is a Utopian idea, and that we can never find men to serve us in the Executive department without paying them well for their services. I conceive this to be a mistake. Some existing facts present themselves to me, which incline me to a contrary opinion. The high-sheriff of a county in England is an honorable office, but it is not a profitable one. It is rather expensive and therefore not sought for. But yet, it is executed and well executed, and usually by some of the principal gentlemen of the county. In France, the office of Counsellor, or member of their judiciary parliament is more honorable. It is therefore purchased at a high price: there are indeed fees on the law proceedings, which are divided among them, but these fees do not amount to more than three per cent on the sum paid for the place. Therefore, as legal interest is there at five per cent, they in fact pay two per cent for being allowed to do the judiciary business of the nation, which is at the same time entirely exempt from the burden of paying them any salaries for their services. I do not, however, mean to recommend this as an eligible mode for our Judiciary department. I only bring the instance to show, that the pleasure of doing good and serving their country, and the respect such conduct entitles them to, are sufficient motives with some minds to give up a great portion of their time to the public, without the mean inducement of pecuniary satisfaction.

Service without pay by the Quakers

"Another instance is that of a respectable society who have made the experiment, and practised it with success more than one hundred years. I mean the Quakers. It is an established rule with them, that they are not to go to law; but in their controversies they must apply to their monthly, quarterly, and yearly meetings. Committees of these sit with patience to hear the parties, and spend much time in composing their differences. In doing this, they are supported by a sense of duty, and the respect paid to usefulness. It is honorable to be so employed, but it is never made profitable by salaries, fees or perquisites. And, indeed, in all cases of public service, the less the profit, the greater the honor.

The example of George Washington

"To bring the matter nearer home, have we not seen the great and most important of our offices, that of General of our armies, executed for eight years together without the smallest salary, by a patriot whom I will not now offend by any other praise; and this, through fatigues and distresses, in common with the other brave men, his military friends and companies, and the constant anxieties peculiar to his station? And shall we doubt finding three or four men in all the United States, with public spirit enough to bear sitting in peaceful council for perhaps an equal term, merely to preside over our civil concerns, and see that our laws are duly executed? Sir, I have a better opinion of our country. I think we shall never be without a sufficient number of wise and good men to undertake and execute well and faithfully the office in question.

"Sir, the saving of the salaries that may at first be proposed is not an object with me. The subsequent mischiefs of proposing them are what I apprehend. And therefore it is, that I move the amendment. If it is not seconded or accepted, I must be contented with the satisfaction of having delivered my opinion frankly and done my duty."

Although Franklin's motion was seconded by

An early print of illustrations from Poor Richard's Almanac

Alexander Hamilton, the delegates postponed discussion on the matter. James Madison commented that "it was treated with great respect, but rather for the author of it, than from any apparent conviction of its expediency or practicability."

Near the end of June, when the Convention seemed to be near the point of breaking up because of the controversy between large and small states as to how the representation should be fixed in Congress, Franklin made a short speech imploring the delegates to ask for Divine guidance:

"Mr. President, The small progress we have made after four or five weeks close attendance and continual reasonings with each other—our different sentiments on almost every question, several of the last producing as many noes as ayes—is, methinks, a melancholy proof of the imperfection of the human understanding. We indeed seem to feel our own want of political wisdom, since we have been running about in search of it. We have gone back to ancient history for models of government, and examined the different forms of those republics which, having been formed with seeds of their own dissolution, now no longer exist. And we have viewed modern states all round Europe, but find none of their constitutions suitable to our circumstances.

"God governs in the affairs of men."

"In this situation of this Assembly, groping as it were in the dark to find political truth, and scarce able to distinguish it when presented to us, how has it happened, Sir, that we have not hitherto once thought of humbly applying to the Father of lights, to illuminate our understandings? In the beginning of the contest with Great Britain, when we were sensible of danger, we had daily prayer in this room for the divine protection. Our prayers, Sir, were heard, and they were graciously answered. All of us who are engaged in the struggle must have observed frequent instances of a superintending Providence in our favor. To that kind Providence we owe this happy opportunity of consulting in peace on the means of establishing our future national felicity. And have we now forgotten that powerful friend? Or do we imagine that we no longer need his assistance? I have lived, Sir, a long time, and the longer I live, the more convincing proofs I see of this truth—*that God governs in the affairs of men.* And if a sparrow cannot fall to the ground without his notice, is it probable that an empire can rise without his aid? We have been assured, Sir, in the sacred writings, that 'except the Lord build the house they labor in vain that build it.' I firmly believe this; and I also believe that without his concurring aid we shall succeed in this political building no better than the builders of Babel. We shall be divided by our little partial local interests; our projects will be confounded; and we ourselves shall become a reproach and by-word down to future ages. And what is worse, mankind may hereafter, from this unfortunate instance, despair of establishing governments by human wisdom, and leave it to chance, war and conquest.

"I therefore beg leave to move—that henceforth prayers imploring the assistance of Heaven, and its blessings on our deliberations, be held in this Assembly every morning before we proceed to business, and that one or more of the clergy of this city be requested to officiate in that service."

Franklin's motion was seconded by Roger Sherman of Connecticut; but, in the discussion that followed, Alexander Hamilton pointed out that the public would suspect that the disagreements in the Convention were greater than they actually were, and Hugh Williamson remarked that there were no funds available to pay the clergymen. So the matter of prayer was dropped without a vote.

"Some of the greatest rogues are the richest."

On August 10, Charles Pinckney made a proposal that the Constitution should require that the President, federal judges, and members of Congress all should declare that they had unencumbered estates of as much as a hundred thousand dollars before being allowed to serve, Franklin took exception to the proposal as being undemocratic. James Madison's journal reports:

"Doctor Franklin expressed his dislike to everything that tended to debase the spirit of the common people. If honesty was often the companion of wealth, and if poverty was exposed to peculiar temptation, it was not less true that the possession of property increased the desire of more property. Some of the greatest rogues he was ever acquainted with were the richest rogues. We should remember the character which the Scripture requires in rulers, that they should be men hating covetousness. This Constitution will be much read and attended to in Europe; and if it should betray a great partiality to the rich, will not only hurt us in the esteem of the most liberal and enlightened men there, but discourage the common people from removing to this country."

After Franklin's statement, Pinckney's proposal was overwhelmingly defeated.

On the last day of the Convention, September 17, 1787, Franklin made an impassioned appeal to the delegates to support the Constitution even though each was not in complete agreement with all parts of the proposed new structure of government. "I cannot help expressing a wish," he said, "that every member of the Convention who may still have objections to it, would with me, on this occasion, doubt a little of his own infallibility, and to make manifest our unanimity, put his name to this instrument."

Less than three months later, a Pennsylvania convention ratified the Constitution on December 12. Franklin, as president of the state, presided over the ceremony the next day at the Philadelphia court house where the ratification was read to a large crowd. As Franklin waited for the other states to ratify the Constitution, he wrote his feelings to a friend:

"I pant for the time when the establishment of the new government, and the safety to individuals which shall arise from it, shall excuse men who like myself wish only to be passengers from performing the duty of sailors on board the political ship in which our all is embarked. I have yielded to a deep sense of the extreme danger of my country, in quitting the cabin for a station at the pump. As soon as the storm is over, and our bark safely moored, the first wish of my heart will be to devote the whole of my time to the peaceable pursuits of science, and to the pleasure of social and domestic life."

Franklin lived to see the new United States government become an actuality, and his friend George Washington the first President. At the age of eighty-four Franklin died at his home in Philadelphia on April 17, 1790.

Courtesy: Phillips Exeter Academy, Davis Library. Library of Congress photo, from the Gilman Family.

Home of Nicholas Gilman
By ARTHUR GILMAN

NICHOLAS GILMAN of NEW HAMPSHIRE

Regarded as the handsomest and most elegant man in New Hampshire, Nicholas Gilman served as a staff officer throughout the Revolutionary War, and he won election to the Congress of the Confederation in its dying days. He became a member of the Constitutional Convention, signed the United States Constitution, and served seventeen years in the United States Congress, first as a Representative and then as a Senator. Politics came to mean more to him than his family. Although his brother, Governor John Taylor Gilman, was leader of his state's Federalist party, Nicholas Gilman became an ardent Democratic-Republican and helped his friend and fellow-signer of the Constitution, John Langdon, win the governorship from his brother.

The blond, blue-eyed Gilman was described as "having the winning grace of Aaron Burr." But however much he may have charmed the ladies, he remained a bachelor all his life. His associates seemed to regard him as a self-seeking politician who preferred the titles of the offices he won to the work they entailed.

Nicholas Gilman was born in Exeter, New Hampshire, on August 3, 1755. His great-great-grandfather, Edward Gilman, had been one of the first settlers of New Hampshire, and the Gilman name was prominent in the colony's affairs for a hundred years before the Revolutionary War. Nicholas Gilman's father and grandfather both bore the name Nicholas and both won a military reputation—his grandfather in Queen Anne's War and his father in the French and Indian War. His mother, Ann Taylor, was the daughter of a minister.

NICHOLAS GILMAN

1755 (Aug. 3) Born in Exeter, N. H.

1776-1782 Served as an officer in the Revolutionary War, rising to rank of captain and assistant adjutant general.

1786-1788 Delegate from New Hampshire to the Congress of the Confederation.

1787 Member of New Hampshire delegation to the Constitutional Convention; signed the United States Constitution.

1789-1797 U. S. Representative in Congress from New Hampshire.

1793, 1797 Presidential elector for New Hampshire.

1805-1814 U. S. Senator from New Hampshire.

1814 (May 2) Died in Philadelphia.

Young Nicholas was the second oldest of three brothers. His elder brother was John Taylor Gilman and his younger brother was Nathaniel Gilman. The boys grew up in a comfortable three-story brick house that overlooked the Exeter River. They were provided a good education, for their father was a wealthy shipowner and merchant.

Twenty years old at the outbreak of the Revolutionary War, Nicholas Gilman volunteered as an officer in Colonel Alexander Scammell's New Hampshire regiment that served with George Washington's Continental Army throughout the war. Gilman rose from lieutenant to captain, and at the Battle of Yorktown in 1781, after Scammell had been captured and slain, he was sent by Wash-

Nicholas Gilman
By John Ramage

ington as deputy adjutant general to receive from Lord Cornwallis an accounting of the number of troops surrendered.

In 1783, Gilman's father died, leaving his extensive estate to be divided among his three sons. John Taylor Gilman inherited the shipbuilding business; Nathaniel Gilman was left the store; and Nicholas Gilman received sufficient property that he did not have to take up any other career than politics.

Nicholas Gilman was chosen by the New Hampshire state legislature as one of its delegates to the Congress of the Confederation from 1786 to 1788. Although he was in his early thirties, he looked more youthful than he actually was. His older colleagues in the Congress of the Confederation resented his cocky attitude and gave him the nickname "Congress" Gilman.

When the Constitutional Convention was called to meet in Philadelphia in 1787, the New Hampshire treasury was so low on funds that no money could be appropriated to pay the expenses of delegates to the meeting. However, John Langdon, the wealthiest man in the state, volunteered to pay his own and Gilman's expenses to the Convention. Delayed, Langdon and Gilman were late in arriving in Philadelphia, taking their seats as New Hampshire's delegates on July 23, nearly two months after the debates had begun. Gilman apparently took little or no part in the discussions, for James Madison's record of the Constitutional Convention does not credit him with a single speech or proposal. William Pierce, one of the delegates from Georgia, wrote that there was "nothing brilliant or striking" about Gilman although he felt there was "something respectable and worthy in the man." Gilman signed the United States Constitution on September 17, 1787, without comment.

Gilman was elected as one of New Hampshire's three U. S. Representatives in Congress in February, 1789, and he continued to be re-elected to that office until 1797 when he publicly declined to serve again. During this same period he also was twice chosen, in 1793 and 1797, as one of New Hampshire's presidential electors.

During the period of his retirement, Gilman had a falling-out with his older brother, John Taylor Gilman, who had been elected governor of New Hampshire in 1794 on the Federalist party ticket. Nicholas Gilman became a member of Thomas Jefferson's Democratic-Republican party and supported his fellow-signer of the Constitution, John Langdon, in the gubernatorial election of 1805. When the votes were counted, Langdon had swept John Taylor Gilman out of office. As a reward for his assistance, the state legislature elected Nicholas Gilman as United States Senator in 1805.

Gilman served in the United States Senate for nine years. He had served only three years of his second term, when, returning to New Hampshire after a session of Congress, he became suddenly ill in Philadelphia and died on May 2, 1814, at the age of fifty-eight.

NATHANIEL GORHAM of MASSACHUSETTS

A successful merchant, Nathaniel Gorham rose to his nation's highest office as president of the Congress of the Confederation in 1786 to 1787. During that time he became convinced that the United States could not continue to hold together under the Articles of Confederation. He even went so far as to write to Prince Henry of Prussia suggesting the possibility that the prince might become King of the United States under a limited monarchy. Gorham went on to take an important role in the writing of the Constitution of the United States. The Anti-Federalists defeated him in his efforts to win office under the new government. After leaving public life, Gorham became involved in a huge land speculation involving more than six million acres of land in western New York, but he lost his fortune when the scheme collapsed. A handsome man, Gorham was described by a fellow-delegate to the Constitutional Convention as "rather lusty" with "an agreeable and pleasing manner."

Nathaniel Gorham was born in Charlestown, Massachusetts, on May 27, 1738. He served an apprenticeship to a merchant in New London, Connecticut, and then at the age of twenty-one he returned to Charlestown and established his own business there.

In 1771, Gorham was elected to the colonial legislature of Massachusetts, where he continued to serve until the beginning of the Revolutionary War. He was elected to the Massachusetts provincial congress in 1774 and 1775, and then served as a member of Massachusetts' board of war during much of the Revolution. In the ten years from 1779 to 1789, Gorham was extremely active in his state's politics, rising to speaker of the state house of representatives, and winning election as judge of the court of common pleas in Middlesex County.

The Massachusetts legislature elected Gorham one of its delegates to the Congress of the Confederation in 1782 and 1783, and again from 1785 to 1787. Congress elected him its president on June 6, 1786. He held this office until February, 1787.

NATHANIEL GORHAM

1738 (May 27) Born in Charlestown, Mass.

1771-1775 Member of Massachusetts colonial legislature.

1774-1775 Delegate to Massachusetts provincial congress.

1779-1789 Member of Massachusetts legislature.

1782-1783; 1785-1787 Delegate to Congress of the Confederation.

1786-1787 President of the Congress of the Confederation.

1787 Member of Massachusetts delegation to the Constitutional Convention; signed the United States Constitution.

1788 Member of Massachusetts constitutional ratification convention.

1796 (June 11) Died in Charlestown, Mass.

Held the next most important office at the convention

Gorham took his seat in the Constitutional Convention in Philadelphia on May 28, 1787, one day after his forty-ninth birthday. Two days later the delegates elected him chairman of the committee of the whole, the office next most important to that of George Washington as president of the convention.

During the course of the Constitutional Convention, Gorham made many practical proposals. He was the first to move that the terms of senators be six years. Like David Brearley of New Jersey, he felt that one of the best ways of preventing the large states from having too much power was

Courtesy: Museum of Fine Arts, Boston. Artist: Charles Willson Peale.

Nathaniel Gorham

Travels in the United States and Canada, by De Roos.

Chester, Massachusetts

to break them up so that all the states would be more equal in population. In July, Gorham was named as a member of John Rutledge's committee of detail, which drew up a constitution based on the various resolutions and proposals that had been discussed by the delegates.

Opposed limitation of voting to property owners

When the convention resumed discussions in August, Gorham strongly opposed an effort by Gouverneur Morris to limit voting rights to property owners. James Madison quoted him as saying: "The people have been long accustomed to this right in various parts of America, and will never allow it to be abridged. We must consult their rooted prejudices if we expect their concurrence in our propositions."

Introduced resolution establishing representation

On the last day of the convention, after the Constitution had been engrossed as was ready to be signed, Gorham proposed one last change in the document. He moved, in order to increase the number of representatives in Congress and gain greater popular support for the Constitution, that one representative be allowed for every thirty thousand people, rather than one for every forty thousand people. For the first time during the four months of deliberations, George Washington rose in his chair as President and spoke in favor of Gorham's motion. As a result, the motion was adopted unanimously—the last change in the Constitution before it was signed by the delegates.

Gorham's last public office was as a delegate to the Massachusetts constitutional ratification convention in 1788, in which he vigorously supported the Constitution. When Gorham ran for election as representative in the new Congress, he was defeated by Elbridge Gerry, a delegate to the Constitutional Convntion, but who had refused to sign the Constitution.

Suffered financial reverses

Like other members of the Constitutional Convention, such as Robert Morris, James Wilson, and William Blount, Gorham was caught up in the belief that huge amounts of money could be made in speculating in vast acreages of land on the western frontier. In 1788, he and a partner, Oliver Phelps, contracted to purchase more than six million acres of land in western New York state for about a million dollars. The land had been ceded to the state of Massachusetts by the state of New York in 1786, although sovereignty was held by New York. Gorham and Phelps had the land surveyed and began selling large tracts of it to other speculators and to settlers. In 1790, they sold more than a million acres to Robert Morris. Then, unable to meet their contract payments to Massachusetts, Gorham and Phelps were forced to turn over to the state the remainder of the land, most of which was still under title to the Indian tribes. The worry over the financial losses that he suffered affected Gorham's health. At the age of fifty-eight he died of apoplexy at Charlestown, Massachusetts, on June 11, 1796.

ALEXANDER HAMILTON of NEW YORK

Nicknamed "The Little Lion" because of his great courage and his short stature, Alexander Hamilton was George Washington's right-hand man in war and in peace. He would have liked Washington to be named as king of the United States with himself as prime minister, and, when he could not achieve such a government in the writing of the Constitution, he set about to come as close to it as he could in the administration of policy. Perhaps Hamilton's greatest contribution to his country came as the first Secretary of the Treasury under President Washington. Hamilton launched a sound economic program by which the new nation honorably paid its war debts.

Favored a strong central government

The conflicting viewpoints of Hamilton and Thomas Jefferson started the two-party political system in the United States, with Hamilton as head of the Federalist party and Jefferson as head of the Democratic-Republican party. Hamilton believed in monarchy, while Jefferson believed in democracy. Hamilton was a spokesman for the industrial northern states, while Jefferson was the leader of the agricultural southern states. Hamilton believed in a strong national government's taking over most power from the states, while Jefferson believed in strong state governments with no stronger a federal government than was absolutely necessary. In foreign affairs, Hamilton favored Great Britain, while Jefferson favored France.

Opinions as to Hamilton's merits and faults are exemplified by statements from Washington and Jefferson. Washington wrote of him: "That he is ambitious I shall readily grant, but it is of that laudable kind which prompts a man to excel in whatever he takes in hand. He is enterprising, quick in his perceptions, and his judgment is intuitively great . . ." On the other hand, Jefferson wrote: "I will not suffer my retirement to be clouded by the slanders of a man whose history, from the moment at which history can stoop to notice him, is a tissue of machinations against the liberty of the country which has not only received and given him bread, but heaped honors on his head."

Thrown upon his own at an early age

Alexander Hamilton was born in Charlestown on the island of Nevis in the British West Indies on January 11 in 1755 or 1757. Historians are not in agreement as to the actual year of his birth, but it seems more likely that he was born in 1755 and later cut two years off his age to save embarrass-

ALEXANDER HAMILTON

1755 or 1757 (Jan. 11) Born in Charlestown on the island of Nevis in the British West Indies.

1772 Came to America.

1773-1775 Attended King's College (now Columbia University).

1776-1777 Captain of artillery in the Continental Army; fought in battles in New York and New Jersey.

1777-1781 Aide-de-camp to George Washington with rank of lieutenant colonel.

1781 Commanded infantry regiment at the Battle of Yorktown.

1782 Admitted to the bar to practice law in New York.

1782-1783 Represented New York in the Congress of the Confederation.

1786-1788 Member of the New York state legislature.

1786 Member of New York delegation to the Annapolis Convention.

1787 Delegate from New York to the Constitutional Convention; signed the United States Constitution.

1787-1788 Collaborated with James Madison and John Jay in writing the series of essays called "The Federalist."

1788 Member of New York state ratification convention.

1789-1795 Secretary of the Treasury.

1798 Appointed major general of the United States Army, second in command to George Washington.

1804 (July 12) Died of wound from a duel with Aaron Burr.

"The Grange," Home of Alexander Hamilton

Library of Congress, Homes of America, Lamb. Photo by Arthur E. Scott.

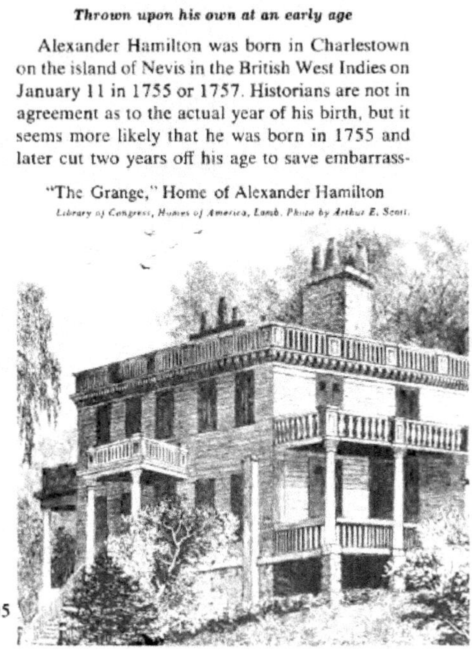

National Gallery of Art, Washington, D. C. Mellon Collection.

Alexander Hamilton
By John Trumbull

ment at attending school with boys younger than himself. His father, James Hamilton, was a Scottish trader. His mother, Rachel Faucette Lavien, was the daughter of a French doctor and wife of a Danish landowner. Her husband divorced her in 1759, but Danish law forbade her from marrying James Hamilton. His father deserted Alexander's mother, and she died in 1769, leaving the boy to fend for himself in the world.

When he was about twelve years old, Alexander Hamilton was apprenticed to a merchant on St. Croix island. Although he performed his work well and was given increasing responsibility, the boy had greater ambitions than to be a small businessman on an out-of-the-way island. Hamilton wrote to a friend of his who had been sent to New York to school: "I confess my weakness, Ned, my ambition is prevalent, so that I contemn the grovelling condition of a clerk or the like, to which my fortune condemns me, and would willingly risk my life, though not my character, to exalt my station . . . I shall conclude by saying, I wish there was a war."

Helped by a Presbyterian minister

A letter that the boy wrote describing a severe hurricane that struck the West Indies in 1772 was published in the local newspaper and so impressed a Presbyterian minister, Hugh Knox, that he helped Alexander borrow enough money to go to America to attend college. Hamilton arrived in America in October and went directly to New Jersey where he presented a letter of introduction from Knox to William Livingston, a prominent Presbyterian layman who later became governor of New Jersey and a fellow-signer with Hamilton of the United States Constitution. Livingston took Hamilton into his home and placed him in school in Elizabethtown.

In 1773, Hamilton began attending King's College (now Columbia University) in New York City, and he was soon caught up in the revolutionary movement. He made an eloquent speech in 1774 before a patriotic meeting in which he defended the actions of the Bostonians in dumping British tea into the harbor. The next year he published two well-written patriotic pamphlets, "A Full Vindication of the Measures of the Congress from the Calumnies of their Enemies" and "The Farmer Refuted." Hamilton did not believe in mob violence, however; and, when a crowd egged on by the Sons of Liberty attacked the home of Myles Cooper, the president of King's College who had openly expressed Tory views, Hamilton and some of his friends helped Cooper escape.

The war which Hamilton had wished for as a boy had now come. He volunteered for military duty and received a commission as captain of artillery in March, 1776. His company fought in the rear guard in the retreat of the Continental Army from Long Island. He then took part in the Battles of White Plains, Trenton, and Princeton.

Served Washington as translator and confidante

The courageous conduct and military skill of the young artilleryman had been called to General Washington's attention, and in March, 1777, he was appointed as one of the commanding general's aides-de-camp and promoted to lieutenant colonel. He quickly became Washington's "principal and most confidential aid," as the general described him; and one of his most useful talents was his knowledge of the French language that enabled him to act as translator with the various French officers who aided the American cause. Hamilton handled Washington's most confidential correspondence and assisted him in his planning. But in February, 1781, a flareup of temper put a temporary end to their friendly relationship. As told by Hamilton, Washington had met him on the stairs of their headquarters and had asked him to come upstairs as soon as he finished his errand. A few minutes later, when he went back up the stairs he met Washington who exclaimed:

"Colonel Hamilton, you have kept me waiting at the head of the stairs these ten minutes; I must tell you, sir, you treat me with disrespect."

"I am not conscious of it, sir," Hamilton replied, "but since you have thought it necessary to tell me so, we part."

"Very well, sire," Washington answered, "if it be your choice."

Fought with distinction at the Battle of Yorktown

Although Washington made efforts to patch up the misunderstanding, Hamilton preferred to return to an active military command where he might win personal military glory. He was given command of a New York infantry regiment, and at the Battle of Yorktown in October, 1781, he distinguished himself by leading a successful night attack on the enemy fortifications.

After the Battle of Yorktown, Hamilton retired from military duty, and went to Albany to join his

Mrs. Alexander Hamilton
By RALPH EARL

wife. In December, 1780, he had married Elizabeth Schuyler, daughter of Major General Philip Schuyler, a wealthy businessman who later became one of New York's first United States Senators. Hamilton applied himself vigorously to the study of law, and in July, 1782, was admitted to the New York bar.

Now, Hamilton entered on his political career. In the same month that he was admitted to the practice of law, the New York legislature elected him as one of its delegates to the Congress of the Confederation meeting in Philadelphia. There he became a close friend of James Madison, who was then one of the Virginia delegates; and he worked closely with Robert Morris, then superintendent of finance, in trying to straighten out the muddled state of affairs of the American economy.

Favored a liberal view toward Tories

Hamilton remained in Congress only a year, then moved his family to New York City where he established himself as a lawyer. Hamilton soon became engaged in a new controversy. A witch-hunt against Loyalists was going forward in New York. Hamilton wrote a series of newspaper articles over the signature "Phocion" which favored a more liberal view toward the Tories, pointing out that America would lose the services of many good minds if all the Loyalists were to be driven from her shores.

In 1786, Hamilton was elected to the New York legislature, and that same year he was sent as one of New York's delegation to the Annapolis Convention. There he joined with Madison in urging that the Articles of Confederation be completely overhauled in order to strengthen the national government. He wrote the report finally adopted by the Convention which called for a Constitutional Convention to consider the matter.

The thirty-year-old Hamilton was elected by the New York legislature as a member of its delegation to the Constitutional Convention of 1787 largely because he was the son-in-law of Schuyler, who was then the president of the New York state senate. The other two members of the New York delegation, Robert Lansing and John Yates, were opposed to strengthening the national government. As a result, Hamilton was placed in the unhappy position of being a minority of one in his state delegation; and, since each state had but a single vote in the Convention, Hamilton knew his voice would not be heard.

Felt that the British government was ideal

Hamilton was present from the beginning of the Constitutional Convention, but it was not until June 18 that he made a speech of any consequence. On that day he took up almost the entire session with a long discussion of his ideas about what the future government of the United States should be, and then he presented the delegates with a proposed outline for the Constitution. He declared that the British Government was "the best in the world" and he doubted "whether anything short of it would do in America."

"Can there be a good government without a good Executive?" he asked, and added that "the English model was the only good one on this subject. The hereditary interest of the King was so interwoven with that of the nation, and his personal emolument was so great, that he was placed above the danger of being corrupted from abroad; and at the same time was both sufficiently independent and sufficiently controlled, to answer the purpose of the institution at home. . . ."

"Let one branch of the Legislature hold their places for life, or at least during good behavior. Let the Executive, also, be for life. . . . It will be objected, probably that such an Executive will be an *elective monarch*, and will give birth to the tumults which characterize that form of government. He would reply that *monarch* is an indefinite term. It marks not either the degree or duration of power."

A little over a week later, on June 26, Hamilton explained his views on representative government. As reported by James Madison, Hamilton said that: "we were not to decide forever the fate of republican government; and that if we did not give to that form due stability and wisdom, it would be disgraced and lost among ourselves, disgraced and lost to mankind forever. He acknowledged himself not to think favorably of republican government; but addressed his remarks to those who did think favorably of it, in order to prevail on them to tone their government as high as possible. He professed himself to be as zealous an advocate for liberty as any man whatever; and trusted he should be as willing a martyr to it, though he differed as to the form in which it was most eligible."

Urged delegates to sign the Constitution

At the end of June, Hamilton returned to New York. He resumed his seat in the middle of August, but took little further part in the debates. He was a member of the committee on style, on which Gouverneur Morris did most of the work in creating the final phraseology of the Constitution. Then on the final day of the Convention, after Edmund Randolph had announced that he was not going to sign the Constitution, Hamilton rose to make his final comments. James Madison reported:

"Mr. Hamilton expressed his anxiety that every member should sign. A few characters of consequence, by opposing, or even refusing to sign the Constitution, might do infinite mischief, by kindling the latent sparks that lurk under an enthusiasm in favor of the Convention which may soon subside. No man's ideas were more remote from the plan than his own were known to be; but is it possible to deliberate between anarchy and convulsion on one side, and the chance of good to be expected from the plan on the other?"

In October, 1787, the month after the Convention, a series of articles explaining and defending the Constitution began appearing in New York newspapers over the name "Publius." These articles continued through the winter and spring of 1788, and were finally published as a two-volume work entitled *The Federalist*. The majority of these articles were written by Hamilton, but some were written by James Madison and John Jay. They are considered among the finest expositions on political science and government ever written.

Hamilton worked even more directly to win ratification of the Constitution, as he was elected to New York's convention called in 1788. Through Hamilton's efforts, his state ratified the Constitution by a narrow margin.

Appointed by Washington as Secretary of the Treasury

In September, 1789, Washington appointed Hamilton as Secretary of the Treasury, and for the next four years his former aide-de-camp worked as a close advisor in helping him shape the new government. Hamilton's first major report in January, 1790, called for the national government to take over those public debts of states that had accumulated during the Revolutionary War. His sec-

The New York Public Library.

View of the spot where Gen. Hamilton fell at Weehawken

ond report, in December, 1790, asked for the establishment of a national bank. His third report, in December, 1791, outlined an elaborate plan to stimulate manufacturing industries. Many years later, Daniel Webster described Hamilton's contribution in these colorful words:

"He smote the rock of the national resources, and abundant streams of revenue gushed forth. He touched the dead corpse of the public credit, and it sprung upon its feet."

Hamilton and Jefferson grew to hate each other. Hamilton felt that Jefferson was trying to thwart his plans for a sound government, and Jefferson felt that Hamilton was trying to maneuver Washington to aid the selfish interests of New York and Philadelphia bankers. When Hamilton's Assistant Secretary of the Treasury, William Duer, was charged with embezzlement and was sent to prison as a speculator who could not pay his debts, Jefferson's supporters made strong efforts to find evidence that Hamilton was involved in wrongdoing. Later, after Hamilton had left the Cabinet, Congressional investigators revealed evidence that Hamilton had been carrying on an illicit romance with the wife of a speculator, and it was charged that he had paid for her favors with government secrets. But Hamilton, who publicly admitted the love affair, denied that he had misused his office; and Jefferson's followers were unable to prove their allegations.

Courtesy: The Boston Athenaeum. Photograph by G. M. Cushing.

John Adams

By MATHER BROWN

Tried to keep John Adams from the presidency

Upon leaving Washington's Cabinet in January, 1795, Hamilton resumed his law practice, but continued to involve himself in politics. He disliked John Adams, so he tried to prevent Adams's winning the presidency in 1796 by trying to maneuver some electoral votes to Thomas Pinckney, the Federalist candidate for vice president. The upshot of his machinations was that Adams nearly lost the presidency and Pinckney did lose the vice-presidency to Jefferson.

When France and the United States nearly went to war in 1798, Adams reluctantly and only at the insistence of Washington appointed Hamilton as a major general in the newly created United States Army. As such, he was second in command only to Washington. With Washington's death in 1799, Hamilton was particularly disappointed because he had hoped to convince the general that he should again run for the office of president in 1800. Hamilton stated: "Perhaps no friend of his has more cause to lament on personal account than myself." Hamilton had further cause to lament in 1800, when France and the United States reached a peaceful settlement of their difficulties, for this destroyed his hopes of reaching military glory at the head of the United States Army.

Maneuvered John Adams out of reelection

Hamilton's distaste for John Adams reached a new height of vituperation in the election of 1800. He circulated to Federalist leaders a series of charges against Adams in a "Letter from Alexander Hamilton Concerning the Public Conduct and Character of John Adams." A copy of the letter fell into the hands of Aaron Burr, the Democratic-Republican candidate for vice president, and he turned it over to the newspapers. This letter split the Federalist party wide open, and Adams lost the election to Jefferson. Many years later Adams still referred to Hamilton as a "bastard brat of a Scotch pedlar."

Hamilton experienced a severe shock in his per-

Library of Congress.

The Narrows Near New York
(1798)

sonal life in 1801, when his oldest son, Philip Hamilton, was slain in a duel that grew out of an argument about Alexander Hamilton's politics. The duel was fought at the same spot where Hamilton himself was to be fatally wounded three years later.

In 1804, Aaron Burr sought the office of the governor of New York, running against another Democratic-Republican candidate. He asked for the support of the Federalist party, but Hamilton urged his friends to vote against Burr, and Burr was defeated. When a newspaper article appeared in an Albany newspaper quoting Hamilton as having called Burr "a dangerous man" and one that "ought not to be trusted," Burr used this as the basis of a challenge for a duel.

Killed in a duel with Aaron Burr

Hamilton accepted Burr's challenge, and melodramatically chose as the scene of the engagement the west bank of the Hudson River near Weehawken, N. J., at the same spot where his son had been slain three years earlier. After the command to fire, Burr's first shot smashed Hamilton to the ground, but Hamilton's shot went wild. When his second reached him, Hamilton said, "I did not intend to fire at him." Hamilton's friends rowed him back across the river to New York City, while Burr fled. The next day, July 12, 1804, at the age of forty-seven or forty-nine, Hamilton died, shortly after being received into the Episcopal Church. His body was buried in the graveyard of Trinity Church.

Courtesy: The Brooklyn Museum.

Winter Scene in Brooklyn
By Francis Guy

Courtesy: Museum of the City of New York.

Old New York
Opening of the Erie Canal

JARED INGERSOLL of PENNSYLVANIA

One of the eight Pennsylvania delegates who signed the Constitution of the United States, Jared Ingersoll won later prominence as a Philadelphia lawyer and as the Federalist Party's unsuccessful candidate for Vice President of the United States in 1812. A conservative by nature as well as in politics, Ingersoll continued to wear a powdered wig and knee breeches long after the fashion had passed out of style.

Horace Binney, who was Ingersoll's law pupil and then his associate, left an excellent description of his friend's manner in court:

"His oratory was of a very high order . . . clear, earnest, logically connected, rarely or never rising to the highest flights, but always on the wing. . . . He never stumbled upon an awkward phrase, nor said a bitter thing, nor uttered a pointless expression, nor began a sentence before the thought was ready for it and the language for the thought. He was not voluble nor rapid. His words did not interfere with each other; nor, in any height of excitement, did his voice bray, nor his arms lash the air, nor his foot explode upon the floor. Neither was he hesitating or slow, as if he was inquiring for the next word, nor monotonous, as if he was reading from a stereotyped memory. But, with just the proper tone and measure, rising sufficiently above the natural key of conversation to give something like air or rhythm to his language, and speaking as from his brain and not from his brief, he proceeded, with proper pauses and variations of time, from beginning to end, without a single break-down or trip in word or thought. . . . Woe betided the adversary that took a false position, or used an illogical argument, or misstated a fact against him. . . . He fastened upon the mistake with the grasp of death, and would repeat and reiterate and multiply his assaults upon it, until there did not remain a shadow of excuse for the blunder."

Jared Ingersoll was born in New Haven, Connecticut, on October 27, 1749, the son of Jared and Hannah Whiting Ingersoll. His great-grandfather, John Ingersoll, had emigrated to America in 1629. The elder Jared Ingersoll was a distinguished lawyer in colonial Connecticut and a friend of Benjamin Franklin. But he fell from popular favor in 1765 when he accepted a commission as a British tax collector under the Stamp Act, and was forced to resign the office by an armed mob of five hundred Sons of Liberty. In 1771, the British appointed the elder Ingersoll as a judge of the court of the vice admiralty in Philadelphia, where he lived until the patriots forced him to return to Connecticut because of his Loyalist sympathies during the Revolutionary War.

Jared Ingersoll
By JOHN SINGLETON COPLEY
Courtesy: C. Jared Ingersoll.
Photo: Society for the Preservation of New England Antiquities, Boston.

JARED INGERSOLL

1749 (Oct. 27) Born in New Haven, Conn.
1766 Graduated from Yale College.
1774-1778 Studied in Europe.
1779 Admitted to the bar in Philadelphia.
1780-1781 Delegate to the Continental Congress from Pennsylvania.
1787 Member of Pennsylvania delegation to the Constitutional Convention; signed the Constitution of the United States.
1790-1799 Attorney general of Pennsylvania.
1798-1801 City solicitor of Philadelphia.
1800-1801 U.S. district attorney for Pennsylvania.
1811-1817 Attorney general of Pennsylvania.
1812 Unsuccessfully ran for Vice President of the United States on the Federalist Party ticket.
1821-1822 Judge of district court of Philadelphia.
1822 (Oct. 31) Died in Philadelphia.

De Witt Clinton

A polished speaker

The younger Jared Ingersoll was reared as a Presbyterian, and received a good education in Connecticut. He was graduated from Yale College in 1766, at the age of sixteen. With the approach of the Revolutionary War, his father decided to send young Jared to Europe to study law. The young man arrived in London in 1774, and studied at the Middle Temple for about two years. He then went to Paris for two more years. While in Europe, young Ingersoll became an ardent supporter of the American patriotic cause.

The 29-year-old Ingersoll returned to America in 1778, and in January, 1779, was admitted to the bar to practice law in Philadelphia. Influential friends of his father helped him build a practice, but his natural abilities also enhanced his reputation as he won notice as a trial lawyer who could sway juries with facility.

Distinguished for his conservatism

Ingersoll entered politics in 1780, when he was elected by the Pennsylvania legislature as a member of the state's delegation to the Continental Congress, and he was a member of that body when the Articles of Confederation went into effect in 1781. Throughout his political career he was distinguished for his conservatism.

At the age of thirty-two, Ingersoll married Elizabeth Pettit. They had four children, all sons, who grew up with such playmates and companions as Philip Hamilton, the son of Alexander Hamilton, and George Washington Parke Custis, the adopted grandson of George Washington. The most distinguished of these sons was Charles Jared Ingersoll, who served in Congress from 1813 to 1815 as a Democratic-Republican and from 1841 to 1849 as a Democrat.

In 1787, Jared Ingersoll won election by the state legislature as one of the deputies to the Constitutional Convention. He apparently took little part in the debates concerning the structure of the new government. However, on the last day of the meeting, September 17, 1787, James Madison's journal records that Ingersoll rose to support Benjamin Franklin's motion that the delegates sign the Constitution. Madison reported:

"Mr. Ingersoll did not consider the signing either as a mere attestation of the fact, or as pledging the signers to support the Constitution at all events; but as a recommendation of what, all things considered, was the most eligible."

An office-holder under the Federalists

As long as the Federalists were in power in Pennsylvania, Ingersoll held important positions. From 1790 to 1799, he was attorney general of Pennsylvania under the administration of Governor Thomas Mifflin, a fellow-signer of the Constitution. Ingersoll also served as city solicitor of Philadelphia from 1798 to 1801. In the last hours of President John Adams's Federalist administration, Ingersoll was appointed as a U.S. circuit court judge for eastern Pennsylvania—one of the "midnight judges"; but he refused the commission.

With the coming to power of Thomas Jefferson's Democratic-Republican Party, Ingersoll retired to private law practice for about ten years. However, he continued as a leader of the Federalist Party in Pennsylvania. In 1812, the Federalists chose him as the Vice Presidential running mate of Governor DeWitt Clinton of New York in the presidential election, but he and Clinton were defeated by the Democratic-Republican ticket of President James Madison and Elbridge Gerry.

Ingersoll again served as attorney general of Pennsylvania from 1811 to 1817, and then at the age of 72 he took his last public office, as presiding judge of the district court of Philadelphia from 1821 to 1822. Just three days after his seventy-third birthday, he died in Philadelphia, on October 31, 1822. Like several other signers of the Constitution, he died a poor man because of speculation in western land.

DANIEL OF ST. THOMAS JENIFER of MARYLAND

A wealthy aristocrat, Daniel of St. Thomas Jenifer had been a trusted lieutenant of the colonial proprietors of Maryland, but switched allegiance at the beginning of the Revolutionary War to head Maryland's patriotic government in its transition from a colony to a state. After the war, Jenifer gladly joined his long-time friend George Washington in efforts to construct a strong national government and became a signer of the United States Constitution.

A witty bachelor

A life-long bachelor who was said to speak "warmly of the Ladies," Jenifer was a witty, friendly man. A fellow-delegate to the Constitutional Convention said of him: "He is always in good humour, and never fails to make his company pleased with him. He sits silent in the Senate, and seems to be conscious that he is no politician. From his long continuance in single life, no doubt that he has made the vow of celibacy."

Daniel of St. Thomas Jenifer was born in 1723 on his father's estate in Charles County, Maryland, across the Potomac River from Washington's Mount Vernon. His father, Daniel Jenifer, was of English descent, and his mother, Elizabeth Hanson Jenifer, was of Swedish descent. His mother's brother, John Hanson, was the first president of the Congress of Confederation after the Articles of Confederation went into effect in 1781.

Jenifer grew up on his father's plantation, Retreat, near Port Tobacco, Md. He was reared as an Episcopalian, and no doubt received most of his education from private tutors, as was customary for the sons of wealthy landowners in colonial days. There are several theories as to why Jenifer was given his unusual middle name "of St. Thomas." He may have received the name because of the nearby church and manor of Saint Thomas that had been maintained by the Jesuits since 1649. Other versions say that an ancestor came from the Isle of St. Thomas off the coast of Cornwall, or that an ancestor stopped at the island of St. Thomas in the West Indies before coming to Maryland. In any event, his middle name distinguished him from his father, from a younger brother, and from a nephew, all of whom were also named Daniel Jenifer.

Mason-Dixon selected by his commission

As a young man, Jenifer helped manage the family plantations. He also served as a justice of

DANIEL OF ST. THOMAS JENIFER

1723 Born in Charles County, Maryland.
1760 Member of a commission to settle a boundary dispute between Pennsylvania and Delaware.
1773-1775 Member of Maryland governor's council.
1775-1777 President of Maryland committee of safety.
1777-1781 President of Maryland senate.
1778-1782 Delegate to Continental Congress from Maryland.
1785 Member of Maryland-Virginia commission that drew up the "Mt. Vernon Compact" to insure free use of the Potomac River and Chesapeake Bay.
1787 Delegate from Maryland to the Constitutional Convention; signed the United States Constitution.
1790 (Nov. 16) Died in Annapolis, Maryland.

Daniel of St. Thomas Jenifer
By HESSELINS
Courtesy: John H. Mitchell.

the peace. The growing respect in which he was held by the proprietors of the colony was evidenced by his appointment in 1760 as a member of a commission to settle a boundary dispute between Pennsylvania and Maryland. This commission led to the hiring of Charles Mason and Jeremiah Dixon to survey the boundary between the two colonies. This boundary came to be called the Mason-Dixon line.

In the years before the Revolutionary War, Jenifer held the office of receiver general for rents and taxes collected for the proprietors. In 1773, he was appointed to the governor's council, the upper house of the Maryland legislature, and became one of the close advisors of the colonial governor, Robert Eden.

With the outbreak of fighting in Massachusetts and the appointment of Washington as commander in chief of the Continental Army, Jenifer decided to join the patriots. From 1775 to 1777, he was president of the Committee of Safety, which governed Maryland during those years. When a state constitution went into effect in 1777, Jenifer became president of the state senate. The legislature elected him a delegate to the Continental Congress from 1778 to 1782.

Handled finances of the state

Because of Jenifer's experience as receiver general for the colonial proprietors, he was appointed intendant of the revenue in 1781, an office similar to that of state treasurer. As such, he was involved in the sale of confiscated British property, the collecting of taxes, and all the other difficult problems of state finance during the hectic days of the Revolution. Jenifer held this office until it expired in 1785, and then he continued to supervise the sale of British property until 1788 as a special agent appointed by the governor.

In 1785, the Maryland legislature elected Jenifer a member of the commission to meet at Mount Vernon with representatives of the state of Virginia to discuss problems of navigation on the Potomac River and Chesapeake Bay. This meeting at George Washington's home resulted in the Mount Vernon Compact, an agreement that Virginia and Maryland would permit free passage of boats and ships on the waters of the Potomac River and Chesapeake Bay. The success of the Mount Vernon meeting led to the Annapolis Convention and ultimately to the Constitutional Convention in Philadelphia two years later.

Was seated as a substitute

Jenifer was not among the original delegates chosen by the Maryland legislature to attend the Constitutional Convention, but he was elected to replace one of the four men who refused to serve. This delay made Jenifer late in going to Philadelphia. He took his seat in the Constitutional Convention on June 2, 1787, after the delegates had been meeting for more than a week.

The 64-year-old Jenifer took little part in the debates on the drawing up of the Constitution. At one point, he proposed that members of the House of Representatives be elected every three years, instead of every two years, because "the too great frequency of elections rendered the people indifferent to them, and made the best men unwilling to engage in so precarious a service." Although his recommendation was adopted by the delegates at the time, they later changed their minds and reduced the term of office to two years. During much of the time that the Convention was meeting Jenifer and Luther Martin were the only two delegates from Maryland present; and, since Jenifer favored the Virginia Plan, while Martin upheld the New Jersey Plan, Maryland's vote was usually split during the controversy between the large and the small states. At the end of the Convention, Jenifer signed the United States Constitution, but Martin refused to do so.

Jenifer's last public service was to aid in winning support for Maryland's ratification of the Constitution, despite the opposition of Martin. Jenifer retired from public life to devote his attention to his extensive landholdings for his remaining years. At the age of 67, he died in Annapolis on November 16, 1790. The place of his burial remains unknown, although it is believed he may have been buried in the graveyard of Old Christ Church at Port Tobacco, Md. This graveyard was later flooded by the waters of the Potomac and all gravestones lost. In his will, he left most of his estate to his nephew Daniel Jenifer, stipulating that his slaves were to be freed by the year 1796. He also left his collection of French books to James Madison, the Father of the Constitution.

Courtesy: Constance Stuart Larrabee.

"Retreat," Home of Daniel of St. Thomas Jenifer

Yale College and State House, New Haven, Connecticut
(From an engraving of the early 1800's)

WILLIAM SAMUEL JOHNSON of CONNECTICUT

Although William Samuel Johnson would not support the idea of American independence from Great Britain in the Revolutionary War, he helped write and later signed the United States Constitution. He also became president of Columbia College in New York City and one of the first United States Senators from Connecticut.

A dark-eyed, delicate-appearing man, Johnson won a reputation as one of the most learned lawyers and scholars of his day. A fellow-delegate to the Constitutional Convention of 1787 described him in these words: "Dr. Johnson possesses the manners of a Gentleman, and engages the Hearts of Men by the sweetness of his temper, and that affectionate style of address with which he accosts his acquaintances."

William Samuel Johnson was born in Stratford, Connecticut, on October 7, 1727. His father, Samuel Johnson, was pastor of the Anglican Church in Stratford, and later, from 1754 to 1763, became the first president of New York City's King's College (now Columbia University). As a boy, young William began studying Latin at the age of eight and Greek when he was ten. In his early teens he was sent to Yale College, where he majored in the classics. At the age of sixteen, in 1744, he was graduated from Yale as third in his class of fifteen. He continued on at Yale to receive a Master of Arts degree in 1747, and later that same year he was awarded an honorary M.A. degree from Harvard College.

Married an heiress, became prominent as attorney

After completing his college studies, Johnson considered becoming a soldier, but his father convinced him that he should instead become a lawyer. After studying law books for two years, Johnson began practicing law in 1749. That same year he married Ann Beach, daughter of a wealthy member of his father's congregation. He and his wife had eleven children, seven of whom died in childhood. The dowry that Johnson acquired with his marriage helped establish him in his profession. Much later he advised one of his sons that to marry an heiress was "the most easy and agreeable method of acquiring a competency." By the time Johnson was twenty-nine, his reputation as an attorney was such that the colonial legislature listed him as one of the dozen leading lawyers of Connecticut.

WILLIAM SAMUEL JOHNSON

1727 **(Oct. 7) Born in Stratford, Conn.**
1744 **Graduated from Yale College.**
1747 **Received Master of Arts degrees from both Yale and Harvard colleges.**
1749 **Began practicing law.**
1765 **Member of general assembly of Connecticut legislature.**
1765 **Delegate to the Stamp Act Congress.**
1766-1775 **Member of the governor's council, the upper house of the Connecticut legislature.**
1767-1771 **Represented Connecticut as special agent in London.**
1774 **Declined election as delegate to the first Continental Congress because he did not believe the colonies should separate from Britain.**
1779 **Arrested for unpatriotic activities, but released after taking an oath of allegiance to the state of Connecticut.**
1785-1787 **Delegate from Connecticut to the Congress of the Confederation.**
1787 **Delegate to the Constitutional Convention; signed the United States Constitution.**
1787-1800 **President of Columbia College in New York City.**
1788 **Member of the Connecticut convention that ratified the United States Constitution.**
1789-1791 **United States Senator from Connecticut.**
1819 **(Nov. 14) Died in Stratford, Conn.**

William Samuel Johnson
By R. E. Pine
Frick Art Reference Library. Mrs. T. Bache Bleecker, owner.

After serving as a member of the town council of Stratford and as a justice of the peace, Johnson was elected to the Connecticut legislature in 1765. When news arrived that the British parliament had established the Stamp Act, Johnson spoke against the tax, but he also applied for the position of assistant tax collector in Stratford. Amidst the clamor and mob violence against the Stamp Act that was raised by the patriotic Sons of Liberty, the Connecticut legislature decided to send Johnson and two other delegates to the Stamp Act Congress in New York City.

At the Stamp Act Congress, Johnson, who was thirty-eight, was younger than a majority of the delegates. However, he may have played a more important role than his two other colleagues from Connecticut because he had previously had contacts as a lawyer with delegates from various other colonies. At this meeting, Johnson developed a particular friendship with Christopher Gadsden of South Carolina, a southern leader of the Sons of Liberty who had much more radical views than those of Johnson.

The next year, in 1766, Johnson received two important honors. He was elected as a member of the governor's council, the upper house of the Connecticut legislature. He also was awarded an honorary degree of Doctor of Civil Law by Oxford University.

Represented Connecticut in Great Britain

On Christmas Day of 1766, Johnson sailed for England as the special agent of the Connecticut legislature, a post he was to fill until 1771. In London, Johnson cooperated with Benjamin Franklin, who during this period was acting as agent for Pennsylvania and several other colonies. As well as working to safeguard Connecticut's legal interests in Great Britain, Johnson greatly broadened himself during his stay abroad. He made several trips to the European continent, attended the theater and the opera, and mingled with such literary figures as Oliver Goldsmith and Samuel Johnson, the lexicographer.

After returning to Connecticut in September, 1771, Johnson resumed his seat in the governor's council, an office that he held until shortly after the outbreak of the Revolutionary War. During 1772 he served as a justice of Connecticut's superior court, but declined reappointment because he felt the salary was too low. He also was commissioned a major in the Connecticut militia in 1772. Johnson had the ambition of becoming chief justice of the colony of New York, and he began correspondence with friends and acquaintances in London with this end in view, but the coming of the revolution wrecked these plans.

Wished to prevent conflict with England

After the Coercive Acts had been imposed against Boston in 1774, Johnson wrote to a friend in the British parliament describing the situation

Library of Congress.

The Dam on the Erie Canal in Rochester, New York

The I. N. Phelps Stokes Collection of American Historical Prints, New York Public Library.

View of Utica from the hotel, September, 1807 Artist: Baroness Hyde de Neuville

in Connecticut: "Contributions are raising in almost all the towns upon the Continent for the support of the poor of Boston who may suffer by the operations of the Port Bill. In a word we are all in motion & the minds of the people are greatly alarmed & highly inflamed. What the end of these things will be I will not pretend to foretell, but the prospect is very gloomy." Johnson also said in this letter that he was determined to "do everything possible to keep the Ardour of my Countrymen within Bounds tho' it is more than possible I shall forfeit their esteem."

Following his resolution to preserve the union between the colonies and Great Britain, Johnson refused to serve when elected by the Connecticut legislature in 1774 as a delegate to the first Continental Congress. He also resigned his commission in the Connecticut militia. After the outbreak of fighting at Lexington and Concord in 1775, the Connecticut legislature sent Johnson and another delegate to visit the British commanding general, Thomas Gage, to investigate whether or not some peaceful solution could be reached. After visiting Gage in Boston, Johnson and his fellow delegate were arrested by the Massachusetts patriots, but they were released after being taken before the Massachusetts provincial congress. Upon his return to Connecticut, Johnson learned that his peace mission had been in vain because the Connecticut legislature had already voted to raise troops and money for the patriotic cause. Late in 1775, Johnson resigned from the legislature, feeling that any action on his part to support the Revolutionary War would be treason to the British government. When Johnson refused to take an oath of allegiance to the independent state of Connecticut in 1777, he was forbidden to continue practicing law.

Took the oath of allegiance to Connecticut in 1779

In 1779, a few of the residents of Stratford circulated a petition asking Johnson to use his influence with the British to obtain a promise that the town would not be plundered by British troops. When word of this action came to the attention of state authorities, Johnson was arrested. In a hearing before the state committee of safety, Johnson denied that he had actually corresponded with the British, and he agreed to take the oath of allegiance to Connecticut. After this, he was permitted to return to Stratford and resume his law practice.

As the Revolutionary War drew to a close, Johnson quickly regained his popularity. The legislature appointed him as one of its attorneys in a land dispute with Pennsylvania over the Wyoming valley area. The legislature elected him from 1785 to 1787 as one of Connecticut's delegates to the Congress of the Confederation, which was meeting in New York City. While there, the trustees of Columbia College in May, 1787, invited him to become president of the institution, following in the footsteps of his father, but he delayed making up his mind for several months.

Represented Connecticut at the Constitutional Convention

The Constitutional Convention had been called to meet in Philadelphia in the spring of 1787, and, although Johnson felt that it was "very problematical" that the convention could solve the nation's problems, he accepted election by the legislature as one of Connecticut's delegates to the convention. He was fifty-nine years old when he took his seat at the convention on June 2, 1787. When the convention deadlocked over the controversy between large and small states regarding how representation was to be determined in the Congress, Johnson became one of the leading spokesmen for the "Connecticut compromise" that resulted in a two-house Congress. On June 29, 1787, he made an address on the subject reported in part by James Madison as saying: "On the whole he thought, that, as in some respects the States are to be considered in their political capacity, and in others as districts of individual citizens, the two ideas embraced on different sides, instead of being opposed to each other, ought to be combined; that in *one* branch the *people* ought to be represented, in the *other* the *States*."

In September, 1787, Johnson was appointed chairman of the committee on style that put the finishing touches to the arrangement and literary form of the United States Constitution. However, most of the work of this committee was performed by Gouverneur Morris, a committee member. On September 17, Johnson along with most of the other delegates signed the United States Constitution.

Accepted appointment as president of Columbia College

After completing his work at the Constitutional Convention, Johnson returned to New York to take his place in Congress. On November 12, 1787, he finally accepted the appointment as president of Columbia College. At the time he became president, Columbia College had three professors and about thirty students. It was located in a three-story building in lower Manhattan.

In January, 1788, Johnson took time out from his new duties as an educator in order to attend the Connecticut convention considering ratification of the United States Constitution. There, he made an impassioned appeal for support of the new form of government:

"Our commerce is annihilated; our national honour, once in so high esteem is no more. We have got to the very brink of ruin; we must turn back and adopt a new system . . . As to the old system, we can go no further with it; experience has shown it to be utterly inefficient. The States were sensible of this, to remedy the evil they appointed the convention. Though no enthusiast, I cannot but impute it to a signal intervention of divine providence, that a convention of States differing in circumstances, interests, and manners, should be so harmonious in adopting one grand system. If we reject a plan of government, which with such favorable circumstances is offered for acceptance, I fear our national existence must come to a final end."

Elected as U.S. Senator from Connecticut

Honoring Johnson's part in drafting the United States Constitution and in winning its ratification, the Connecticut legislature elected him as one of the state's first two United States Senators in 1789. Because the new Congress met in New York City, Johnson was able to function both as a college

Home of William Samuel Johnson
By CHARLES LAY
Courtesy: Columbia University, New York. Owner: Miss Geraldine Carmalt.

The I. N. Phelps Stokes Collection of American Historical Prints, New York Public Library.

A View of Flushing, Long Island
This home was built in 1661

president and as a U.S. Senator. At the age of sixty-one, Johnson was the oldest man in the United States Senate, and he was described by William Maclay, the Senator from Pennsylvania, as a "thorough-paced courtier." This last remark was reflected by Johnson's service on a committee that recommended that President George Washington should be addressed as "His Highness." While serving in the Senate, Johnson aided in the admission of Vermont and Kentucky as states. He was particularly interested in the admission of Vermont, where he had money invested in land at a town that was later named after him as Johnson, Vt. Johnson also aided in the passage of Alexander Hamilton's fiscal program including the assumption by the federal government of the state's war debts. Johnson's interest in the latter may have been influenced by the fact that he and one of his sons had invested about fifty thousand dollars in state securities that increased in value several times with the passage of the federal legislation. Less than a month after the fiscal legislation had been passed in 1791, Johnson resigned his senate seat to devote full time to education.

As president of Columbia College, Johnson added a "School of Physic" to teach medicine, and employed the school's first professor of law. Johnson himself from time to time taught courses in logic, rhetoric, and literature. After more than twelve years at the college, ill health forced Johnson to resign in July, 1800.

The last nineteen years of his life were spent in quiet retirement at Stratford, Conn. His first wife had died in 1796, and Johnson re-married in December, 1800. His second wife was Mrs. Mary Beach, the widow of his first wife's brother. A severe case of palsy forced Johnson to give up letter writing, so there is little information available about his late years. At the age of ninety-two, he died on November 14, 1819, in Stratford.

RUFUS KING of MASSACHUSETTS

Rufus King helped write the United States Constitution, and served in public office under the first six Presidents of the United States as a Senator and as a diplomat, devoting a span of more than forty years to his country's service. A staunch Federalist, he was twice that party's unsuccessful candidate for vice president and once for president. Strongly opposed to slavery, he introduced the measure in the Congress of Confederation that forbade slavery in the new states of the Northwest Territory, and thirty-five years later he opposed the Missouri Compromise that permitted Missouri to join the Union as a slave state.

In recommending to President George Washington that he appoint King as United States Minister to England in 1796, Alexander Hamilton wrote:

"Mr. King is a remarkably well informed man, a very judicious one, a man of address, a man of fortune and economy, whose situation affords just ground of confidence; a man of unimpeached probity where he is known, a firm friend to the government, a supporter of the measures of the President; a man who cannot but feel that he has strong pretensions to confidence and trust."

Courtesy: Yale University Art Gallery.

Rufus King

By John Trumbull

A Harvard graduate

Rufus King was born on March 24, 1755, in Scarboro, Massachusetts (now in Maine). He was the son of a well-to-do merchant. After attending a preparatory school at Newburyport, Mass., he was sent to Harvard College at the age of eighteen. His education was briefly interrupted when the outbreak of the Revolutionary War closed Harvard, but when the institution reopened in 1777, he returned and received his degree.

After serving briefly in the war of 1778 as an aide to Brigadier General John Glover in the Continental Army's unsuccessful attempt to take Rhode Island from the British occupation forces, King began the study of law under Theophilus Parsons, who later became chief justice of Massachusetts. At the age of twenty-five, King was admitted to the bar and began practicing law in Newburyport. His first case in court is said to have been one in which his opposing counsel was Parsons, but King made such a good showing as an orator that he quickly rose to local prominence in his profession.

RUFUS KING

1755 (March 24) Born in Scarboro, Massachusetts (now Maine).

1777 Graduated from Harvard College.

1778 Served as an aide to General John Glover in the attempt to recapture Rhode Island from the British.

1780 Admitted to the bar to practice law.

1784 Elected to the Massachusetts legislature.

1784-1787 Delegate from Massachusetts to the Congress of the Confederation.

1787 Delegate from Massachusetts to the Constitutional Convention; signed the United States Constitution.

1789 Elected to the New York legislature.

1789-1796 United States Senator from New York.

1794 Wrote a series of essays with Alexander Hamilton defending the Jay Treaty with Great Britain.

1796-1803 United States Minister to Great Britain.

1804, 1808 Federalist party candidate for Vice President of the United States.

1813-1825 United States Senator from New York.

1816 Federalist party candidate for President of the United States.

1825-1826 United States Minister to Great Britain.

1827 (April 29) Died in Jamaica, New York.

Introduced resolution forbidding slavery in Northwest Territory

In 1784, King was elected to the Massachusetts legislature, and that same year was chosen to represent his state in the Congress of the Confederation. He never again returned to the practice of law. On March 16, 1785, he introduced in Congress a resolution forbidding slavery in any new states to be formed northwest of Ohio, a proposal that Thomas Jefferson had also made at an earlier date. This provision was incorporated in the Northwest Ordinance that King helped draft, and that was approved by Congress in 1787.

King was elected by the Massachusetts legislature in 1787 to represent the state at the Constitutional Convention in Philadelphia. He was described at this time by a contemporary writer: "He was an uncommonly handsome man, in face and form; he had a powerful mind, well cultivated, and was a dignified and graceful speaker. He had the appearance of one who was a gentleman by nature, and who had well improved all her gifts. It is a rare occurrence to see a finer assemblage of personal and intellectual qualities, cultivated to best effect, than were seen in this gentleman."

Favored a strong national government

King took his seat at the opening of the Constitutional Convention on May 25, 1787, and remained all summer, taking a lively part in the debates. He favored establishing a strong national government, and explained his position in a speech on June 19, as reported by James Madison:

"He conceived that the import of the term 'States,' 'sovereignty,' 'national,' and 'federal,' had been often used and implied in the discussions

View of Niagara Falls (From an early drawing)

Library of Congress.

Courtesy: The Long Island Historical Society.

Mrs. Rufus (Mary) King

inaccurately and delusively. The States were not "sovereigns" in the sense contended for by some. They did not possess the peculiar features of sovereignty, – they could not make war, nor peace, nor alliances, nor treaties. Considering them as political beings, they were dumb, for they could not speak to any foreign sovereign whatever. They were deaf, for they could not hear any propositions from such sovereign. They had not even the organs or faculties of defence or offence, for they could not of themselves raise troops or equip vessels, for war. On the other side, if the union of the States comprises the idea of a confederation, it comprises that also of consolidation. A union of the States is a union of the men composing them, from whence a national character results to the whole. Congress can act alone without the States; they can act, and their acts will be binding, against the instructions of the States. If they declare war, war is *de jure* declared; captures made in pursuance of it are lawful; no acts of the States can vary the situation or prevent the judicial consequences. If the States, therefore, retained some portion of their sovereignty, they had certainly divested themselves of essential portions of it. If they formed a confederacy in some respects, they formed a nation in others. The Convention could clearly deliberate on and propose any alterations that Congress could have done under the Federal Articles. And could not Congress propose, by virtue of the last Article, a change in any article whatever,–and as well that relating to the equality of suffrage, as any other? He made these remarks to obviate some scruples which had been expressed. He doubted much the practicability of annihilating the States; but thought that much of their power ought to be taken from them."

Spokesman for the northern states

Throughout the Convention, King was a spokesman for the large northern states. He frequently pointed out that although much was said about the division of interests between the large and the small states, in his opinion the country really divided between North and South. He opposed permitting the importation of slaves to continue, particularly if Congress did not have the power to tax the products of slave labor that were exported. Concerning slavery, he said, "The admission of slaves was a most grating circumstance to his mind, and he believed would be so to a great part of the people of America."

King made the last motion of the Convention on September 17, just before the United States Constitution was signed by himself and most of the other delegates. He proposed that the journals of the Convention be deposited with the President for safekeeping, because a "bad use" of them might be made in the ensuing public debates on ratification. The Convention approved his motion. After the signing, King went to New York, where the Congress of the Confederation was meeting, and helped vote approval of the Constitution and the forwarding of it to the states for ratification.

When the Massachusetts ratification convention was held in 1788, King was elected a member from Newburyport. He fought for the Constitution and helped obtain its ratification–by the close vote of 187 to 168.

When the Massachusetts legislature met in the fall of 1788 to elect the state's first United States senators, King was ruled as ineligible for the office on the basis that he was not a resident of the state. In 1786 he had married sixteen-year-old Mary Alsop, the only child of a wealthy New York merchant, and, although King had authorized a friend to purchase him a house in Boston, he and his wife had made New York their residence.

Elected to the U. S. Senate by New York

Angered over his treatment by the Massachusetts legislators, King ran for office in New York and was elected to the state legislature there in 1789. A special session of the legislature was called in July, 1789, to elect New York's Senators, and King was one of those elected, defeating Lewis Morris, the signer of the Declaration of Independence. He took his seat in the United States Senate on July 16, 1789.

As an ardent Federalist, King worked closely with Alexander Hamilton in supporting his measures in the new Congress. When the controversial Jay Treaty was signed, he and Hamilton appeared before a public meeting in New York to explain the provisions of the treaty with Great Britain, but they were shouted down by an angry crowd. They then co-authored a series of newspaper articles called "Essays on the Treaty" over the signature "Camillus." King was re-elected to the Senate in 1795, but he resigned the next year to accept an appointment by George Washington as U.S. Minister to England.

Minister to England under Washington and Adams

King served for seven years in England, during the last years of Washington's second term, throughout John Adams' administration, and during the first years of Thomas Jefferson's administration. These were times of great crisis in which Great Britain and France were at war, and the United States was endeavoring to maintain its neutrality and prevent the impressment of American seamen into the service of the British navy.

Upon the termination of his ambassadorship in 1803, King returned to find the United States much changed. When he left, the Federalists had been firmly in control of both the national and state government. But now Washington was dead, John Adams was in retirement, and Jefferson's Democratic-Republican party dominated the political scene. King purchased a farm on Long Island, near Jamaica, and retired there with his family. One of his sons, Charles King, later wrote of this period of his father's retirement:

"Mr. King possessed, in a remarkable degree, all the tastes that fit one for the enjoyment of country life. He had a large and well selected library, particularly rich in its books relating to the Americas . . . With these true, tried, unwavering and unwearying friends—and such good books are —Mr. King spent much time; varying, however, his studious labors with out-door exercise on horseback, to which he was much addicted; and in judgment of the qualities, as well as in the graceful management of a horse, he was rarely excelled. He loved, too, his gun and dog; was rather a keen sportsman and good shot; though often, when the pointer was hot upon the game, his master's attention would be diverted by some rare or beautiful shrub or flower upon which his eye happened to light, and of which—if not the proper season for transplanting it into his border—he would carefully mark the place, and make a memorandum thereof, so as to be enabled to return at the fitting time and secure his prize. . . ."

Twice the unsuccessful vice presidential candidate

During his ten years of retirement from public office, King was twice the unsuccessful vice presidential candidate of the Federalist party, both times as the running mate of Charles Cotesworth Pinckney of South Carolina, a fellow-signer of the Constitution. In the election of 1804, in which the Pinckney-King ticket ran against Thomas Jefferson and George Clinton of New York, he received only 14 electoral votes—those of Connecticut, Delaware, and two of Maryland's votes. In the election of 1808, in which the Pinckney-King ticket ran against James Madison and Clinton, they won 47 out of 175 electoral votes, carrying the states of New Hampshire, Massachusetts, Rhode Island, Connecticut, and Delaware.

When the nation was plunged into the War of 1812, King offered his services to his country. Martin Van Buren, then a state senator in New York, later described King's action:

"At this momentous crisis, which applied the touchstone to the hearts of men, when many of the stoutest were appalled, and the weak despaired of the republic, Mr. King was neither idle nor dismayed. His love of country dispelled his attachments to party. In terms of the warmest solicitude and in strains of the most impassioned eloquence, he remonstrated in his correspondence with the leaders of the opposition in this state and in the east, on the folly, the madness, and the mischief of their course; he contributed largely of his means to the loans to government; he infused confidence into the desponding, and labored to divest the timid of their fears . . ."

Again elected to the U. S. Senate

The legislature of New York elected King to the United States Senate in 1813. Three years later he campaigned as the Federalist candidate for president against James Monroe of the Democratic-Republican party. But King was heavily defeated, winning only 34 out of 217 electoral votes, and carrying only the states of Massachusetts, Connecticut, and Delaware.

When King's six-year term as Senator was completed in 1819, the New York legislature fell into such disagreement over his re-election that the Senate seat was vacated for a year, and he was not re-elected until 1820. King strongly fought Missouri's admission as a slave-holding state in 1821, and insisted on a provision that the Missouri legislature could not take away the constitutional rights of Negro citizens in the state. Thomas Hart Benton, a new Senator from Missouri, described King at this period:

"Mr. King had his individuality of character, manners, and dress . . . a high model of courtly refinement. He always appeared in the Senate in full dress; short small clothes, silk stockings, and shoes, and was habitually observant of all the courtesies of life. His colleague in the Senate, during the chief time that I saw him there, was Mr. Van Buren: and it was singular to see a great State represented in the Senate at the same time by the chiefs of opposite political parties; Mr. Van Buren was much the younger, and it was delightful to behold the deferential regard which he paid to his elder colleague, always returned with marked kindness and respect."

Served as Minister to England under John Q. Adams

After John Quincy Adams became President in 1825, Adams persuaded the seventy-year-old King to accept appointment as U.S. Minister to Great Britain, the same diplomatic position he had held under Adams's father, John Adams, some twenty-five years earlier. King was well received in London, but after a few months he became ill and asked to be relieved of his duties. He returned to the United States, and on April 29, 1827, the seventy-two-year-old King died at his farm on Long Island.

Courtesy: The Long Island Historical Society.

King Manor, Jamaica

New York Public Library. Photo by Francis G. Mayer.

The First Methodist Episcopal Church in America

This building was erected in 1768, on Golden Hill, now John Street, City of New York.

Library of Congress. Atlantic Neptune.

Boston Harbor

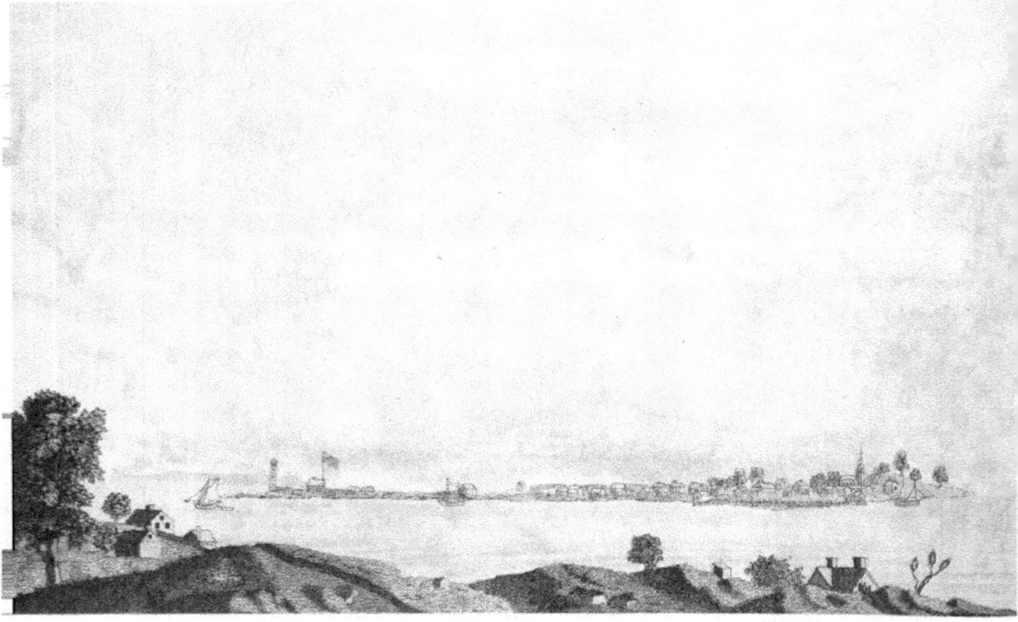
Library of Congress. Atlantic Neptune.

View of Newcastle, New Hampshire, on the Piscataqua River

JOHN LANGDON of NEW HAMPSHIRE

The richest man in one of the poorest states, John Langdon distinguished himself for his patriotism, generosity, and liberalism, in more than thirty-five years service to his state and to the nation. In 1774, more than four months before the Battles of Lexington and Concord, Langdon roused the patriots of New Hampshire to seize 100 barrels of powder from the royal fort in Portsmouth harbor. He helped build John Paul Jones' *Ranger*, the first American warship to fly the United States Flag. He financed with his own funds the raising of New Hampshire troops in 1777, then went with them to fight at the Battles of Bennington and Saratoga. When New Hampshire could not provide the money to send a representative to attend the Constitutional Convention, Langdon paid all the expenses for himself and his fellow delegate Nicholas Gilman so that New Hampshire's voice would be heard in Philadelphia. As the first president *pro tempore* of the United States Senate, he counted the first electoral votes and informed George Washington of his election as President of the United States. He served many years as a U. S. senator and then as governor of his state, declining a post in Thomas Jefferson's cabinet and refusing the candidacy for vice president under James Madison. In writing of Langdon, Madison said:

JOHN LANGDON

1741 (June 25) Born in Portsmouth, N. H.

1774 (Dec. 14) Helped lead seizure of powder from British Fort William and Mary in Portsmouth, N. H.

1775-1782 Member of New Hampshire legislature; speaker of house of representatives from 1776-1781.

1775-1776 Delegate from New Hampshire to the Continental Congress.

1776 Appointed agent of Continental Congress for building warships in New Hampshire.

1777-1778 Served as an officer in the militia at the Battles of Bennington and Saratoga and in the attempt to recapture Rhode Island.

1785-1786 President of New Hampshire.

1787 Delegate to the Continental Congress and to the Constitutional Convention; signed the United States Constitution.

1788-1789 President of New Hampshire.

1789-1801 United States Senator from New Hampshire; president pro tempore of the U. S. Senate from 1789-1793.

1801-1805 Member of New Hampshire legislature; speaker of the house of representatives from 1804-1805.

1805-1809; 1810-1812 Governor of New Hampshire.

1819 (Sept. 18) Died in Portsmouth, N. H.

Independence National Historical Park Collection.
JOHN LANGDON
Attributed to James Sharples, Sr.

"He was a true patriot and a good man, with a noble way of thinking and a frankness and warmth of heart that made his friends love him much, as it did me in a high degree, and disarmed his enemies of some of the asperities indulged toward others."

Was from a fifth generation American family

John Langdon was born in Portsmouth, N. H., on June 25, 1741. His ancestors had come to America five generations earlier, and the family included many honest farmers and hardworking sailors. The youngest son in a family of six children, young John received a grammar school education, and then was apprenticed as a clerk to a merchant by the name of Daniel Rindge.

After completing his apprenticeship, he went to sea as a supercargo. An ambitious youth, he invested his money in trading goods, and soon was able to go into business for himself. As his business prospered, he also became a shipbuilder as well as a merchant. He married Elizabeth Sherburne, and they settled down in one of the most substantial homes in Portsmouth. By the time of

Essex Institute.

Home of Governor John Langdon

the Revolutionary War, the 33-year-old Langdon was reputed to be the wealthiest merchant of New Hampshire.

Helped take gunpowder from a British fort

On December 13, 1774, word reached the committee of correspondence in Portsmouth that the British had forbidden the export of gunpowder, and that they were going to send a warship to protect the supply of powder at Fort William and Mary in Portsmouth harbor. The next day, Langdon and John Sullivan led about four hundred men to the fort, overpowered the British soldiers, captured 100 barrels of powder and other supplies, and carried them away for safekeeping. Word of this daring act of rebellion spread throughout the colonies, and made Langdon one of the leaders of the patriotic movement in his state.

In the spring of 1775, Langdon served briefly in the last session of the colonial legislature until it was dissolved and the royal governor fled aboard a British warship. Then he and Sullivan were elected by a provincial patriotic convention as delegates to the Continental Congress in Philadelphia. After reaching Philadelphia, Sullivan was chosen as one of the brigadier generals for the Continental Army, while Langdon remained to represent New Hampshire.

Built the first U. S. Warship, **The Ranger**

Because of Langdon's knowledge of shipbuilding, he was appointed by the Continental Congress as an agent for marine to build and outfit warships for a Continental Navy. Among the ships he built was the *Ranger*, an 18-gun warship that Langdon turned over to Captain Paul Jones in June, 1777. The Ranger carried the first United States Flag on an American warship.

When Langdon was re-elected to Congress in January, 1776, he was so occupied with his efforts to build a navy that he wrote to the New Hampshire legislators:

"Nothing can give greater satisfaction than to have the approbation of your Honorable House of having done my duty as far as my poor abilities would admit of. I think myself under every tie of

Honour and Gratitude to strain every nerve in my Country's cause at this important day, more especially when I receive such repeated honour from my Country. When I shall have finished the business in which I have the honour to be immediately employed by the Continent, or have it in such forwardness to leave, I shall attend in my place at the General Congress where it will be my greatest pride to serve in any way that may be in my power, this Colony in particular and the Continent in general. I lament that my abilities are not greater. All I can say is, I shall employ such as I have (to the utmost) in the service of my Country."

Helped finance the army at the Battle of Saratoga

Langdon was elected speaker of the house of representatives in the state legislature in December, 1776, and continued to hold that office for the next five years. In this capacity, Langdon performed one of the most dramatic acts of his career in the summer of 1777 when word reached New Hampshire that British General John Burgoyne was leading an army south from Canada down Lake Champlain to attack New England. The militia was called out, but at a meeting of the state legislature it was discovered that there was no money in the treasury to purchase necessary supplies for the troops. At this point, Langdon volunteered to finance the project, saying:

"I have a thousand dollars in hard money. I will pledge my plate for three thousand more. I have seventy hogsheads of Tobago rum, which will be sold for the most they will bring. They are at the service of the state. If we succeed in defending our firesides and our homes, I may be remunerated; if we do not, then the property will be of no value to me. Our friend Stark who so nobly maintained the honor of our state at Bunker Hill may safely be entrusted with the enterprise and we will check the progress of Burgoyne."

Not content with merely providing money and supplies, Langdon took his musket and joined the New Hampshiremen as a captain at the Battle of Bennington in August, 1777, and at the decisive victory over Burgoyne at Saratoga in October, 1777. He later served as a colonel under Sullivan in the attempt to recapture Rhode Island from the British.

Offered to finance trip to Philadelphia

The legislature elected Langdon as president of New Hampshire in 1785, but after serving for a year he was defeated for re-election by Sullivan. Like all the other colonies, New Hampshire suffered from the inflation brought on by the war, and when the Constitutional Convention was called in 1787, the New Hampshire treasury was so poor that there was no money to send delegates to the meeting. Again rising to the occasion, Langdon offered to pay his own way and that of Nicholas Gilman. Both were also elected to the Congress of the Confederation, meeting in New York City.

Because of the delay caused by New Hampshire's financial plight, Langdon and Gilman were a month late arriving in Philadelphia, taking their seats in the Constitutional Convention on Monday, June 23, 1787. Langdon repeatedly interjected his practical New England point of view

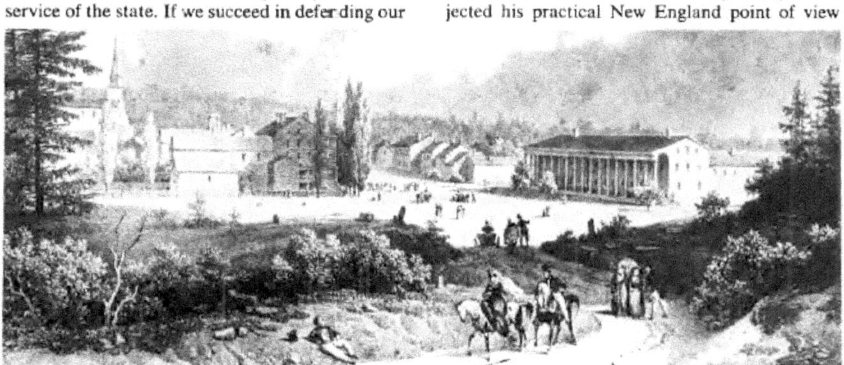

The I. N. Phelps Stokes Collection of American Historical Prints, New York Public Library.

The Plains of Saratoga, New York

into the ensuing debates. When it was proposed that under the new Constitution the states should pay the members of Congress, he pointed out the inequity of distant states, such as New Hampshire, having to pay greater travel expenses than states near to the national capital. In the discussion as to whether the Congress should have the right to issue paper money, Langdon spoke out sharply to say that he would "rather reject the whole plan, than to retain the three words, 'and emit bills.' " When it looked for a time as though taxes would be collected from each state in proportion to the number of representatives it was allocated in Congress, Langdon said this "would bear unreasonably hard on New Hampshire" and he pointed out that he "was not here when New Hampshire was allowed three members. It was more than her share; he did not wish for them." Several times he expressed amazement at the continual arguments over whether the national government would be taking over the rights of states governments, and discussing this matter late in August he said:

"The General and State Governments are not enemies to each other, but different institutions for the good of the people of America. As one of the people, I can say, the National Government is mine, the State Government is mine. In transferring power from one to the other, I only take out of my left hand what it cannot so well use, and put it into my right hand where it can be better used."

Helped persuade the state legislature to ratify

After signing the Constitution on September 17, 1787, Langdon and Gilman traveled to the meeting of the Congress of the Confederation in New York City, where they voted to send the new Constitution to the states for ratification. When the New Hampshire ratification convention met in February, 1788, Langdon wrote to George Washington that "a small majority of (say, four) persons appeared against the system." Rather than risk having the state convention turn down the Constitution, Langdon succeeded in having the convention adjourned until June, and in the interval, he and other Federalists succeeded in convincing enough members of the opposition to cre-

The I. N. Phelps Stokes Collection of American Historical Prints, New York Public Library.

White Hall on Lake Champlain

ate a majority in favor of ratification. As a result New Hampshire became the ninth state to ratify the Constitution, the necessary number to place the new government into operation.

Langdon again was elected president of New Hampshire in 1788, and he also was elected by the legislature to serve as one of the first Senators in the new Congress. He resigned as president of the state in January, 1789, and left for New York the next month. A newspaper of the day reported of his journey:

"His excellency was escorted as far as Greenland (where a collation was provided) by a number of respectable gentlemen, citizens of this town." The article went on to say that bad weather kept others from paying "that respect, on his quitting the town, which has exertions in that cause of freedom and good government, so justly entitled him to receive."

Elected president of Congress

Only seven other Senators were present with Langdon when Congress was supposed to convene on March 4, 1789. They waited until a quorum finally gathered on April 6, and then elected Langdon as president for the "sole purpose of opening and counting the votes for President of the United States." Before both house of Congress, Langdon personally opened the electoral votes, counted them, and declared George Washington elected as President and John Adams elected as vice president. The Senate then elected Langdon president *pro tempore*. Langdon sent the following notification to Washington:

"*Be it Known*, That the Senate and House of Representatives of the United States of America, being convened in the City and State of New York, the sixth day of April, in the year of our Lord one thousand seven hundred and eighty-nine, the underwritten appointed President of the Senate for the sole purpose of receiving, opening, and counting the votes of the electors, did, in the presence of the said Senate and House of Representatives, open all the certificates and count all the votes of the Electors for a President and for a vice president; by which it appears that George Washington, esquire, was unanimously elected, agreeably to the Constitution, to the office of President of the United States of America.

"In testimony whereof I have hereunto set my hand and seal."

John Langdon

The I. N. Phelps Stokes Collection of American Historical Prints, New York Public Library.

Northwest view of The Citadel at Halifax (c. 1781)

A follower of the policies of Thomas Jefferson

As a Senator, Langdon became one of the Democratic-Republican followers of Thomas Jefferson, voting against the policies of Washington, Adams, and Alexander Hamilton. Langdon served twelve years in the Senate, until Jefferson became President in 1801. He declined Jefferson's offer of appointment as Secretary of the Navy, in order to return to New Hampshire, where he was elected to the state legislature.

New Hampshire had been under the control of the Federalist party since 1794, and Langdon now set about building a strong Democratic-Republican party in the state. That he was successful is testified by his election as speaker of the house of representatives in 1804 and as governor in 1805.

Langdon was re-elected annually as governor from 1805 to 1812, except for one year, 1809, when he was defeated by the Federalist candidate Jeremiah Smith. In the presidential election of 1808, Langdon received nine Democratic-Republican electoral votes for vice president–those of Vermont and Ohio. In the presidential election of 1812, he was offered the Democratic-Republican candidacy as vice president on the ticket with James Madison, but he declined the honor.

Retiring from office in 1812, Langdon spent his old age in the enjoyment of his family in Portsmouth. He died there at the age of seventy-eight on September 18, 1819.

New York Public Library, Prints Division. Engraving by Sidney L. Smith.

A View of Wall Street, New York, Trinity Church, and the First Presbyterian Church. (c. 1825)

WILLIAM LIVINGSTON of NEW JERSEY

A member of the rich and powerful Livingston family of New York, William Livingston made his fortune as a successful New York City lawyer and won fame as a writer of liberal political essays. At the age of 49, he retired to New Jersey to enjoy the life of a country gentleman; but the coming of the Revolutionary War called him into service, first as a delegate to the Continental Congress, second as commander of the New Jersey militia, and finally for fourteen years as the first governor of the state of New Jersey. Describing himself as "a long-nosed, long-chinned, ugly-looking fellow," Livingston won the nickname of "Doctor Flint" as he courageously led his war-torn state through the Revolutionary War. After the war, he attended the Constitutional Convention, signed the United States Constitution, and urged his state to early ratification of the Constitution.

William Livingston was born at Albany, N. Y., in November, 1723, apparently on about the last day of the month. He was the fifth of nine children of Philip and Catharine Van Brugh Livingston. His father was a wealthy landowner whose estate south of Albany stretched from the Hudson River to the Massachusetts border.

WILLIAM LIVINGSTON

1723 (Nov. 30?) Born at Albany, N. Y.

1741 Graduated from Yale College.

1748 Admitted to the bar to practice law in New York City.

1752-1753 Published The Independent Reflector, a weekly newspaper of political comment.

1754 Appointed to board of governors of King's College (now Columbia University), but he refused to serve because he believed the Episcopalian Church was given too much power in the founding of the college.

1754-1755 Wrote and edited a series of essays called "The Watch Tower."

1765 Wrote a series of essays called "The Sentinel."

1768-1769 Wrote essays under the title "The American Whig."

1770 Elected president of The Moot, a New York lawyer's club.

1772 Retired from the practice of the law and moved to a country estate near Elizabethtown, N. J.

1774-1776 Delegate from New Jersey to the Continental Congress.

1776 Brigadier general in command of New Jersey militia.

1776-1790 First state governor of New Jersey.

1787 Delegate from New Jersey to the Constitutional Convention; signed the United States Constitution.

1790 (July 25) Died at Elizabethtown, N. J.

Spent a year among the Mohawks

While still a boy, Livingston had the unusual experience of living with the Mohawk Indians for a year. As he described the adventure in a letter written several years later, he said, "I spent a year among the Mohawks, with a missionary of the Society for propagating the Gospel, under whom I then studied their language, and had a good opportunity to learn the genius and manners of the natives."

At the age of thirteen, Livingston was sent to Yale College at New Haven, Conn. The boy is said to have wanted to go to Italy to study painting and become an artist, but his parents persuaded him that he should prepare for a career as a lawyer. In 1741, the seventeen-year-old Livingston was graduated from Yale at the head of his class. He could read and write fluently in Greek, Latin, French, and Dutch, as well as English.

William Livingston
Governor of New Jersey
The Long Island Historical Society.

New York Public Library.

Greenwich and Dey Streets in New York (1810)

Ambitious to be an author

After graduation, Livingston went to New York City where two of his older brothers already were successful merchants; and there he became the indentured clerk of James Alexander, a prominent attorney. Soon, however, Livingston's desire to become a writer interfered with his law studies. He wrote a play in 1744 that he described in a letter to a friend by saying "kissing constitutes a great part of its entertainment." He followed this play with two essays in a newspaper in which he criticized eminent lawyers who neglected to teach law to their clerks. Livingston's mentor, Alexander, took offense at the essays, and terminated the youth's clerkship. As a result, Livingston entered the law office of William Smith, the attorney general of the state; but he continued his writing, publishing in 1747 a 700-line poem entitled "Philosophic Solitude, or the Choice of Rural Life. A Poem by a Gentleman educated at Yale College." At the age of twenty-five, Livingston completed his law studies and was admitted to the bar on October 14, 1748.

While still a law clerk, Livingston married Susanna "Surkey" French, the daughter of a prominent New Jersey family. In their forty-four years of marriage they had thirteen children. One of his sons, Brockholst Livingston, later became an associate justice of the Supreme Court of the United States; and one of his daughters, Sarah Van Brugh Livingston, married John Jay, who became Chief Justice of the United States. Livingston's youngest son, John Lawrence Livingston, died during the Revolutionary War while serving as a midshipman aboard the warship *Saratoga*.

Wrote articles critical of the church

Livingston rose rapidly in the legal profession in New York City and at the same time became known as a writer on controversial subjects. In 1752, Livingston and his close friend William Smith, Jr., were appointed by the colonial legislature to compile and publish all the colony's laws that had been passed between 1691 and 1751. On November 30, 1752, Livingston began publishing a weekly periodical called *The Independent Reflector*. Many of his essays in this periodical were critical of efforts by the Episcopalian Church to control a new college for which money was being raised by lotteries. Livingston, a Presbyterian, saw these moves by the Episcopalians as the forerunner of an effort to establish the Episcopalian Church as the official religion in the colony. The printer refused to continue publication of Livingston's essays in November, 1753, after the mayor of New York recommended that the grand jury investigate *The Independent Reflector* for libel. Livingston later had this to say of these essays:

"A mighty clamour was raised against me under

pretence that I transgressed the bounds of my design, in writing against the Church of England. Of the falsity of this charge, whoever reads my weekly productions with an unprejudiced mind will be easily convinced. But to say something in vindication of myself:—I do declare that I never wrote a syllable with a view of censuring the church as such: I have only exposed her unreasonable encroachments. When one religious persuasion, in defiance of the equal rights of the rest, and in contradiction to the plain dictates of law and reason, openly advances a claim destructive of those rights; to sit as a calm and unconcerned spectator would, in a writer of my class, have been a treasonable neglect of the interest of the community. At this conduct indeed I took the alarm: it was my duty, my bounden, my indispensable duty."

When King's College (now Columbia University) was finally chartered in 1754, Livingston was named as one of the board of governors, apparently in an effort to silence his opposition. However, the majority of the board was made up of Episcopalians, so Livingston refused to accept the office, explaining: "As I could not conscientiously take the oaths of office, I never frequented their meetings."

Livingston again wrote weekly essays in 1754 to 1755 under the title of "The Watch Tower." In 1757, he published a pamphlet in London entitled "A Review of the Military Operations in North America from the commencement of French hostilities, on the frontiers of Virginia in 1753, to the surrender of Oswego, on the 14th of April, 1756." Among his other writings of this period, Livingston wrote a love poem to a young lady called Eliza.

A Whig liberal

Livingston served in a political office for the first time from 1758 to 1760 as a member of the colonial legislature of New York. His brother, Philip Livingston also was elected as a member of this legislature. The Livingston brothers became leaders of the Whig party, representing the liberal views of the colonists and opposing abuses by the British administrators.

In 1765, Livingston resumed publication of weekly essays, this time calling them "The Senti-

Library of Congress, Magazine of American History.

Liberty Hall
Residence of Governor Livingston, Elizabethtown, N. J.

New York Public Library. I. N. Phelps Stokes Collection.

The "Clermont" Making a Landing at Cornwall on the Hudson (1810)

nel." These essays ceased suddenly as the dispute over the Stamp Act heated the tempers of the people. Although no records confirm it, a general belief arose that Livingston was devoting his time to the organization of the Sons of Liberty, a secret patriotic organization that violently opposed the Stamp Act and later British tyrannies.

The Episcopalian Church began an active campaign in 1767 to send bishops to the colonies and to establish the Church of England as the official religion. Livingston leaped to the attack. His essays appeared under the title of "The American Whig" in the *New York Gazette*, and he encouraged the establishment of similar papers in Boston and Philadelphia to fight the issue. In a letter he wrote in 1768, Livingston clearly explained his position:

"As this country is good enough for me, and I have no notion of removing to Scotland, whence my ancestors were banished by this set of men, I cannot without terror reflect on a bishop's setting his foot on this continent."

In 1770, Livingston was elected president of The Moot, a newly established club of leading New York lawyers. Among the members of this club were John Jay and Gouverneur Morris, both of whom played important roles in the later establishment of the United States.

Decided to retire at forty-nine

At the age of forty-nine, Livingston decided to retire, having accumulated a fortune of more than eight thousand pounds. It is believed that he was disgusted with the political administration of New York, and this was what led him to purchase an estate of about 120 acres near Elizabethtown, N. J. He and his family moved to Elizabethtown in May, 1772, and the next year he completed a mansion that he called "Liberty Hall."

Shortly after Livingston moved to New Jersey, a homeless sixteen-year-old boy came to his door, bringing with him letters of introduction from a Presbyterian minister in the West Indies, where the boy had been born. Livingston put the boy in school in Elizabethtown and later sent him to King's College in New York. This act of kindness had an important effect on American history, because the boy was Alexander Hamilton.

When the British closed the port of Boston in

1774 in retaliation against the "Boston Tea Party," a committee of correspondence was formed in Newark, N. J., with Livingston as a member. Shortly afterward he was elected as one of the New Jersey delegates to attend the first Continental Congress. Livingston did not take a prominent part in the Congress, and apparently was one of the majority who believed that appeals to the reason of the British government could solve the difficulties. Several years later in describing his feelings about this Congress, Livingston revealed his own views of the times:

"I had not, sir, been in Congress a fortnight before I discovered that parties were forming, and that some members had come to that assembly with views altogether different from what America professed to have, and that, bating a designing junto, she really had. Of these men, her independency upon Great Britain at all events was the most favourite project. By these the pulse of the rest was felt on every favourable occasion, and often upon no occasion at all; and by these men measures were concerted to produce what we all professed to deprecate; nay, at the very time that we universally invoked the Majesty of Heaven to witness the purity of our hearts, I had reason to believe that the hearts of many of us gave our invocation the lie . . . I cannot entertain the most favourable opinion of a man's veracity, who intended to do it [declare independence] when he swore he did not, and when he represented a people who were actually pursuing measures to prevent the necessity of doing it."

Livingston also served in the second Continental Congress of 1775 to 1776. Although he served on nearly a dozen committees, his activities were overshadowed by those of the more prominent delegates from Virginia and Massachusetts. In June, 1776, as the Congress was moving closer to declaring the colonies independent of Great Britain, Livingston left Philadelphia to take command of the New Jersey militia, having been commissioned a brigadier general the previous December. Some persons, including John Adams, felt that his departure indicated opposition to the Declaration of Independence, although his brother Philip, a delegate from New York, signed it.

Deprecated his military abilities

Because New Jersey feared an invasion by sea by the British, General Livingston began gathering the militia and constructing defenses at Elizabethtown. He wrote to a friend of his military activities in August, 1776:

"You would really be astonished to see how grand I look, while at the same time I can assure you I was never more sensible (to use a New England phrase) of my own *nothingness* in military affairs . . . My ancient corporeal fabric is almost tottering under the fatigue I have lately undergone: constantly rising at 2 o'clock in the morning to examine our lines . . ."

The New Jersey legislature had jailed the royal governor, William Franklin, the natural son of Benjamin Franklin and, unlike his father, a dedicated loyalist. Now, on August 31, 1776, the legislature elected Livingston as the state's first governor—an office he was to hold for the next fourteen years. In his first speech to the legislature, Livingston won the nickname "Doctor Flint" because he exhorted the legislators and state officials to provide an example for the citizenry by "setting our faces . . . like a flint against that dissoluteness of manners and political corruption which will ever be the reproach of any people."

A reward for his capture

Livingston's task as governor of New Jersey was not an easy one, because the state lay strategically between two main objects of British attack —New York City and Philadelphia. British troops poured into New Jersey shortly after Livingston took office, and he and the legislature fled from town to town with the redcoats in pursuit. The British offered a reward for Livingston's capture, and throughout the war he had many narrow escapes from being taken prisoner. He received word that his home in Elizabethtown had been partly burned and that "the very hinges, locks, and panes of glass, are taken away."

Throughout the war Livingston continued to write. Most of his essays appeared in the *New Jersey Gazette*. Many were satirical, and others were appeals to patriotism. In 1778, he published a long poem in honor of George Washington that said in part:

"Thy worth unequalled, thy heroic deeds,
Thy patriot virtues, and high-soaring fame
Prompt irresistibly my feeble arm
To grasp the long-forgotten lyre, and join
The universal chorus of thy praise."

Favored abolition of slavery

Livingston was an early advocate of the aboli-

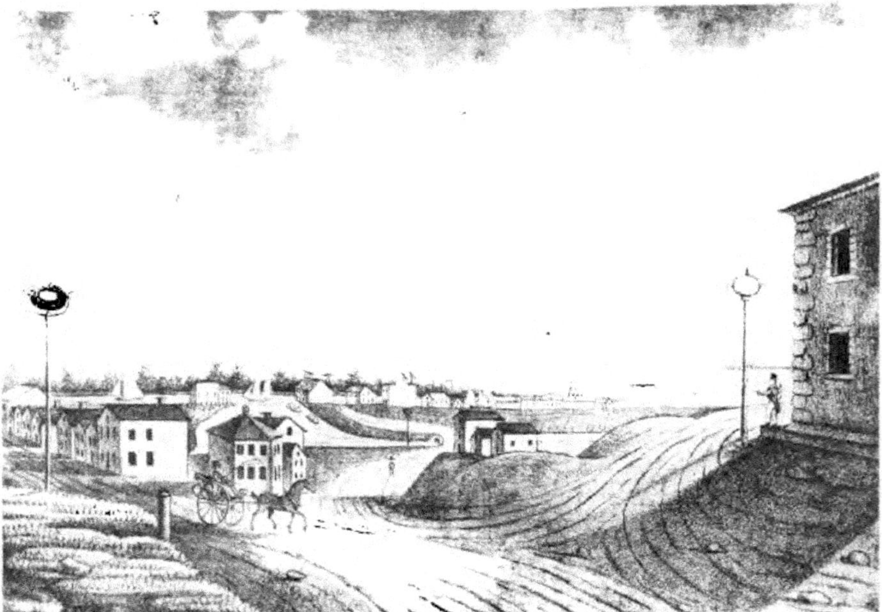

The I. N. Phelps Stokes Collection of American Historical Prints, New York Public Library.

Buffalo Harbor from the village

tion of slavery. Although he owned two slaves in 1778, he wrote that he believed slavery was "utterly inconsistent with the principles of Christianity and humanity, and in Americans, who have almost idolized liberty, peculiarly odious and disgraceful." Eight years later, in 1786, Livingston joined the New York anti-slavery society and freed his two slaves. In March, 1786, he succeeded in having the New Jersey legislature forbid the importation of slaves into the state.

At the age of sixty-three, Livingston was chosen as one of New Jersey's delegates to the Constitutional Convention of 1787. Because of his duties as governor, he did not attend the full meeting of the convention; but he devoted as much time to attending the convention as was possible. Livingston strongly supported the position of the small states in demanding equal representation in the Senate, but he did not take much part in the debates. After signing the United States Constitution in September, Livingston returned to New Jersey and supported its ratification as an ardent Federalist.

Livingston continued to hold office as governor of New Jersey until his death. He received a cherished honor in 1788 when Yale College granted him an honorary degree of doctor of laws; but he received a blow the next year when his beloved wife died after a long illness. He became ill in June, 1790, with pains in his chest and a severe cough that confined him to his home. At the age of sixty-six, Livingston died in Elizabethtown on July 25, 1790.

JAMES MADISON of VIRGINIA

As the "Father of the Constitution" at the age of thirty-six, James Madison helped draft the "Virginia Plan" that laid the groundwork for the United States Constitution, worked tirelessly guiding the debates in the Constitutional Convention, and then helped win ratification by writing many of *The Federalist* essays and by taking part in the Virginia ratification convention. Later, as a Congressman, he wrote and helped push through to adoption the Bill of Rights amendments to the Constitution. A fellow-delegate to the Convention, William Pierce of Georgia, said that what was "very remarkable" about Madison was that "every Person seems to acknowledge his greatness." Pierce further explained why Madison was so effective at the Convention: "He blends together the profound politician, with the scholar. In the management of every great question he evidently took the lead in the Convention, and tho' he cannot be called an orator, he is a most agreeable, eloquent, and convincing speaker. . . . From a spirit of industry and application which he possesses in a most eminent degree, he always comes forward the best informed man of any point in debate. The affairs of the United States, he perhaps has the most correct knowledge of, of any man in the Union."

JAMES MADISON

1751 (March 16) Born at Port Conway, Va.

1771 Graduated from the College of New Jersey (now Princeton University).

1776 Member of Virginia's patriotic convention that drafted the state constitution.

1778-1779 Member of Virginia governor's council.

1780-1783 Delegate to the Congress of the Confederation.

1784-1786 Member of Virginia's state legislature.

1786 Delegate from Virginia to the Annapolis Convention.

1787 Member of Virginia's delegation to the Constitutional Convention; signed the United States Constitution.

1787-1788 Delegate to the Congress of the Confederation.

1787-1788 Cooperated with Alexander Hamilton and John Jay in writing "The Federalist" essays.

1788 Member of Virginia's constitutional ratification convention.

1789-1797 Representative from Virginia in the U. S. Congress.

1799-1800 Member of Virginia's state legislature.

1801 Virginia presidential elector; voted for Thomas Jefferson.

1801-1809 Secretary of State of the United States.

1809-1817 Fourth President of the United States.

1820 Co-chairman of Virginia's state constitutional convention.

1836 (June 28) Died at Montpelier in Orange County, Virginia.

Last of the Founding Fathers to die

Living longer than any other of the Founding Fathers, Madison served for eight years as Secretary of State under President Thomas Jefferson, and then succeeded Jefferson as the fourth president of the United States. During Madison's administration as president, the British burned the Capitol in Washington, D.C., in the War of 1812, which was called "Mr. Madison's War" by his opponents. He lived to see the United States grow from thirteen to twenty-five states, and its population expand from four million to fifteen million persons. He also saw the birth of the transportation revolution that made greater westward expansion possible—the invention of the railroad, the steamboat, and the steamship.

Had ability as a storyteller

The short, blue-eyed Madison was described as follows by a friend who knew him in his later years: "In person Mr. Madison was below the middle size; though his face was ordinarily homely, when he smiled it was so pleasing as to be almost handsome. His manner with strangers was reserved, which some regarded as pride, and others as coldness; but, on further acquaintance, these impressions were completely effaced. His temper seemed to be naturally a very sweet one, and to have been brought under complete control. When excited, he seldom showed any stronger indication of anger than a slight flush on the cheek. . . . With great powers of argument, he had a fine vein of humor. He abounded in anecdote, told his stories very well, and they had the advantage of being such as were never heard before, except perhaps from himself."

James Madison was born on March 16, 1751, at Port Conway, Va., at the home of his maternal grandfather, where his mother was then visiting. His father, also named James Madison, was a wealthy plantation owner, and his mother, Eleanor Conway Madison, was the daughter of an aristocratic Virginia family.

Young James grew up at his family's plantation,

The Pennsylvania Academy of Fine Arts.

Dolley Madison
By Gilbert Stuart

Montpelier, in Orange County in the foothills of the Blue Ridge mountains. When he was twelve, he was sent to a boarding school in a neighboring county for a few years, and then he returned home to be prepared for college by a local Church of England minister, the Reverend Thomas Martin.

Attended Princeton University

When Madison was eighteen years old, he went away to the College of New Jersey (now Princeton University), a school that was receiving an increasingly good reputation because of its new president, the Reverend John Witherspoon, who soon was to become the only clergyman to sign the Declaration of Independence. He completed his college work in two years, receiving his bachelor of arts degree in 1771 at the age of twenty; but the intensive work required to compress his college studies into such a short span undermined his health. He remained at Princeton an extra six months until he was feeling better, before he returned to Virginia.

Helped draft Virginia's first constitution

Madison had been exposed to revolutionary thinking about politics at Princeton, had become a member of the Whig party, and upon his return to Virginia began to take an active part in the patriotic cause. He was elected to the committee of safety of Orange County in 1774, a group that became the unofficial local government. In 1776, he won election to the general patriotic convention of Virginia that organized the new state government. There he served on the committee with George Mason that drafted Virginia's first constitution; and he was particularly responsible for revising the Declaration of Rights section on freedom of religion where he added the word "toleration," having in mind the recent persecutions of Baptists under the royal government in Virginia. Madison next served in the first state legislature under Governor Patrick Henry; there he met and began his long friendship with Thomas Jefferson, who had just returned to Virginia from writing the Declaration of Independence.

Defeated because of refusal to buy votes with liquor

Madison failed to win re-election to the legislature, largely because he refused to follow the political custom of the times of providing large quantities of liquor for his supporters on election day; but his friends in the legislature elected him as a member of the governor's advisory council where he served for two years, under Governors Patrick Henry and Thomas Jefferson.

At the age of twenty-eight, Madison was elected by the legislature as a member of its delegation to Congress. He traveled to Philadelphia, took his seat in the assembly in March, 1780, and continued to serve there until the end of the Revolutionary War in 1783. He took an important part in helping organize the government of the United States under the Articles of Confederation, which went into effect in 1781. He became a close friend of Alexander Hamilton, who was serving as a member of Congress from New York; and they mutually agreed that the Articles did not provide a satisfactorily strong government for the nation.

Because the Articles of Confederation provided that a delegate to Congress could serve only one term of three years, Madison returned to Virginia at the expiration of his term, and from 1784 to

1786 he was elected as a member of the Virginia legislature. In 1786, the legislature sent Madison as a member of its delegation to the Annapolis Convention to consider what changes in the federal laws were needed to encourage trade between the states. At the Annapolis Convention, he resumed his friendship with Hamilton, and worked with the New Yorker in promoting the need for a Constitutional Convention.

Kept record of the Constitutional Convention

The Virginia legislature chose Madison as a member of its delegation to the Constitutional Convention of 1787 and named George Washington as the head of the delegation. Madison was present from the beginning of the Convention on May 25, 1787. He viewed the historic importance of drawing up a new Constitution as one "on which would be staked . . . the cause of liberty throughout the world." Therefore, he determined to keep accurate records of the meeting.

"In pursuance of the task I had assumed," Madison later wrote, "I chose a seat in front of the presiding member, with the other members on my right and left hands. In this favorable position for hearing all that passed, I noted, in terms legible and in abbreviations and marks intelligible to myself, what was read from the Chair or spoken by the members; and losing not a moment unnecessarily between the adjournment and reassembling of the Convention, I was enabled to write out my daily notes during the session, or within a few finishing days after its close, in the extent and form preserved in my own hand on my files."

Although Madison did not consider himself an orator, nor did his friends, he spoke more often than any other member of the Convention; and it is remarkable that he was able to make so many speeches and still keep such elaborate and detailed notes of the proceedings.

Worked on the Virginia Plan with Randolph

On May 29, Edmund Randolph, the governor of Virginia, presented the Virginia Plan which he and Madison had worked out as a basis for action for the Convention. This plan called for the Articles of Confederation to be "corrected and enlarged" to provide for a two-house "National Legislature," a "National Executive" with the authority "to execute the national laws," and a "National Judiciary." That same day, Charles Pinckney of South Carolina, presented his draft of a proposed

Thomas Gilcrease Institute of American History and Art, Tulsa, Oklahoma. Frick Art Reference Library.

James Madison
By CHARLES WILLSON PEALE

Federal Constitution, which incorporated most of the ideas of the Virginia Plan, but added many details.

Two days later, when the committee of the whole was discussing the various provisions of the Virginia Plan, Roger Sherman of Connecticut and Elbridge Gerry of Massachusetts attacked the proposal that one branch of Congress be elected by the people, saying that they would prefer to see the representatives to Congress continue to be appointed by the state legislatures. At this point, Madison made a strong appeal for democracy, as he later reported in his Journal of the Constitutional Convention:

"Mr. Madison considered the popular election of one branch of the National Legislature as essential to every plan of free government. He observed, that in some of the States one branch of the Legislature was composed of men already removed from the people by an intervening body of electors. That if the first branch of the General Legislature should be elected by the State Legislatures . . . the people would be lost sight of altogether; and the necessary sympathy between them and their rulers and officers too little felt. . . . He thought, too, that the great fabric to be raised would be more stable and durable, if it should rest on the solid foundation of the people themselves, than if it should stand merely on the pillars of the Legislatures."

Madison served as a member of the committee of style that drew up the final version of the United States Constitution; and then, after it had been signed on September 17, he went to New York where Congress was meeting, having also been elected by the Virginia legislature as a delegate to the Congress of the Confederation. In Congress, he voted for acceptance of the Constitution and its submission to the states for ratification.

Wrote The Federalist along with Hamilton and Jay

In the next several months, Madison joined Alexander Hamilton and John Jay in writing the series of essays defending and explaining the Constitution that became known as *The Federalist*. Then, Madison returned to Virginia and was elected to the state ratification convention where, despite the opposition of Patrick Henry, he won approval of the Constitution by the narrow margin of 89 to 79 by giving assurances that he would help see to it that Bill of Rights amendments would be incorporated in the Constitution.

When the Virginia legislature met in the fall of 1788 to elect Senators to the new United States Congress, Madison's name was proposed, but Patrick Henry took the floor to denounce him as "unworthy of the confidence of the people," and declared that Madison's election "would terminate in producing rivulets of blood throughout the land." As a result, Madison was defeated for Senator. Henry was also determined that Madison should not be elected to the U. S. House of Representatives, and arranged the districting of the state in such a way that Madison's county was

Montpelier

From an original etching by Don Swann.

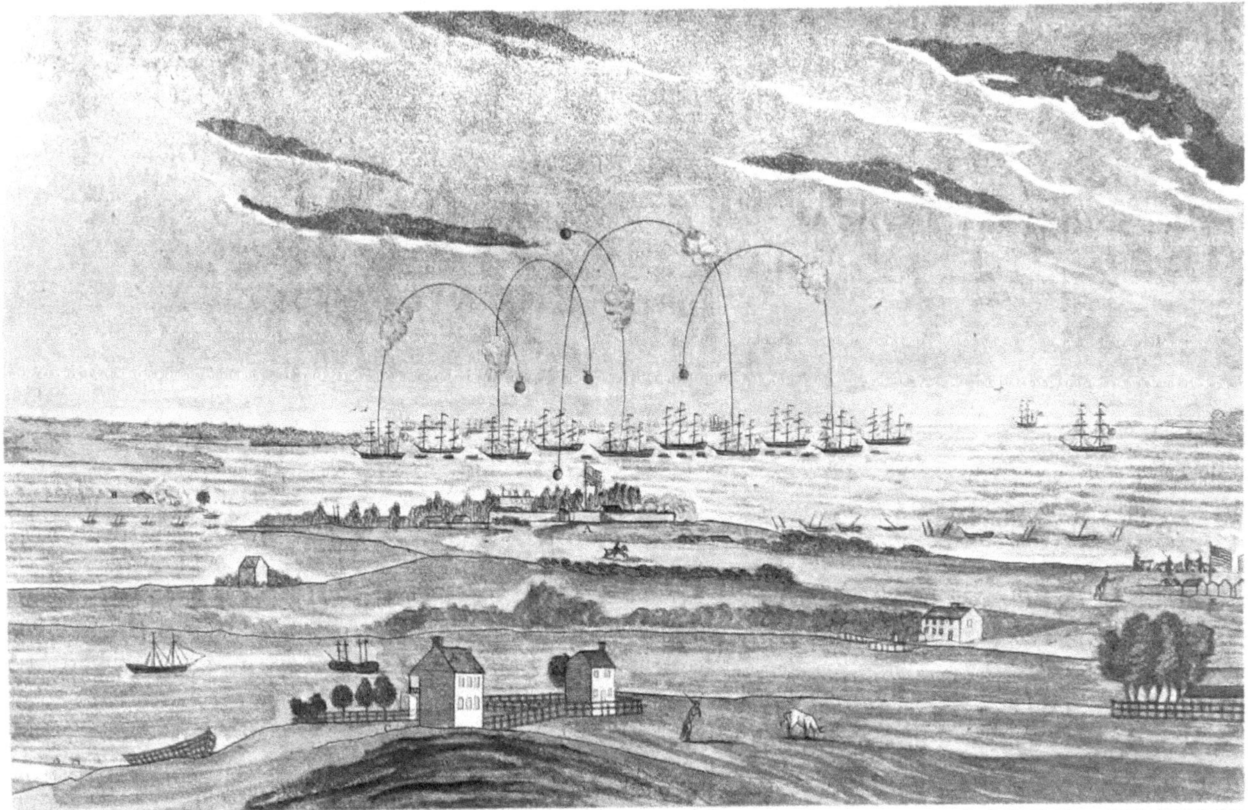

New York Public Library. Photo by Francis G. Mayer.

A View of the Bombardment of Fort McHenry, near Baltimore, September 13, 1814.
This view from the observatory shows the shelling which lasted twenty-four hours. During the bombardment, the British used between 1,500 and 1,800 shells in an attempt to force a landing. It was during this engagement that Francis Scott Key composed *The Star Spangled Banner*.

Battle of New Orleans and death of Major-General Packenham
(January 8th, 1815)

thrown in with others where he was not known to be popular. However, Madison wrote to Washington that he was "disposed to serve the public," so he carried on a vigorous election campaign against his opponent, James Monroe, and won by a majority of about three hundred votes.

Helped prepare speeches for George Washington

Madison was of invaluable aid to President Washington and to the nation during his service in the new United States Congress from 1789 to 1797. He helped Washington write his inaugural address at the outset of the administration, and advised Washington in the preparation of his "Farewell Address" at the close of his term of office. Acting as majority leader in the House of Representatives, Madison played a major part in writing the bills that created the various executive departments of the government and in writing the ten "Bill of Rights" amendments to the Constitution.

In 1794, at the age of forty-three, Madison married Mrs. Dolley Payne Todd, the twenty-six-year-old widow of a Philadelphia lawyer. She was a Quaker, but was expelled by the Society of Friends because of her marriage to Madison, who was not a Quaker. Madison and his wife had no children of their own, but they reared her son by her previous marriage.

After completing his term in Congress in 1797, Madison and his wife retired to "Montpelier" in Virginia, but he did not remain absent from public affairs for long. Angered at the Alien and Sedition Acts passed in 1798 under President John Adams, Madison wrote the "Virginia Resolution" passed by the Virginia legislature which declared that the Acts violated the United States Constitution. Kentucky passed a similar resolution that was prepared by Thomas Jefferson, but other states were unwilling to go along with the idea that the power to nullify an act of Congress lay with the states. Madison was then elected to the state legislature, serving during 1799 and 1800.

Served as Secretary of State under Jefferson

Madison was one of Virginia's presidential electors in 1801, voting for Thomas Jefferson; and then he was appointed by Jefferson as Secretary of State, an office that he held for the next eight years. His greatest achievement in this period was his supervision of the negotiations that resulted in the Louisiana Purchase. Throughout Jefferson's administration there were many difficulties with France and Britain brought about by the recurring wars in Europe, and Madison was constantly engaged in efforts to maintain American neutrality. Mrs. Madison, meanwhile, became the social leader of Washington, often acting as First Lady for the widowed President Jefferson.

In the presidential election of 1808, Madison was the nominee of the Democratic-Republican party and his running-mate was George Clinton of New York, who had served as Vice-President during Jefferson's second administration. Madison defeated Charles Cotesworth Pinckney, the Federalist party's nominee for President, with an electoral vote of 122 to 47.

War of 1812 declared despite absence of preparation

Relationships with Great Britain became steadily worse during the early years of Madison's administration as President. A group of Western and Southern Congressmen, designated the "War Hawks" by Jefferson, urged that war be declared on Britain. Madison finally gave in to the demands, and on June 1, 1812, he asked Congress to declare war. More than two weeks later, on June 18, Congress declared war, even though American military forces were ill-prepared to fight a war. Later that year, Madison won an overwhelming re-election to four more years as President, despite Federalist party opposition to the war.

The war with Britain dragged on for two years, largely because the British were engaged in fighting Napoleon on the continent of Europe and could not spare men and supplies to send to America. With the defeat of Napoleon in 1814, the British sent reinforcements to America. A British army landed in Maryland, and in August, 1814, defeated United States troops near Washington at the Battle of Bladensburg. A letter from Mrs. Madison to her sister written on August 23 and 24, 1814, gives a dramatic presentation of her plight:

"Dear Sister,—My husband left me yesterday morning to join General Winder.—He inquired anxiously whether I had courage, or firmness, to remain in the president's house until his return, on the morrow, or succeeding day, and on my assurance that I had no fear but for him and the success of our army, he left me, beseeching me to take care of myself, and of the cabinet papers, public and private.—I have since received two despatches from him, written with a pencil; the last is alarming, because he desires I should be ready at a moment's warning to enter my carriage and leave the city; that the enemy seemed stronger than had been reported, and that it might happen that they would reach the city, with intention to destroy it. . . . I am accordingly ready; I have pressed as many cabinet papers into trunks as to fill one carriage; our private property must be sacrificed, as it is impossible to procure wagons for its transportation. I am determined not to go myself, until I see Mr. Madison safe and he can accompany me, —as I hear of much hostility towards him . . . disaffection stalks around us. . . . My friends and acquaintances are all gone . . .

"*Wednesday morning, twelve o'clock.*—Since sunrise I have been turning my spy-glass in every direction and watching with unwearied anxiety, hoping to discern the approach of my dear husband and his friends; but, alas, I can descry only groups of military wandering in all directions, as if there was a lack of arms, or of spirit to fight for their own firesides!

"*Three o'clock.*—Will you believe it, my sister? We have had a battle or skirmish near Bladensburgh, and I am still here within sound of the cannon! Mr. Madison comes not; may God protect him! Two messengers covered with dust, come to bid me fly; but I wait for him. . . . At this late hour, a waggon has been procured; I have had it filled with the plate and most valuable portable articles belonging to the house; whether it will reach its destination, the Bank of Maryland, or fall into the hands of British soldiery, events must determine.

Dolley Madison saved the painting of George Washington

"Our kind friend, Mr. Carroll, has come to hasten my departure, and is in a very bad humor with me, because I insist on waiting until the large picture of General Washington is secured, and it requires to be unscrewed from the wall. This process was found too tedious for these perilous moments; I have ordered the frame to be broken and the canvass taken out; it is done,—and the precious portrait placed in the hands of two gentlemen of New York, for safe keeping. And now, dear sister, I must leave this house, or the retreating army will make me a prisoner in it, by filling up the road I am directed to take. When I shall again write to you, or where I shall be tomorrow, I cannot tell!!"

The British captured Washington, and burned the Capitol and part of the White House; but Dolley Madison made good her escape with the portrait of George Washington. Peace negotiations already were underway in Europe at the time of the capture of Washington, and a peace treaty was signed in December, 1814. But word of peace did not reach the United States in time to prevent the Battle of New Orleans in January, 1815, in which Andrew Jackson became a hero.

The remaining two years of Madison's administration were filled with prosperity as the movement to the West expanded and new manufacturing industries were built. In 1816, Madison named James Monroe, his secretary of state, to succeed him in the presidency, and Monroe easily won the election over the Federalist candidate Rufus King.

Retiring to Montpelier in 1817, at the age of sixty-six, Madison spent his latter years quietly in Virginia. After the death of Jefferson, in 1826, Madison succeeded him as rector, or president, of the University of Virginia. In 1829, Madison served for a few months as co-chairman of a state convention to draft a new Constitution for Virginia. The last survivor of the signers of the United States Constitution, Madison died at the age of eighty-five on June 28, 1836, at Montpelier.

After Madison's death, his widow sold to the government his report on the debates in the Constitutional Convention, which he had kept secret until the death of all those who had participated in it. His report was finally published in 1840, more than fifty years after the fateful summer that had been the most important of his life.

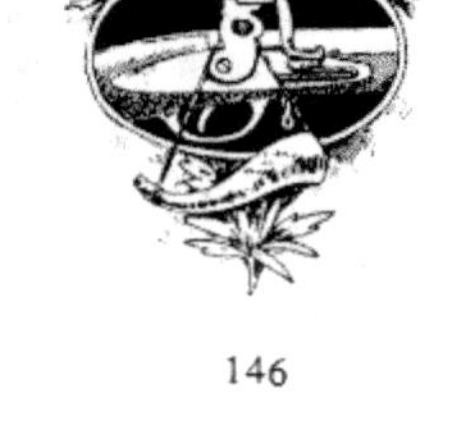

JAMES McHENRY of MARYLAND

Although he was not one of the greatest of the Founding Fathers, James McHenry took part in many of the most important events of the Revolutionary War and the post-war period of organizing the new government of the United States. An Irishman who came to America at the age of seventeen, McHenry threw himself into the struggle against Great Britain, serving first as an army surgeon, then as a secretary and aide to General George Washington and the Marquis de Lafayette. After the war, he was one of Maryland's delegates in the Constitutional Convention and signed the United States Constitution. Toward the end of Washington's second term as President, McHenry was appointed Secretary of War, an office that he also held during most of John Adams' administration. Fort McHenry at Baltimore, Md., where the "Star-Spangled Banner" was inspired, was named for McHenry.

Studied medicine under Dr. Benjamin Rush

James McHenry was born in Ballymena, Ireland, on November 16, 1753, the son of Daniel McHenry, a prosperous merchant. As a boy, he attended a classical academy in Dublin, but illness forced him to stop his studies. His parents sent him to America in 1771 in hope that the change would improve his health. He lived for a time at the home of William Allison in Philadelphia, attended school for a while in Newark, Del., then began studying medicine under Benjamin Rush in Philadelphia. His parents and his younger brother John followed him to America and opened a general store in Baltimore in 1773.

JAMES McHENRY

1753 (Nov. 16) Born at Ballymena, Ireland.

1771 Immigrated to America at the age of 17.

1775-1781 Served in the Continental Army during the Revolutionary War.

1781-1786 Member of state senate of Maryland.

1783-1785 Delegate from Maryland to the Congress of the Confederation.

1787 Member of Maryland's delegation to the Constitutional Convention; signed the United States Constitution.

1788-1790 Member of the lower house of the Maryland legislature.

1791-1796 Member of the Maryland state senate.

1796-1800 Secretary of War of the United States under Presidents Washington and Adams.

1816 (May 3) Died at Baltimore, Md.

Frick Art Reference Library. Owner: James McHenry.

James McHenry

By CHARLES WILLSON PEALE

Caught up with the patriotic enthusiasm of the times, the twenty-one-year-old McHenry set off for Boston in July, 1775, to join the Continental Army that was besieging Boston. He served as a volunteer surgeon in army hospitals for about a year, and then he was appointed as surgeon of the Fifth Pennsylvania Battalion at Fort Washington, N. Y. When the fort was captured by the British in November, 1776, McHenry was captured along with about 2,000 American troops. He attended sick and wounded American prisoners in New York for about two months; then, on January 27, 1777, he was paroled by the British and permitted to go to Baltimore to live with his family. More than a year went by before he was freed from the parole in March, 1778, by the exchange of a British doctor that the American forces had taken prisoner. McHenry resumed his military duties, becoming senior surgeon at the Valley Forge army hospital.

Became Washington's secretary

General Washington had become familiar with McHenry and admired some of the reports he had

Frick Art Reference Library. Owner: James McHenry.

Mrs. James McHenry
(Margaret Caldwell)
By CHARLES WILLSON PEALE

written, and in June, 1778, McHenry became Washington's secretary, writing orders and letters. In this capacity he came to know many of the most important men of the day. Alexander Hamilton, who also was serving as an aide to Washington, became his best friend. In August, 1780, McHenry was transferred to the staff of the Marquis de Lafayette, as his aide.

While McHenry was in camp at the siege of Yorktown in 1781, the legislature of Maryland elected him to the state senate. After the British surrendered at Yorktown, McHenry resigned from the army and went to Annapolis, Md., where he began serving in the legislature in January, 1782. The next year, the legislature elected McHenry as one of the state's representatives in the Congress of the Confederation, and for the next several years he held office both in the state senate and in the national Congress. McHenry's term in Congress ended in 1785, and he was ineligible under state law for a second term. He resigned from the state senate in 1786 to devote his attention to the family's business affairs, his wife having died.

Faint praise from a fellow delegate

McHenry married twenty-one-year-old Margaret "Peggy" Caldwell on January 8, 1784. She was the step-daughter of William Allison, in whose home in Philadelphia McHenry had lived as an immigrant Irish boy; and McHenry had carried on correspondence with her for several years before the marriage. Both McHenry and his wife were devoted Presbyterians, and their mutual interest in religion contributed to their long, happy marriage. They had five children, two of whom died in childhood.

McHenry was elected by the state legislature as one of Maryland's delegates to the Constitutional Convention in 1787; but he was absent from the meeting for about half its sessions because of the illness of his younger brother in Baltimore. He took little part in the debates of the Convention, and endeavored to take a middle stand between opposing factions in the Maryland delegation. A fellow delegate, William Pierce of Georgia, described McHenry: "He is a man of Specious talents with nothing of genius to improve them. As a politician there is nothing remarkable in him, nor has he any of the graces of the Orator. He is however, a very respectable young Gentleman, and deserves the honor which his country has bestowed on him."

"I distrust my own judgment"

After signing the Constitution with the other delegates on September 17, 1787, McHenry wrote in his diary: "Being opposed to many parts of the system I make a remark why I signed it and mean to support it. 1stly. I distrust my own judgement, especially as it is opposite to the opinion of a majority of gentlemen whose abilities and patriotism are of the first cast; and as I have already frequent occasions to be convinced that I have not always judged right. 2dly. Alterations may be obtained, it being provided that the concurrence of ⅔ of the congress may at any time introduce them. 3dly. Comparing the inconveniences and the evils which we labor under and may experience from the present confederation, and the little good we can expect from it, with the possible evils and probable benefits and advantages promised us by the new system, I am clear that I ought to give it all the support in my power . . ."

McHenry became an active Federalist for the rest of his life. He was elected to the Maryland state ratification convention, and helped win approval of the United States Constitution by his state. In October, 1788, McHenry ran on a Federalist ticket for a seat in the house of delegates of the state legislature, and successfully won over the Anti-Federalist candidate, Samuel Chase. McHenry was re-elected in 1789, but retired from public office during the winter of 1790-1791. He was elected to the state senate in 1791, an office that he held for the next five years.

Appointed Secretary of War by Washington

Toward the end of his second term as President, George Washington had great difficulty in finding qualified men to serve in the important appointive offices in the national government; so in January, 1796, McHenry received a letter from President Washington saying "it would now give me sincere pleasure if you will fill the office of Secretary of War." In the same letter Washington frankly explained that three other persons already had been asked to serve, but they had refused. McHenry accepted the appointment, writing to Washington: "I cannot say that I have ever experienced so much hesitation between giving way to inclination and attachment to you personally and my own interest and ease, as has taken place during the two past days. It is now, however, all over and it is right I should confess that the soothing idea of serving under you, more particularly at this crisis, has effectually and irresistably silenced all opposition. Such then as I am and with a heart truly devoted to you and the public good, dispose of as you please." In order to insure that there would be no conflict of interest in his public office and his private business, McHenry sold the two partnerships that he had in the mercantile business in Baltimore before setting out for the nation's capital in Philadelphia.

McHenry was sworn into office as Secretary of War on February 8, 1796. When John Adams became President in 1797, McHenry and the other members of Washington's cabinet continued in office. Throughout his service as a cabinet officer, McHenry kept in close touch with his old friend Alexander Hamilton, who was now the leader of the Federalist party. McHenry often asked Hamilton's advice on important matters and used Hamilton's comments as the basis of his actions. Most of the official records that would have revealed McHenry's effectiveness in office were burned when the War Office building was destroyed by fire in November, 1800.

Relations between France and the United States nearly reached a state of war during Adams's administration, and McHenry was kept busy trying to create a United States Navy and enlarge the United States Army. He supervised the construction and launching of the first United States warships, the frigates *Constellation*, *United States*, and *Constitution*. He persuaded George Washington to return to active duty as lieutenant general in command of the new army, and won a commission for his friend Alexander Hamilton as a major general and second in command.

An inefficient administrator

McHenry, who had never had much experience as an administrator, was swamped with paperwork, and annoyed his old friends by delays and confusions that occurred in his War Department. Hamilton wrote to Washington, complaining: "My friend McHenry is wholly inefficient for his place with the additional misfortune of not having the least suspicion of the fact. This generally will not surprise you, when you take in view the large scale upon which he is now to act. But you, perhaps, may not be aware of the whole extent of the insufficiency. It is so great as to leave no probability that the business of the War Department can make an tolerable progress in his hands." Washington replied to Hamilton, saying that the opinion "respecting the unfitness of a certain gentleman for the office he holds, accords with mine and it is to be regretted sorely, at this time, that these opinions are so well founded. I early discovered, after he entered upon the duties of his office, that his talents were unequal to great exertions, or deep resources. In truth, these were not expected, for the fact is, it was a Hobson's choice."

A more charitable view of McHenry was expressed by his fellow cabinet officer, Oliver Wolcott, Jr., the Secretary of the Treasury, who wrote: "He is a man of honour and entirely trustworthy; he is also a man of sense, and delivers correct opinions when required, but he is not skilled in the details of Executive business and he is at the head of a difficult and unpopular department. The diffidence which he feels, exposes his business to delays and he sometimes commits mistakes, which his enemies employ to impair his influence."

Relieved of his office by Adams

As the presidential election of 1800 approached, Adams's relationship with Wolcott and McHenry

Saint John's College, Annapolis, Maryland

cooled because he felt they were working too closely with Hamilton, who Adams knew was trying to prevent his winning of a second term as President. On May 5, 1800, Adams called McHenry into his office, charged him with promoting Hamilton's interests over his own, and demanded McHenry's resignation. McHenry later described the interview as "a most mortifying scene, and insults which I shall never forget." Of Adams, he said, "At times he would speak in such a manner of certain men and things, as to persuade one that he was actually insane." The ensuing battle between Adams and Hamilton destroyed the Federalist party, and it never again won control of the national government.

At the age of forty-six, McHenry retired from both public and business affairs. For the next sixteen years he lived most of the time at his estate of Fayetteville just west of Baltimore, keeping in touch with his many friends by extensive correspondence. The only office that he held in his later years was as president of the Bible Society of Baltimore. In 1812, McHenry was stricken with paralysis of both his legs, and he was confined to bed for the rest of his life. On May 3, 1816, on his estate near Baltimore, McHenry died at the age of sixty-two.

THOMAS MIFFLIN of PENNSYLVANIA

As Pennsylvania's leading general of the Revolutionary War, Thomas Mifflin had great popular support all his life in spite of his many faults. At the beginning of the war, he served as George Washington's first aide-de-camp at the siege of Boston, and then he rose swiftly to the rank of major general as the Continental Army's first quartermaster general. In this office, the youthful Mifflin won the nickname of "Tommy the Quartermaster". In addition, he increased his fortune with the commissions he received on the purchase of supplies for the troops. After a falling-out with Washington over the defense of Philadelphia, Mifflin became a ringleader of the Conway Cabal that Washington believed was trying to oust him from command. But even the dispute with Washington did not dim Hifflin's political popularity. He was elected President of the Congress of the Confederation and as such signed the peace treaty with Great Britain at the end of the war. In later years he helped write the United States Constitution, presided over his state's constitutional convention, and repeatedly was elected president and governor of Pennsylvania despite charges he was an embezzler and "an habitual drunkard."

Headquarters of Maj. Gen. Thomas Mifflin

THOMAS MIFFLIN

1744 (Jan. 10) Born in Philadelphia, Pa.

1760 Graduated from College of Philadelphia (now University of Pennsylvania).

1764-1765 Toured France and England.

1772-1775 Member of Pennsylvania colonial legislature.

1774-1775 Member of Pennsylvania patriotic convention.

1774-1775 Delegate from Pennsylvania to the Continental Congress.

1775 Appointed first aide-de-camp to General George Washington, with rank of major.

1775-1777 First quartermaster-general of Continental Army; rose to rank of major general.

1778-1781 Member of Pennsylvania legislature.

1782-1784 Delegate from Pennsylvania to Congress of the Confederation.

1783-1784 President of the Congress of the Confederation; received Washington's resignation of his commission and signed the peace treaty with Great Britain.

1785-1788 Speaker of the Pennsylvania state legislature.

1787 Delegate from Pennsylvania to the Constitutional Convention; signed United States Constitution.

1788-1790 President of Pennsylvania.

1789-1790 President of Pennsylvania state constitutional convention.

1790-1799 Governor of Pennsylvania.

1799-1800 Member of Pennsylvania house of representatives.

1800 (Jan. 20) Died in Lancaster, Pa.

Possessed genius, knowledge, eloquence, patriotism

His fellow-Pennsylvanian Benjamin Rush,once said: "Those who knew this man in the close of the Revolution and in the evening of life will scarcely believe" that Mifflin once "possessed genius, knowledge, eloquence, patriotism, courage, self-government and an independent spirit in the first years of the war." A newspaper article a few years after Mifflin's death, described his appearance:

"He stood very erect; dressed as a citizen in rich apparel such as became a gentleman of his circle; was of the middle size, with a handsome rotund but active person; evidently 'with good capon lined,' a hearty claret color, or rather ruddy complexion, and a keen coal black eye. He moved in a kind of quick step, and conversed with a brisk and easy sort of elocution, when stopping with some of the 'great ones of the city," who encounter him on the way."

Thomas Mifflin was born in Philadelphia on January 10, 1744. His father, John Mifflin, was a well-to-do merchant. Young Thomas attended a Quaker school, and then went to the College of

The Historical Society of Pennsylvania.

Governor and Mrs. Thomas Mifflin
By John Singleton Copley

Philadelphia (now the University of Pennsylvania), where he was graduated at the age of sixteen.

After completing his college education in 1760, Mifflin received practical business training as a clerk in the countinghouse of William Coleman for four years. Then he went on a year-long tour of England and France. Upon his return from his trip to Europe, Mifflin opened a store in Philadelphia in partnership with his brother George.

Married his cousin

A successful young businessman at the age of twenty-three, Mifflin married his cousin, Sarah Morris, in 1767. They had a daughter, Emily, who married Joseph Hopkinson, a son of the signer of the Declaration of Independence, Francis Hopkinson. Mifflin's son-in-law later won fame as the author of the patriotic song "Hail! Columbia."

When he was twenty-eight, Mifflin won election to the colonial legislature of Pennsylvania, where he continued to serve until his military service in the Revolutionary War caused him to resign. In the legislature, Mifflin aligned himself with the patriotic minority in this largely conservative assembly. He also won election in 1774 and 1775 to the patriotic conventions held in Philadelphia, and was appointed to the committees of correspondence that kept in touch with patriots in other colonies.

"A sprightly and spirited speaker"

In 1774, Mifflin was elected by the Pennsylvania legislature as a member of its delegation to the first Continental Congress. There, John Adams described the thirty-year-old Mifflin as a "sprightly and spirited speaker." Mifflin was a member of the congressional committee that drew plans for the Continental Association to enforce an American boycott of trade with Great Britain.

Soon Mifflin moved from politics into active military duty. When word came to Philadelphia in 1775 that fighting had begun at Lexington and Concord, he helped organize an infantry company and was elected its major. He told a meeting of Philadelphians, "Let us not be bold in declarations and afterwards cold in action. Let not the patriotic feeling of today be forgotten tomorrow; nor have it said of Philadelphia, that she passed noble resolutions, slept upon them, and afterwards neglected them." He took his seat in the Continental Congress that met in May, served on a committee chaired by George Washington to organize military supplies for defense, helped elect Washington as commander in chief of the Continental Army, and then was honored by being chosen as Washington's first aide-de-camp. While Mifflin was helping Washington at the siege of Boston in July, a Quaker meeting in Philadelphia "separated" him from the church because of his military activities.

Appointed as quartermaster of the army

In surveying his military forces drawn up before Boston, Washington quickly recognized the need of organizing the purchase of clothing, powder, and other supplies. He appointed Mifflin as quartermaster general because of his experience as a merchant. Congress authorized Mifflin to pay his expenses by collecting a five per cent commission on all supplies he purchased. Within a few months, Mifflin was appointed a colonel, then in May, 1776, he was appointed a brigadier general.

Mifflin performed his most important service to the revolutionary cause in the winter of 1776-1777, after the Continental Army had lost New York City and the spirit of defeat filled the air. During this time Mifflin made recruiting speeches in and around Philadelphia, raising troops that aided Washington in his sorely needed victories at Trenton and Princeton. For his services, Congress promoted Mifflin to major general in February, 1777.

During the summer of 1777, the British were momentarily expected to march through New Jersey and attack Philadelphia. Mifflin was stationed in Philadelphia to raise troops and defend the city from the frontal attack, while Washington planned to attack from the rear. The British did not attack as expected. Instead they boarded ships, sailed south from New York, came up Chesapeake Bay, and finally attacked Philadelphia from the south. Washington's forces lost the Battle of the Brandywine in September and Philadelphia was captured by the enemy. Disgusted by the loss of the nation's capital, and tired of his duties as quartermaster general, Mifflin submitted his resignation to Congress on October 8, 1777, pleading ill health as his excuse.

The Conway Cabal, a conspiracy ending with resignation

It soon developed that Mifflin was more interested in resigning his job as quartermaster general rather than his commission as a major general. In November, Congress appointed him as a mem-

The Historical Society of Pennsylvania.

Thomas Mifflin House, Philadelphia
By WHITEFIELD

ber of the Board of War, the executive department administering the war effort, and let him retain his commission. Major General Horatio Gates also was appointed to the Board of War as its president. Now began the period of the Conway Cabal in which Washington believed that Mifflin was conspiring with Brigadier General Thomas Conway to overthrow him as commander in chief in favor of Gates.

In January, 1778, Congress ordered Mifflin to "render an account to Congress of all his public expenditures" as quartermaster. Records for many of the purchases had not been kept in good order, and Mifflin dallied in getting his report in. In June, 1778, Congress decided to hold an inquiry into the quartermaster's department and order a court-martial if necessary. In August, Mifflin again offered to resign as major general, but Congress delayed consideration of the matter. In September, Congress appropriated a million dollars to Mifflin to settle his outstanding accounts, and four months later Washington was directed to proceed with a court-martial of his former aide-de-camp. By the time Washington received this directive, Congress had accepted Mifflin's resignation, so he was no longer under Washington's jurisdiction, and the matter was dropped.

Mifflin's military career having come to an inglorious close, he now returned to politics. From 1778 to 1781, he twice won election to the Pennsylvania state legislature, and then in 1782 he was named as a member of his state's delegation to the Congress of the Confederation.

Elected president of Congress

On November 3, 1783, the thirty-nine-year-old Mifflin won the highest political office in the nation with his election as President of the Congress, an office that he held for a little more than a year. The war now being over, George Washington appeared before the Congress, meeting in Annapolis, Md., to "resign with satisfaction the appointment

I accepted with diffidence." Mifflin's historic answer to Washington was as follows:

"Sir: The United States in Congress assembled receive, with emotions too affecting for utterance, the solemn resignation of the authorities under which you have led their troops with success through a perilous and doubtful war. Called upon by your country to defend its invaded rights, you accepted the sacred charge, before it had formed alliances, and whilst it was without funds or a government to support you. You have conducted the great military contest with wisdom and fortitude, invariably regarding the rights of the civil power through all disasters and changes. You have, by the love and confidence of your fellow-citizens, enabled them to display their martial genius, and transmit their fame to posterity. You have persevered till these United States, aided by a magnanimous king and nation, have been enabled, under a just Providence, to close the war in freedom, safety, and independence; on which happy event we sincerely join you in congratulations.

"The glory of your virtues will not terminate."

"Having defended the standard of liberty in this new world; having taught a lesson useful to those who inflict and to those who feel oppression, you retire from the great theatre of action, with the blessings of your fellow-citizens; but the glory of your virtues will not terminate with your military command; it will continue to animate remotest ages.

"We feel with you our obligations to the army in general, and will particularly charge ourselves with the interests of those confidential officers, who have attended your person to this affecting moment.

"We join you in commending the interests of our dearest country to the protection of Almighty God, beseeching him to dispose the hearts and minds of its citizens to improve the opportunity afforded them of becoming a happy and respectable nation. And for you we address to him our earnest prayers, that a life so beloved may be fostered with all his care; that your days may be happy as they have been illustrious; and that he will finally give you that reward which this world cannot give."

On January 14, 1784, Congress ratified the peace treaty with Great Britain, and President Mifflin signed three copies of the ratified treaty to make sure that one of them would reach Paris for the final formalities. Despite these precautions, bad weather and ship disasters delayed the arrival of the ratified agreements in Europe until May, when the war was formally ended.

Succeeded Benjamin Franklin as President of Pennsylvania

After completing his duties in Congress, Mifflin again was elected to the Pennsylvania legislature, where he was chosen as speaker of the assembly. He served under Benjamin Franklin, who was president of the state. Both Mifflin and Franklin were elected as members of the Pennsylvania delegation to the Constitutional Convention of 1787, but Mifflin took little part except to sign the United States Constitution after it had been drafted. In 1788, he succeeded Franklin as president of Pennsylvania, an officer elected by the legislature.

In 1789-1790, Mifflin presided at a state convention which revised the old state constitution, establishing a two-house legislature with a governor to be elected by the people. In 1790, the forty-six-year-old Mifflin won a statewide election as the state's first governor. Benjamin Rush declared that Mifflin won "by the basest acts of familiarity with the meanest of the people."

Mifflin held the governorship for three three-year terms, from 1790 to 1799. During most of this time, both the state and national government had their capitals in Philadelphia, so social and governmental affairs were sometimes considerably entwined. Governor Mifflin lived just down the street from President Washington; members of the Congress and members of the state legislature mixed socially; and the problems of the national government often were similar to the problems of the state government.

A close friend of Thomas Jefferson, Mifflin was generally more sympathetic to the Democratic-Republican party than to the Federalist party of Alexander Hamilton. However, in the Whisky Rebellion of 1794, he vigorously called up the state militia and marched at their head to western Pennsylvania to help enforce the collection of federal excise taxes. During Mifflin's administration, the city of Philadelphia was struck several times by epidemics of yellow fever, and Mifflin generally relied more on the advice of the doctors who opposed Benjamin Rush than he did on that eminent doctor who was so critical of Mifflin's conduct.

A heavy drinker who tapped the public treasury

Political campaigns in the 1790's were conducted with so much abuse and so little regard for

The New York Public Library, The I. N. Phelps Stokes Collection.

View of Pittsburgh

the truth that it is sometimes difficult to separate fact from fancy; however, there seems to have been grounds for some of the charges against Mifflin as a heavy drinker and of dipping into the public till occasionally. The United States Secretary of the Treasury, Oliver Wolcott, in a personal letter said of Mifflin: "The governor is an habitual drunkard. Every day, and not unfrequently in the forenoon, he is unable to articulate distinctly." Mifflin also often excused himself from various duties on the grounds of being sick, although his illness was never identified. Likewise, Mifflin was charged with having drawn funds from the Bank of Pennsylvania illegally, and having covered the matter up by replacing the funds when he was about to be exposed.

During Mifflin's last year as governor, the state capital was moved to Lancaster, Pa. There Mifflin completed his term in December, 1799, and accepted appointment as major general and commander in chief of the militia of Philadelphia. He then took his seat in the Pennsylvania house of representatives to which he had been elected, and served there about a month, until his death at the age of fifty-six, on January 20, 1800. His fortune dissipated, he was given a funeral at public expense and buried in the graveyard of a Lutheran church at Lancaster.

GOUVERNEUR MORRIS of PENNSYLVANIA

An accomplished orator and writer, Gouverneur Morris made more speeches than any other man at the Constitutional Convention of 1787, even though he was absent for about a month. A fellow-delegate described Morris's speeches as "fickle and inconstant—never pursuing one train of thinking—nor ever regular," but he contributed many ideas to the United States Constitution and was given the honor of writing it in its final form. James Madison, the "Father of the Constitution," said of him: "The finish given to the style and arrangement of the Constitution, fairly belongs to the pen of Mr. Morris."

An amputee at an early age

A younger brother of Lewis Morris, the signer of the Declaration of Independence, Gouverneur Morris signed the Articles of Confederation as a Congressional representative of New York, and nine years later he signed the Constitution as a delegate from Pennsylvania. Morris had lost one of his legs in an accident when he was in his twenties, and he wore a plain wooden peg-leg that gave him a piratical appearance. A gay bachelor until he was fifty-seven, one story said his leg was amputated as the result of an injury from jumping off a balcony to escape an irate husband. Another story said the leg was amputated after he fell from his carriage

Gouverneur Morris was born on January 31, 1752, at Morrisania, the family estate located in what is now the Bronx of New York City. His father, Lewis Morris, died when Gouverneur was only ten years old, leaving the bulk of his estate to the eldest son, also named Lewis Morris, but providing in his will that Gouverneur should have "the best education that is to be had in England or America." He received his early education from tutors, then was sent to King's College (now Columbia University) where he was graduated at the age of sixteen. He already showed his proficiency as a writer, winning praise for compositions on the subjects "Wit and Beauty" and "Love."

After receiving his college degree, Morris took up the study of law under William Smith, chief justice of New York. His ability as a student of the law was demonstrated by his winning admittance to practice at the bar at the age of twenty.

Gave a rousing speech for independence

With the coming of the Revolutionary War,

GOUVERNEUR MORRIS

1752 (Jan. 31) Born in Morrisania, N. Y.
1768 Graduated from King's College (now Columbia University).
1771 Admitted to the bar to practice law
1775-1777 Member of New York's provincial patriotic congress.
1776 Member of New York state constitutional convention.
1778-1779 Delegate from New York to the Continental Congress; signed the Articles of Confederation.
1781-1785 Assistant superintendent of finance of the Congress of the Confederation.
1787 Member of Pennsylvania's delegation to the Constitutional Convention; signed the United States Constitution.
1788 Traveled to France as an agent for Robert Morris.
1789 Special agent for George Washington in Great Britain.
1792-1794 United States Minister to France.
1800-1803 U.S. Senator from New York.
1810 Appointed chairman of the Erie Canal commission.
1816 (Nov. 6) Died at Morrisania, N. Y.

Gouverneur Morris
By JAMES SHARPLES

National Archives

Morris took an active part in the patriotic movement in New York. He was elected to the provincial congress, serving from 1775 to 1777, and was a member of the convention in 1776 that wrote the state's first constitution. Many delegates to the New York convention were doubtful of the advisability of declaring themselves independent of Great Britain, and were hopeful of an early settlement of the dispute, but a speech by the twenty-four-year-old Morris helped convince some of the doubters. In it he said:

"Experience has taught those powers, and will teach them more clearly every day, that an American war is tedious, expensive, uncertain, and ruinous. Three thousand miles of a boisterous ocean are to be passed over, and the vengeful tempests which whirl along our coasts are daily to be encountered in such expeditions. At least three months' expense must be incurred before one gun can be fired against an American village; and three months more before each shattered armament can find an asylum for repose. A hardy, brave people, or else a destructive climate, must be subdued, while the troops, exhausted by fatigue, find at every step that desertion and happiness are synonymous terms . . .

'To trust the King is madness'

"Now let me earnestly ask, why should we hesitate? Have you the least hope in treaty? Will you even think of it before certain acts of Parliament are repealed? Have you heard of any such repeal? Will you trust these commissioners? Is there any act of Parliament passed to ratify what they shall do? No, they come from the King. We have no business with the King. We did not quarrel with the King. He has officiously made himself a party in the dispute against us. And now he pretends to be the umpire. Trust crocodiles, trust the hungry wolf in your flock, or a rattlesnake in your bosom, you may yet be something wise. But trust the King, his ministers, his commissioners, it is madness in the extreme!"

Early in 1778, Morris was elected as a delegate to Congress. Shortly after reaching Congress, he was sent to investigate conditions in Washington's camp at Valley Forge. He wrote to his friend John Jay in February of this experience: "The skeleton of an Army presents itself to our eyes in a naked, starving condition, out of health, out of spirits." On July 9, 1778, he signed his name as a delegate from New York to the Articles of Confederation, which set up the first national government of the United States.

Suggested the word "cent" to replace "penny"

After Morris' term in Congress ended in 1779, he continued to live in Philadelphia, where he became a close friend of the wealthy merchant, Robert Morris (no relation). When Robert Morris was appointed superintendent of finance by Congress in 1781, Gouverneur Morris was named as his assistant, a position in which he served until 1785. In 1782, Gouverneur Morris proposed the first decimal system of coinage for the United States and made up the word "cent" to replace the English word "penny."

The thirty-five-year-old Gouverneur Morris had won such distinction during the short time he had lived in Philadelphia that he was chosen by the state legislature in 1787 as one of Pennsylvania's delegates to the Constitutional Convention. William Pierce, a delegate from Georgia who did not remain to the end of the Convention, noted his personal observations of Morris as follows:

"Mr. Gouverneur Morris is one of those Genius's in whom every species of talents combine to render him conspicuous and flourishing in public debate:—He winds through all the mazes of rhetoric, and throws around him such a glare that he charms, captivates, and leads away the senses of all who hear him. With an infinite stretch of fancy he brings to view things when he is engaged in deep argumentation, that render all the labor of reasoning easy and pleasing."

"Let the rich mix with the poor."

Morris attended the first meeting of the Constitutional Convention in May, then he was called away to New York on personal business. He returned and resumed his seat on July 2, at a time when the meeting was split on the question of whether each state should have an equal vote in one branch of the Congress. He immediately rose and made one of the longest speeches heard by the Convention—one such as Pierce must have had in mind in his description above. As reported by James Madison, Pierce said:

"Mr. Gouverneur Morris thought a Committee advisable, as the Convention had been equally divided. He had a stronger reason also. The mode of appointing the second branch tended, he was sure, to defeat the object of it. What is this object? To check the precipitation, changeableness, and

"Morrisania," Home of Gouverneur Morris

excesses of the first branch. Every man of observation had seen in the democratic branches of the State Legislatures, precipitation – in Congress, changeableness – in every department, excesses against personal liberty, private property, and personal safety. What qualities are necessary to constitute a check in this case? *Abilities* and *virtue* are equally necessary in both branches. Something more, then, is now wanted. In the first place, the checking branch must have a personal interest in checking the other branch. One interest must be opposed to another interest. Vices, as they exist, must be turned against each other. In the second place, it must have great personal property; it must have the aristocratic spirit; it must love to lord it through pride. Pride is, indeed, the great principle that actuates both the poor and the rich. It is this principle which in the former resists, in the latter abuses, authority. In the third place it should be independent. In religion the creature is apt to forget its Creator. That it is otherwise in political affairs, the late debates here are an unhappy proof. The aristocratic body should be as independent, and as firm, as the democratic. If the members of it are to revert to a dependence on the democratic choice, the democratic scale will preponderate. All the guards contrived by America have not restrained the Senatorial branches of the Legislature from a servile complaisance to the democratic. If the second branch is to be dependent, we are better without it. To make it independent, it should be for life. It will then do wrong, it will be said. He believed so; he hoped so. The rich will strive to establish their dominion, and enslave the rest. They always did. They always will. The proper security against them is to form them into a separate interest. The two forces will then control each other. Let the rich mix with the poor, and in a commercial country they will establish an oligarchy. Take away commerce, and the democracy will triumph. Thus it has been all the world over. So it will be among us. Reason tells us we are but men; and we are not to expect any particular interference of Heaven in our favor. By thus combining, and setting apart, the aristocratic interest, the popular interest will be combined against it. There will be a mutual check and mutual security. In the fourth place, an independence for life, involves the necessary permanency. If we change our measures nobody will trust us—and how avoid a change of measures, but by avoiding a change of men? Ask any man if he confides in Congress—if he confides in the State of Pennsylvania—if he will lend his money, or enter into contract? He will tell you, no. He sees no stability. He can repose no confidence. If Great Britain were to explain her refusal to treat with us, the same reasoning would be employed. He disliked the exclusion of the second branch from holding offices. It is dangerous. It is like the imprudent exclusion of the military officers, during the war, from civil appointments. It deprives the Executive of the principal source of influence. If danger be apprehended from the Executive, what a left-handed way is this of obviating it! If the son, the brother, or the friend can be appointed, the danger may be even increased, as the disqualified father, &c. can then boast of a disinterestedness which he does not possess. Besides, shall the best, the most able, the most virtuous citizens not be permitted to hold offices? Who then are to hold them? He was also against paying the Senators. They will pay themselves, if they can. If they cannot, they will be rich, and can do without it. Of such the second branch ought to consist; and none but such can compose it, if they are not to be paid. He contended that the Executive should appoint the Senate, and fill up vacancies. This gets rid of the difficulty in the present question. You may begin with any ration you please, it will come to the same thing. The members being independent, and for life, may be taken as well from one place as from another. It should be considered, too, how the scheme could be carried through the States. He hoped there was strength of mind enough in this House to look truth in the face. He did not hesitate, therefore, to say that loaves and fishes must bribe the demagogues. They must be made to expect higher offices under the General, than the State Governments. A Senate for life will be a noble bait. Without such captivating prospects, the popular leaders will oppose and defeat the plan. He perceived that the first branch was to be chosen by the people of the States, the second by those chosen by the people. Is not here a government by the States—a government by compact between Virginia in the first and second branch, Massachusetts in the first and second branch, &c.? This is going back to mere treaty. It is no government at all. It is altogether dependent on the States, and will act over again the part which Congress has acted. A firm government alone can protect our liberties. He fears the influence of the rich. They will have the same effect here as elsewhere, if we do not, by such a government, keep them within their proper spheres. We should remember that the people never act from reason alone. The rich will take the advantage of their passions, and make there the instruments

A view of English Ships in New York Harbor (c. 1775)

New York Public Library.

New York Public Library. Photo by Francis G. Mayer.

The Clermont

Although it was called "Fulton's Folly" by the crowds along the shore, it moved successfully in September, 1807, running between New York and Albany.

New York Public Library. Photo by Francis G. Mayer.

A view of the lake and Fort Erie from Buffalo Creek, c. 1810.
by Edward Walsh.

New York Public Library.

A View of the City of New York from Long Island

for oppressing them. The result of the contest will be a violent aristocracy, or a more violent despotism. The schemes of the rich will be favoured by the extent of the country. The people in such distant parts cannot communicate and act in concert. They will be the dupes of those who have more knowledge and intercourse. The only security against encroachments, will be a select and sagacious body of men, instituted to watch against them on all sides. He meant only to hint these observations, without grounding any motion on them."

Favored election by the people

When the Southern States argued that representation in Congress should be based on population and that the slaves should be counted as part of the population, Morris countered by insisting "that taxation shall be in proportion to representation." He forcefully opposed a proposal that the President be chosen by Congress, suggesting instead that the chief executive be chosen by the "citizens of the United States."

At the end of July, the Convention adjourned for ten days while John Rutledge and his committee on detail sorted out the various resolutions that had been agreed to, and organized them into a draft of a constitution. Since Morris was not a member of this committee, he and George Washington were free to spend several days taking an excursion to Valley Forge. There Washington rode about looking at the scene where his army had suffered so greatly nearly ten years earlier, and Morris spent some time fishing for trout. Washington's biographer, Douglas Southall Freeman, believed that the fact Washington and Morris were so intimate as to take this trip together belied the truth of a much-told story—that during the Convention Morris accepted a bet that he would not dare to slap Washington on the back, did so, and received such an icy stare from the general that he "retreated abashed and sought refuge in the crowd."

Proposed the President's Cabinet

After the Convention reconvened, Morris was not so long-winded in his speeches as he had been during July, and his proposals were more concrete. On August 20, he made what was in effect the first proposal for the President's Cabinet. Morris called it a "Council of State" and recommended that the President appoint to it the Chief Justice of the Supreme Court, a Secretary of Domestic Affairs, a Secretary of Commerce and Finance, a Secretary of Foreign Affairs, a Secretary of War, and a Secretary of Marine.

Credited with wording the preamble

On September 8, the Convention having reached general agreement on the content of the Constitution, a committee on style was appointed to revise the material and put the Constitution in final form. The chairman of this committee was Samuel Johnson, and the other members were Morris, Alexander Hamilton, James Madison, and Rufus King. During the next four days most of the work of the styling and rewriting was left in Morris' hands. He particularly is given credit for the dignified wording of the preamble to the Constitution:

"We the people of the United States, in Order to form a more perfect Union, establish Justice, insure domestic Tranquility, provide for the common defence, promote the general Welfare, and secure the Blessings of Liberty to ourselves and our Posterity, do ordain and establish this Constitution for the United States of America."

The Constitution as revised by Morris was presented to the Convention on September 12. Several changes were made, and then it was ordered that the Constitution be engrossed on parchment. When the Convention met on September 17, James Wilson read Benjamin Franklin's impassioned speech calling for unanimity among the delegates. Edmund Randolph announced that he could not sign the document because he was sure nine states would not ratify it and that this would result in much public confusion. Morris rose and answered him, as reported by Madison:

"Mr. Gouverneur Morris said, that he too had objections, but considering the present plan as the best that was to be attained, he should take it with all its faults. The majority had determined in its favor, and by that determination he should abide. The moment this plan goes forth, all other considerations will be laid aside, and the great question will be, shall there be a National Government, or not? and this must take place, or a general anarchy will be the alternative. He remarked that the signing, in the form proposed, related only to the fact that *the States* present were unanimous."

Appointed Minister to France

In November, 1788, Morris traveled to France as an agent for the commercial enterprises of Robert Morris, and during the next year he also visited England. While he was there in the fall of 1789, he received a letter from George Washington asking him to sound out the British government to determine whether commercial treaties might be worked out between the countries in "harmony and mutual satisfaction." The negotiations

New York Public Library.

Hudson Falls at the Village of Glen Falls, New York

dragged on and got nowhere. In December, 1791, Washington appointed Morris as Minister to France, and the appointment was confirmed by the Senate in January, 1792. Washington warned Morris that he must be more discreet in his remarks as a diplomat than he had been at the Constitutional Convention, commenting, "that the promptitude, with which your lively and brilliant imagination displays itself, allows too little time for deliberation and correction, and is the primary cause of those sallies, which too often offend, and of that ridicule of character, which begets enmity not easy to be forgotten, but which might easily be avoided, if it were under the control of more caution and prudence."

Witnessed the French Revolution

During the three years Morris spent as United States Minister to France, he witnessed much of the greatest turmoil of the French Revolution. "We stand on a vast volcano," he wrote. "We feel it tremble—we hear it roar. But how and when and where it will burst, and who may be destroyed by its eruptions, it is beyond the ken of mortal foresight to discover." Morris involved himself in private efforts to enable the French king to escape from the revolutionists, and tried to obtain the release of Washington's friend the Marquis de Lafayette; but these activities destroyed his usefulness as a diplomat. In 1794, he was replaced by James Monroe, but he remained in Europe on private business for the next several years.

In 1798, Morris' brother, Lewis Morris, died, and Gouverneur Morris returned to America to take up his residence at the family estate at Morrisania. He created quite a stir on his arrival home, wearing his hair in curls and bringing with him French servants and a French travelling companion.

Campaigned against Thomas Jefferson

Morris was appointed as a United States Senator from New York in April, 1800, to fill out the unexpired term of a Senator who had resigned. He served until March, 1803, using his oratorical powers in the cause of the Federalist party in campaigning against Thomas Jefferson's election as President.

On Christmas Day in 1809, the fifty-seven-year-old Morris invited his relatives to Morrisania and surprised them by marrying Anne Carey Randolph, a member of the aristocratic Virginia family. A year later he summoned his relatives to the baptism of the first child of the marriage, and it is said that one of the witty relatives who had been anticipating the inheritance of Morris' fortune remarked, "I think he had better call his boy after his Russian friend, Kutusoff."

The I. N. Phelps Stokes Collection of American Historical Prints, New York Pub

(1810)
View of West Point on the Hudson River showing the Steamboat, *The Clermont*, going up the River
Litho by F. Berthane à Djòn

In his latter years, Morris devoted considerable time to the construction of the Erie Canal, linking the Great Lakes and the Huron River. He was chairman of the commission to establish a route for the canal in 1810, and his report helped stir public support for the plan. He also was often called upon to make funeral orations, and to speak at various public celebrations. In 1816 he was elected president of the New York Historical Society. At the age of sixty-four, Morris died at Morrisania on November 6, 1816. His friend De Witt Clinton, who completed the Erie Canal while serving as governor of New York, eulogized Morris as follows:

"Morris' intellectual character was distinguished by versatile and great qualities – his colloquial powers were unrivalled—at the Bar or in the Senate he was preeminent – he united wit, logic, pathos, and intelligence, and he wielded the passions and feelings of his audience at pleasure."

The I. N. Phelps Stokes Collection of American Historical Prints, New York Public Library.

South Street from Maiden Lane in New York City

ROBERT MORRIS of PENNSYLVANIA

EDITOR'S NOTE: *Because Robert Morris was one of the six men who signed both the Declaration of Independence and the United States Constitution, a biography of his life is included in Volume I of* FOUNDERS OF FREEDOM, *and the following article is concerned only with his role in the writing of the United States Constitution.*

One of the wealthiest men in the United States, the fifty-three-year-old Robert Morris was vitally interested in seeing to it that his country obtained a strong national government. Prior to the Constitutional Convention, he nominated Benjamin Franklin as a member of Pennsylvania's delegation, knowing that having the name of that elder statesman associated with the new plan for government would help win acceptance for the new Constitution. On the opening of the Convention, he nominated George Washington as President of the meeting, and then helped escort Washington to the rostrum after his election.

Although Morris took little part in the debates on the floor of the Convention, it is safe to assume that he made his influence felt in the discussions between the delegates that took place outside the State House, for his opinion was highly respected in the area of finance. No one could forget that he had contributed mightily to the winning of the Revolutionary War by time and again pledging his personal credit to obtain needed supplies for Washington's soldiers.

Robert Morris
From an engraving by J. B. Longacre and H. B. Hall

ROBERT MORRIS

1734 (Jan. 31) Born in Liverpool, England.

1747 Came to America.

1754-1793 Partner of Thomas Willing as a Philadelphia merchant.

1775 Appointed member of Pennsylvania's committee of safety.

1775-1778 Delegate from Pennsylvania to the Continental Congress; signed the Declaration of Independence and the Articles of Confederation.

1779-1780 Member of the Pennsylvania legislature.

1781-1784 Superintendent of finance and agent of marine for the Congress of the Confederation.

1781 Founded the Bank of North America at Philadelphia.

1785-1786 Member of the Pennsylvania legislature.

1786 Delegate of Pennsylvania to the Annapolis Convention.

1787 Member of Pennsylvania delegation to the Constitutional Convention; signed the United States Constitution.

1789-1795 United States Senator from Pennsylvania.

1798-1801 Jailed for debt after losing his fortune in land speculations.

1806 (May 8) Died in Philadelphia.

Washington's constant companion

Throughout the Convention, Morris was Washington's companion. When Washington arrived in Philadelphia on May 13, 1787, he moved into Morris's mansion on Market Street. This imposing house had once been the home of the proprietary governor Richard Penn, and had later been the headquarters of Sir William Howe during the British occupation of Philadelphia. Morris and Washington went on fishing trips to New Jersey during some of the weekends during the Convention, and, on the Sunday before the United States

THE STATE HOUSE AS IT APPEARED IN 1774.

Constitution was signed, they held a private celebration at The Hills, Morris's country home near Philadelphia.

James Madison said that from the outset of the Convention, Morris favored a plan in which the small states would be denied an equal vote, because he feared that the small states could combine to prevent any measures that were not favorable to them. The only other mention of Morris's participation in the debates in Madison's records came on June 25 when Morris seconded a motion by George Read of Delaware that members of the Senate should be given terms for life "during good behavior."

An honest effort by honest men

After the Constitution had been signed, Morris wrote the following opinion of it to a friend: "This paper has been the subject of infinite investigation, disputation, and declamation. While some have boasted it as a work from Heaven, others have given it a less righteous origin. I have many reasons to believe that it is the work of plain, honest men, and such, I think, it will appear."

Morris took an active role in the new government of the United States, winning office as a U.S. Senator from Pennsylvania from 1789 to 1795. During this term, he succeeded in getting the national capital moved from New York City to Philadelphia.

In his later years he became deeply involved in speculation in western lands, lost his fortune, served a term in debtor's prison, and died a poor man at the age of seventy-two on May 8, 1806.

Library of Congress. Travels Through North America, Isaac Weld.

View of Bethlehem, a Moravian settlement.

WILLIAM PATERSON of NEW JERSEY

The son of an Irish pots and pans peddler, William Paterson rose to become one of the main authors of the United States Constitution, governor of New Jersey, United States senator, and finally, an associate justice of the Supreme Court of the United States. From the outbreak of the Revolutionary War, he devoted more than thirty years of his life to public service. A fellow delegate to the Constitutional Congress, William Pierce, thus described Paterson:

"Paterson is one of those kind of men whose powers break in upon you and create wonder and astonishment. He is a man of great modesty, with looks that bespeak no great talents, but he is a classic, a lawyer and an orator—and of a disposition so favorable to his advancement that every one seemed ready to exalt him with their praises. He is very happy in the choice of time and manner in engaging in debate and never speaks but when he understands his subject well. This gentleman is about thirty-four years of age [he actually was forty-one] and very low in stature."

Son of a door-to-door salesman

William Paterson was born in County Antrim, Ireland, on December 24, 1745, the son of Richard and Mary Paterson. About ten years earlier, Richard Paterson's two brothers had established themselves in America as tinsmiths, and they became so successful that they persuaded Richard to bring his family to the colonies in 1748. Richard Paterson settled in Princeton, N. J., where he opened a small store that he used as headquarters from which he followed a peddler's route from Philadelphia to New England selling pots and pans and other household articles as a door-to-door salesman.

Having been reared as a Presbyterian, it was natural for fourteen-year-old William Paterson to be enrolled in the Presbyterian-sponsored College of New Jersey (now Princeton University). Besides, Nassau Hall, as the college was popularly called, was directly across the street from his father's store. At that time the Reverend Aaron Burr, Sr., was president of the college; and his son, Aaron Burr, Jr., the future vice president of the United States under Thomas Jefferson, later became a law student under Paterson. At the age of seventeen, Paterson was graduated from college;

WILLIAM PATERSON

1745 (Dec. 24) Born in County Antrim, Ireland.
1748 Came to America with his parents.
1763 Graduated from the College of New Jersey (now Princeton).
1766 Received Master of Arts degree from College of New Jersey.
1769 Admitted to practice law before the New Jersey Supreme Court.
1775-1776 Secretary of New Jersey's provincial congress; member of committee that arrested the royal governor, William Franklin.
1776-1783 Attorney general of New Jersey.
1780-1781 Delegate from New Jersey to the Continental Congress.
1786 Delegate from New Jersey to the Annapolis Convention.
1787 Member of New Jersey delegation to the Constitutional Convention; signed the United States Constitution.
1789-1790 U. S. Senator from New Jersey.
1790-1793 Governor of New Jersey.
1793-1806 Associate Justice of the Supreme Court of the United States.
1806 (Sept. 9) Died in Albany, N. Y.

William Paterson
By James Sharples
U. S. Supreme Court.

but he continued his studies and received a Master of Arts degree from the College of New Jersey in 1766.

Studied law under Richard Stockton

Paterson took up the study of law under Richard Stockton, who later became a signer of the Declaration of Independence; and in 1769, at the age of twenty-three, Paterson was admitted to practice law before the Supreme Court of New Jersey. After unsuccessfully trying to start a combination general store and law office in New Bromley, N. J., Paterson moved to Raritan, N. J., where he went into partnership with his brother Thomas in a store and a legal practice.

As troubles with the British government mounted in the 1770's, Paterson took an active part in the patriotic movement. He became secretary of the New Jersey committee of safety responsible for raising and equipping a militia, and in 1775 he was elected as a delegate to a provincial congress of New Jersey patriots. Paterson was elected as secretary of the provincial congress, and in 1776 he was appointed as one of a four-man committee who arrested the royal governor, William Franklin, the natural son of Benjamin Franklin. Paterson also helped in drawing up the state constitution that was adopted in 1776. That same year he was appointed as attorney general under the new state government, an office that he held for the next seven years.

Bought a Loyalist estate with Continental currency

At the age of thirty-three, Paterson married Cornelia Bell. They lived on a four-hundred-acre estate near Raritan, N. J., that had been confiscated by the state of New Jersey from a Loyalist and had in turn been purchased by Paterson with $60,000 of inflated Continental currency. They had three children, two daughters and a son. After his first wife died, Paterson was married again in 1785, this time to Euphemia White.

Paterson was elected by the legislature as one of the state's delegation to the Continental Congress in 1780-1781, but his duties as attorney general of New Jersey were so arduous that he was unable to devote much attention to the national office. After he retired as attorney general, he was chosen as a New Jersey delegate to the Annapolis Convention of 1786 that paved the way for a revision of the Articles of Confederation. Then in 1787 he was named as a member of the state's delegation to the Constitutional Convention in Philadelphia.

Opposed the "Virginia Plan"

At the Constitutional Convention, Paterson became the leading spokesman for the small states, opposing the plans of the three large states (Virginia, Massachusetts, and Pennsylvania) to base the number of members in the national legislature from each state entirely on the size of their populations. After the Convention had been in session for nearly two weeks, Paterson denounced the "Virginia Plan" saying in part, as reported by James Madison:

"New Jersey will never confederate on the plan before the Committee. She would be swallowed up. He had rather submit to a monarch, to a despot, than to such a fate. He would not only oppose the plan here, but on his return home do every thing in his power to defeat it there."

Proposed the "New Jersey Plan"

On June 15, 1787, Paterson presented the Convention with the "New Jersey Plan" which called for maintaining the existing Congress of the Confederation with an equal representation from each state but extending its powers and adding a na-

View of the White House in 1807.

Library of Congress.

Library of Congress, Itineraire Pittoresque, J. Milbert.

View in Albany, House of the first Dutch Governors

tional executive and a national judiciary. Paterson argued that the delegates to the Convention had only been authorized to amend the Articles of Confederation, whereas in his opinion the "Virginia Plan" would create a government that was not federal in character.

The debate between the large states and the small states dragged into the middle of the hot Philadelphia summer, and, on July 16, Paterson suggested that the Convention should adjourn and the members should return home. His suggestion was disregarded, however, and the debate continued until July 26 when a Committee of Detail was appointed with John Rutledge as chairman to put together all the various plans into a Constitution. At this point, Paterson returned to New Jersey and did not come back to the Convention until September, when he signed the Constitution with the other delegates.

Helped organize the federal court system

In November, 1788, Paterson was elected by the state legislature as one of New Jersey's first U. S. Senators. In the year and a half that Paterson served as a Senator, his most important contribution was as a member of the committee that drew up legislation that established the system of federal courts. He did not enjoy life in New York away from his family, writing to Mrs. Paterson:

"Gay life has never been my wish; my disposition is naturally pensive and in general I had much rather take a solitary walk in a grove or among tombs than mingle in the festivities and pleasures of a ball. I hope soon to take my leave of my present station and return to private life."

Paterson was not to get his wish, for he never again returned to private life, except for a few months before his death. In 1790, the governor of New Jersey, William Livingston, died; and in November of that year the legislature elected Paterson to take his place. He resigned from the Senate on November 23, 1790, and immediately was sworn into office as the state's chief executive.

Revised, translated, and codified the New Jersey laws

During Paterson's administration as governor

two noteworthy events took place. In 1792, the legislature assigned him the task of revising and codifying all the laws of the state, translating into English the Latin and French phrases that appeared in old colonial laws and British laws. This assignment took Paterson eight years to complete, the revised laws finally being published in 1800. Also in 1792, Governor Paterson signed the charter establishing Paterson, N. J., which was named after him; this city was planned to become the largest manufacturing center in the country under a plan proposed by Alexander Hamilton.

Associate justice of the U.S. Supreme Court

In 1793, Paterson left the office of governor and donned the robes of a judge when President George Washington appointed him as an associate justice of the Supreme Court of the United States. Paterson served in this judicial role with distinction. One of the most notable cases that appeared before him was the trial of the ringleaders of Pennsylvania's Whisky Rebellion.Washington tried to persuade Paterson to step down from the bench and become his Secretary of State in 1795, but Paterson declined because he did not wish to become involved in the political controversies then raging.

In 1804, Paterson was critically injured when a team of horses ran away with his carriage and upset it. He was bedridden for many weeks, and when he returned to his judicial duties his health was broken. He retired in July, 1806; and two months later, on September 9, 1806, he died at the age of sixty-one while on a visit to the home of his daughter in Albany, N. Y.

Library of Congress.

View of the Mohawk River, about six miles from Albany.

CHARLES PINCKNEY of SOUTH CAROLINA

One of the youngest as well as one of the most active members of the Constitutional Convention, Charles Pinckney was the author of the *Pinckney Plan*—a draft for a national constitution that included about thirty of the provisions ultimately agreed upon in the United States Constitution. Because no completely authentic copy of the original *Pinckney Plan* has ever been found, all of Pinckney's exact contributions to the form of the United States government are not known. But historians are generally agreed that he deserves considerable credit for many of the terms and features of the Constitution.

Supported Thomas Jefferson for the presidency

A cousin of Charles Cotesworth Pinckney, a fellow-signer of the Constitution, Charles Pinckney became a leader of the Democratic-Republican party and helped win the presidency for Thomas Jefferson. As a result, Federalists nicknamed him "Blackguard Charlie" to distinguish him from his cousin, who was a prominent Federalist. Charles Pinckney's career as a brilliant lawyer and politician extended nearly fifty years, from the outbreak of the Revolutionary War to the Missouri Compromise, which he opposed. He was elected four times as governor of South Carolina, served as a United States Senator and as U. S. Minister to Spain. His final public service was as U. S. Representative in Congress.

Charles Pinckney was born in Charleston, S.C., on October 26, 1757. His father, Colonel Charles Pinckney, was a wealthy lawyer and plantation owner, a leader in the colonial legislature, and commander of Charleston's military fortifications. Like his cousins, Charles Cotesworth Pinckney and Thomas Pinckney, Charles Pinckney was sent to England for his education. He was a remarkable student, and won admittance to law training

CHARLES PINCKNEY

1757 (October 26) Born in Charleston, S. C.

1775-1776 Member of three-man executive council in charge of South Carolina's revolutionary government.

1776 Member of committee that drafted South Carolina's first state constitution.

1779-1780 Member of South Carolina state legislature.

1780-1781 Captain of militia in Revolutionary War; captured by British and imprisoned at St. Augustine, Fla.

1784-1787 Delegate to the Congress of the Confederation.

1786-1787 Member of the South Carolina legislature.

1787 Member of the South Carolina delegation to the Constitutional Convention; drafted the Pinckney Plan; signed the United States Constitution.

1788 Led Federalist forces at South Carolina ratification convention.

1789-1792 Governor of South Carolina.

1790 President of South Carolina state constitutional convention.

1792-1796 Member of South Carolina state legislature.

1796-1798 Governor of South Carolina.

1798-1801 United States Senator from South Carolina.

1801-1805 United States Minister to Spain.

1805-1806 Member of South Carolina state legislature.

1806-1808 Governor of South Carolina.

1810-1814 Member of South Carolina legislature.

1819-1821 U.S. Representative from South Carolina in Congress.

1824 (October 29) Died in Charleston, S. C.

Charles Pinckney
Attributed to GILBERT STUART
Frick Art Reference Library, American Scenic and Historic Preservation Society Collection.

From a watercolor by A. B. Bibb, Carolina Art Association, Gibbes Gallery, Charleston, S. C.

Residence of Charles Pinckney
(Washington was entertained here)

at the Middle Temple in London when he was only fifteen years old.

Imprisoned by the British

Returning to South Carolina at the outset of the Revolutionary War, young Pinckney was admitted to the bar. He immediately plunged into patriotic activities, aided by his father who was chairman of the colony's Committee of Safety and president of the colony's patriotic congress. When his father retired from public life because he did not believe in independence for the colonies from Great Britain, eighteen-year-old Charles Pinckney stepped into his father's shoes. He served as a member of the temporary three-man executive council that administered the affairs of South Carolina in 1775 and in early 1776, and then aided the committee that drafted the first constitution for the new state in 1776. He was elected to the state legislature in 1779. The next year, while serving as a captain of militia, he was captured by the British during the siege of Charleston. With other "dangerous" revolutionary leaders, he was sent to the British prison at St. Augustine, Fla., and remained there until he won his freedom in an exchange of prisoners in 1781.

After the war, Pinckney's family influence and his legal abilities won him a successful law practice. In 1784, when he was twenty-seven years old, he was elected by the state legislature as a delegate to the Congress of the Confederation. Like Alexander Hamilton and James Madison, Pinckney realized the need for changes in the Articles of Confederation to provide a stronger national government, and he began urging that a convention be called to revise the Articles. In 1786, he was appointed chairman of a congressional sub-committee that drew up recommendations for a series of amendments to the Articles that would have given Congress power to collect taxes.

Originated the Pinckney Plan

When the Constitutional Convention was called in Philadelphia in 1787, the twenty-nine-year-old Pinckney was elected by the state legislature as a member of the South Carolina delegation; and in the weeks before the meeting he spent many hours drawing up a detailed plan of government. On May 29, the fifth day of the convention, he presented this *Pinckney Plan* to the delegates immediately after Edmund Randolph had pre-

Library of Congress.

The victorious Colonial Army in New York, 1783.

sented the *Virginia Plan*. Apparently because Randolph had submitted his proposal first, it was taken up first. Discussion dragged on for many weeks, while Pinckney's plan was never discussed as such by the delegates as a whole. However, on July 26, the Virginia resolutions, the *Pinckney Plan*, and a plan submitted by William Paterson of New Jersey all were turned over to John Rutledge's committee of detail to draw up a complete constitution.

Constitution adopted many of Pinckney's ideas

The actual form and wording of the *Pinckney Plan* is an historical mystery that has never been solved. The official journal of the convention did not contain a copy of the plan, and neither did James Madison's report on the debates in the convention. In 1818, John Quincy Adams, who was then Secretary of State, wrote to Pinckney and asked him if he had a copy of the original plan that might be placed in the national archives. Pinckney replied: "It is impossible for me now to say which of the 4 or 5 draughts I have is the one. But enclosed I send you the one I believe was it." The plan which Pinckney sent Adams was an elaborate constitution with a preamble and sixteen articles, containing much the same language as the United States Constitution finally approved. Considerable doubt as to the authenticity of this plan was raised when it was discovered that Pinckney had written it on paper that carried a watermark of 1797—ten years after the Constitutional Convention had been held. Further, it

Henry Laurens

was disclosed that Pinckney had written to a friend in 1788 saying, "I would with pleasure send you a copy of my system on which these observations are founded . . . but I have not one —the original being laid before the Convention, and the copy I gave to a gentleman to the Northward." In the early 1900's, historians discovered notes taken by James Wilson, who was a member of the convention's committee of detail, which are believed to represent the contents of the *Pinckney Plan*. Based on these notes, some historians believe that Pinckney's original plan may have been used as the copy on which the committee of detail made its report that was delivered to a printer, set in type, and then lost. However, even though the *Pinckney Plan* as such may be lost to history, it seems safe to assume that Pinckney's draft of a constitution contained many ideas that were used by the Founding Fathers in drafting the final document.

A lengthy speech supporting Constitution

After signing the United States Constitution in September, 1787, Pinckney returned to South Carolina where he became a leader of the forces calling for ratification. He presented the new Constitution to the state legislature in a lengthy speech in January, 1788, in which he concluded that the new plan of government "is better calculated to answer the great ends of public happiness than any that has yet been devised." Two weeks before the state ratification convention met in 1788, Pinckney married Mary Eleanor Laurens, daughter of Henry Laurens, the wealthiest merchant in Charleston and a former president of the Continental Congress. He then attended the ratification convention where he harangued the delegates with his reasons for believing the Constitution should be approved. He said in part:

"The advantages of a republic are, liberty—exemption from needless restrictions—equal laws—public spirit—averseness to war—frugality—above all, the opportunities afforded to men of every description, of producing their abilities and counsels to public observation, and the exciting to the service of the commonwealth the faculties of its best citizens. . . .

"The citizens of the United States would reprobate, with indignation, the idea of a monarchy. But the essential qualities of a monarchy—unity of council — vigor — secrecy — and despatch, are qualities essential in every government.

Laws executed with energy and despatch

"While, therefore, we have reserved to the people, the fountain of all power, the periodical election of their first magistrate—while we have defined his powers, and bound them to such limits as will effectually prevent his usurping authorities dangerous to the general welfare—we have, at the same time, endeavored to infuse into this department that degree of vigor which will enable the president to execute the laws with energy and despatch. . . .

"To the philosophic mind how new and awful an instance do the United States, at present, exhibit in the political world! They exhibit, sir, the first instance of a people, who, being dissatisfied with their government unattached by foreign force, and undisturbed by domestic uneasiness—coolly and deliberately resort to the virtue and good sense of their country, for a correction of their public errors. . . ."

Elected governor of South Carolina

In January, 1789, Pinckney was elected governor of South Carolina by the state legislature. He wrote to a friend that he probably could have been elected one of the state's first United States Senators, but that "considerations of a private nature prevented me from becoming a candidate. In 1790, Pinckney was elected president of a convention that wrote a new constitution for South Carolina. He was elected to a second term as governor in 1791.

Acquired the nickname of "Blackguard Charlie"

After completing his administration as governor in 1792, Pinckney took a seat in the state legislature for the next four years. During this period he shifted from the Federalist party and became a Democratic-Republican. When George Washington announced the signing of the Jay Treaty with Great Britain, Pinckney called for John Jay's impeachment as Chief Justice of the United States. Pinckney's former friends in the Federalist party retaliated by pinning the nickname "Blackguard Charlie" on him.

Rewarded by Thomas Jefferson for his backing

Pinckney won re-election as governor in 1796, the first Democratic-Republican to hold the office. He continued his success in 1798, being elected by the state legislature as a United States Senator. In the presidential election of 1800, Pinckney promised federal jobs to many South Carolina legislators if they would support electors favorable to Thomas Jefferson. Jefferson won the state's eight electoral votes and with them, the presidency, even though Pinckney's cousin, Charles Cotesworth Pinckney, was John Adams' running-mate for Vice President on the Federalist ticket. As a reward, President Jefferson appointed Charles Pinckney as U.S. Minister to Spain in 1801.

After his return from his diplomatic mission, Pinckney served about a year in the state legislature. He then won his fourth election as governor in 1806, an office that he held until 1808. During the War of 1812, Pinckney was a member of the state legislature. He held his last major political office as a U.S. Representative from South Carolina in the 16th Congress, from 1819 to 1821. There he distinguished himself by his opposition to the Missouri Compromise.

At the age of sixty-seven, Pinckney died in Charleston, S.C., on October 29, 1824. He was buried in the graveyard of St. Philip's church, apparently near the grave of his father. Vandals apparently defaced his gravestone, and there is some doubt as to his exact resting place.

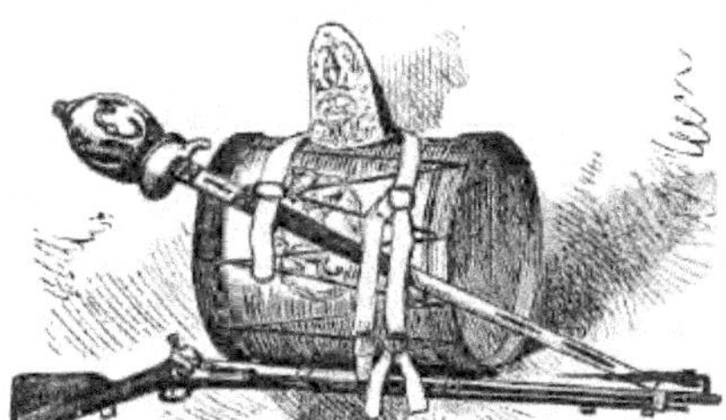

Library of Congress.

Reproduction of a Colonial poster

Courtesy: Carolina Art Association. A Charleston Sketchbook, Charles Fraser.

The South View of Fort Mechanic, Charleston
(July 4th, 1796)

Courtesy: Carolina Art Association. A Charleston Sketchbook, Charles Fraser.

A Basin and Storehouse in the Santee Canal
(1803)

Courtesy: Louisiana State Museum

A sugar refinery on a Louisiana plantation
The refinery is the red building at the right

CHARLES COTESWORTH PINCKNEY of SOUTH CAROLINA

A wealthy lawyer and plantation owner, Charles Cotesworth Pinckney distinguished himself among the Founding Fathers as a soldier, a diplomat, and a politician. He took an active part in the fighting during the Revolutionary War, rising from captain to brigadier general; and he spent more than a year as a British prisoner after the capture of Charleston, S. C. He helped write the United States Constitution and two constitutions for his own state. He won national prominence as an American diplomat in Paris, when he upheld his country's honor by exposing the X Y Z Affair in which French representatives attempted to obtain bribes from the United States, occasioning the coining of the slogan, "Millions for defense, but not one cent for tribute!" When war seemed imminent with France in 1798, he was appointed third in command of the new United States Army, ranking only after George Washington and Alexander Hamilton. As the leader of the Federalist party in the South, he was that party's candidate for President against Thomas Jefferson in 1800 and against James Madison in 1804, but was unsuccessful. His friend Christopher E. Gadsden said of Pinckney:

"He was an early, decided, and devoted promoter of the revolution, courting the scenes of difficult duty and danger, and *chusing* to be the companion of Washington. The friendship of these illustrious individuals was never interrupted, and the younger enjoyed a series of marks of confidence . . . greater than were bestowed upon any other man. . . . According to the judgment of that great man, General Pinckney was qualified for every variety of elevated station, executive, judicial, diplomatic or military. He was invited into the cabinet on two occasions; was offered a seat on the bench of the Supreme Court; sent on a foreign embassy of extraordinary importance, and twice called to prominent offices in the army. . . .

CHARLES COTESWORTH PINCKNEY

1746 (Feb. 25) Born in Charleston, S. C.

1753-1769 Educated in England and France.

1770 Admitted to the bar to practice law in Charleston, S. C.

1773 Appointed assistant attorney general of South Carolina.

1775 Member of the South Carolina patriotic provincial congress.

1776-1783 Served as an officer in the Revolutionary War, rising to rank of brevet brigadier general.

1780-1782 Prisoner of the British.

1787 Delegate from South Carolina to the Constitutional Convention; signed the United States Constitution.

1789 Presidential elector for South Carolina.

1790 Member of convention that wrote new state constitution.

1796-1798 United States diplomatic representative in France.

1798-1800 Major general and third in command of new United States Army.

1800 Federalist party candidate for vice president.

1804, 1808 Federalist party candidate for president.

1825 (Aug. 1) Died in Charleston, S. C.

"His private life was exemplary."

"His private life was . . . exemplary as the head of a family, the kindest of brothers, a sincere and constant and generous friend, a good citizen, fulfilling alike his duties to the government and to the community, and placing his great influence zealously, and firmly, and perseveringly, on the side of law, and order, of morality and religion. Political measures when approved, he fearlessly vindicated, and those which he disapproved, he as fearlessly canvassed, and by peaceable and constitutional means sought to have them corrected....

"In general intercourse, the law of kindness was on his lips. It was the hand of a hearty well-wisher which was extended to you. It was the freedom of a man, who recognized you as his fellow citizen, which welcomed you. You saw no look of half-subdued pride. You heard no whisper of vanity. The most suspicious searched in vain for the least symptom of insincerity. The door of hospitality was widely thrown open, and when you entered it you were instantly made happy by a pure benevolence, and saw around you as much happiness as falls to the lot of humanity, affectionate children, domestics obviously well governed and well provided for, and at the head of this scene, the venerable patriarch with a countenance glowing with satisfaction."

The son of a remarkable mother

Charles Cotesworth Pinckney was born in Charleston, S. C., on February 25, 1746. His father, Charles Pinckney, was chief justice of the colony. His mother, Elizabeth Lucas Pinckney,

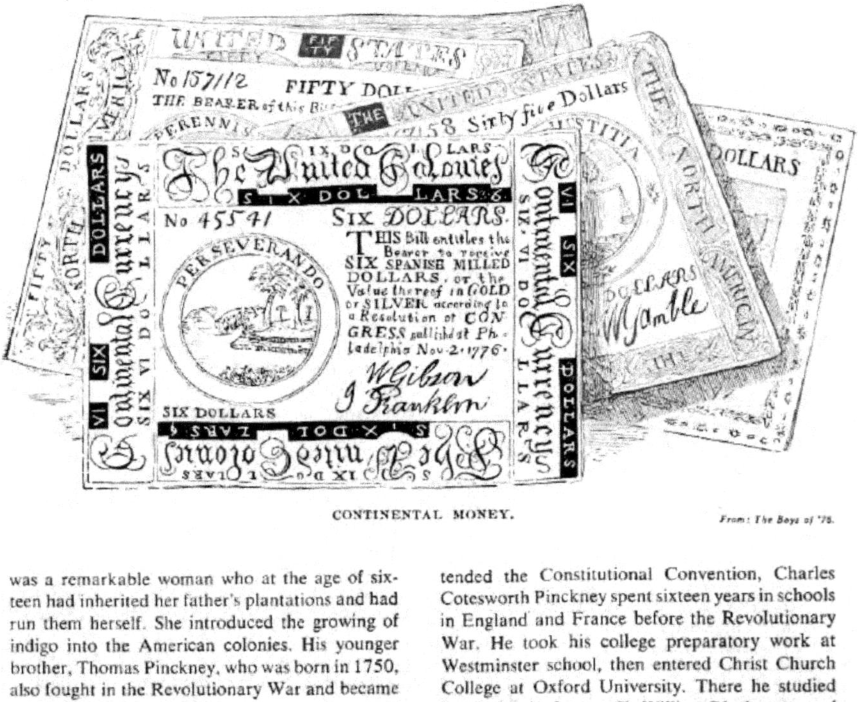

CONTINENTAL MONEY.

From: The Boys of '76.

was a remarkable woman who at the age of sixteen had inherited her father's plantations and had run them herself. She introduced the growing of indigo into the American colonies. His younger brother, Thomas Pinckney, who was born in 1750, also fought in the Revolutionary War and became governor of South Carolina.

In 1753, Chief Justice Pinckney went to Great Britain as an agent for South Carolina, and he took with him his wife and children. When he and Mrs. Pinckney returned to South Carolina in 1758, the boys were left in England to continue their education. Upon his return to America, Chief Justice Pinckney found that his plantations had been mismanaged during his absence; he so over-exerted himself trying to put them in order that he died. The resourceful Mrs. Pinckney took over the plantations, managing them until her death in 1793.

Spent sixteen years in schools in England and France

One of the most highly educated men who attended the Constitutional Convention, Charles Cotesworth Pinckney spent sixteen years in schools in England and France before the Revolutionary War. He took his college preparatory work at Westminster school, then entered Christ Church College at Oxford University. There he studied law under the famous Sir William Blackstone, and took four volumes of notes on the lectures of this first professor of English law. After completing his work at Oxford University at the age of eighteen, Pinckney continued the study of law at the Temple in London. Finally, he rounded off his education with a tour of France and Germany and nine months of training at the Royal Military Academy of Caen in France.

Returning to South Carolina at the age of twenty-three, Pinckney was admitted to the bar to practice law in 1770. Three years later, the attorney general of the colony recognized the young lawyer's ability by appointing him his deputy to act for him in district courts.

Charles Cotesworth Pinckney
By JAMES EARL

Charles Cotesworth Pinckney
Attributed to JAMES SHARPLES, SR.

A true southern aristocrat

By birth and by marriage he was a member of the aristocracy of South Carolina. He married Sarah Middleton, the daughter of Henry Middleton, the wealthiest planter in the colony. By this marriage he became the brother-in-law of two men who were to sign the Declaration of Independence —Edward Rutledge, who married Sarah's sister Henrietta, and Arthur Middleton, Sarah's brother. Charles Cotesworth Pinckney was also a cousin of Charles Pinckney, a fellow-signer of the United States Constitution.

With the outbreak of the Revolutionary War in Massachusetts, Charles Cotesworth Pinckney plunged into patriotic and military activities. He was elected to the patriotic convention of South Carolina in 1775, and that same year was elected captain in one of two regiments of infantry. He was advanced to lieutenant colonel by the next year when he helped in the successful defense of Charleston from a British attack by sea. In 1778, he commanded a regiment in an unsuccessful expedition against the British forces in Florida. During the siege of Charleston in 1780 when a council of the leading officers was called, Pinckney is said to have exclaimed:

"I will not say, if the enemy attempt to carry our lines by storm, that we shall be able to resist them successfully: but am convinced we shall so cripple the army before us, that although we may not live to enjoy the benefits ourselves, yet to the United States they will prove incalculably great. Considerations of self are out of the question. They cannot influence any member of this council. My voice is for rejecting all terms of capitulation, and for continuing hostilities to the last extremity."

Taken prisoner by the British

Pinckney's advice was not taken—Charleston surrendered to the British in May, 1780, and Pinckney and many other prisoners were taken to a prison camp on Haddrel's Point, about two miles from the city. Pinckney became ill from the privations he suffered in the camp, and was granted leave to visit his family. Upon returning to Charleston, he found that his only son had just died; but before he could bury the child, the British cancelled his leave and forced him to return to the prison camp. Pinckney finally was released in an exchange of prisoners in February, 1782. He took part in no more fighting, but in November of the next year he was promoted to the rank of brevet brigadier general.

After the war, Pinckney resumed his law practice. His chief competitors were his cousin Charles Pinckney, his brother Thomas Pinckney, and his brother-in-law Edward Rutledge. He served rich and poor alike, and it was said he never sent a bill for his services to a widow; but the annual income from his law practice rose to four thousand guineas (about twenty thousand dollars), a huge sum for the time.

A delegate to the Constitutional Convention

In 1787, Pinckney was chosen as one of the members of South Carolina's delegation to the Constitutional Convention. He took his seat at the opening of the meeting on May 25 and remained throughout the summer, aiding in the deliberations with the wisdom of his extensive legal background.

At the outset of the Convention, Pinckney doubted that the delegates were authorized to set up an entirely new form of government rather than merely suggest changes in the Articles of Confederation; and, when he saw that the other delegates were determined to move ahead, he warned them not to set up a national government that took too many powers away from the state legislatures. He

The I. N. Phelps Stokes Collection of American Historical Prints, New York Public Library.

Launching the steam frigate, *Fulton the First*, at New York, 29 October, 1814

made this clear in a speech on June 6, as reported by James Madison:

"General Pinckney wished to have a good National Government, and at the same time to leave a considerable share of power in the States. An election of either branch by the people, scattered as they are in many States, particularly in South Carolina, was totally impracticable. He differed from gentlemen who thought that a choice by the people would be a better guard against bad measures, than by the Legislatures. A majority of the people in South Carolina were notoriously for paper-money, as a legal tender; the Legislature had refused to make it a legal tender. The reason was, that the latter had some sense of character, and were restrained by that consideration. The State Legislatures, also, he said, would be more jealous, and more ready to thwart the National Government, if excluded from a participation in it. The idea of abolishing these Legislatures would never go down."

Urged protection for the system of slavery

Pinckney consistently urged that larger representation be given to the Southern States in Congress, claiming that the Northern States were trying to set themselves up to control the wealth of the South. On July 23, he warned the Convention that if it failed "to insert some security to the Southern States against an emancipation of slaves, and taxes on exports," he would be forced to vote against the Constitution. He also got the Convention to agree to extend from 1800 to 1808 the period under which Congress might not prohibit the importation of slaves. After signing the United States Constitution, he returned to South Carolina where he helped rally support for it in the state ratification convention.

In the years after the Constitution had been ratified and George Washington was organizing the new government, Pinckney repeatedly declined invitations from the president to take important offices. In 1791, he was offered a seat on the Supreme Court, and in 1795 he was offered the position of Secretary of War, then that of Secretary of State; but each time he replied that his personal affairs stood in the way of accepting a federal appointment.

Then, in July, 1796, he responded favorably to an especially urgent appeal from Washington that he accept the position of envoy to France, replacing James Monroe. Taking his wife and daughter with him, Pinckney arrived in September in Philadelphia, where he conferred with Washington. He and his family then embarked for France, arriving in Paris in December.

Pinckney received a cold reception in Paris from the revolutionary Directory then in power. He was informed that France refused to recognize him as a representative, and he was ordered to leave the country. So Pinckney and his family retired to the Netherlands to await further instructions.

"It is no, no! Not a sixpence."

John Adams had succeeded Washington as president in March, 1797, and he now appointed John Marshall and Elbridge Gerry to join Pinckney in a new effort "to dissipate umbrages, remove prejudices, rectify errors, and adjust all differences by a treaty between the two powers." The three reached Paris in October, 1797. They were met with a demand that President Adams apologize for certain remarks he had made about France, that bribes of about a quarter of a million dollars be paid to French officials, and that the United States should underwrite a loan of about thirteen million dollars—all this as a price of resuming friendly relations. The negotiations with the American envoys were carried on by unofficial representatives of France who were identified only as X, Y, and Z. When the French insisted on a reply to their request for money, Pinckney replied, "It is no, no! Not a sixpence!"

The public disclosure of the XYZ Affair caused a great public outcry against France in the United States. A magazine writer coined the slogan, "Millions for defense, but not one cent for tribute!" Preparations for a possible war with France were rushed.

"Let us first dispose of our enemies."

When Pinckney arrived back in the United States in October, 1798, he found that upon the recommendation of Washington, President Adams had appointed him major general in the new United States Army, third in command after Washington and Alexander Hamilton. Washington had been fearful that Pinckney might reject the appointment, because at the end of the Revolutionary War he had held a higher rank than Hamilton, who had been a colonel; but Pinckney accepted the commission, stating:

"I am confident that General Washington had sufficient reasons for this preference. Let us first dispose of our enemies, we shall then have leisure to settle the question of rank."

For the next several months Pinckney was busy aiding Washington and Hamilton in the plans for the new army, appointing officers, ordering supplies, and recruiting men. Then, in December, 1799, Washington died, and a few months later a new American diplomatic mission to France reached a peaceful settlement of the difficulties.

A losing candidate for vice president

A Congressional caucus of Federalists in May, 1800, chose Pinckney as the vice presidential candidate to run with President Adams against the Democratic-Republican candidates, Thomas Jefferson for president and Aaron Burr for vice president. A split between Adams and Hamilton wrecked the Federalist party, and the Jefferson-Burr ticket won the election.

After Adams retired and Hamilton was killed in a duel with Burr, Pinckney became the leading figure in the Federalist party. He ran as the Federalist candidate for president against Jefferson in 1804 and against James Madison in 1808, but both times the Federalists were severely beaten.

In the remaining years of his life, Pinckney spent much of his time at his country estate, Pinckney Island, where he conducted scientific experiments in chemistry and botany. From 1805 until his death, Pinckney was president of the Society of the Cincinnati, the association of officers who had served in the Revolutionary War. He also was president of the Bible Society of Charleston for the last fifteen years of his life. At the age of seventy-nine, he died in Charleston on August 1, 1825.

GEORGE READ of DELAWARE

Editor's Note: *Because George Read was one of the six men who signed both the Declaration of Independence and the United States Constitution, a biography of his life is included in Volume I of* Founders of Freedom, *and the following article is concerned only with his role in the writing of the United States Constitution.*

Fifty-three-year-old George Read, who headed Delaware's delegation to the Constitutional Convention, was a distinguished lawyer who believed so strongly in the need for a more powerful national government that he favored abolishing the states, and allowing the President to appoint the members of the Senate. He attended the Convention regularly from the first day to the last, taking an active part in the debates.

Spokesman for equal voting rights

From the outset of the Convention, Read was an important spokesman for the small states in their effort to preserve their voting rights against the larger states. On the fourth day of the Convention, Wednesday, May 30, 1787, James Madison had moved, and Gouverneur Morris had seconded, a resolution providing "that the equality of suffrage established by the Articles of Confederation ought not to prevail in the National Legislature; and that an equitable ratio of representation ought to be substituted." Madison's journal of the debates angrily notes that his resolution "being generally relished, would have been agreed to," but Read moved that the motion be postponed, reminding the delegates "that the Deputies from Delaware were restrained by their commission from assenting to any change of the rule of suffrage, and in case such a change should be fixed on, it might become their duty to retire from the Convention." Fearing that if Delaware walked out of the Convention before it was a week old, the entire plan for a new government might fail, the rest of the delegates gave in to Read's demand and postponed consideration of the matter of how the states were to be represented in the new Congress.

Advocated a strong central government

On June 6, during a debate on whether the first branch of Congress should be elected by the people or by the state legislatures, Read made his first plea for a strong national government instead of a federal government, saying: "Too much attachment is betrayed to the State Governments. We must look beyond their continuance. A National Government must soon of necessity swallow them all up. They will soon be reduced to the mere office of electing the National Senate." He was against patching up the old Federal system,

GEORGE READ

1733 (Sept. 18) Born on his father's plantation near North East, Md.

1753 Admitted to the bar to practice law.

1763-1774 Attorney general for the crown for Delaware.

1765-1780 Member of the Delaware legislature.

1774-1779 Delegate from Delaware to the Continental Congress; signed the Declaration of Independence.

1776 President of the Delaware state constitutional convention.

1777-1778 Acting president of Delaware.

1782-1789 Judge of the court of appeals in admiralty cases.

1786 Delegate from Delaware to the Annapolis Convention.

1787 Member of the Constitutional Convention; signed the United States Constitution.

1789-1793 United States Senator from Delaware.

1793-1798 Chief justice of Delaware.

1798 (Sept. 21) Died at New Castle, Del.

Courtesy: Frick Art Reference Library. Owner: Mrs. George Clymer

George Read
By R. E. Pine

The Historical Society of Delaware, Wilmington.
From a pencil sketch by Dr. Allan V. Lesley. Photo by Sanborn Studio.

Residence of George Read
Newcastle, Delaware

and hoped the idea would be dismissed. "It would be like putting new cloth on an old garment. The confederation was founded on temporary principles. It cannot last: it cannot be amended. If we do not establish a good government on new principles, we must either go to ruin, or have the work to do over again. The people at large are wrongly suspected of being averse to a General Government. The aversion lies among interested men who possess their confidence."

The next day, when the debate continued on whether one or both branches of Congress should be elected by the state legislatures, Read made the unusual proposal that "the Senate should be appointed by the Executive magistrate, out of a proper number of persons to be nominated by the individual Legislatures." Madison's journal records Read's opinions: "He thought it his duty to speak his mind frankly. Gentlemen, he hoped, would not be alarmed at the idea. Nothing short of this approach towards a proper model of government would answer the purpose, and he thought it best to come directly to the point at once." However, no other delegate seconded or supported Read's proposal, and it was dropped.

Favored elimination of state boundaries

The next Monday, June 11, Read again called for eliminating the states as part of the new government. In debate on a resolution that called for "guaranteeing republican government and territory to each State," Read said that he disliked the idea of guaranteeing the territory of each state. He said, "It abetted the idea of distinct States, which would be a perpetual source of discord. There can be no cure for this evil but in doing away with States altogether, and uniting them all into one society." This time Read's proposal was

Library of Congress. Itinéraire Pittoresque, J. Milbert.

Foundry on Tone's Creek near Baltimore

accepted, and the territorial guarantee of the states was dropped from the resolution.

Read favored a long term for Senators in the new government. On June 25, he proposed that Senators should serve for life "during their good behavior," but his idea failed to win acceptance. The next day he proposed that the term be for nine years. He pointed out that longer terms of office would give the Senators more of a national viewpoint. He said that he "wished it to be considered by the small States that it was their interest that we should become one people as much as possible; that State attachments should be extinguished as much as possible; that the Senate should be so constituted as to have the feelings of citizens of the whole." After Read's proposal won support from only Pennsylvania and Virginia, as well as his own state of Delaware, he then voted for a six-year term for Senators.

Refused the prayers of a clergyman

At the end of June, the Convention still seemed unable to agree on how the number of representatives in the new Congress should be divided among the states, and had even been unwilling to accept Benjamin Franklin's suggestion that they employ a clergyman to lead them in prayer. Read again called for the abolition of the states in the new government. Madison reported Read's opinions as follows:

"He should have no objection to the system if it were truly national, but it has too much of a federal mixture in it. The little States, he thought, had not much to fear. He suspected that the large States felt their want of energy, and wished for a General Government to supply the defect. Massachusetts was evidently laboring under her weakness, and he believed Delaware would not be in much danger if in her neighborhood. Delaware had enjoyed tranquillity, and he flattered himself would continue to do so. He was not, however, so selfish as not to wish for a good General Government. In order to obtain one, the whole States must be incorporated. If the States remain, the representatives of the large ones will stick together, and carry every thing before them. The Executive, also, will be chosen under the influence of this practicality, and will betray it in his administration. These jealousies are inseparable from the scheme of leaving the States in existence. They must be done away. The ungranted lands, also, which have been assumed by particular States, must be given up." Read then went on to say that he preferred Alexander Hamilton's plan of government, which called for a national executive and a Senate, both elected for life.

Served on the committee of apportionment

On July 9, Read was appointed to a committee of eleven members, one from each state, to consider how the number of representatives in the House of Representatives should be apportioned among the states. The next day, the committee reported that it favored a total of sixty-five representatives, with ten allocated to Virginia as the largest state, and only one each to Delaware and Rhode Island, the smallest states. Read made an effort to have the number doubled for all the states, but was supported only by Virginia.

Once the important question of representation in Congress between the large and small states had been settled, Read took less part in the debates of the Convention. He continued to voice his opinion on various minor matters, but made no further major speeches. On the last day of the Convention, Read signed both for himself and his friend John Dickinson, who had been forced to leave early because of sickness.

Read aided in the campaign that resulted in Delaware's being the first state to ratify the new United States Constitution. He then served for more than four years as one of the state's first U.S. Senators, but resigned that office in 1793 to become chief justice of Delaware's supreme court. Read died at the age of sixty-five on September 21, 1798.

The Old Colony Seal.

JOHN RUTLEDGE of SOUTH CAROLINA

A distinguished lawyer who seldom lost a case, John Rutledge won the nickname of "Dictator John" as the chief executive officer of South Carolina throughout most of the Revolutionary War. The fame of his eloquence was such that no less an authority than Patrick Henry called him "by far the greatest orator" in the first Continental Congress. Rutledge's legal knowledge was used extensively in the writing of the United States Constitution, which he also signed. He served for a short while as an associate justice of the Supreme Court of the United States, and an even shorter time as acting Chief Justice of the United States. He felt so strongly in favor of the federal union that he named one of his sons "States" Rutledge.

Yale University Art Gallery

John Rutledge
By John Trumbull

The son of a child bride

John Rutledge was born in Charleston (then called Charles Town), S.C., in 1739, probably in the month of September. His Irish father, also named John Rutledge, was a ship's doctor. His mother, Sarah Hext Rutledge, was only fifteen years old when John was born, but she was the wealthiest heiress in South Carolina. The marriage between the elder John Rutledge and his child bride had been arranged by the doctor's brother, Andrew Rutledge, who had married Sarah's widowed mother and was determined to keep the fortune in the family.

The boy's early education was gained from tutors, and from being taken by his father to read books in the local library. He was said to have shown special interest in mathematics, but developed a life-long aversion to reading books. John's father died when the boy was eleven years old. The next year he talked his uncle Andrew into letting him start studying law in his office. Young John also learned the ins and outs of political life by attending every session of the South Carolina legislature, where his uncle was the speaker of the lower house. John Rutledge learned well his uncle's favorite saying, which was "Care not who reigns; think only of who rules."

Studied law in England

At the age of eighteen, John Rutledge sailed to England to study law at the Middle Temple in

---

JOHN RUTLEDGE

1739 (September ?) Born in Charleston, S. C.
1758-1760 Studied law at Middle Temple in London, England.
1761 Admitted to bar to practice law in South Carolina.
1761-1776 Member of South Carolina legislature.
1764-1765 Attorney general of South Carolina.
1765 Delegate to the Stamp Act Congress.
1774-1775 Delegate to the Continental Congress.
1776-1778 President and commander in chief of South Carolina.
1779-1782 Governor of South Carolina.
1782-1783 Representative of South Carolina in the Congress of the Confederation.
1784-1791 Judge of the court of chancery of South Carolina.
1787 Chief delegate of South Carolina to the Constitutional Convention; signed the United States Constitution.
1789-1791 Associate justice of the Supreme Court of the United States.
1791-1795 Chief justice of South Carolina.
1795 Acting Chief Justice of the United States; was refused confirmation of appointment by the United States Senate.
1798-1799 Member of the South Carolina state legislature.
1800 (July 18) Died in Charleston, S.C.

Carolina Art Association, Charleston, S.C. Photograph by George H. Van Anda.

Home of John Rutledge

London. There, he demonstrated unusual legal ability, winning several cases before he was twenty-one years old. He arrived home in South Carolina on Christmas eve in 1760, bringing back the first news that George II was dead and that George III was now King of England.

Upon his return home, he discovered that his mother had mismanaged the estate. His uncle had died meanwhile, and John decided to go to work at once in order to forestall the selling off of the family's plantations to pay its debts. He was admitted to the bar in January, 1761, and two months later was elected to a seat in the colonial legislature. He quickly won prominence as a lawyer by successfully prosecuting the first "heart-balm" case in America, acting as attorney for a young lady who sued a prosperous merchant for breaking his promise to marry her. Rutledge's eloquence in winning this unusual case impressed the wealthy merchants of Charleston, and he immediately became the most sought-after attorney in the colony. Court records show that during Rutledge's second year as a practicing attorney he handled about a fourth of all the cases heard in Charleston, and that he did not lose a single one.

On May 1, 1763, Rutledge married Elizabeth Grimké, the nineteen-year-old daughter of a well-to-do planter. During their thirty years of marriage, they had ten children. Their son John Rutledge III became a general in the South Carolina militia and a representative in the United States Congress.

Attorney general of South Carolina at age of twenty-five

At the age of twenty-five, Rutledge was appointed attorney general of South Carolina—the youngest man ever honored with this office. As attorney general, his most sensational case was the prosecution of a white overseer for killing a female Negro slave. Rutledge's oratory in this case resulted in, for that time, the unusual finding of a decision of guilty and the hanging of the overseer. Rutledge resigned after serving for less than a year as attorney general because he could not live on the salary he was paid.

In 1765 the Stamp Act Congress was called to meet in New York to discuss what the colonies should do about the taxation by the British parliament; and Rutledge advised the legislature that South Carolina should be represented at the meeting. The legislature agreed with his recommendation, and appointed him as one of its three delegates to attend the congress. Just before his twenty-sixth birthday, Rutledge sailed for New York. Despite his youth, the South Carolinian impressed the delegates from the other colonies with his eloquence and his legal knowledge. It is believed that he wrote the memorial to the British House of Lords that was adopted by the Congress and had an important influence in causing the repeal of the Stamp Act.

Defended a patriot for killing a Tory

During the next several years, Rutledge improved his practice as an attorney, strengthened his political leadership in the colonial legislature, and provided for the education of his younger brothers. In 1771, he won fame throughout the colonies for his successful defense in a murder trial of a member of the patriotic Sons of Liberty who had killed the son of the royalist chief justice of New York in a duel.

By 1774, arguments between the royalist governor and the colonial legislature of South Carolina had reached such proportions that the royal governor dismissed the legislators and locked the door of their assembly room. Undaunted, the legislature convened as a Committee of Public Safety in a vacant lot called The Corner, and elected delegates to attend the first Continental Congress with Rutledge as head of the delegation. When the question arose as to what instructions should be given to the delegates, Rutledge proposed that "no instructions" should be given other than that the delegates should use their own discretion. When one of the legislators asked what would be the result if the delegates made "bad use of this authority," Rutledge quickly snapped the answer, "Hang them!" He made his point, and the delegates went to Philadelphia without further instructions.

When the delegates to the first Continental Congress gathered in Philadelphia, the representatives from New England were suspicious of those from the southern colonies. John Adams of Massachusetts wrote in his diary: "John Rutledge still maintains that air of reserve, design and cunning."

Achieving a sense of unity

Although the first Continental Congress ended on a rather weak note by merely petitioning the King of England to listen to the grievances of the colonies and by deciding on cutting off trade with Great Britain, the delegates did achieve a sense of

Virginia State Library.

Residence of Edward Rutledge
Charleston, South Carolina

unity; and John Adams credited Rutledge with a major role in this regard:

"After several days deliberation, we agreed upon all the articles excepting one, and that was the authority of Parliament, which was indeed the essence of the whole controversy; some were for a flat denial of all authority; others for denying the power of taxation only; some for denying internal, but admitting external, taxation. After a multitude of motions had been made, discussed, negatived, it seemed as if we should never agree upon anything. Mr. John Rutledge of South Carolina, one of the Committee, addressing himself to me, was pleased to say, 'Adams, we must agree upon something; you appear to be as familiar with the subject as any one of us, and I like your expressions,—"The necessity of the case," and "excluding all ideas of taxation, external and internal"; I have a great opinion of that same idea of the necessity of the case, and I am determined against all taxation for revenue. Come, take the pen and see if you can't produce something that will unite us.' Some others of the committee seconding Mr. Rutledge, I took a sheet of paper and drew up an article. When it was read, I believe not one of the committee was fully satisfied with it; but they all soon acknowledged that there was no hope of hitting on anything in which we could all agree with more satisfaction. All therefore agreed to this, and upon this depended the union of the Colonies."

Advised other colonies on problems of management

Rutledge also was a delegate to the second Continental Congress in 1775 where he served on various committees. Perhaps his most important service was as chairman of the committee on government that advised the various colonies how to set up their governments during the crisis.

Learning that opposing loyalist and patriotic forces in South Carolina were nearing the point of civil war, Rutledge returned to Charleston in August, 1775, and used his influence to smooth out the difficulties. He had left his wife behind in Philadelphia, and returned there in September to bring her back to South Carolina. Upon his return to Charleston in November, Rutledge asked to be relieved of his duties as a delegate to the Congress; but his younger brother Edward Rutledge remained in Philadelphia and became one of the signers of the Declaration of Independence.

Rutledge was a moderate who attempted to steer a middle course between the extreme patriots and the rabid loyalists. He was worried about the future of South Carolina because the most radical patriots had won control of the legislature; so he set about to win back his dominance of the legislature. First, he won appointment by the legislature as chairman of a committee to draft a state constitution. Second, in writing the constitution he provided that the chief executive of the state should be a president and should be commander in chief of the state's armed forces. Third, when the new constitution had been approved, he succeeded in having the legislature elect him as the state's first president, on March 26, 1776.

Achieved a military victory

Rutledge's military judgment was responsible for one of the few American victories in 1776. A British fleet of about fifty warships arrived off Charleston in June with plans to subdue the South Carolinians and place Lord William Campbell back in charge of the government as the royal governor. The Americans had constructed a large fort of palmetto logs on Sullivan's Island in

Charleston harbor, and the British decided to destroy this fort as an object lesson to the people of Charleston. Major General Charles Lee, George Washington's chief of staff, was in command of armed forces in South Carolina, and he decided that American troops should evacuate the fort. Rutledge disagreed with this plan, and in his role as commander in chief of South Carolina wrote the following order to Colonel William Moultrie, the fort's commander: "General Lee wishes you to evacuate the fort. You will not without an order from me. I would sooner cut off my hand than write one." On June 28, British warships dropped anchor close by the fort and began bombarding it, but the palmetto logs of the fort acted like sponges and absorbed the British cannonballs. On the other hand, the careful aim of American artillerymen in the fort wreaked havoc on the British fleet: Lord William Campbell, the royal governor of South Carolina, was fatally wounded; Commodore Peter Parker, the commander of the fleet, was wounded twice; and hundreds of British sailors were killed. As a result, the British fleet hauled in its anchors and fled.

Frick Art Reference Library. Courtesy: Mrs. Overton F. Price.

Mrs. John Rutledge (Septima Sexta Middleton)
By E. D. Marchant

Resigned as president of the legislature

For the next year and a half, Rutledge was in firm control of South Carolina with his brother Hugh Rutledge as speaker of the upper house of the legislature and his brother-in-law John Mathews as speaker of the lower house of the legislature. During this period, the South Carolina militia fought a successful war with the Cherokee Indians on the frontier. Meanwhile, Rutledge's opponents succeeded in having a new state constitution drawn up that provided for a governor as chief executive, and ended the Church of England's role as an official religion in the state. When the legislature adopted this constitution in March, 1778, Rutledge resigned as president because he believed the constitution could not be legally adopted without having it ratified by the people and because he felt that the religious provisions were directed at him because of his membership in the Anglican Church.

Rutledge served in both houses of the South Carolina legislature during 1778, having been elected to the lower house from one district and to the state senate from another district. During this period, Rawlins Lowndes served as interim president of the state.

On January 11, 1779, Lowndes called an emergency joint session of the legislature to announce that he was stepping down as chief executive officer because the new constitution had been ratified at the last election. He further pointed out that a British army that had captured Savannah, Ga., was now advancing through South Carolina toward Charleston. "Your affairs will now in all probability be conducted more by arms than by councils," Lowndes said, "and their success, in a great measure, depends upon military ability and experience, and you should look to these qualities in choice of a Chief Executive . . ."

Elected as South Carolina's first governor

Rutledge was unanimously elected by the legislature as the state's first governor, and he immediately set about preparing to save Charleston from the British. Rutledge rode about the countryside on horseback recruiting militiamen to come to the defense of the city. Then, when the British, under General Augustine Prevost, had reached the outskirts of Charleston, Rutledge offered to surrender the city; but he managed to delay the negotiations for several days until Benjamin Lincoln, the south-

John Jay
First Chief Justice of the United States

ern commander of the Continental Army, arrived with enough troops to drive Prevost away.

In 1780, Rutledge received the almost unlimited authority from the legislature that won him the nickname of "Dictator John." In February of 1780, Sir Henry Clinton landed a British army about thirty miles south of Charleston and blockaded the capital. The legislators decided to disband to their homes, granting Rutledge "power to do everything necessary for the public good, except the taking away of the life of a citizen without a legal trial." The British finally captured Charleston in May, but Rutledge slipped through the blockade and rode north to the temporary national capital in Baltimore where he appealed to Congress for aid. Rutledge worked tirelessly throughout 1780 and 1781 urging recruits to join the guerrilla forces of Francis Marion, Thomas Sumter, James Williams, and other commanders. The battle of King's Mountain in October, 1780, brought a decisive defeat to the British forces, and Washington's victory at Yorktown in 1781 brought an end to the fighting in the South.

"Delayed justice is injustice."

Rutledge retired as governor in 1782, turning that office over to his brother-in-law John Mathews. Rutledge served as a delegate to the Congress of Confederation from 1782 to 1783; and then in 1784 he accepted appointment as chancellor, or judge of the chancery court, of the state of South Carolina. In the seven years that Rutledge served as judge of the chancery court, he conscientiously pushed cases that came before him to a quick decision. His favorite saying became, "Delayed justice is injustice."

Rutledge's most important contribution to his country came in 1787 when he was forty-eight years old and headed South Carolina's delegation to the Constitutional Convention in Philadelphia. From the outset of the meeting in May, Rutledge played a leading role. On the first day he seconded the nomination of George Washington as president of the Convention and escorted the former commander in chief of the Continental Army to the rostrum. During the convention he spoke out strongly for the interests of the slave states, saying, "If the Convention thinks that North Carolina, South Carolina, and Georgia, will ever agree to the plan, unless their right to import slaves be untouched, the expectation is vain. The people of those States will never be such fools, as to give up so important an interest." On July 24, Rutledge was appointed chairman of a five-man committee of detail that was given the task of drafting a Constitution that incorporated all the various resolutions in the first two months of discussion. The draft of the Constitution produced by this committee was largely written by Edmund Randolph and James Wilson, but their work was extensively edited and revised by Rutledge. After signing the United States Constitution with the other delegates in September, Rutledge returned to South Carolina where he led the support for ratification.

Appointed associate justice of Supreme Court

In 1789, Rutledge received six of South Carolina's electoral votes for Vice President of the

New York Public Library. Photo by Francis G. Mayer.

Burning of Savannah

New York Public Library. Photo by Francis G. Mayer.

The Monument to General DeKalb

Erected August 16, 1780, in the Town of Camden, South Carolina. The cornerstone was laid March 9, 1825, by General Lafayette.

United States; then a few months later he accepted an appointment by President Washington as an associate justice of the Supreme Court of the United States. Rutledge never attended a session of the Supreme Court, although he handled several cases in federal circuit court. In 1791, he resigned his federal post to accept appointment as Chief Justice of the Supreme Court of South Carolina.

When John Jay resigned as Chief Justice of the United States in 1795, Rutledge sent a messenger by a slave to President Washington saying that he would be willing to accept an appointment as Chief Justice of the United States. Washington, who at this time was having great difficulty finding outstanding men to serve in high federal offices, immediately made out a commission appointing Rutledge as Chief Justice, and Rutledge's slave carried the commission back to his master in South Carolina. The commission was dated July 1, 1795, and was an *ad interim* appointment because Congress was not then in session.

Rejected as Chief Justice by the U. S. Senate

Shortly after being appointed Chief Justice, Rutledge injudiciously spoke out violently against the recently negotiated Jay Treaty that provided for the federal government to pay debts to British merchants that had been contracted before the Revolutionary War. At once the Federalist party which favored the Jay Treaty began a violent campaign against Rutledge, declaring that he was mentally ill. On December 15, 1795, The United States Senate, which was controlled by the Federalists, refused to confirm Rutledge's appointment.

The action by the Senate seemed to shatter Rutledge's spirit and make him old before his time. He had lost his law practice and most of his fortune in the service of his country. His constituents elected him once more to the state legislature in 1798 to 1799, but a severe kidney ailment prevented much activity on his part. He suffered a further blow when his younger brother Edward, then serving as governor, died in January, 1800. Six months late, on July 18, John Rutledge died in Charleston at the age of sixty-one.

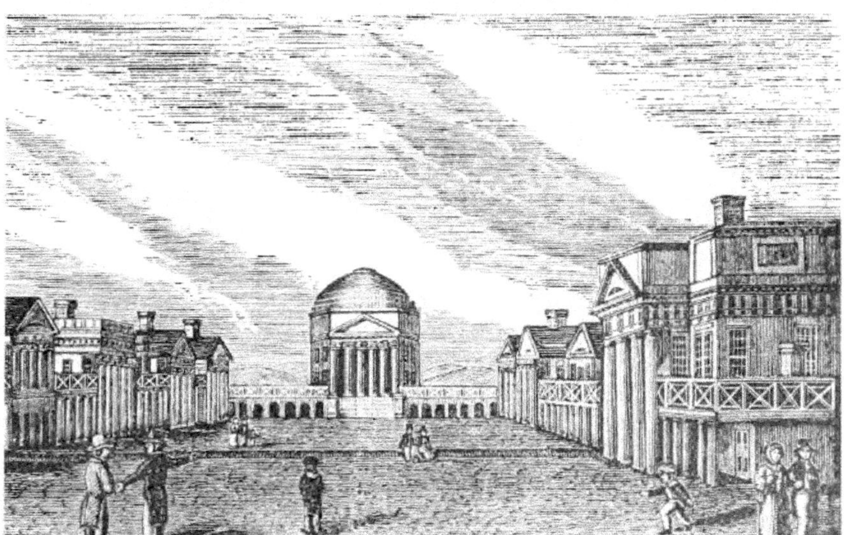

Library of Congress.

University of Virginia, Charlottesville, Virginia

Library of Congress. Itinéraire Pittoresque, J. Milbert.

View of Boston and the South Boston Bridge

ROGER SHERMAN of CONNECTICUT

EDITOR'S NOTE: *Because Roger Sherman was one of the six men who signed both the Declaration of Independence and the United States Constitution, a biography of his life is included in Volume I of* FOUNDERS OF FREEDOM, *and the following article is concerned only with his role in the writing of the United States Constitution.*

Sixty-six-year-old Roger Sherman had had more than thirty years' experience as a lawyer, legislator, and judge when he took part in the Constitutional Convention, and helped construct the "Connecticut Compromise" between the large and small states. He was the only man present at the meeting who had signed the Articles of Association of 1774, the Declaration of Independence in 1776, and the Articles of Confederation in 1778; and his words were listened to carefully. William Pierce, a delegate to the Convention from Georgia, described Sherman as follows:

Had a reputation for succeeding

"He is awkward, un-meaning, and unaccountably strange in his manner. But in his train of thinking there is something regular, deep and comprehensive; yet the oddity of his address, the vulgarisms that accompany his public speaking, and that strange New England cant which runs through his public as well as his private speaking make everything that is connected with him gross and laughable; —and yet he deserves infinite praise,—no Man has a better Heart nor a clearer Head. If he cannot embellish he can furnish thoughts that are wise and useful. He is an able politician, and extremely artful in accomplishing any particular object; —it is remarked that he seldom fails."

Favored a stronger government but moderate

Sherman was among the delegates who were late arriving in Philadelphia, and did not take his seat in the Constitutional Convention until Wednesday, May 30, 1787, the fourth day of the meeting. On this day, the delegates were meeting as a Committee of the Whole, debating whether they

Roger Sherman

ROGER SHERMAN

1721 (April 19) Born in Newton, Mass.
1743 Moved to New Milford, Conn., where he worked as a cobbler.
1745 Appointed county surveyor.
1754 Admitted to the bar to practice law.
1755-1761 Member of the Connecticut legislature.
1759-1761 Judge of the court of common pleas of Litchfield County.
1765 Judge of the court of common pleas of New Haven County.
1766-1785 Member of the governor's council of Connecticut.
1766-1789 Judge of the superior court of Connecticut.
1766-1776 Treasurer of Yale College.
1774-1781 Delegate from Connecticut to the Continental Congress; signed the Declaration of Independence and the Articles of Confederation.
1781-1789 Delegate from Connecticut to the Congress of the Confederation.
1784-1793 Mayor of New Haven, Conn.
1787 Member of the Constitutional Convention; signed the United States Constitution.
1789-1791 Representative from Connecticut in the United States Congress.
1791-1793 U.S. Senator from Connecticut.
1793 (July 23) Died in New Haven, Conn.

were merely to correct and enlarge the Articles of Confederation or were to establish a new national government. According to James Madison's journal. Sherman commented on this matter: ". . . the Confederation had not given sufficient power to Congress, and that additional powers were necessary; particularly that of raising money, which he said would involve many other powers. He admitted also, that the general and particular jurisdictions ought in no case to be concurrent. He seemed, however, not to be disposed to make too great inroads on the existing system; intimating, as one reason, that it would be wrong to lose every amendment by inserting such as would not be agreed to by the States."

Distrusted the vote of the people

The next day, when the delegates began discussing whether one house of Congress should be elected by the people, Sherman firmly opposed a popular election, insisting that representatives should be elected by the state legislatures. "The people," he said, "should have as little to do as may be about the government. They want information, and are constantly liable to be misled."

A week later, on June 6, when the matter of whether the House of Representatives should be elected by the people or by the state legislatures was still being discussed, Sherman amplified his views against popular elections thus:

"If it were in view to abolish the State Governments, the election ought to be by the people. If the State Governments are to be continued, it is necessary in order to preserve harmony between the National and State Governments, that the elections to the former should be made by the latter. The right of participating in the National Government would be sufficiently secured to the people by their election of the State Legislatures." The objects of the Union, he thought were few: first, defence against foreign danger; secondly, against internal disputes, and a resort to force;

The Old Corner Bookstore Boston

Atlantic Neptune, Library of Congress.
Portsmouth Harbor, New Hampshire

thirdly, treaties with foreign nations; fourthly, regulating foreign commerce, and drawing revenue from it. These, and perhaps a few lesser objects, alone rendered a confederation of the States necessary. All other matters, civil and criminal, would be much better in the hands of the States. "The people are more happy in small than in large States. States, may, indeed, be too small, as Rhode Island, and thereby be too subject to faction. Some others are, perhaps, too large, the powers of government not being able to pervade them." He was for giving the General Government power to legislate and execute within a defined province.

When the delegates began to consider how many votes each state should have in the Congress, Sherman proposed on June 11 that "the proportion of suffrage in the first branch should be according to the respective numbers of free inhabitants; and that in the second branch, or Senate, each State should have one vote and no more."

Favored annual elections of representatives

Sherman repeatedly proposed that the members of the House of Representatives be elected annually. He explained that he thought, "the Representatives ought to return home and mix with the people. By remaining at the seat of government, they would acquire the habits of the place, which might differ from those of their constituents."

As the arguments between the large and small states continued late in June, Sherman, on June 28, attempted to express a philosophy of compromise. "The question is," he said, "not what rights naturally belong to man, but how they may be most equally and effectually guarded in society. And if some give up more than others, in order to obtain this end, there can be no room for complaint. To do otherwise, to require an equal concession from all, if it would create danger to the rights of some, would be sacrificing the end to the means. The rich man who enters into society along with the poor man gives up more than the poor man, yet with an equal vote he is equally safe. Were he to have more votes than the poor man, in proportion to his superior stake, the rights of the poor man would immediately cease to be secure." Later that day, when Benjamin Franklin proposed that the delegates ask Divine help by daily prayer, Sherman seconded the motion; but the proposal was not voted upon after it was pointed out that the Convention had no funds with which to pay a clergyman.

On July 2, the Convention was deadlocked on the issue of representation between the large and small states in Congress. "We are now at a full stop," Sherman said, "and nobody means that we should break up without doing something." He therefore supported a plan proposed by Charles Cotesworth Pinckney to refer the problem to a committee of members from all of the states. Although Sherman was not elected to this Committee of Eleven, he sat in for his fellow-delegate from Connecticut, Oliver Ellsworth, who was ill. In the committee, Sherman moved that if each state were to be given an equal vote in the Senate "that no decision therein should prevail unless the majority of States concurring should also comprise a majority of the inhabitants of the United

States." This particular proposal was not approved by the committee. The committee, however, finally reached a compromise that was agreeable to the delegates. It called for representation based on population in the House of Representatives, and an equal number of representatives for each state in the Senate.

Favored election of the President by Congress

When the Convention began considering how the President of the United States was to be chosen, Sherman again expressed his distrust of popular elections, favoring election of the chief executive by Congress rather than by the people at large. "The latter," he said, "will never be sufficiently informed of characters, and besides will never give a majority of votes to any one man. They will generally vote for some man in their own State, and the largest State will have the best chance for the appointment. If the choice be made by the Legislature, a majority of voices may be made necessary to constitute an election."

On August 18, Sherman was appointed to the Grand Committee of Eleven to consider whether the new national government should assume the war debts of the states. Sherman felt that Congress should be authorized to assume the state debts, but that it should not be required to do so.

Opposed slavery as "iniquitous"

Sherman spoke out strongly against slavery, which he said he regarded as "iniquitous." But he suggested that the Convention should "leave the matter as we find it," in order to have "as few objections as possible to the proposed scheme of government." He noted that "the abolition of slavery seemed to be going on in the United States, and that the good sense of the several States would probably by degrees complete it." He opposed placing a tax on the import of slaves, saying that to do so would be to imply that they were property. He also opposed using the word "slaves" in the Constitution, because, as he said, the term was "not pleasing to some people."

Completely opposed to the issuance of paper money, which had caused disastrous inflation during the Revolutionary War, Sherman moved on August 28 that the Constitution prohibit the use of anything but gold and silver as legal tender. He said he felt the time was opportune "for crushing paper money," and pointed out that, if the Constitution permitted Congress to approve the issuance of paper money, then "the friends of paper money would make every exertion to get into the Legislature in order to license it."

As the Convention drew to a close, Sherman expressed his opinion that the Constitution should not go into effect until it had been ratified by all the states. This motion failed to win support. He then moved that ten states should be required to ratify. His motion failed, and he finally agreed to a motion from the Virginia delegation calling for ratification by at least nine states.

The elder statesman from Connecticut made dozens of other contributions to the writing of the Constitution; and, after it had been finally approved by the delegates, he returned to Connecticut to work actively for his state's ratification. He served as a U.S. Representative from Connecticut in the first United States Congress under the Constitution, and later was appointed to the U.S. Senate, where he served until his death on July 23, 1793 at the age of seventy-two.

THE CHARTER OAK.

RICHARD DOBBS SPAIGHT of NORTH CAROLINA

A hot-blooded Southern gentleman, Richard Dobbs Spaight was one of the three Founding Fathers who died as the result of a duel over politics—the others being Alexander Hamilton and Button Gwinnett. Spaight was only twenty-nine when he signed the United States Constitution, but he already had distinguished himself as an officer in the Revolutionary War and as speaker of the house of representatives in the state legislature. Spaight went on to become the first native-born governor of North Carolina. He also served as a Democratic-Republican representative from his state in the United States Congress. At the age of forty-four, he died of wounds after a duel with a Federalist party Congressman.

Educated in England

Richard Dobbs Spaight was born in New Bern, North Carolina, on March 25, 1758. His father, Richard Spaight, was a well-to-do Irishman, who was a member of the royal governor's council and was treasurer, secretary, and clerk to Arthur Dobbs, the royal governor of North Carolina. His mother, Margaret Dobbs, was the governor's sister. Both of his parents died when young Richard was only eight years old; and, since his uncle, the governor, had died a year earlier, he was placed in the hands of a guardian. At the age of nine he was sent to Great Britain for his education.

Spaight was attending the University of Glasgow when the Revolutionary War began. It might have been expected that because of his royalist heritage he would prefer to remain in the British Isles; however, it was evidence of his love of his native land that he hurried home at the age of twenty and volunteered for military service. He was appointed as aide-de-camp to Richard Caswell, the governor of North Carolina and major general in command of its military forces. Spaight served with Caswell at the Battle of Camden in 1780, and later rose to lieutenant colonel in a regiment of artillery.

Opposed Jefferson on the slavery issue

Entering politics at the age of twenty-three, Spaight was elected to represent the town of New Bern in the state legislature from 1781 to 1783. He was appointed one of North Carolina's delegates to the Congress of the Confederation in 1783, and continued to serve in that body until 1785. Thomas Jefferson, who was a member of Congress at this time, had proposed that slavery should not be allowed in any new states formed

RICHARD DOBBS SPAIGHT

1758 (Mar. 25) Born in New Bern, N. C.
1778-1780 Aide-de-camp to Major General Richard Caswell in the Revolutionary War.
1781-1783 Representative in the North Carolina state legislature.
1783-1785 Delegate from North Carolina to the Congress of the Confederation.
1785-1787 Speaker of the North Carolina house of representatives.
1787 Member of North Carolina's delegation to the Constitutional Convention; signed the United States Constitution.
1792 Representative in the North Carolina state legislature.
1792-1795 Governor of North Carolina.
1793 Presidential elector for North Carolina.
1798-1801 U. S. Representative from North Carolina.
1801-1802 Member of North Carolina state senate.
1802 (Sept. 6) Died in New Bern, N. C.

Richard Dobbs Spaight
By James Sharples
Eastern National Park & Monument Association.

in the western territories after the year 1800; but Spaight successfully moved to kill this provision, and Jefferson later blamed him as the man responsible for the spread of slavery in the western states. Spaight was elected to the state legislature from 1785 to 1787, as a representative of Craven County, and at the age of twenty-seven he was chosen as speaker of the state house of representatives.

"A worthy man of some ability and fortune."

In 1787, Spaight was elected by the legislature as a member of its delegation to the Constitutional Convention in Philadelphia. He took his seat on the opening day of the meeting and remained throughout the summer as the delegates shaped the new form of government. A fellow-delegate described Spaight as "a worthy man, of some abilities, and fortune." He apparently regarded seven as a lucky number, for he unsuccessfully proposed that the terms of both Senators and the term of the President should be seven years. Spaight also was the first to suggest that Senators should be chosen by the state legislatures, a proposal that was added to the Constitution and remained in effect until the Seventeenth Amendment providing for popular election of Senators was adopted in 1913. Spaight also supported efforts to have the President appointed by Congress. At the conclusion of the Convention in September, he signed the United States Constitution along with most of the other delegates.

After the Constitutional Convention, Spaight took some part in the efforts to achieve ratification in North Carolina, but ill health forced him to retire from politics for the next several years. He traveled to the West Indies, where the warm climate aided in his recovery.

The first native born governor of North Carolina

In 1792, Spaight was again elected to the state legislature as a representative of New Bern. In that same year the legislature elected him governor —the first North Carolina-born man to serve in that office. In the first year of his administration, the capital of the state was moved permanently from New Bern to Raleigh. While governor, he also served as a presidential elector in 1793.

After his term as governor expired in 1795, Spaight again temporarily retired from politics. That year he married Mary Leach of Homesburg, Pennsylvania. They had two sons and a daughter. His eldest son, Richard Dobbs Spaight, Jr., later became governor of the state, from 1835 to 1837.

In 1798, Spaight won election on the Democratic-Republican ticket as one of his state's Representatives in the United States Congress. He was re-elected to Congress in 1799, but illness made his attendance irregular. In 1801, when the disputed election of Thomas Jefferson and Aaron Burr was given to the House of Representatives to decide, Spaight supported Jefferson for the presidency. Spaight declined re-election to Congress in 1801, preferring instead to accept election to the state senate.

Died from wounds incurred in a duel

In 1802, John Stanly, who had been elected on the Federalist ticket to succeed Spaight in Congress, made accusations that Spaight had used his health as an excuse to avoid voting on controversial issues in Congress, such as the Alien and Sedition Acts. Spaight indignantly published handbills defaming Congressman Stanly's character. Stanly in turn declared that the handbills contained "humiliating filth" and issued a challenge for a duel that Spaight accepted. They met on a field outside New Bern on Sunday afternoon, September 5. The antagonists fired four times, and on the final volley, Spaight was fatally wounded. He died the next day at the age of forty-four. Stanly was charged with murder, but was pardoned by the governor.

Mount Vernon, Estate of George Washington. (c. 1790)

Engraved by N. Green.

General Washington
By J. Trumbull

GEORGE WASHINGTON of VIRGINIA

George Washington stands alone as the man most responsible for the founding of freedom in the United States. As commander in chief of the Continental Army, his personal determination overcame unbelievable odds to win independence from Great Britain during the Revolutionary War. As presiding officer of the Constitutional Convention of 1787, he again used the force of his personality to draw together the bickering states into a permanent union under the United States Constitution. Then, as the first President of the United States, he established democratic traditions of government that breathed life into the words of the Declaration of Independence and the United States Constitution.

A living example to the world

He set the crowned heads of the rulers of the world shaking in amazed disbelief when he first laid down his sword as a successful general and turned the government of his country over to civilians. Again they could hardly believe it, when, after eight years as president, he stepped down and let his successor be chosen by the orderly democratic procedures of the Constitution. More than all the words written on paper, his living example made it possible for oppressed people throughout the world to believe that liberty and freedom were goals that could be achieved.

Worshipped almost as a god during his own lifetime, Washington was epitomized upon his death by John Adams: "For himself, he had lived long enough to life and to glory; for his fellow citizens, if their prayers could have been answered, he would have been immortal." His wife, Abigail Adams, echoed: "History will not produce to us a parallel. . . . Simple truth is his best, his greatest eulogy. She alone can render his fame immortal." But perhaps the most well-rounded and perceptive summation of Washington was written in a letter by Thomas Jefferson in 1814:

"His mind was great and powerful, without being of the very first order; his penetration strong, though not so acute as that of a Newton, Bacon, or Locke; and as far as he saw, no judgment was ever sounder. It was slow in operation, being little aided by invention or imagination, but sure in conclusion. . . . Perhaps the strongest feature in his character was prudence, never acting until every circumstance, every consideration, was maturely weighed; refraining when he saw a doubt, but, when once decided, going through with his purpose whatever obstacles opposed. His integrity was most pure, his justice the most inflexible I have ever known, no motives or interest or consanguinity, of friendship or hatred being able to bias his decision. He was indeed, in every sense of the words, a wise, a good and a great man. . . . On the whole, his character was, in its mass, perfect, in nothing bad, in few points indifferent; and it may truly be said, that never did nature and fortune combine more perfectly to make a man great, and to place him in the same constellation with whatever worthies have merited from man an everlasting remembrance."

George Washington was born on February 22, 1732, at his father's farm on Pope's Creek in Westmoreland County, Virginia. He was the oldest of six children of Augustine and Mary Ball Washington. He also had two older half-brothers by his father's first marriage. George Washington's great-grandfather had settled in Virginia in the 1650's, and had left his descendants large landholdings. Washington's father, whose nickname was "Gus," owned several plantations and one of America's earliest ironworks.

The origin of the cherry tree story

Some light on Washington's early childhood is shed by the famous anecdote about the cherry tree,

---

GEORGE WASHINGTON

1732 (Feb. 22) Born on Pope's Creek Farm in Westmoreland County, Virginia.

1749 Surveyor for Culpeper County, Virginia.

1751 Accompanied his brother Lawrence on a visit to the British West Indies.

1753-1758 Rose from major to colonel in command of Virginia militia in the French and Indian War.

1759-1774 Member of Virginia House of Burgesses.

1774-1775 Delegate from Virginia to the Continental Congress.

1775-1783 Commander in Chief of the Continental Army during the Revolutionary War.

1787 President of the Constitutional Convention; signed the United States Constitution.

1789-1797 First President of the United States

1798-1799 Commander-in-Chief of the United States Army.

1799 (Dec. 14) Died at Mount Vernon in Fairfax County, Virginia.

even though historians view it as largely fiction. It first appeared in a biography of Washington written about 1800 by an Episcopal parson, M. L. Weems, and, according to Weems, it was told to him by an acquaintance of Washington as follows:

" 'When George,' said she, 'was about six years old, he was made the wealthy master of a hatchet! of which, like most little boys, he was immoderately fond, and was constantly going about chopping every thing that came in his way. One day, in the garden, where he often amused himself hacking his mother's pea-sticks, he unluckily tried the edge of his hatchet on the body of a beautiful young English cherry-tree, which he barked so terribly, that I don't believe the tree ever got the better of it. The next morning the old gentleman, finding out what had befallen his tree, which, by the by, was a great favorite, came into the house; and with much warmth asked for the mischievous author, declaring at the same time, that he would not have taken five guineas for his tree. Nobody could tell him any thing about it. Presently George and his hatchet made their appearance. "George," said his father, "do you know who killed that beautiful little cherry tree yonder in the garden?" This was a tough question; and George staggered under it for a moment; but quickly recovered himself; and looking at his father, with the sweet face of youth brightened with the inexpressible charm of all-conquering truth, he bravely cried out, "I can't tell a lie, Pa; you know I can't tell a lie. I did cut it with my hatchet."–"Run to my arms, you dearest boy," cried his father in transport, "run to my arms! Glad am I, George, that you killed my tree; for you have paid me for it a thousand fold. Such an act of heroism in my son is worth more than a thousand trees, though blossomed with silver, and their fruits of purest gold." '

Worshipped his older brother

When George was about seven years old, he moved with his family from his birthplace to a large plantation on the Rappahannock River called Ferry Farm. This farm was just across the river from Fredericksburg, Va., where he went to school for the next seven or eight years. When

Site of Washington's Birthplace

LIFE IN EASTERN VIRGINIA.
The Home of the Planter

LIFE IN WESTERN VIRGINIA.
The Home of the Mountaineer.

Library of Congress.

George was eleven, his father died, leaving him about a fifth of his estate of 10,000 acres and fifty slaves. However, the largest share of the estate went to George's oldest half-brother, Lawrence Washington. George grew up hero-worshipping Lawrence, who was fourteen years older than himself, was a member of the Virginia House of Burgesses, and was adjutant of the Virginia militia.

Because he was not particularly interested in schoolwork, George, at the age of fourteen, developed a desire to go to sea. Lawrence Washington encouraged him with plans to win him a place in the British Navy as a midshipman; but George's mother refused to let him go. Balked in his plans to become a sailor, young George decided that the next best thing was to be a surveyor and explore the western wilderness. So he dropped out of school at the age of fifteen, and the next year was employed as part of a surveying party that spent a month in western Virginia mapping lands of Lord Thomas Fairfax, who held royal grants for millions of acres of Virginia land. When Washington was seventeen, he received an appointment as the Culpeper County surveyor, and that same year helped survey the new town of Alexandria, Va.

A gay youth

As a youth, George Washington apparently had many flirtations and brief romances. He sometimes wrote poems and letters to these girls, such as this unfinished acrostic he wrote at the age of sixteen to a Frances Alexander:

"*F*rom your bright sparkling Eyes, I was undone;
*R*ays, you have more transparent than the sun,
A midst its glory in the rising Day,
*N*one can you equal in your bright array;
*C*onstant in your calm and unspotted Mind;
*E*qual to all, but will to none Prove kind,
*S*o Knowing, seldom one so Young, you'll Find

*A*h! woe's me, that I should love and conceal,
*L*ong have I wish'd, but never dare reveal,
*E*ven though severly Loves Pains I feel;
*X*erxes that great, wasn't free from Cupid's Dart,
*A*nd all the greatest Heroes, felt the smart . . ."

Meanwhile, Lawrence Washington had become ill with tuberculosis, and in 1751 he asked George to go with him to the British West Indies in hope that the climate might produce a cure. Shortly after arriving at Barbados Island, George caught smallpox. His fortunate recovery left him immune for the rest of his life to this dread disease that killed so many persons each year in the colonies. Upon regaining his health, George returned to Virginia, never again to make a trip outside the United States.

Library of Congress.

Lawrence Washington, George Washington's older half brother

Commissioned a major at the age of 20

Upon Lawrence Washington's death in 1752, George Washington applied to the governor for the post of adjutant of the militia which his half-brother had held, and at the age of twenty he was commissioned a major in the Virginia militia. Anxious for more exciting duty than drilling and training the rural militia, Washington volunteered in October, 1753, for a dangerous mission. French forces from Canada were said to have invaded western territory near the Ohio River, and Virginia's British governor, Robert Dinwiddie, was planning to send them a message to get out. Hearing all this, Washington went to Williamsburg, the Virginia capital, where he won the governor's appointment to carry the message. Leaving in November, Washington took almost two months to make the hazardous journey through the wilderness and winter snows to the French Fort Le Boeuf (near present-day Erie, Pa.) and back to Virginia. Upon his return, he delivered to the governor the French commander's blunt reply: "As to the summons you send me to retire, I do not think myself obliged to obey it." Washington also told the governor that he believed the French were likely to establish a fort on the Ohio River at about the location of present-day Pittsburgh. Dinwiddie already had sent men to the place to build a British fort, and Washington's report convinced him that he should send troops to protect these workers from a possible invasion by the French.

Promoted to lieutenant colonel

In March, 1754, the twenty-two-year-old Washington was appointed by the governor as lieutenant colonel and second in command of a task force to be sent to the Ohio River to hold it for Britain. The next month, Washington set off on the march at the head of less than two hundred poorly trained militia. But after a month on the road, and after covering only a third of the distance to the Ohio, he received word that the French had already captured the uncompleted British fort that was his objective.

Soon Washington took part in the first skirmish of what was to become the long-protracted French and Indian War. Although dismayed by news of the French advance to the Ohio, Washington pressed forward to meet them. Late in May, while leading a small party of his militiamen, Washington encountered his first French troops. In his own words:

"I was the first man that approached them, and the first whom they saw, and immediately they ran to their arms, and fired briskly till they were defeated. . . . I fortunately escaped without any wound; for the right wing, where I stood, was exposed to, and received, all the enemy's fire; and it was the part where the man was killed and the rest wounded. I heard the bullets whistle, and, believe me, there is something charming in the sound."

When this quotation of Washington's about the "charming" sound of bullets reached the ears of King George II later that year, he is said to have commented: "He would not say so, if he had been used to hear many." Many years later Washington was asked about his quotation, and remarked only that it had been made "when I was young."

A skirmish, a victory, and a promotion

In the brief fight in May, 1754, Washington's troops had killed ten Frenchmen and captured twenty-one, while losing only one Virginian. The commanding officer of the French force had been slain in the fight; and among his papers was a letter which indicated that his mission was to pretend to be carrying a dispatch to Governor Dinwiddie while in reality he would be surveying the strength of British forces in Virginia. Therefore, Washington arrested the Frenchmen as spies and sent them under guard to Dinwiddie. He then set about building a stockade fort, which he named Fort Necessity, in anticipation of a retaliatory at-

General George Washington
From a painting by Charles Willson Peale, 1770

tack by the French. Governor Dinwiddie rewarded Washington for his early success by raising him to the rank of colonel and placing him in command of the expedition to the Ohio.

Defeated and humiliated

On July 4, 1754, exactly twenty-two years before the United Colonies were to declare themselves independent of British rule, Washington suffered his first great humiliation as a military commander—one that he never forgot. On July 3, a large French force surrounded Washington and his men in the uncompleted Fort Necessity; firing back and forth went on all afternoon; later, as evening came, there began, in Washington's words, "the most tremendous rain that be conceived." The Virginians' powder was wet and they were cold—so cold that they broke into the fort's supply of rum and became too tipsy to obey Washington's orders to continue the fight. After twice refusing to discuss surrender, Washington gave in about midnight and sent a French-speaking Dutchman to see what terms the French would offer. Washington's lack of education stood him in poor stead when the French sent back their written terms, for he had to depend on the faulty translation of his Dutch interpreter. As he heard the terms, they seemed honorable to Washington; so he signed them; and on the morning of July 4 he surrendered Fort Necessity to the French. They allowed him and his men to march out of the fort and back to Virginia, carrying with them their arms but leaving behind two hostages, on condition that they would not invade French lands for a year and

Gen. Edward Braddock

that Virginia would release the French prisoners Washington had taken earlier. It was not until later that Washington learned to his chagrin that the French had tricked him into signing a surrender document in which he admitted the "assassination" of the commander of the French soldiers he had captured in May—an admission the French were to broadcast widely in justification of their actions in the French and Indian War that followed for the next nine years.

Cleared of blame for the defeat

Washington hurried back to Williamsburg to give a firsthand report to Governor Dinwiddie. There, he was acclaimed for his soldierly courage. The loss of Fort Necessity was blamed on the fact that other colonies had not responded to Dinwiddie's appeals for help with enough men and supplies, and the signing of the "assassination" statement in the surrender was blamed on the interpreter.

The summer of 1754 was spent by Washington with his troops at Alexandria. The Virginia House of Burgesses refused to provide sufficient supplies for the soldiers, and Washington found it difficult to maintain discipline among the discouraged militia, many of whom deserted. Then, in October, Washington learned that word had come from England that Governor Horatio Sharpe of Maryland was to be placed in charge of all military operations, and that all officers of the Virginia militia were to be reduced in rank, with none being higher than captain of a company. In prospect of coming demotion, Washington resigned his commission and returned to the life of a planter.

Joined General Braddock's staff

In the spring of 1755, Major General Edward Braddock arrived from England with a regiment of regular British troops to march to the Ohio and capture Fort Duquesne from the French. Hearing of Washington's courage and previous experience, Braddock invited the young Virginian to join his staff as an aide-de-camp, and Washington proudly accepted. The troops for the expedition assembled at Fort Cumberland, Md., and then began advancing toward the French Fort Duquesne at the end of the first week in June. The march across the Allegheny Mountains was a slow undertaking because roads had to be built as the army moved forward. On July 9, Braddock's forces crossed the Monongahela River, southeast of present-day Pittsburgh, and were immediately attacked by the French and Indians. Braddock was fatally wounded, the British soldiers were routed, and Washington was lucky to escape with his life. With the death of Braddock, Washington's service as aide was ended, so he again returned home. His discouragement and a summary of his military career to date were expressed in a letter to his half-brother Augustine Washington, who then was serving in the Virginia House of Burgesses:

"I was employed to go a journey in the winter, when I believe few or none would have undertaken it, and what did I get by it? —my expenses borne! I was then appointed, with trifling pay, to conduct a handful of men to the Ohio. What did I get by that? Why, after putting myself to a considerable expense in equipping and providing necessaries for the campaign, I went out, was soundly beaten, and lost all! Came in, and had my commission taken from me; or, in other words, my command reduced, under pretence of an order from home (England). I then went out a volunteer with General Braddock, and lost all my horses, and many other things. But this being a voluntary act, I ought not to have mentioned it; nor should I have done it, were it not to show that I have been on the losing order ever since I entered the service, which is now nearly two years."

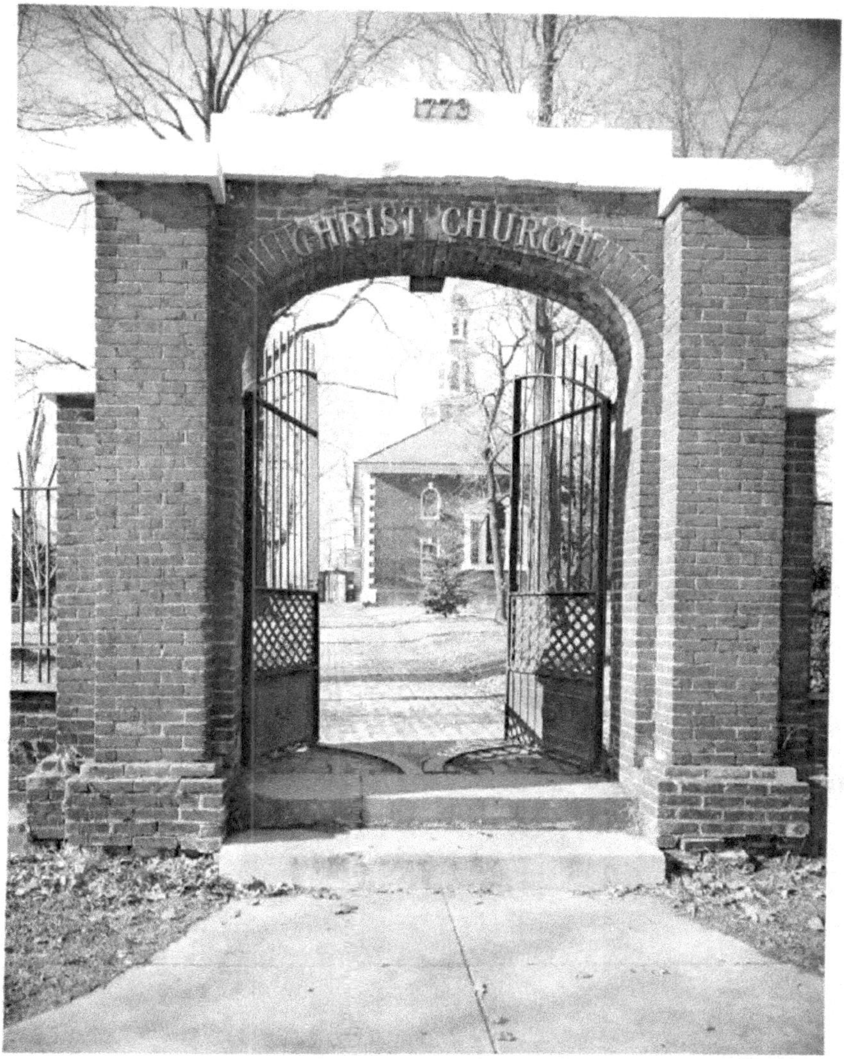

Photo by Marler.

Christ Church, Alexandria, Virginia
(Where General George Washington was a Vestryman)

Courtesy: National Gallery of Art. Mellon Collection.

The Washington Family
By Savage

Appointed commander in chief of Virginia militia

By now, the twenty-three-year-old Washington was the most experienced military officer in Virginia. Recognizing this, Governor Dinwiddie appointed Washington as commander in chief of Virginia militia, restoring his rank as colonel. Early in 1756, Washington traveled on horseback to Philadelphia, New York, and Boston, to confer with northern military commanders on actions to be taken in the war with the French. During this trip, he created an impression on northern colonial leaders that was not forgotten nineteen years later when he was chosen to command the Continental Army. Upon his return, Washington was busily engaged on the Virginia frontier defending settlers from the marauding French and Indians. Finally, in November, 1758, Washington took part in a successful campaign in which his troops captured Fort Dusquene and re-named it Fort Pitt. With the French having been driven north, the frontiers of Virginia were safe from attack, and Washington retired from military service.

Romance with a wealthy young widow

Meanwhile, Washington had fallen in love with an attractive young widow, Mrs. Martha Dandridge Custis. On January 6, 1759, they were married at her plantation home, the White House. Martha brought to the marriage a large fortune inherited from her husband, as well as two small children, John Parke Custis and Martha Parke Custis, whom Washington adopted. George Washington had no children of his own.

While Washington was serving on the Virginia frontier, he was elected as a member of the colony's House of Burgesses, an office that he continued to hold until the beginning of the Revolutionary War. When he first took his seat in the legislature early in 1759, the legislators passed a resolution: "That the thanks of the House be given to George Washington, Esq.; a member of this

Library of Congress.

Loudon Street, Winchester, Virginia

Mrs. George Washington
(Martha Dandridge)

House, late Colonel of the First Virginia Regiment, for his faithful Services to his Majesty, and this Colony, and for his brave and steady behavior, from the first Encroachments and hostilities of the French and their Indians, to his Resignation, after the happy Reduction of Fort Duquesne." It is reported that Washington rose to reply, but could find no words to express his gratitude. The speaker of the house then said, "Sit down, Mr. Washington, your modesty equals your valor, and that surpasses the power of any language I possess."

A striking figure of a man

About this time, a fellow-member of the House of Burgesses, George Mercer, described Washington as follows:

"He may be described as being straight as an Indian, measuring 6 feet 2 inches in his stockings, and weighing 175 lbs. when he took his seat in the Houses of Burgesses in 1759. His frame is padded with well developed muscles, indicating great strength. His bones and joints are large as are his hands and feet. He is wide shouldered but has not a deep or round chest; is neat waisted, but is broad across the hips, and has rather long legs and arms. His head is well shaped, though not large, but is gracefully poised on a superb neck. A large and straight rather than a prominent nose; blue-grey penetrating eyes which are widely separated and overhung by a heavy brow. His face is long rather than broad, with high round cheek bones, and terminates in a good firm chin. He has a clear tho rather colorless pale skin which burns with the sun. A pleasing and benevolent tho a commanding countenance, dark brown hair which he wears in a cue. His mouth is large and generally firmly closed, but which from time to time discloses some defective teeth. His features are regular and placid with all the muscles of his face under perfect control, tho flexible and expressive of deep feeling when moved by emotions. In conversation he looks you full in the face, is deliberate, deferential and engaging. His demeanor at all times composed and dignified. His movements and gestures are graceful, his walk majestic, and he is a splendid horseman."

One of the richest men in the colonies

In the years between the French and Indian War and the Revolutionary War, he lived the life of a Virginia plantation owner, steadily increasing his fortune and his land holdings until he was one of the richest men in the colonies. Upon the death of his half-brother Lawrence's widow and daughter, Washington inherited the family estate of Mount Vernon, where he and Martha made their home for the rest of their life.

As relations between Great Britain and the American colonies became progressively worse in the 1760's, Washington spoke seldom; but his thoughts began to turn to the possibility that the colonists would have to resort to military force in order to protect their liberty. Washington wrote of this to his friend George Mason on April 5, 1769:

"At a time when our lordly masters in Great Britain will be satisfied with nothing less than the deprivation of American freedom, it seems highly necessary that something should be done to avert the stroke, and maintain the liberty which we have derived from our ancestors. But the manner of doing it, to answer the purpose effectually, is the point in question. That no man should scruple, or hesitate a moment in defense of so valuable a blessing, is clearly my opinion; yet arms should be the last resource—the *dernier ressort*. We have already, it is said, proved the inefficacy of addresses to the throne, and remonstrances to Parliament. How far their attention to our rights and interests is to be awakened, or alarmed, by starving their trade and manufactures, remains to be tried."

Offered to raise and finance an army of 1,000

After the British had established a blockade of Boston in retaliation for the Boston Tea Party, a patriotic convention was called in 1774 in Virginia of which Washington was a member. He is said to have told this meeting that he was ready to raise a thousand men at his own expense and march at their head to the relief of Boston. Although he was not taken up on this offer, he was elected as a member of Virginia's delegation to the first Continental Congress to meet in Philadelphia in September.

It is difficult to know how large a part Washington took in the Continental Congress because no complete records were kept of the meetings. His diary reveals that he attended many dinners with the other delegates and that he often gambled at cards, winning seven pounds during his stay in Philadelphia. Comments in letters and diaries by the other delegates indicate they were impressed by Washington, and particularly by his military reputation. After the meetings were completed in

The I. N. Phelps Stokes Collection of American Historical Prints, New York Public Library.

A view of the City of Boston, drawn on the spot, by His Excellency, Governor Pownal. (c. 1758)

National Gallery of Art, Washington, D.C. Mellon Collection.

George Washington (Vaughan Portrait)
By Gilbert Stuart

October, Patrick Henry was said to have been asked who was the greatest man in the Congress, replying: "If you speak of eloquence, Mr. (John) Rutledge, of South Carolina, is by far the greatest orator; but if you speak of solid information and sound judgment, Colonel Washington is unquestionably the greatest man on that floor."

While attending the Congress, Washington received a letter from Boston from a Captain Robert Mackenzie who had served under Washington in the French and Indian War and was now stationed as one of the British occupation troops in Boston. Mackenzie had spoken in his letter of the "rebellious" men of Massachusetts who were seeking "total independence." In his carefully worded reply to Mackenzie on October 9, 1774, Washington no doubt expressed many of the same views that he used on the floor of Congress. His letter to Mackenzie was as follows:

"Permit me with the freedom of a friend (for you know I always esteemed you), to express my sorrow that fortune should place you in a service that must fix curses, to the latest posterity upon the contrivers, and, if success (which, by the by, is impossible) accompanies it, execrations upon all those who have been instrumental in the execution . . . When you condemn the conduct of the Massachusetts people, you reason from effects, not causes, otherwise you would not wonder at a people, who are every day receiving fresh proofs of a systematic assertion of an arbitrary power, deeply planned to overturn the laws and constitution of their country, and to violate the most essential and valuable rights of mankind, being irritated, and with difficulty restrained, from acts of the greatest violence and intemperance.

People will not submit to loss of rights

"For my own part, I view things in a very different point of light from the one in which you seem to consider them; and though you are led to believe, by venal men, that the people of Massachusetts are rebellious, setting up for independency, and what not, give me leave, my good friend, to tell you that you are abused, grossly abused. . . . I think I can announce it as a fact, that it is not the wish or interest of that government, or any other upon this continent, separately or collectively, to set up for independence; but this you may at the same time rely on, that none of them will ever submit to the loss of their valuable rights and privileges, which are essential to the happiness of every free state, and without which, life, liberty, and property, are rendered totally insecure.

"These, sire, being certain consequences, which must naturally result from the late acts of Parliament relative to America in general and the government of Massachusetts in particular, is it to be wondered at that men who wish to avert the impending blow, should attempt to oppose its progress, or prepare for their defense, if it cannot be averted? Surely I may be allowed to answer in the negative; and give me leave to add, as my opinion, that more blood will be spilled on this occasion, if ministry are determined to push matters to extremity, than history has ever yet furnished instances of in the annals of North America; and such a vital wound will be given to the peace of this great country, as time itself cannot cure, or eradicate the remembrance of."

Washington attended the second Virginia patriotic convention that was held in a church in Richmond, Va., in March, 1775. There, Patrick Henry introduced resolutions calling for the establishment of a well-trained Virginia militia, declaring, "We must fight!" And adding his famous words: "I know not what course others may take; but as for me, give me liberty or give me death!" Washington joined in support of Henry's resolutions and was appointed to the twelve-man committee to organize the colony's military forces. Washington also was re-elected as a delegate to the second Continental Congress. Washington wrote to one of his brothers that ". . . it is my full intention to devote my life and fortune in the cause we are engaged in, if need be."

Proposed by John Adams as commander in chief

When the second Continental Congress met in Philadelphia in May, it was roused to fever pitch by the fighting that had begun the Revolutionary War at Lexington and Concord in Massachusetts. Wearing his red and blue uniform of the French and Indian War, Washington was made chairman of the various military committees established by the Congress. On June 14, John Adams proposed that Washington should be the commander in chief of the armed forces being raised by the colonies. Adams later wrote describing his action of that day:

"I had no hesitation to declare, that I had but one gentleman in my mind for that important command, and that was a gentleman from Virginia, who was among us and very well known to all of

General Washington on Christmas Day, 1776, in Trenton, New Jersey

us; a gentleman, whose skill and experience as an officer, whose independent fortune, great talents, and excellent universal character, would command the approbation of all America, and unite the cordial exertions of all the colonies better than any other person in the Union. Mr. Washington, who happened to sit near the door, as soon as he heard me allude to him, from his usual modesty, darted into the library-room. Mr. Hancock, who was our president, which gave me an opportunity to observe his countenance, while I was speaking on the state of the colonies, the army at Cambridge, and the enemy, heard me with visible pleasure; but when I came to describe Washington for the commander, I never remarked a more sudden and striking change of countenance. Mortification and resentment were expressed as forcibly as his face could exhibit them.

"When the subject came under debate, several delegates opposed the appointment of Washington; not from personal objections, but because the army were all from New England, and had a general of their own, General Artemas Ward, with whom they appeared well satisfied; and under whose command they had proved themselves able to imprison the British army in Boston; which was all that was to be expected or desired."

Unanimously elected commander in chief

The next day, June 15, the Congress unanimously elected Washington; and, on June 16, Washington accepted the position, reading the following statement to the Congress:

"Mr. President: Tho' I am truly sensible of the high Honour done me in this Appointment, yet I feel great distress from a consciousness that my abilities and Military experience may not be equal to the extensive and important Trust: However, as the Congress desires I will enter upon the momentous duty, and exert every power I Possess In their Service for the Support of the glorious Cause: I beg they will accept my most cordial thanks for this distinguished testimony of their Approbation.

"But lest some unlucky event should happen unfavourable to my reputation, I beg it may be remembered by every Gentleman in the room, that I this day declare with the utmost sincerity, I do not think my self equal to the Command I am honoured with.

Service without pay

"As to pay, Sir, I beg leave to Assure the Congress that as no pecuniary consideration could have tempted me to have accepted this Arduous employment (at the expence of my domestic ease and happiness) I do not wish to make any profit from it: I will keep an exact Account of my expences; those I doubt not they will discharge and that is all I desire."

After this session, John Adams wrote in a letter to a friend: "There is something charming to me in the conduct of Washington, a gentleman of one of the first fortunes upon the continent, leaving his delicious retirement, his family and friends, sacrificing his ease, and hazarding all, in the cause of his country. His views are noble and disinterested. He declared, when he accepted the mighty trust, that he would lay before us an exact account of his expenses, and not accept a shilling of pay."

Washington set off for Boston on June 23, accompanied by his aide, Thomas Mifflin; his secretary, Joseph Reed; and by Major General Charles Lee and Philip Schuyler. He traveled by way of New York City, and finally arrived at Cambridge, his headquarters in Massachusetts, on July 2, 1775. Washington soon learned that there was such a shortage of gunpowder that it was impos-

I. N. Phelps Stokes Collection of Historical Prints, New York Public Library.

A sketch of the Battle at Charlestown, Massachusetts, June 17, 1775.

An advanced party of about 700 provincials stood an attack, made by 11 Regiments and a Train of Artillery, and after an engagement of 2 hours, retreated to their main body at Cambridge, leaving 1100 of the enemy killed and wounded upon the field. The key to the numbering is as follows: 1. Boston, 2. Charlestown, 3. Breeds Hill, 4. Provincial Brestwork, 5. Retreating Regulars, 6. Frigate, 7. Somerset, 8. Gunnery Officer, 9. General Putnam.

sible to contemplate an attack on the British in Boston, and that it was doubtful that his army would have sufficient ammunition to withstand a concerted attack by the British. He sent out urgent appeals for military supplies to the Continental Congress and to the various colonies. Early in March, 1776, Washington fortified Dorchester Heights overlooking the city of Boston; from this position his artillery commanded the British positions; but, in turn, the British cannons could not fire at the new fortifications. On March 17, the British troops boarded ships and sailed away, leaving Washington a victory in the siege of Boston.

Announcing Independence to the troops

In April, 1776, Washington went to New York City, where he expected that the British would strike next. He was there when word officially came on July 9 that the Congress had declared the colonies independent of Great Britain, and that evening the troops were drawn up to hear the Declaration of Independence. A few days later the British fleet moved into Hudson River, carrying an army of fifteen thousand men. Then followed a series of retreats and lost battles in which Washington and his men were driven from New York into New Jersey. By December, Washington's army had been reduced to only about five thousand men, and many persons were saying that the war was lost. Washington knew that some battle must be won to improve the morale of the patriotic cause, and on the day after Christmas he led a surprise attack on Hessian troops at Trenton, capturing more than nine hundred without the loss of a single American soldier. He followed this victory up with another eight days later, when he successfully attacked British forces at Princeton, inflicting a loss of about three hundred men on the British, and only about forty American soldiers killed.

Defeat at Brandywine Creek

Washington and his army spent the first few months of 1777 in winter quarters at Morristown, N.J. The next spring and summer were largely occupied in marching back and forth across New Jersey in anticipation of a British frontal attack on Philadelphia that did not materialize. In Sep-

The Hon. Horatio Gates
Major General of the American Forces

tember, the British landed troops south of Philadelphia, and Washington led his forces to meet them, but was unsuccessful in stopping the British in the Battle of Brandywine Creek on September 11. After this defeat, with its subsequent loss of the American capital, Washington rallied his forces in October for an attack on Germantown, Pa., where Britsh forces were quartered; but the weather on the morning of October 4 turned Washington's surprise attack into an American defeat as his troops became confused in the fog.

The flagging American spirits were boosted in October when Major General Horatio Gates succeeded in capturing British General John Burgoyne and his army of about five thousand men at the Battle of Saratoga in New York. Soon there were whispers that Washington should be replaced as commander in chief by Gates, and Gates himself was suspected by Washington of being part of the Conway Cabal, a plot that was attempting to replace him. But Gates's victory also brought France into the war on America's side, and, with help from France, Washington felt that victory was assured.

Misery at Valley Forge

Washington spent the winter of 1777-1778 in camp with his army at Valley Forge, Pa., near Philadelphia. His troops were ill-housed, ill-clothed and ill-fed. Washington wrote of this winter: "For some days past there has been little less than a famine in the camp. A part of the army has been a week without any kind of flesh, and the rest three or four days. Naked and starving as they are, we cannot enough admire the incomparable patience and fidelity of the soldiery, that they have not been, ere this, excited by their suffering to a general mutiny and desertion."

In June, 1778, the British decided to leave Philadelphia and marched across New Jersey to New York City. Washington moved his troops into New Jersey to harass the British march. Washington planned to attack the British army at Monmouth, N.J., on June 28, but an important battle was lost when Major General Charles Lee disobeyed orders and called for a retreat at a time when an important victory might have been won. Washington ordered Lee courtmartialed, and in August the court found Lee guilty of disobedience of orders, sentencing him to suspension from the army.

For the next three years, Washington's forces were largely engaged in keeping the British bottled up in New York City, and Washington's job became one of holding his army together in the face of discouraging inaction, lack of supplies, mutinies, and desertions. In a letter in 1780, Washington wrote to one of his brothers: "It is impossible for any person at a distance to have an idea of my embarrassments, or to conceive how an Army can be kept together under any such circumstances as ours is."

Victory at Yorktown

In the summer of 1781, Washington kept close watch on the British army of Lord Charles Cornwallis that was raising havoc in Virginia. He also kept a force under the Marquis de Lafayette in pursuit of Cornwallis. In August, Washington learned that a French fleet in command of Admiral de Grasse was being sent to his aid, and that it would be carrying about three thousand French troops. Washington immediately began planning a concentration of forces to trap Cornwallis. Washington led his army to Virginia. By early October, the Continental Army and its French allies had surrounded Cornwallis's troops at Yorktown, Va. On October 19, Cornwallis surrendered his more than seven thousand troops, and Washington had the pleasure of dispatching the following report to the President of Congress, Thomas McKean:

"Sir, I have the Honor to inform Congress, that a Reduction of the British Army under the Command of Lord Cornwallis, is most happily effected. The unremitting Ardor which actuated every Officer and Soldier in the combined Army in this Occasion, has principally led to this Important Event, at an earlier period than my most sanguine Hope had induced me to expect. . . ."

When word of Cornwallis's surrender was delivered to the British Prime Minister, Lord North, in London, he exclaimed, "Oh God! It is all over!" Peace negotiations dragged on between American and British representatives for more than two years, but the war in effect was over.

Surrendered his commission

On December 23, 1783, Washington appeared before the Congress of the Confederation at Annapolis, Md., and surrendered his commission as commander in chief to the President of Congress, Thomas Mifflin, his former aide with whom he had had a falling out over the affair of the Conway Cabal. Washington's speech was as follows:

"Mr. President: The great events on which my resignation depended having at length taken place, I have now the honor of offering my sincere con-

Library of Congress. Itineraire Pittoresque, J. Milbert.

Haverstraw Landing on the Hudson River

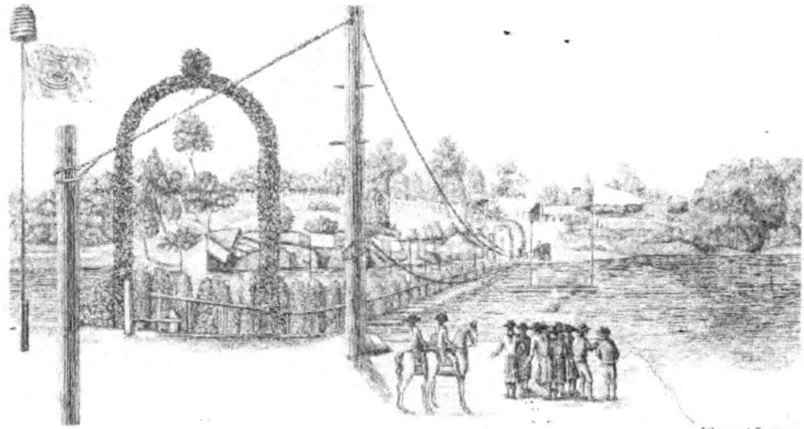

Library of Congress.

The reception of General Washington showing the triumphal arch erected at Gray's Ferry, near Philadelphia, April 20th, 1789.

gratulations to Congress, and of presenting myself before them, to surrender into their hands the trust committed to me, and to claim the indulgence of retiring from the service of my country.

"Happy in the confirmation of our independence and sovereignty, and pleased with the opportunity afforded the United States of becoming a respectable nation, I resign with satisfaction the appointment I accepted with diffidence; a diffidence in my abilities to accomplish so arduous a task; which however was superseded by a confidence in the rectitude of our cause, the support of the supreme power of the Union, and the patronage of Heaven.

"The successful termination of the war has verified the most sanguine expectations; and my gratitude for the interposition of Providence, and the assistance I have received from my countrymen, increases with every review of the momentous contest.

"While I repeat my obligations to the army in general, I should do injustice to my own feelings not to acknowledge, in this place, the peculiar services and distinguished merits of the gentlemen who have been attached to my person during the war. It was impossible the choice of confidential officers to compose my family should have been more fortunate. Permit me, sir, to recommend, in particular, those who have continued in the service to the present moment, as worthy of the favorable notice and patronage of Congress.

"I consider it an indispensable duty to close this last act of my official life by commending the interests of our dearest country to the protection of Almighty God, and those who have the superintendence of them to his holy keeping.

"Having now finished the work assigned me, I retire from the great theatre of action, and bidding an affectionate farewell to this august body, under whose orders I have so long acted, I here offer my commission, and take my leave of all the employment of public life."

A member of Congress who witnessed Washington's surrender of his commission was James McHenry, one of his secretaries during the war and later a signer of the United States Constitution. He described the scene in a letter to his bride-to-be as follows:

"To day, my love, the General at a public audience made a deposit of his commission and in a very pathetic manner took leave of Congress. It was a solemn and affecting spectacle; such an one as history does not present. The spectators all wept, and there was hardly a member of Congress who did not drop tears. The General's hand which held the address shook as he read it. When he spoke of the officers who had composed his family, and recommended those who had continued in it to the present moment to the favorable notice of Congress he was obliged to support the paper with both hands. But when he commended the interest of his dearest country to almighty God, and those who had the superintendence of them to his holy keeping, his voice faultered and sunk, and the whole house felt his agitations. After the pause which was necessary for him to recover himself, he proceeded to say in the most penetrating manner, 'Having now finished the work assigned me, I retire from the great theatre of action, and bidding an affectionate farewell to this august body, under whose orders I have so long acted, I here offer my commission, and take my leave of all the employments of public life.' So saying, he drew out from his bosom his commission and delivered it up to the president of Congress. He then returned to his station, when the president read the reply that had been prepared—but I thought without any show of feeling, tho' with much dignity."

A country gentleman at Mount Vernon

The fifty-one-year-old Washington retired to Mount Vernon to take up again the life of the country gentleman. He wrote to Lafayette: "Free from the bustle of a camp and the busy scenes of public life, I am solacing myself with those tranquil enjoyments which the soldier, who is ever in pursuit of fame; the statesman, whose watchful days and sleepless nights are spent in devising schemes to promote the welfare of his own, perhaps the ruin of other countries—as if this globe was insufficient for us all; and the courtier, who is always watching the countenance of his prince in hopes of catching a gracious smile, can have very little conception. I have not only retired from all public employments, but I am retiring within myself, and shall be able to view the solitary walk, and tread the paths of private life with heartfelt satisfaction. Envious of none, I am determined to be pleased with all; and this, my dear friend, being the order of my march, I will move gently down the stream of life until I sleep with my fathers."

But it soon became apparent to Washington and other leaders that the government of the United States that had been organized under the Articles of the Confederation was not strong enough to provide a lasting peace. Trade and commerce were breaking down between the states and open revolt had broken out in Massachusetts in Shays' Rebellion. His friends, including James Madison and Alexander Hamilton, urged him to exert his leadership. Despite his wishes to remain a private citizen, he accepted election by the Virginia legislature as head of his state's delegation to the Constitutional Convention of 1787.

Presided over the Constitutional Convention

At the opening of the Constitutional Convention on May 25, 1787, Washington was unanimously elected president. As such, he presided over the heated debates with calmness and dignity; his presence alone did much to hold together the disputing delegates. James Madison in his journal of the debates in the Convention, noted that only once did Washington enter into the discussion, and that was on the final day when he told the delegates that it would "give him much satisfaction" if they made the Constitution more democratic by increasing the number of representatives in the House of Representatives – allowing one representative for every thirty thousand people instead of for every forty thousand as had been proposed. This amendment was approved just before the Constitution was signed by Washington and the other delegates on September 17.

Although Washington took no direct part in the campaign for ratification of the Constitution by the various states, the facts that he had presided at the Constitutional Convention and had endorsed the Constitution with his signature were among the most potent arguments in its favor. Gouverneur Morris, who wrote the final draft of the Constitution, told Washington in a letter that he was convinced "that if you had not attended the convention, and the same paper had been handed out to the world, it would have met with a colder reception, with fewer and weaker advocates, and with more and more strenuous opponents."

Favored for selection as President

As one state after another ratified the Constitution, everyone began to take it for granted that Washington was the most logical person to become president under the new Constitution. His friends kept Washington informed of this growing opinion, and he wrote of it to Alexander Hamilton:

"In taking a survey of the subject, in whatever point of light I have been able to place it, I have always felt a kind of gloom upon my mind, as often as I have been taught to expect I might, and perhaps must ere long, be called upon to make a decision. You will, I am well assured, believe the assertion, though I have little expectation it would gain credit from those who are less acquainted with me, that, if I should receive the appointment,

Residence and Tomb of Washington, Mount Vernon.

Library of Congress.

and if I should be prevailed upon to accept it, the acceptance would be attended with more diffidence and reluctance than ever I experienced before in my life. It would be, however, with a fixed and sole determination of lending whatever assistance might be in my power to promote the public weal, in hopes that, at a convenient and early period, my services might be dispensed with, and that I might be permitted once more to retire, to pass an unclouded evening, after the stormy day of life, in the bosom of domestic tranquility."

A triumphal procession

Washington bowed to public opinion and accepted the unanimous vote that was given him for president in 1789. He was officially notified of his election in April, and after a triumphal procession from Mount Vernon to New York City, he was inaugurated on April 30. In a letter to Edward Rutledge, a signer of the Declaration of Independence, Washington wrote of his uncertainty in his new office:

"I walk, as it were, on untrodden ground, so many untoward circumstances may intervene in such a new and critical situation, that I shall feel an insuperable diffidence in my own abilities. I feel, in the execution of my arduous office, how much I shall stand in need of the countenance and aid of every friend to myself, of every friend to the revolution, and of every lover of good government."

Washington surrounded himself with outstanding men to aid him in the formation of the new government. These men included Thomas Jefferson as Secretary of State, Alexander Hamilton as Secretary of the Treasury, Henry Knox as Secretary of War, Edmund Randolph as Attorney General, and John Jay as Chief Justice of the United States. He also relied heavily on advice from James Madison, who was majority leader in the House of Representatives.

Distressed at the rise of political parties

During the eight years of his administration, Washington managed to maintain neutrality for the United States in the war raging between Great Britain and France, but only at the expense of criticism by the partisans for each of the combatants. He was particularly distressed by the rise of political parties headed by Jefferson and by Hamilton. In his "Farewell Address" published on September 17, 1796, he warned that in the future the government should have "as little political connection as possible" with other countries and that the people should avoid the "ill founded jealousies and false alarms" of political parties.

After John Adams was inaugurated as the second President of the United States on March 4, 1797, Washington once again retired to Mount Vernon. He had been there only a little more than a year when the hostile actions of the revolu-

Library of Congress. History of the United States Capitol, by Glenn Brown.

Thornton's West Elevation
showing alternate design for the dome of the Capitol. This was not adopted
although it was quite similar to the plan that was accepted.

tionary government in France once more called him to public office; this time as commander in chief of the new United States Army being formed as a defensive force against a possible French invasion. Washington took an active part in planning the new army in cooperation with his two major generals, Alexander Hamilton and Charles Cotesworth Pinckney.

Approved the establishment of West Point

The last letter that Washington wrote before his death was to Hamilton, on Dec 12, 1799. In it he complimented Hamilton on plans he had proposed for the West Point military academy. He said that he believed it was "an object of primary importance to this country." Later that day, Washington went horseback riding in the snow, ate dinner in his damp clothes, and caught cold. The next day, his secretary, Tobias Lear, suggested that he take something for the cold, but he replied: "No, you know I never take anything for a cold. Let it go as it came."

By December 14, the sixty-seven-year-old Washington was seriously ill with a sore throat that present-day doctors believe may have been a streptococcic infection. Three doctors were sent for, and they tried the standard practice of bleeding the patient extensively. About five o'clock in the afternoon, Washington spoke to one of the doctors, James Craik, who had once served with him at Fort Necessity in the French and Indian War. He said: "Doctor, I die hard, but I am not afraid to go. I believed, from my first attack, that I should not survive it—my breath cannot last long." However, he continued to linger until shortly after ten o'clock. When word of his death reached the public, the nation was plunged into mourning. His body was interred with military honors in the family tomb at Mount Vernon.

"First in war, first in peace"

The most famous eulogy to Washington's memory was that delivered by one of Washington's former officers, Henry "Light Horse Harry" Lee, at a funeral ceremony held by Congress on December 26, 1799, at which Lee described Washington in these words:

"First in war, first in peace, and first in the hearts of his countrymen, he was second to none in the humble and endearing scenes of private life: pious, just, humane, temperate, and sincere, uniform, dignified, and commanding, his example was as edifying to all around him as were the effects of that example lasting."

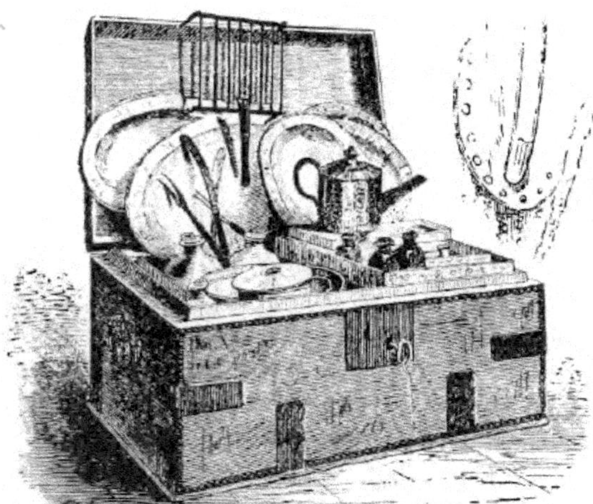

WASHINGTON'S CAMP CHEST.

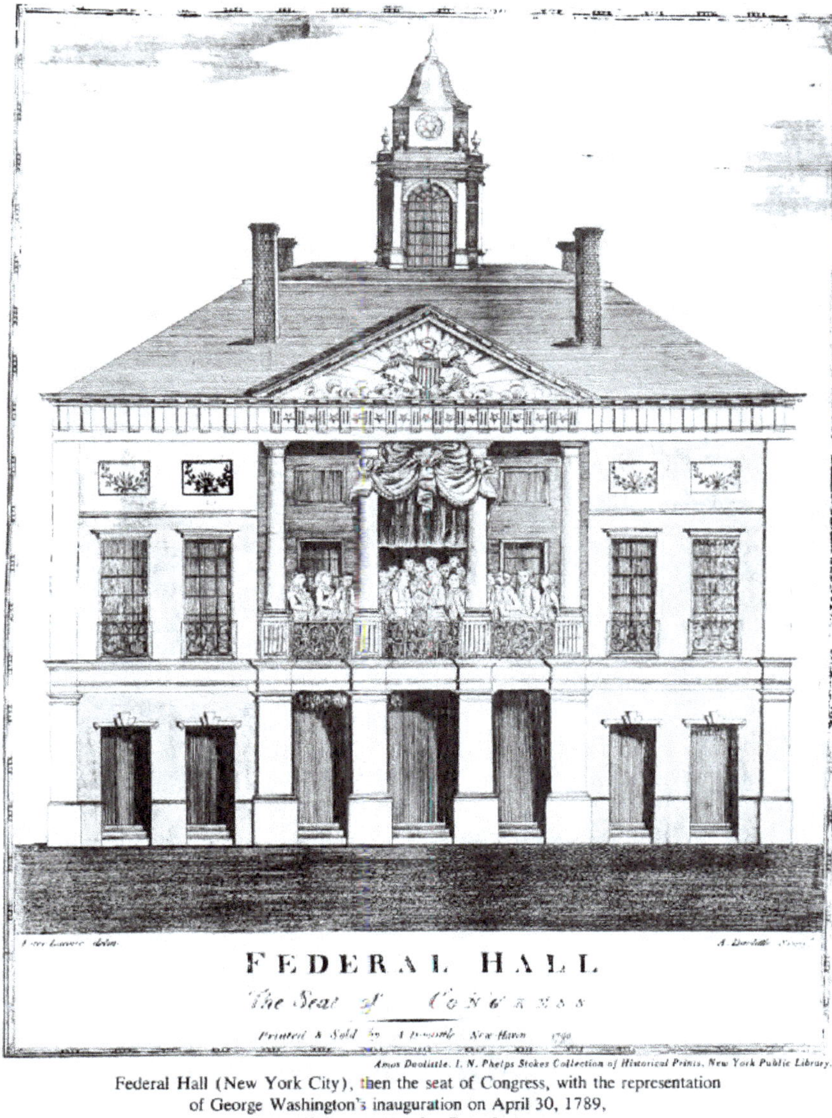

Amos Doolittle. I. N. Phelps Stokes Collection of Historical Prints, New York Public Library.

Federal Hall (New York City), then the seat of Congress, with the representation of George Washington's inauguration on April 30, 1789, from a line engraving after Peter Lacour.

Library of Congress. Itineraire Pittoresque, J. Milbert.
The Plain of West Point during a dress parade.

New York Public Library. Photo by Francis G. Mayer.

A view of Norfolk from Gosport, Virginia
By J. Shaw

New York Public Library. Photo by Francis G. Mayer.

A Scene of the Hudson at West Point
1828

HUGH WILLIAMSON of NORTH CAROLINA

Fifty-one years old at the time he signed the United States Constitution, Hugh Williamson was a versatile, well-educated man who had been a minister, a professor, a physician, an astronomer, a merchant, and a legislator. He served in the Revolutionary War as surgeon general for North Carolina's troops, and after the war represented North Carolina in the Congress of the Confederation. After the ratification of the United States Constitution, he became North Carolina's first U.S. representative in the new Congress.

Abrupt in manner

A strong-featured man, with dark gray eyes, a long, thin nose, and a prominent chin, Williamson had no patience with anyone he suspected of "ignorance, want of moral character, or a disregard to religious truth." A friend said of Williamson that to such persons "both his language and manner might be considered as abrupt, if not possessing a degree of what might be denominated Johnsonian rudeness." However, a fellow-delegate to the Constitutional Convention said of Williamson that "in his manners there is a strong trait of the Gentleman." A good example of his impatience with flatterers and favor-seekers came in 1792, while Williamson was serving in Congress, when an Italian sculptor, Joseph Ceracchi, wrote him the following note:

"Mr. Ceracchi requests the favour of Mr. Williamson to sit for his bust, not on account of getting Mr. Williamson's influence in favour of the National Monument; this is a subject too worthy to be recommended; but merely on account of his distinguished character, that will produce honour to the artist, and may give to posterity the expressive features of the American Cato."

Williamson replied with the following caustic letter:

"Mr. Hugh Williamson is much obliged to Mr. Ceracchi for the polite offer of taking his bust. Mr. Williamson could not possibly suppose that Mr. Ceracchi had offered such a compliment by way of a bribe; for the man in his public station who could accept of a bribe, or betray his trust, ought never to have his likeness made, except from a block of *wood*.

"Mr. Williamson, in the mean time, cannot avail himself of Mr. Ceracchi's services, as he believes that posterity will not be solicitous to know what were the features of his face. He hopes, nevertheless, for the sake of his children, that posterity will do him the justice to believe, that his conduct was upright, and that he was uniformly influenced by a regard to the happiness of his fellow citizens, and those who shall come after them."

From Irish parents

Hugh Williamson was born in West Nottingham township, Chester County, Pennsylvania, on December 5, 1735. His father, John Williamson, was a clothing merchant, who had come to America five years earlier from Dublin, Ireland. His mother, Mary Davison Williamson, had also come from Ireland with her father, and on the voyage to America in 1717 had been captured and robbed by the notorious pirate Blackbeard. Hugh was the eldest son of ten children.

An outstanding scholar

After learning how to read and write, young Hugh was sent to an academy operated by the Reverend Francis Allison at New London, Pennsyl-

---

HUGH WILLIAMSON

1735 (Dec. 5) Born in West Nottingham township, Pennsylvania.

1757 Graduated from the College of Philadelphia (now the University of Pennsylvania).

1759 Licensed as a Presbyterian minister.

1760 Granted a Master of Arts Degree by the College of Philadelphia.

1760-1763 Professor of mathematics at the College of Philadelphia.

1764-1768 Studied in Europe; received a Doctor of Medicine degree from the University of Utrecht.

1772-1776 Toured West Indies and Europe to raise funds for an academy at Newark, Delaware.

1777-1780 Became a merchant and practiced medicine in North Carolina.

1780-1781 Surgeon general of North Carolina troops in the Revolutionary War.

1782-1785, 1788 Member of North Carolina state legislature.

1782-1785, 1787-1789 Delegate from North Carolina to the Congress of the Confederation.

1786 Delegate from North Carolina to the Annapolis Convention.

1787 Member of North Carolina delegation to the Constitutional Convention; signed the United States Constitution.

1790-1793 First Representative from North Carolina in the United States Congress.

1819 (May 22) Died in New York City.

Harper's Ferry from the Blue Ridge. *Library of Congress.*

vania. There, he learned Latin and Greek, and became acquainted with a fellow-student, Thomas McKean, who later was to be one of the signers of the Declaration of Independence. Williamson entered the College of Philadelphia (now the University of Pennsylvania) when he was seventeen. Among his fellow students were two future signers of the Declaration of Independence–Francis Hopkinson and William Paca. Williamson's ability as a scholar was quickly recognized, and while still an undergraduate he was employed as a teacher of Latin and English. He received his Bachelor of Arts degree in 1757 at the college's first graduation ceremony.

The same year that he received his college degree, Williamson's father died, and for about two years he lived with his mother at Shippensburg, Pennsylvania, while he helped settle his father's estate, collecting debts and providing for his younger brothers and sisters.

An intensely religious young man, Williamson took up the study of divinity under the guidance of the Reverend Samuel Finley, an uncle of Benjamin Rush. In 1759, Williamson went to Connecticut for further study, and there he was licensed as a minister. Upon his return to Pennsylvania, he preached as a Presbyterian minister, but did not take on the duties of a pastor of a congregation.

Meanwhile, he had resumed his studies at the College of Philadelphia, specializing in mathematics, and, in 1760, he was granted a Master of Arts degree. That same year he was appointed as a professor of mathematics in the institution. In addition to teaching classes, he now took up the study of medicine.

Studied medicine in British Isles

Desirous of obtaining a better education in medicine than could be obtained in the colonies, Williamson resigned his professorship and traveled to Scotland in 1764. There he enrolled in the University of Edinburgh. After studying there for some time, he became severely ill with chest pains, and decided to move to London to pursue his studies. After studying in London for about a year, he went to the Netherlands, where he completed his medical education and received his Doctor of Medicine degree from the University of Utrecht in 1768.

Returning to Philadelphia at the age of thirty-two, Williamson took up the practice of medicine. He became a member of the American Philosophical Society, and was appointed to a committee in

1769 to observe the transits of Venus and Mercury across the face of the sun. That same year he made important observations on a great comet that had appeared in the sky; and propounded the theory that the tail of the comet was not a mass of fire, as believed by most scientists of the time, but was in reality merely the atmosphere of the comet reflecting light from the sun. From this theory he concluded that comets were as habitable as the earth, and on this subject he wrote the following interesting comment:

"Having ventured an opinion that every planet and every comet in our system is inhabited, we have only taken a very imperfect view of the astonishing works of the divine architect. There are about three thousand fixed stars visible by the naked eye. Every one of those stars is doubtless a sun, and each of those suns affords light and heat to another system of worlds. Let us only suppose that each of those suns illuminates as many orbs as belong to our system. We shall state the number at two hundred, though it is believed that twice this number of comets, beside the planets, have already been discovered. This would give three hundred thousand worlds. But three hundred thousand is a small number when compared with the whole number of stars that have been discovered. The relative places of fifty thousand stars have been determined by the help of telescopes. Fifty thousand solar systems, each containing at least one hundred worlds! Five millions of worlds all inhabited by rational beings! How do we seem to dwindle into littleness? How small, how few, are the ephemerons of this little globe, when compared with the countless myriads who inhabit five millions of worlds? All those worlds, and every one of their inhabitants, are under the constant care of the Divine Being. Not one of them is neglected. 'Great and marvellous are his works: how terrible his power!'"

A noted scientist

The next year, Williamson published a scientific paper on the change of climate in North America with observations showing that winters had become milder over the period of the previous fifty years. These observations and the papers he had written on astronomy won him recognition in Europe for his scientific efforts, and he was awarded a Doctor of Laws degree by the University of Leyden.

Williamson had become a trustee of an academy at Newark, Delaware, that later was to become the University of Delaware, and in 1772 he made a trip to the West Indies to raise money for the school. He was successful in subscribing money for the academy, and decided to make a similar fund-raising trip to Europe.

While in Boston awaiting the sailing of a ship in December of 1773, Williamson was present at the Boston Tea Party and met such leaders of the patriotic cause as John and Samuel Adams and James Otis. The ship in which he sailed to England was owned by John Hancock.

Warned the British of the possibility of war

Upon his arrival in England, Williamson was closely questioned by officials of the British government as to the circumstances of the Boston Tea Party. He told the British officials that if Parliament passed the Coercive Acts against Boston that "the time was not far distant when his native country would be deluged with blood." Later, British Prime Minister Lord North said that Williamson was the first person who had ever told him that there was a possibility of civil war in the colonies.

Williamson took an important part in another incident, not disclosed until after his death, that heaped fuel on the growing flames of the Revolution. Williamson had learned that the British gov-

Library of Congress.

View of Leesburg, Virginia.

ernor of Massachusetts, Thomas Hutchinson, had been carrying on secret correspondence urging that the Parliament take away some of the liberties of the colonists. Williamson boldly went to the British bureau where he had been told the letters were filed and asked for them, pretending he had been sent by another department of the government. After the letters had been handed over to him, he presented them to Benjamin Franklin who promptly published them, bringing great indignation against Hutchinson among the people of Massachusetts.

Captured by the British but escaped

Upon learning that the Declaration of Independence had been signed, Williamson returned to America in 1777. On his homeward voyage, his ship was captured by a British cruiser, but Williamson and another passenger escaped in a row boat and made their way to shore.

Philadelphia was captured by the British in the fall of 1777, so Williamson decided to move to North Carolina. He settled at the port of Edenton where he and a younger brother established a shipping company, trading with the West Indies. Williamson also established a successful medical practice in Edenton.

In 1780, Williamson was appointed surgeon general of the North Carolina militia. He was with the militia at the Battle of Camden in South Carolina in August, 1780, when American troops under Major General Horatio Gates were severely beaten by Lord Cornwallis. About 300 North Carolina militiamen were captured in the fight, and Williamson volunteered to go under a flag of truce to care for their wounds. He remained with them for two months, then returned to his regular duties.

A delegate to Congress

In the spring of 1782, Williamson was elected to the North Carolina state legislature. Shortly afterward, that body elected him as one of its delegates to the Congress of the Confederation. He served in Congress for the next three years—the longest continuous period a delegate was allowed to serve under the Articles of the Confederation. Unlike most of the representatives of the Southern States, Williamson voted to prohibit slavery in the western territories of the United States. Thomas Jefferson, who was a delegate to Congress from Virginia at this time, remarked of Williamson: "We served together in congress, at Annapolis, during the winter of 1783 and 4; there I found

Library of Congress.

Shannondale Springs in the Blue Ridge Mountains.

him a very useful member, of an acute mind, attentive to business, and of an high degree of erudition."

In 1786, Williamson was elected a delegate from North Carolina to the Annapolis Convention that set the stage for the framing of the United States Constitution, and the next year he was elected as a member of North Carolina's delegation to the Constitutional Convention.

First to propose a six year senatorial term

Williamson took his seat in Philadelphia on the opening day of the Constitutional Convention in May, 1787, and remained there throughout the summer, aiding in the preparation of the Constitution. He was the first to propose that the term of a United States Senator should be six years—a view that eventually won out over efforts by some of the delegates to make the office a lifetime appointment. Williamson spoke regularly during the meeting, but usually made only brief comments. On the last day of the Convention, when several members, including his fellow-delegate from North Carolina, William Blount, had objected to signing the document, Williamson proposed that the delegates could merely sign the covering letter forwarding the Constitution to Congress; but he added that he did "not think a better plan was to be expected, and had no scruples against putting his name to it."

Williamson also had been elected by the state legislature as a member of the Congress of Confederation in 1787, so he went to New York where Congress was meeting and remained there until the spring of 1789. Because the North Carolina state ratification convention refused to ratify the Constitution in 1788, there was some doubt about Williamson's status when the new Constitution went into effect on March 4, 1789. On March 23, after the new Congress had failed to reach a quorum, he wrote to the governor of North Carolina: "Hitherto I consider myself in the service of the State as a Member of Congress and shall continue so to do until the New Government is in Operation, hence I claim the right of Franking Letters . . ." After the new government of the United States finally was formed in April, Williamson returned to North Carolina.

Married at 53

In January, 1789, the fifty-three-year-old Williamson married Maria Apthorpe, daughter of a well-to-do New Yorker. They had two sons, but his wife died only a few days after the birth of the second boy. Williamson never re-married.

He returned to North Carolina to attend the state's second ratification convention in November, 1789, and aided in finally convincing North Carolina that it should join the Union. Elections for North Carolina's representatives to the new Congress were held in February, 1790, and Williamson won a place in the state's five-man delegation. He apparently was already in New York City when news of the election came, because he was the first of the state's Congressmen to take his seat—on March 19, 1790. The next year he was elected to the second Congress.

Voted for tax on whisky

In 1791, when the bill establishing an excise tax on whisky came up for a vote, Williamson voted for it because, as he said, he "was not without the hope that one of its effects would be to lessen the use of a poison which was destructive of the morals and health of a numerous class of the people." Williamson realized that his vote would not be popular with his constitutents, and he told a colleague: "Sir, my vote was in its favour; I have discharged my duty to my conscience, but I have lost my popularity. I shall never again be elected to congress."

Williamson retired from public life in 1793, at the age of fifty-seven, and established his home in New York City. He devoted the rest of his life to medicine, philosophy, and writing. He gave a particularly large proportion of his time to the New York Hospital, the City Dispensary, and to the Humane Society. He published a book on the climate of North America in 1811 and a two-volume work on the history of North Carolina in 1812; in addition, he wrote many scientific papers.

His old age was saddened by the death of his two sons in early manhood, and in the last years of his life he was afflicted with a severe case of dropsy that prevented his sleeping in a bed. Shortly before his death, he wrote: "I have not any apprehension of a long confinement by sickness; men of my habits usually drop off quickly, therefore I count it my duty to be constantly in a state of preparation, whether I may be called off in the morning, at noon, or at midnight." At the age of eighty-three, Williamson died in New York City on May 22, 1819.

BOSTON,

Plymouth & Sandwich

MAIL STAGE,

CONTINUES TO RUN AS FOLLOWS:

LEAVES Boston every Tuesday, Thursday, and Saturday mornings at 5 o'clock, breakfast at Leonard's, Scituate; dine at Bradford's, Plymouth; and arrive in Sandwich the same evening. Leaves Sandwich every Monday, Wednesday and Friday mornings; breakfast at Bradford's, Plymouth; dine at Leonard's, Scituate, and arrive in Boston the same evening.

Passing through Dorchester, Quincy, Wyemouth, Hingham, Scituate, Hanover, Pembroke, Duxbury, Kingston, Plymouth to Sandwich. *Fare*, from Boston to Scituate, 1 doll. 25 cts. From Boston to Plymouth, 2 dolls. 50 cts. From Boston to Sandwich, 3 dolls. 63 cts.

.N. B. Extra Carriages can be obtained of the proprietor's, at Boston and Plymouth, at short notice.—
☞STAGE BOOKS kept at Boyden's Market-square, Boston, and at Fessendon's, Plymouth.

LEONARD & WOODWARD.

BOSTON, *November* 24, 1810.

The I. N. Phelps Stokes Collection of American Historical Prints, New York Public Library

A poster advertising the mail stage.

JAMES WILSON of PENNSYLVANIA

EDITOR'S NOTE: *Because James Wilson was one of the six men who signed both the Declaration of Independence and the United States Constitution, a biography of his life is included in Volume I of* FOUNDERS OF FREEDOM, *and the following article is concerned only with his role in the writing of the United States Constitution.*

James Wilson was forty-five-years-old at the time he signed the United States Constitution, and regarded as the leading lawyer of Philadelphia. He was one of the hardest-working and most vocal delegates to the Constitutional Convention, speaking almost every day on every subject being debated. He firmly championed the rights of the people to elect members of Congress and the President, scathingly denouncing the more "aristocratic" delegates who would have preferred to have the members of Congress appointed by the state legislatures, and to have the President appointed by Congress. Wilson also often acted as the spokesman for his good friend Benjamin Franklin, reading the elder statesman's speeches to the Convention.

On the first day of the Convention, May 25, 1787, Wilson nominated Temple Franklin, Benjamin Franklin's grandson who had acted as his grandfather's secretary in Paris, for Secretary of the Convention. However, Alexander Hamilton nominated Major William Jackson, a Revolutionary War officer who had been secretary to John Laurens on his mission to France in 1781, and the delegates elected Jackson by a vote of five to two.

Favored direct election of both houses

On the fifth day of the meeting, May 31, after Roger Sherman of Connecticut had said, "The people should have as little to do as may be about the government," and Elbridge Gerry of Massachusetts had declared, "The evils we experience flow from the excess of democracy," Wilson spoke out strongly in favor of direct election of both

JAMES WILSON

1742 (Sept. 14) Born near St. Andrews, Scotland.

1765 Emigrated to America.

1766 Taught Latin at the College of Philadelphia.

1766-1767 Studied law under John Dickinson was admitted to the bar.

1774-1775 Member of the Pennsylvania provincial convention.

1775-1777 Delegate to the second Continental Congress; signed the Declaration of Independence.

1779-1782 Advocate-general of France in the United States.

1781 Appointed a director of the Bank of North America.

1782-1783 Delegate from Pennsylvania to the Congress of the Confederation.

1785-1787 Delegate to Congress.

1787 Delegate from Pennsylvania to the Constitutional Convention; signed the United States Constitution.

1787 Member of Pennsylvania state ratification convention.

1789-1790 Member of the Pennsylvania state constitutional convention; helped write the new state constitution.

1789-1798 Associate justice of the Supreme Court of the United States.

1790-1791 First professor of law at the College of Philadelphia (now the University of Pennsylvania).

1798 Served in federal circuit court. Died at Edenton, N.C. (Aug. 21).

National Collection of Fine Arts, Smithsonian Institution.

James Wilson

houses of Congress, saying, "No government can long subsist without the confidence of the people."

The next day, Wilson moved that the executive power of the new government be vested in a single person. His proposal was immediately opposed by Edmund Randolph of Virginia, who said he would regard a single chief executive "as the foetus of monarchy." Wilson warmly replied that to the contrary of the Virginian's opinion, a single executive "would be the best safeguard against tyranny." Having reached an impasse, the delegates decided to postpone consideration of this matter to another day, and took up the question of how the executive or executives were to be chosen. On this, Wilson locked horns with Sherman, George Mason of Virginia, and John Rutledge of South Carolina, all of whom favored appointment of the executive by Congress. Wilson pointed out that he favored direct election both of the members of Congress and the executive as the best way "to make them as independent as possible of each other, as well as of the States." When the debate on the matter continued on June 2, Wilson proposed the Electoral College system to choose the President, with the people voting for electors who would in turn elect the chief executive. But at this time the Convention turned down the proposal by a vote of eight to two, preferring instead to have the President chosen by Congress.

National Archives. Courtesy: Mr. Cooper Dawson.

Mrs. George Mason (Anne Eilbeck)
Copy by D. W. Boudet from Hesselins

Argued for a single chief executive

The delegates on June 4 again took up the question of whether there should be a single chief executive or a triumvirate to administer the laws of the new national government. Wilson forcibly argued in favor of the single chief executive, pointing out that Randolph's opposition to the idea was based on the reasoning that it would be unpopular with the people. "On examination," Wilson said, "I can see no evidence of the alleged antipathy of the people. On the contrary, I am persuaded that it does not exist. All know that a single magistrate is not a king. One fact has great weight with me. All the thirteen States, though agreeing in scarce any other instance, agree in placing a single magistrate at the head of the government. The idea of three heads had taken place in none." He proceeded to state that with three equal executives he saw nothing but "uncontrolled, continued and violent animosities; which would not only interrupt the public administration but diffuse their poison through the other branches of government, through the states, and at length through the people at large." As a result of Wilson's forceful arguments, the delegates voted seven to three in favor of the single executive. Only New York, Delaware, and Maryland voted in opposition.

Favored the veto power

When the delegates took up a discussion of the powers to be given to the President, Wilson and Alexander Hamilton joined in a motion that the chief executive be given an absolute veto over any legislation passed by Congress. Franklin differed from his colleague on this issue, pointing out that under the colonial government of Pennsylvania, the governor had used such power to force the legislature to vote him money and tax exemptions on his personal property to win his approval of legislation. The states voted unanimously against Wilson's suggestion.

On June 6, Charles Pinckney of South Carolina moved "that the first branch of the National Legislature be elected by the State Legislatures, and not by the people." Wilson immediately de-

The I. N. Phelps Stokes Collection of American Historical Prints, New York Public Library.

A View of Boston, taken on the road to Dorchester
(Drawn by William Pierrie. Engraved by James Newton)

clared his opposition to the Southerner's motion, stating that it was his opinion that the authority of the government must "flow immediately from the legitimate source of all authority . . . the people at large." Wilson was supported by Madison and many other delegates, and Pinckney's motion was defeated eight to three, being supported only by Connecticut, New Jersey, and South Carolina. The next day, Wilson endeavored to defeat John Dickinson's proposal that the Senate be elected by the state legislatures, arguing that both branches of Congress be elected by the people. This time, however, Wilson was on the losing end of the argument, and Dickinson's motion passed unanimously.

Favored proportional representation in the Senate

Wilson was a strong advocate of proportional representation in Congress based on population. On June 11 he made a motion in the Committee of the Whole that in the House of Representatives there should be an "equitable ratio of representation in proportion to the whole number of white and other free citizens and inhabitants of every age, sex and condition, including those bound to servitude for a term of years, and three-fifths of

Library of Congress. Itineraire Pittoresque, J. Milbert.

Machine for the Portage on the Susquehanna

all other persons not comprehended in the foregoing description, except Indians not paying taxes, in each State." His motion carried over the opposition of the two small states of New Jersey and Delaware. That same day Wilson and Alexander Hamilton joined in a motion that the right of suffrage in the Senate should be according to the same proportionate representation already agreed to for the House of Representatives. Again, the motion carried, but this time by a six to five vote, with Connecticut, New York, New Jersey, Delaware, and Maryland voting against it.

Government for men—not for states

The decisions of the Committee of the Whole in accepting Wilson's proposals brought terror to the smaller states, who feared they were about to be swallowed up by the large states. As a result, they combined behind the New Jersey Plan that was laid before the Convention on June 15 by William Paterson. Wilson, Hamilton, and Madison were the chief spokesmen in denouncing the New Jersey Plan during the next several days. The heated argument focused on whether or not the states might have an equal vote in the Senate. On June 30, Wilson declared that the question before the delegates was "Shall less than one-fourth of the United States withdraw themselves from the Union, or shall more than three-fourths renounce the inherent, indisputable and unalienable rights of men, in favor of the artificial system of States?" He pointed out that with equal votes for each state seven states would be able to control six states and that the seven smallest states contained less than one-third of the people of the United States. "Can we forget for whom we are forming a Government?" he asked "Is it for *men*, or for the imaginary beings called *States?*" When a motion by Oliver Ellsworth of Connecticut allowing one vote for each state in the Senate was put to a vote on July 2, it lost by an equal division of votes, five to five with Georgia's vote divided. Despite Wilson's objections, the delegates voted to send the matter to a committee to achieve a compromise.

When the committee made its report on July 5, it advised that the House of Representatives should have one member for each forty thousand persons in the country, and the Senate should provide an equal vote for each state. Wilson immediately objected that the committee had exceeded its powers in making such a recommendation. After several more days of debate in which various compromises were suggested, the question of the proportion of representation was referred to a new committee of eleven delegates. The report of this committee, which called for a sixty-five-member House of Representatives, with ten representatives for the largest state, Virginia, ranging down to one representative each for Delaware and Rhode Island. This report was approved by the Convention on July 10 with no further objection by Wilson.

Opposed wealth as a criterion in representation

Wilson made a dramatic speech on July 13 in support of a motion to strike out the word "wealth" as one of the criteria in future reapportionment of representation in the House of Representatives. Madison's report of Wilson's speech is as follows:

"If a general declaration would satisfy any gentleman, he had no disposition to declare his sentiments. Conceiving that all men, wherever placed, have equal rights and are equally entitled to confidence, he viewed without apprehension the period when a few States should contain the superior number of people. The majority of people, wherever found, ought in all questions, to govern the minority. If the interior country should acquire this majority, it will not only have the right, but will avail itself of it, whether we will or no. This jealousy misled the policy of Great Britain with regard to America. The fatal maxims espoused by her were, that the Colonies were growing too fast, and that their growth must be stinted in time. What were the consequences? First, enmity on our part, then actual separation. Like consequences will result on the part of the interior settlements, if like jealousy and policy be pursued on ours. Further, if numbers be not a proper rule, why is not some better rule pointed out? No one has yet ventured to attempt it. Congress have never been able to discover a better. No State, as far as he had heard, had suggested any other. In 1783, after elaborate discussion of a measure of wealth, all were satisfied then, as they now are, that the rule of numbers does not differ much from the combined rule of numbers and wealth. Again, he could not agree that property was the sole or primary object of government and society. The cultivation and improvement of the human mind was the most noble object. With respect to property, they could not vary much from the precise measure. In no point of view, however,

THE CHEW HOUSE, GERMANTOWN.

From: The Boys of '76.

could the establishment of numbers, as the rule of representation in the first branch, vary his opinion as to the impropriety of letting a vicious principle into the second branch."

After hearing Wilson's strong argument, the delegates voted to strike out the word "wealth" as a measure for deciding future proportionate representation in the House of Representatives.

Against equal representation for all states

On Saturday, July 14, Wilson continued to argue passionately against equal representation for all states in the Senate. He declared again that it would enable the minority to rule. "A vice in the representation," he said, "like an error in the first concoction, must be followed by disease, convulsions, and finally death itself. . . .Will not our constituents say, we sent you to form an efficient government, and you have given us one, more complex, indeed, but having all the weakness of the former government?"

On Monday, July 16, the Convention approved equality of representation in the Senate by a vote of five states to four, with Massachusetts's vote divided and New York not represented. The large states, Pennsylvania, Virginia, South Carolina, and Georgia all voted against the motion.

The delegates indicated the respect with which they viewed Wilson on July 24 by electing him to the five-man Committee of Detail, headed by John Rutledge, which was charged with the task of drawing up a Constitution based upon the multitude of resolutions that had been approved by the Convention. The meeting adjourned for nearly two weeks, in order to give the committee time to draw up the document. During this time Wilson drafted the new Constitution, and it was edited and revised by Rutledge. A printed copy of this Constitution was given to each delegate when the Convention resumed on Monday, August 6.

Argued that nine years citizenship sufficed

Gouverneur Morris on August 9 proposed that members of the Senate should have been citizens of the United States for fourteen years before they could be elected. Wilson rose to point out his own Scottish birth and the "peculiar feelings" that came to him as he heard ideas put forward that might rule him out from holding office "under the very Constitution which he had shared in the trust of making." The delegates decided to reduce the restriction to nine years as a citizen.

In the succeeding weeks of the Convention, Wilson continued to take an active part in the discussions on the many small issues that were adjusted and compromised. Wilson read Franklin's plea for unanimous consent to the Constitution on the final day of the meeting, and then signed the document with most of the other delegates.

Wilson was elected to Pennsylvania's ratification convention, and was credited with a major role in obtaining his state's ratification on December 12, 1787. The last years of his life were spent as an associate justice of the Supreme Court of the United States and as a law professor at the College of Philadelphia. Like several other signers of the Constitution, Wilson speculated heavily in Western land, and when their value collapsed he was ruined financially. He died a poor man at the age of fifty-six on August 21, 1798.

THE ARTICLES OF CONFEDERATION

The first formal government of the United States was formed under the Articles of Confederation. This plan of government was drawn up by a committee of the Continental Congress appointed in June, 1776. The Articles were approved by Congress on November 15, 1777, but they did not formally go into effect until March 2, 1781, because Maryland, the last state to ratify the Articles, delayed empowering its delegates to sign the document until that year. Following is a copy of the Articles of Confederation:

The following have been critically compared with the original Articles of Confederation in the Department of State, and found to conform minutely to them in text, letter, and punctuation. It may therefore be relied upon as a true copy.

First formal government of the United States

TO ALL TO WHOM THESE PRESENTS SHALL COME, WE THE UNDERSIGNED DELEGATES OF THE STATES AFFIXED TO OUR NAMES, SEND GREETING.–Whereas the Delegates of the United States of America in Congress assembled did on the 15th day of November in the Year of our Lord 1777, and in the Second Year of the Independence of America agree to certain articles of Confederation and perpetual Union between the States of New Hampshire, Massachusetts-bay, Rhode-island and Providence Plantations, Connecticut, New-York, New-Jersey, Pennsylvania, Delaware, Maryland, Virginia, North-Carolina, South-Carolina, and Georgia, in the words following, viz.

"ARTICLES OF CONFEDERATION AND PERPETUAL UNION BETWEEN THE STATES OF NEW-HAMPSHIRE, MASSACHUSETTS-BAY, RHODE-ISLAND AND PROVIDENCE PLANTATIONS, CONNECTICUT, NEW-YORK, NEW-JERSEY, PENNSYLVANIA, DELAWARE, MARYLAND, VIRGINIA, NORTH-CAROLINA, SOUTH-CAROLINA, AND GEORGIA.

ARTICLE I. The Stile of this confederacy shall be "The United States of America."

ARTICLE II. Each state retains its sovereignty, freedom and independence, and every Power, Jurisdiction and right, which is not by this confederation expressly delegated to the united states, in congress assembled.

ARTICLE III. The said states hereby severally enter into a firm league of friendship with each other, for their common defence, the security of their Liberties, and their mutual and general welfare, binding themselves to assist each other, against all force offered to, or attacks made upon them, or any of them, on account of religion, sovereignty, trade, or any other pretence whatever.

ARTICLE IV. The better to secure and perpetuate mutual friendship and intercourse among the people of the different states in this union, the free inhabitants of each of these states, paupers, vagabonds, and fugitives from Justice excepted, shall be entitled to all privileges and immunities of free

From: The Boys of '76.

Interior of Washington's Headquarters at Newburgh, New York

citizens in the several states; and the people of each state shall have free ingress and regress to and from any other state, and shall enjoy therein all the privileges of trade and commerce, subject to the same duties, impositions and restrictions as the inhabitants thereof respectively, provided that such restriction shall not extend so far as to prevent the removal of property imported into any state, to any other state of which the Owner is an inhabitant; provided also that no imposition, duties or restriction shall be laid by any state, on the property of the united states, or either of them.

Agreement of Extradition

If any person guilty of, or charged with treason, felony, or other high misdemeanor in any state, shall flee from Justice, and be found in any of the united states, he shall upon demand of the Governor or executive power, of the state from which he fled, be delivered up and removed to the state having jurisdiction of his offence.

Full faith and credit shall be given in each of these states to the records, acts and judicial proceedings of the courts and magistrates of every other state.

ARTICLE V. For the more convenient management of the general interest of the united states, delegates shall be annually appointed in such manner as the legislature of each state shall direct, to meet in congress on the first Monday in November, in every year, with a power reserved to each state, to recal its delegates, or any of them, at any time within the year, and to send others in their stead, for the remainder of the Year.

No state shall be represented in congress by less than two, nor by more than seven members; and no person shall be capable of being a delegate for more than three years in any term of six years; nor shall any person, being a delegate, be capable of holding any office under the united states, for which he, or another for his benefit receives any salary, fees or emolument of any kind.

Each state shall maintain its own delegates in any meeting of the states, and while they act as members of the committee of the states.

In determining questions in the united states, in congress assembled, each state shall have one vote.

Delegates given special protection

Freedom of speech and debate in congress shall not be impeached or questioned in any Court, or place out of congress, and the members of congress shall be protected in their persons from arrests and imprisonments, during the time of their going to and from, and attendance on congress, except for treason, felony, or breach of the peace.

ARTICLE VI. No state without the Consent of the united states in congress assembed, shall send any embassy to, or receive any embassy from, or enter into any conference, agreement, alliance or treaty with any King prince or state; nor shall any person holding any office of profit or trust under the united states, or any of them, accept of any present, emolument, office or title of any kind whatever from any king, prince or foreign state; nor shall the united states in congress assembled, or any of them, grant any title of nobility.

No two or more states shall enter into any treaty, confederation or alliance whatever between them, without the consent of the united states in congress assembled, specifying accurately the purposes for which the same is to be entered into, and how long it shall continue.

No state shall lay any imposts or duties, which may interfere with any stipulations in treaties, entered into by the united states in congress assembled, with any king, prince or state, in pursuance of any treaties already proposed by congress, to the courts of France and Spain.

State militia should be adequate but limited in size

No vessels of war shall be kept up in time of peace by any state, except such number only, as shall be deemed necessary by the united states in congress assembled, for the defence of such state, or its trade; nor shall any body of forces be kept up by any state, in time of peace, except such number only, as in the judgment of the united states, in congress assembled, shall be deemed requisite to garrison the forts necessary for the defence of such state; but every state shall always keep up a well regulated and disciplined militia, sufficiently armed and accoutred, and shall provide and have constantly ready for use, in public stores, a due number of field pieces and tents, and a proper quantity of arms, ammunition and camp equipage.

No state shall engage in any war without the consent of the united states in congress assembled, unless such state be actually invaded by enemies, or shall have received certain advice of a resolution being formed by some nation of Indians to invade such state, and the danger is so imminent as not to admit of a delay, till the united states in congress assembled can be consulted: nor shall any state grant commissions to any ships or vessels of war, nor letters of marque or reprisal, except it be after a declaration of war by the united states in congress assembled, and then only against the kingdom or state and the subjects thereof, against which war has been so declared, and under such regulations as shall be established by the united states in congress assembled, unless such state be infested by pirates, in which case vessels of war may be fitted out for that occasion, and kept so long as the danger shall continue, or until the united states in congress assembled shall determine otherwise.

ARTICLE VII. When land-forces are raised by any state for the common defence, all officers of or under the rank of colonel, shall be appointed by the legislature of each state respectively by whom such forces shall be raised, or in such manner as such state shall direct, and all vacancies shall be filled up by the state which first made the appointment.

ARTICLE VIII. All charges of war, and all other expenses that shall be incurred for the common defence or general welfare, and allowed by the united states in congress assembled, shall be defrayed out of a common treasury, which shall be supplied by the several states, in proportion to the value of all land within each state, granted to or surveyed for any Person, as such land and the buildings and improvements thereon shall be estimated according to such mode as the united states in congress assembled, shall from time to time, direct and appoint. The taxes for paying that proportion shall be laid and levied by the authority and direction of the legislatures of the several states within the time agreed upon by the united states in congress assembled.

States taxed in proportion to the value of the land

ARTICLE IX. The united states in congress assembled, shall have the sole and exclusive right and power of determining on peace and war, except in the cases mentioned in the 6th article—of sending and receiving ambassadors—entering into treaties and alliances, provided that no treaty of commerce shall be made whereby the legislative power of the respective states shall be restrained from imposing such imposts and duties on foreigners, as their own people are subjected to, or from prohibiting the exportation or importation of any species of goods or commodities whatsoever—of establishing rules for deciding in all cases, what captures on land or water shall be legal, and in what manner prizes taken by land or naval forces in the service of the united states shall be divided or appropriated—of granting letters of marque and reprisal in times of peace—appointing courts for the trial of piracies and felonies committed on the high seas and establishing courts for receiving and determining finally appeals in all cases of captures, provided that no member of congress shall be appointed a judge of any of the said courts.

Procedure for settling disputes between states

The united states in congress assembled shall also be the last resort on appeal in all disputes and differences now subsisting or that hereafter may arise between two or more states concerning boundary, jurisdiction or any other cause whatever; which authority shall always be exercised in the manner following. Whenever the legislative or executive authority or lawful agent of any state in controversy with another shall present a petition to congress, stating the matter in question and praying for a hearing, notice thereof shall be given by order of congress to the legislative or executive authority of the other state in controversy, and a day assigned for the appearance of the parties by their lawful agents, who shall then be directed to appoint by joint consent, commissioners or judges to constitute a court for hearing and determining the matter in question: but if they cannot agree, congress shall name three persons out of each of the united states, and from the list of such persons each party shall alternately strike out one, the petitioners beginning, until the number shall be reduced to thirteen; and from that number not less than seven, nor more than nine names as congress shall direct, shall in the presence of congress be drawn out by lot, and the persons whose names shall be so drawn or any five of them, shall be commissioners or judges, to hear and finally determine the controversy, so always as a major part of the judges who shall hear the cause shall agree in the determination: and if either party shall neglect to attend at the day appointed, without showing reasons, which congress shall

Designer: William Barton, 1782.
Library of Congress.

The Great Seal of the United States
as Adopted by the Continental Congress June 20, 1782

Courtesy: Essex Institute. Photo by Eric Muller

Launching of the Ship *Fame*

judge sufficient, or being present shall refuse to strike, the congress shall proceed to nominate three persons out of each state, and the secretary of congress shall strike in behalf of such party absent or refusing; and the judgment and sentence of the court to be appointed, in the manner before prescribed, shall be final and conclusive; and if any of the parties shall refuse to submit to the authority of such court, or to appear or defend their claim or cause, the court shall nevertheless proceed to pronounce sentence, or judgment, which shall in like manner be final and decisive, the judgment or sentence and other proceedings being in either case transmitted to congress, and lodged among the acts of congress for the security of the parties concerned: provided that every commissioner, before he sits in judgment, shall take an oath to be administered by one of the judges of the supreme or superior court of the state, where the cause shall be tried, "well and truly to hear and determine the matter in question, according to the best of his judgment, without favour, affection or hope of reward:" provided also that no state shall be deprived of territory for the benefit of the united states.

All controversies concerning the private right of soil claimed under different grants of two or more states, whose jurisdictions as they may respect such lands, and the states which passed such grants are adjusted, the said grants or either of them being at the same time claimed to have originated antecedent to such settlement of jurisdiction, shall on the petition of either party to the congress of the united states, be finally determined as near as may be in the same manner as is before prescribed for deciding disputes respecting territorial jurisdiction between different states.

The right of minting and regulating coin

The united states in congress assembled shall also have the sole and exclusive right and power of regulating the alloy and value of coin struck by their own authority, or by that of the respective states—fixing the standard of weights and measures throughout the United States—regulating the trade and managing all affairs with the Indians, not members of any of the states, pro-

From: History of New York City.

The Bowling Green and Fort George, in 1783

vided that the legislative right of any state within its own limits be not infringed or violated—establishing or regulating post-offices from one state to another, throughout all the united states, and exacting such postage on the papers passing thro' the same as may be requisite to defray the expenses of the said office—appointing all officers of the land forces, in the service of the united states, excepting regimental officers—appointing all the officers of the naval forces, and commissioning all officers whatever in the service of the united states—making rules for the government and regulation of the said land and naval forces, and directing their operations.

"A Committee of the States"

The united states in congress assembled shall have authority to appoint a committee, to sit in the recess of congress, to be denominated "A Committee of the States," and to consist of one delegate from each state; and to appoint such other committees and civil officers as may be necessary for managing the general affairs of the united states under their direction—to appoint one of their number to preside, provided that no person be allowed to serve in the office of president more than one year in any term of three years; to ascertain the necessary sums of Money to be raised for the service of the united states, and to appropriate and apply the same for defraying the public expenses—to borrow money, or emit bills on the credit of the united states, transmitting every half year to the respective states an account of the sums of money so borrowed or emitted,—to build and equip a navy—to agree upon the number of land forces, and to make requisitions from each state for its quota, in proportion to the number of white inhabitants in such state; which requisition shall be binding, and thereupon the legislature of each state shall appoint the regimental officers, raise the men and cloath, arm and equip them in a soldier like manner, at the expense of the united states; and the officers and men so cloathed, armed and equipped shall march to the place appointed, and within the time agreed on by the united states in congress assembled: But if the united states in congress assembled shall, on consideration of circumstances judge proper that any state should not raise men, or should raise a smaller number than its quota, and that any other state should raise a greater number of men than the quota thereof, such extra number shall be raised, officered, cloathed, armed and equipped in the same manner as the quota of such state, unless the legislature of such state shall judge that such extra number cannot be safely spared out of the same, in which case they shall raise officer, cloath, arm and equip as many of such extra number as they judge can be safely spared. And the officers and men so cloathed, armed and equipped, shall march to the place appointed, and within the time agreed on by the united states in congress assembled.

Majority Rule

The united states in congress assembled shall never engage in a war, nor grant letters of marque and reprisal in time of peace, nor enter into any treaties or alliances, nor coin money, nor regulate the value thereof, nor ascertain the sums and expenses necessary for the defence and welfare of the united states, or any of them, nor emit bills, nor borrow money on the credit of the united states, nor appropriate money, nor agree upon the number of vessels of war, to be built or purchased, or the number of land or sea forces to be raised, nor appoint a commander in chief of the army or navy, unless nine states assent to the same: nor shall a question on any other point, except for adjourning from day to day be determined, unless by the votes of a majority of the united states in congress assembled.

The Congress of the united states shall have power to adjourn to any time within the year, and to any place within the united states, so that no period

View of Pawtucket Falls *New York Public Library. I. N. Phelps Stokes Collection of American Historical Prints. Engraved by J. Milbert and T. B. Smith.*

of adjournment be for a longer duration than the space of six months and shall publish the Journal of their proceedings monthly, except such parts thereof relating to treaties, alliances or military operations, as in their judgment require secrecy; and the yeas and nays of the delegates of each state on any question shall be entered on the Journal, when it is desired by any delegate; and the delegates of a state, or any of them, at his or their request shall be furnished with a transcript of the said Journal, except such parts as are above excepted, to lay before the legislatures of the several states.

ARTICLE X. The committee of the states, or any nine of them, shall be authorized to execute, in the recess of congress, such of the powers of congress as the united states in congress assembled, by the consent of nine states, shall from time to time think expedient to vest them with; provided that no power be delegated to the said committee, for the exercise of which, by the articles of confederation, the voice of nine states in the congress of the united states assembled is requisite.

Canada granted rights in the Confederation

ARTICLE XI. Canada acceding to this confederation, and joining in the measures of the united states, shall be admitted into, and entitled to all the advantages of this union: but no other colony shall be admitted into the same, unless such admission be agreed to by nine states.

ARTICLE XII. All bills of credit emitted, monies borrowed and debts contracted by, or under the authority of congress, before the assembling of the united states, in pursuance of the present confederation, shall be deemed and considered as a charge against the united states, for payment and satisfaction whereof the said united states, and the public faith are hereby solemnly pledged.

ARTICLE XIII. Every state shall abide by the determinations of the united states in congress assembled, on all questions which by this confederation is submitted to them. And the Articles of this confederation shall be inviolably observed by every state, and the union shall be perpetual; nor shall any alteration at any time hereafter be made in any of them; unless such alteration be agreed to in a congress of the united states, and be afterwards confirmed by the legislatures of every state.

Acts of Congress shall bind all

And Whereas it hath pleased the Great Governor of the World to incline the hearts of the legislatures we respectively represent in congress, to approve of, and to authorize us to ratify the said articles of confederation and perpetual union. Know Ye that we the undersigned delegates, by virtue of the power and authority to us given for that purpose, do by these presents, in the name and in behalf of our respective constituents, fully and entirely ratify and confirm each and every of the said articles of confederation and perpetual union, and all and singular the matters and things therein contained: And we do further solemnly plight and engage the faith of our respective constituents, that they shall abide by the determinations of the united states in congress assembled, on all questions, which by the said confederation are submitted to them. And that the articles thereof shall be inviolably observed by the states we respectively represent, and that the union shall be perpetual. In witness whereof we have hereunto set our hands in Congress. Done at Philadelphia in the state of Pennsylvania the 9th Day of July in the Year of our Lord, 1778, and in the 3d year of the Independence of America.

Josiah Bartlett,	John Wentworth, jun. August 8th, 1778,	On the part and behalf of the state of New Hampshire.
John Hancock, Samuel Adams, Elbridge Gerry,	Francis Dana, James Lovell, Samuel Holten,	On the part and behalf of the state of Massachusetts-Bay.
William Ellery, Henry Marchant,	John Collins,	On the part and behalf of the state of Rhode-Island and Providence Plantations.
Roger Sherman, Samuel Huntington, Oliver Wolcott,	Titus Hosmer, Andrew Adam,	On the part and behalf of the state of Connecticut.
Jas Duane, Fras Lewis,	William Duer, Gouvr Morris,	On the part and behalf of the state of New-York.
Jno Witherspoon,	Nathl Scudder,	On the part and behalf of the state of New-Jersey, November 26th, 1778.
Robt Morris, Danie Roberdeau, Jona Bayard Smith,	William Clingan, Joseph Reed, 22d July, 1778,	On the part and behalf of the state of Pennsylvania.
Tho. M'Kean, Feb. 12, 1779, John Dickinson, May 5, 1779,	Nicholas Van Dyke,	On the part and behalf of the state of Delaware.
John Hanson, March 1st, 1781,	Daniel Carroll, March 1st, 1781,	On the part and behalf of the state of Maryland.
Richard Henry Lee, John Banister, Thomas Adams,	Jno Harvie, Francis Lightfoot Lee,	On the part and behalf of the state of Virginia.
John Penn, July 21st, 1778,	Corns Harnett, Jno Williams,	On the part and behalf of the state of North-Carolina.
Henry Laurens, William Henry Drayton, Jno Matthews,	Richd Hutson, Thos. Heyward, jun.	On the part and behalf of the state of South-Carolina.
Jno Walton, 24th July, 1778,	Edwd Telfair, Edwd Langworthy,	On the part and behalf of the state of Georgia.

THE VIRGINIA PLAN

Edmund Randolph of Virginia opened the main business of the Constitutional Convention on May 29, 1787, by introducing the Virginia Plan for a new government of the United States. This plan had been devised by the several delegates from Virginia, including James Madison, who had arrived in Philadelphia about two weeks before the sessions got underway. The Virginia Plan provided the basis for the debates in the Convention for the first several weeks. Following is a copy of the text of the Virginia Plan as presented by Randolph:

Limitations as to age and terms

1. *Resolved*, that the Articles of Confederation ought to be so corrected and enlarged as to accomplish the objects proposed by their institution; namely, common defence, security of liberty, and general welfare.

2. *Resolved*, therefore, that the rights of suffrage in the National Legislature ought to be proportioned to the quotas of contribution, or to the number of free inhabitants, as the one or the other rule may seem best in different cases.

3. *Resolved*, that the National Legislature ought to consist of two branches.

4. *Resolved*, that the members of the first branch of the National Legislature ought to be elected by the people of the several States every --- for the term of ---; to be of the age of --- years at least; to receive liberal stipends by which they may be compensated for the devotion of their time to the public service; to be ineligible to any office established by a particular State, or under the authority of the United States, except those peculiarly belonging to the functions of the first branch, during the term of service, and for the space of --- after its expiration; to be incapable of re-election for the space of --- after the expiration of their term of service, and to be subject to recall.

5. *Resolved*, that the members of the second branch of the National Legislature ought to be elected by those of the first, out of a proper number of persons nominated by the individual Legislatures, to be of the age of --- years at least; to hold their offices for a term sufficient to ensure their independency; to receive liberal stipends, by which they may be compensated for the devotion of their time to the public service; and to be ineligible to any office established by a particular State, or under the authority of the United States, except those peculiarly belonging to the functions of the second branch, during the term of service; and for the space of --- after the expiration thereof.

6. *Resolved*, that each branch ought to possess the right of originating acts; that the National Legislature ought to be empowered to enjoy the legislative rights vested in Congress by the Confederation, and moreover to legislate in all cases to which the separate States are incompetent, or in which the harmony of the United States may be interrupted by the exercise of individual legislation; to negative all laws passed by the several States contravening, in the opinion of the National Legislature, the Articles of Union, or any treaty

subsisting under the authority of the Union; and to call forth the force of the Union against any member of the Union failing to fulfil its duty under the Articles thereof.

7. *Resolved*, that a National Executive be instituted; to be chosen by the National Legislature for the term of ——; to receive punctually, at stated times, a fixed compensation for the services rendered, in which no increase nor diminution shall be made, so as to affect the magistracy existing at the time of increase or diminution; and to be ineligible a second time; and that, besides a general authority to execute the national laws, it ought to enjoy the executive rights vested in Congress by the Confederation.

8. *Resolved*, that the Executive, and a convenient number of the national Judiciary, ought to compose a Council of Revision, with authority to examine every act of the National Legislature, before it shall operate, and every act of a particular Legislature before a negative thereon shall be final; and that the dissent of the said Council shall amount to a rejection, unless the act of the National Legislature be again passed, or that of a particular Legislature be again negatived by —— of the members of each branch.

9. *Resolved*, that a National Judiciary be established; to consist of one or more supreme tribunals, and of inferior tribunals to be chosen by the National Legislature; to hold their offices during good behaviour, and to receive punctually, at stated times, fixed compensation for their services, in which no increase or diminution shall be made, so as to affect the persons actually in office at the time of such increase or diminution. That the jurisdiction of the inferior tribunals shall be to hear and determine, in the first instance, and of the supreme tribunal to hear and determine, in the dernier ressort, all piracies and felonies on the high seas; captures from an enemy; cases in which foreigners, or citizens of other States, applying to such jurisdictions, may be interested; or which respect the collection of the national revenue; impeachments of any national officers, and questions which may involve the national peace and harmony.

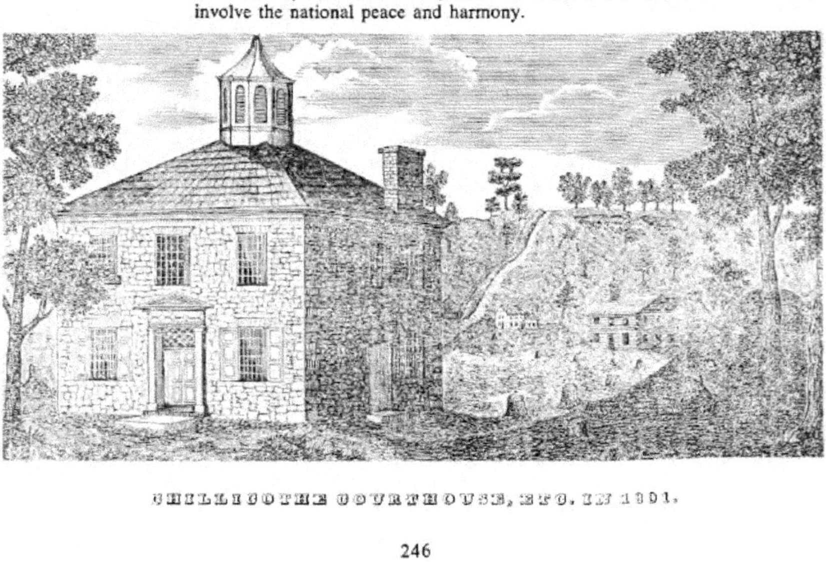

CHILLICOTHE COURTHOUSE, ETC. IN 1801.

THE PINCKNEY PLAN

On May 29, 1787, Charles Pinckney of South Carolina presented to the Constitutional Convention a plan for a federal constitution. No copy of this Pinckney Plan was found in James Madison's records of the meeting, but Pinckney himself presented the United States government in 1818 with what he said was a draft of his plan. Historians cast doubt on the authenticity of the 1818 version because of its close resemblance to the finished Constitution. However, in 1904, historian Andrew C. McLaughlin published what he believed to be an authentic outline of Pinckney's Plan as gleaned from notes made during the Convention by Pennsylvania delegate James Wilson. McLaughlin's outline of the Pinckney Plan is as follows:

An authentic outline

1. A Confederation between the free and independent States of N.H., etc., is hereby solemnly made uniting them together under one general superintending Government for their common Benefit and for their Defense and Security against all Designs and Leagues that may be injurious to their interests and against all force and Attacks offered to or made upon them or any of them.

2. The Stile.

3. Mutual Intercourse—Community of Privileges—Surrender of Criminals —Faith to Proceedings, etc.

4. Two Branches of the Legislature—Senate—House of Delegates—Together the U. S. in Congress assembled.

H. D. to consist of one Member for every thousand Inhabitants 3/5 of Blacks included.

Senate to be elected from four Districts—to serve by Rotation of four years—to be elected by the H. D. either from among themselves or the people at large.

5. The Senate and H. D. shall by joint Ballot annually (septennially) chuse the Presidt. U. S. from among themselves or the people at large.—In the Presdt. the executive authority of the U. S. shall be vested.—His Powers and Duties—He shall have a Right to advise with the Heads of the different Departments as his Council.

6. Council of Revision, Consisting of the Presidt. S. for for. Affairs, S. of War, Heads of the Departments of Treasury and Admiralty or any two of them togr wt the Presidt.

7. The members of S. and H. D. shall each have one Vote, and shall be paid out of the common Treasury.

8. The Time of the Election of the Members of the H. D. and of the meeting of U. S. in C. assembled.

9. No state to make Treaties—lay interfering Duties—keep a naval or land Force Militia excepted to be disciplined etc. according to the Regulations of the U. S.

10. Each State retains its Rights not expressly delegated—But no Bill of the Legislature of any State shall become a law till it shall have been laid before S. and H. D. in C. assembled and received their Approbation.

11. The exclusive Power of S. and H. D. in C. Assembled.

12. The S. and H. D. in C. ass. shall have exclusive Power of regulating trade and levying Imposts—Each State may lay Embargoes in Times of Scarcity.

13. —of establishing Post-Offices.

14. S. and H. D. in C. ass. shall be the last Resort on Appeal in Disputes between two or more States; which Authority shall be exercised in the following Manner etc.

15. S. and H. D. in C. ass. shall institute offices and appoint officers for the Departments of for. Affairs, War, Treasury and Admiralty.

They shall have the exclusive power of Declaring what shall be Treason and Misp. of Treason agt. U. S.—and of instituting a federal judicial Court, to which an Appeal shall be allowed from the judicial Courts of the several States in all Causes wherein Questions shall arise on the Constructions of Treaties made by U. S.—or on the Laws of Nations—or on the Regulations of U. S. concerning Trade and Revenue—or wherein U. S. shall be a Party. The Court shall consist of Judges to be appointed during good Behavior—S. and H. D. in C. ass. shall have the exclusive Right of instituting in each State a Court of Admiralty and appointing the Judges etc of the same for all maritime Causes which may arise therein respectively.

16. S. and H. D. in C. ass. shall have the exclusive Right of coining Money—regulating its Alloy and Value—fixing the Standard of Weights and Measures throughout U. S.

17. Points in which the Assent of more than a bare Majority shall be necessary.

18. Impeachments shall be by the H. D. before the Senate and the Judges of the Federal Judicial Court.

19. S. and H. D. in C. ass. shall regulate the Militia thro' the U. S.

20. Means of enforcing and compelling the Payment of the Quota of each State.

21. Manner and Conditions of admitting new States.

22. Power of dividing annexing and consolidating States, on the consent and Petition of such States.

23. The assent of the Legislature of States shall be sufficient to invest future additional Powers in U. S. in C. ass. and shall bind the whole Confederacy.

24. The Articles of Confederation shall be inviolably observed, and the Union shall be perpetual: unless altered as before directed.

25. The said States of N. H. etc. guarantee mutually each other and their Rights against all other Powers and against all Rebellion, etc.

SEALS OF NEW AMSTERDAM AND NEW YORK.

THE NEW JERSEY PLAN

The delegates of the small states at the Constitutional Convention were fearful that the Virginia Plan for the new government would swallow up the small states by not permitting them an equal vote with the large states in the new Congress. Therefore, delegates from New Jersey, Delaware, Connecticut, New York, and Maryland drew up what came to be called the New Jersey Plan, which was presented to the Convention on June 15, 1787, by William Paterson of New Jersey Following is a copy of the text of the New Jersey Plan:

1. *Resolved,* That the Articles of Confederation ought to be so revised, corrected and enlarged, as to render the federal Constitution adequate to the exigencies of government, and the preservation of the Union.

Raising Revenue

2. *Resolved,* That, in addition to the powers vested in the United States in Congress by the present existing Articles of Confederation, they be authorized to pass acts for raising a revenue, by levying a duty or duties on all goods or merchandises of foreign growth or manufacture, imported into any part of the United States; by stamps on paper, vellum, or parchment; and by a postage on all letters or packages passing through the general post-office;—to be applied to such federal purposes as they shall deem proper and expedient: to make rules and regulations for the collection thereof; and the same, from time to time, to alter and amend in such manner as they shall think proper: to pass acts for the regulation of trade and commerce, as well with foreign nations as with each other;—provided that all punishments, fines, forfeitures, and penalties, to be incurred for contravening such acts, rules, and regulations, shall be adjudged by the common-law judiciaries of the state in which any offence contrary to the true intent and meaning of such acts, rules, and regulations, shall have been committed or perpetrated, with liberty of commencing in the first instance all suits and prosecutions for that purpose in the superior common-law judiciary in such state; subject, nevertheless, for the correction of all errors, both in law and fact, in rendering judgment, to an appeal to the judiciary of the United States.

3. *Resolved,* That whenever requisitions shall be necessary, instead of the rule for making requisitions mentioned in the Articles of Confederation, the United States in Congress be authorized to make such requisitions in proportion to the whole number of white and other free citizens and inhabitants, of every age, sex, and condition, including those bound to servitude for a term of years, and three fifths of all other persons not comprehended in the foregoing description, except Indians not paying taxes; that, if such requisitions be not complied with in the time specified therein, to direct the collection thereof in the non-complying states, and for that purpose to devise and pass acts directing and authorizing the same;—provided, that none of the powers hereby vested in the United States in Congress shall be exercised without the consent of at least —— states; and in that proportion, if the number of confederated states should hereafter be increased or diminished.

4. *Resolved,* That the United States in Congress be authorized to elect a federal executive, to consist of — — persons; to continue in office for the term of — — years; to receive punctually, at stated times, a fixed compensation for their services, in which no increase no diminution shall be made so as to affect the persons composing the executive at the time of such increase or diminution; to be paid out of the federal treasury; to be incapable of holding any other office or appointment during their time of service, and for — — years thereafter; to be ineligible a second time, and removable by Congress, on application by a majority of the executives of the several states: that the executive, besides their general authority to execute the federal acts, ought to appoint all federal officers not otherwise provided for, and to direct all military operations;— provided, that none of the persons composing the federal executive shall, on any occasion, take command of any troops, so as personally to conduct any military enterprise, as general, or in any other capacity.

A Supreme Court

5. *Resolved,* That a federal judiciary be established, to consist of a supreme tribunal, the judges of which to be appointed by the executive, and to hold their offices during good behaviour; to receive punctually, at stated times, a fixed compensation for their services, in which no increase nor diminution shall be made so as to affect the persons actually in office at the time of such increase or diminution. That the judiciary so established shall have authority to hear and determine, in the first instance, on all impeachments of federal officers, and, by way of appeal, in the dernier ressort, in all cases touching the rights of ambassadors; in all cases of captures from an enemy; in all cases of piracies and felonies on the high seas; in all cases in which foreigners may be interested; in the construction of any treaty or treaties, or which may arise on any of the acts for the regulation of trade, or the collection of the federal revenue: that none of the judiciary shall, during the time they remain in office, be capable of receiving or holding any other office or appointment during their term of service, or for — — thereafter.

6. *Resolved,* That all acts of the United States in Congress, made by virtue and in pursuance of the powers hereby, and by the Articles of Confederation, vested in them, and all treaties made and ratified under the authority of the United States, shall be the supreme law of the respective states, so far forth as those acts or treaties shall relate to the said states or their citizens; and that the judiciary of the several states shall be bound thereby in their decisions, any thing in the respective laws of the individual states to the contrary notwithstanding; and that if any state, or any body of men in any state, shall oppose or prevent the carrying into execution such acts or treaties, the federal executive shall be authorized to call forth the power of the confederated states, or so much thereof as may be necessary, to enforce and compel an obedience to such acts, or an observance of such treaties.

7. *Resolved,* That provision be made for the admission of new states into the Union.

8. *Resolved,* That the rule for naturalization ought to be the same in every state.

9. *Resolved,* That a citizen of one state, committing an offence in another state of the Union, shall be deemed guilty of the same offence as if it had been committed by a citizen of the state in which the offence was committed.

10. *Resolved,* that provision ought to be made for the admission of States lawfully arising within the limits of the United States, whether from a volun-

tary junction of government and territory, or otherwise, with the consent of a number of voices in the National Legislature less than the whole.

11. *Resolved,* that a republican government, and the territory of each State, except in the instance of a voluntary junction of government and territory, ought to be guaranteed by the United States to each State.

12. *Resolved,* that provision ought to be made for the continuance of Congress and their authorities and privileges, until a given day after the reform of the Articles of Union shall be adopted, and for the completion of all their engagements.

13. *Resolved,* that provision ought to be made for the amendment of the Articles of Union, whensoever it shall seem necessary; and that the assent of the National Legislature ought not to be required thereto.

14. *Resolved,* that the legislative, executive, and judiciary powers, within the several States ought to be bound by oath to support the Articles of Union.

15. *Resolved,* that the amendments which shall be offered to the Confederation, by the Convention ought, at a proper time or times, after the approbation of Congress, to be submitted to an assembly or assemblies of representatives, recommended by the several Legislatures to be expressly chosen by the people to consider and decide thereon. . . . It was then *resolved,* that the House will to-morrow resolve itself into a Committee of the Whole House, to consider of the state of the American Union; and that the propositions by Mr. Randolph be referred to said Committee.

From: History of New York City. Engraved by J. McNevin and J. Rogers.

Reception of President Washington at New York, April 23, 1789

GENERAL INDEX

E

F

G

H

I

J

K

L

S

T

U

V

W

X

Y

IN CONGRESS, JULY 4.
The unanimous Declaration of the thirteen united States of

When in the course of human events it becomes necessary for one people to dissolve the political bands which have connected them with another, and to assume among the powers of the earth, the separate and equal station to which the Laws of Nature and of Nature's God entitle them, a decent respect to the opinions of mankind requires that they should declare the causes which impel them to the separation. — We hold these truths to be self-evident, that all men are created equal, that they are endowed by their Creator with certain unalienable Rights, that among these are Life, Liberty and the pursuit of Happiness. — That to secure these rights, Governments are instituted among Men, deriving their just powers from the consent of the governed, — That whenever any Form of Government becomes destructive of these ends, it is the Right of the People to alter or to abolish it, and to institute new Government, laying its foundation on such principles and organizing its powers in such form, as to them shall seem most likely to effect their Safety and Happiness. Prudence, indeed, will dictate that Governments long established should not be changed for light and transient causes; and accordingly all experience hath shewn, that mankind are more disposed to suffer, while evils are sufferable, than to right themselves by abolishing the forms to which they are accustomed. But when a long train

Article the ninth

the tenth

Frederick Augustus Muhlenberg

John Adams

In Convention. Monday September 17th 1787.
Present
The States of

New Hampshire, Massachusetts, Connecticut, Mr. Hamilton from New York, New Jersey, Pennsylvania, Delaware, Maryland, Virginia, North Carolina, South Carolina and Georgia.

Resolved

That the preceding Constitution be laid before the United States in Congress assembled, and that it is the Opinion of this Convention, that it should afterwards be submitted to a Convention of Delegates, chosen in each State by the People thereof, under the Recommendation of its Legislature, for their Assent and Ratification;

Congress of the United States
begun and held at the City of New-York, on
Wednesday the fourth of March, one thousand seven hundred and

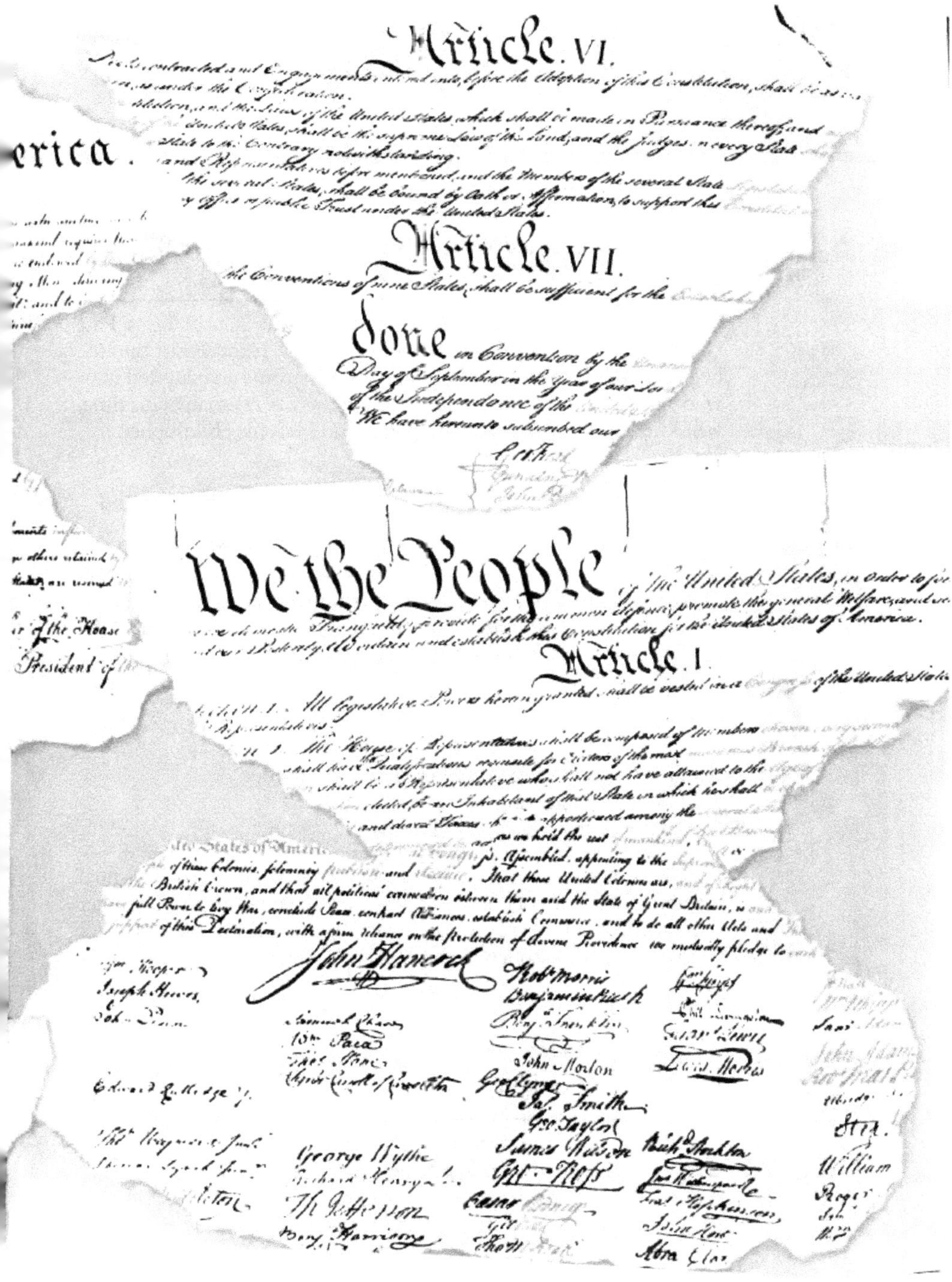

Article. VI.
Article. VII.
done
We the People
of the United States, in Order to
Article. I
John Hancock

Related Titles from Westphalia Press

Ancient Mysteries and Modern Masonry: The Collected Writings of Jewel P. Lightfoot, Edited by Billy J. Hamilton Jr.

Jewel P. Lightfoot. Former Attorney General of the State of Texas. Past Grand Master of the Masonic Grand Lodge of Texas. From humble beginnings in rural Arkansas, he worked to become an educated man who excelled in law and Freemasonry. He was a gentleman of his time, well-known as a scholar, public speaker, and Masonic philosopher.

Essay on The Mysteries and the True Object of The Brotherhood of Freemasons
by Jason Williams

This isn't a reprint of a classic. It's a new rendition with new life breathed into it, to be enjoyed both by the layperson trying to understand the Craft and Masonic scholars taking a deeper dive into the fraternity's golden years—when the concepts of liberty and equality were still fresh.

Female Emancipation and Masonic Membership: An Essential Collection
By Guillermo De Los Reyes Heredia

Female Emancipation and Masonic Membership: An Essential Combination is a collection of essays on Freemasonry and gender that promotes a transatlantic discussion of the study of the history of women and Freemasonry and their contribution in different countries.

Freemasonry, Heir to the Enlightenment
by Cécile Révauger

Modern Freemasonry may have mythical roots in Solomon's time but is really the heir to the Enlightenment. Ever since the early eighteenth century freemasons have endeavored to convey the values of the Enlightenment in the cultural, political and religious fields, in Europe, the American colonies and the emerging United States.

Freemasonry: A French View
by Roger Dachez and Alain Bauer

Perhaps one should speak not of Freemasonry but of Freemasonries in the plural. In each country Masonic historiography has developed uniqueness. Two of the best known French Masonic scholars present their own view of the worldwide evolution and challenging mysteries of the fraternity over the centuries.

Worlds of Print: The Moral Imagination of an Informed Citizenry, 1734 to 1839
by John Slifko

John Slifko argues that freemasonry was representative and played an important role in a larger cultural transformation of literacy and helped articulate the moral imagination of an informed democratic citizenry via fast emerging worlds of print.

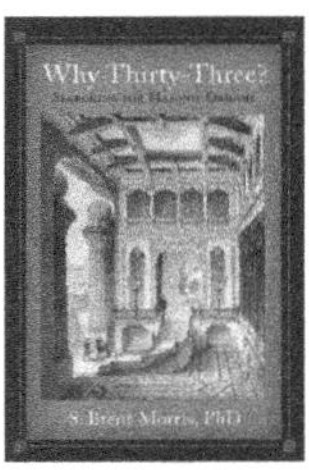

Why Thirty-Three?: Searching for Masonic Origins
by S. Brent Morris, PhD

What "high degrees" were in the United States before 1830? What were the activities of the Order of the Royal Secret, the precursor of the Scottish Rite? A complex organization with a lengthy pedigree like Freemasonry has many basic foundational questions waiting to be answered, and that's what this book does: answers questions.

The Great Transformation: Scottish Freemasonry 1725-1810
by Dr. Mark C. Wallace

This book examines Scottish Freemasonry in its wider British and European contexts between the years 1725 and 1810. The Enlightenment effectively crafted the modern mason and propelled Freemasonry into a new era marked by growing membership and the creation of the Grand Lodge of Scotland.

Getting the Third Degree: Fraternalism, Freemasonry and History
Edited by Guillermo De Los Reyes and Paul Rich

As this engaging collection demonstrates, the doors being opened on the subject range from art history to political science to anthropology, as well as gender studies, sociology and more. The organizations discussed may insist on secrecy, but the research into them belies that.

Policy Studies Organization

The Policy Studies Organization (PSO) is a publisher of academic journals and book series, sponsor of conferences, and producer of programs.

Policy Studies Organization publishes dozens of journals on a range of topics, such as European Policy Analysis, Journal of Elder Studies, Indian Politics & Polity, Journal of Critical Infrastructure Policy, and Popular Culture Review.

Additionally, Policy Studies Organization hosts numerous conferences. These conferences include the Middle East Dialogue, Space Education and Strategic Applications Conference, International Criminology Conference, Dupont Summit on Science, Technology and Environmental Policy, World Conference on Fraternalism, Freemasonry and History, and the Internet Policy & Politics Conference.

For more information on these projects, access videos of past events, and upcoming events, please visit us at:

www.ipsonet.org

www.ingramcontent.com/pod-product-compliance
Lightning Source LLC
Chambersburg PA
CBHW051528020426
42333CB00016B/1823
* 9 7 8 1 6 3 7 2 3 5 5 9 1 *